Economic Policy and Income Distribution in Colombia

Westview Replica Editions

This book is a Westview Replica Edition. The concept of Replica Editions is a response to the crisis in academic and informational publishing. Library budgets for books have been severely curtailed; economic pressures on the university presses and the few private publishing companies primarily interested in scholarly manuscripts have severely limited the capacity of the industry to properly serve the academic and research communities. Many manuscripts dealing with important subjects, often representing the highest level of scholarship, are today not economically viable publishing projects. Or, if they are accepted for publication, they are often subject to lead times ranging from one to three years. Scholars are understandably frustrated when they realize that their first-class research cannot be published within a reasonable time frame, if at all.

Westview Replica Editions are our practical solution to the problem. The concept is simple. We accept a manuscript in camera-ready form and move it immediately into the production process. The responsibility for textual and copy editing lies with the author or sponsoring organization. If necessary we will advise the author on proper preparation of footnotes and bibliography. We prefer that the manuscript be typed according to our specifications, though it may be acceptable as typed for a dissertation or prepared in some other clearly organized and readable way. The end result is a book produced by lithography and bound in hard covers. Initial edition sizes range from 500 to 800 copies, and a number of recent Replicas are already in second printings. We include among Westview Replica Editions only works of outstanding scholarly quality or of great informational value, and we will continue to exercise our usual editorial standards and quality control.

Economic Policy and Income Distribution in Colombia

edited by R. Albert Berry and Ronald Soligo

Contributors to this book assess the impact of economic policy on income distribution by examining several examples from Colombia. Their focus on one country allows quantitative comparisons of the effects of different policies, as well as some tentative conclusions. Colombia was chosen for several reasons: it is one of the few less developed countries for which there is substantial data on the distribution of income over time; its distribution of wealth is unequal in the extreme; and, despite extended government commitment to distributional reform, evidence suggests that the disparities continue and, in fact, increase.

R. Albert Berry, professor of political economy at the University of Toronto, has served as an economic adviser in Colombia and as an economist at the World Bank. Ronald Soligo is professor of economics at Rice University, where he was director of the Program of Development Studies for four years.

Economic Policy and Income Distribution in Colombia

edited by R. Albert Berry
and Ronald Soligo

Routledge
Taylor & Francis Group
LONDON AND NEW YORK

First published 1980 by Westview Press

Published 2018 by Routledge
52 Vanderbilt Avenue, New York, NY 10017
2 Park Square, Milton Park, Abingdon, Oxon OX14 4RN

Routledge is an imprint of the Taylor & Francis Group, an informa business

Library of Congress Catalog Card Number: 79-28068
ISBN: 0-89158-558-3

ISBN 13: 978-0-367-02149-8 (hbk)

ISBN 13: 978-0 367-17136-0 (pbk)

CONTENTS

PREFACE

This decade has been marked by a growing interest on the part of development economists and international aid agencies in the problems of distributional equity and, more specifically, the poor in less developed countries. For the first time aid and lending agencies are giving significant weight in their decisions to the impact of grants and loans on the income levels of the poor and on the overall distribution of income in the recipient country. At the same time LDC governments have also exhibited increasing interest in these issues and have made some attempts to formulate specific policies to address them. Unfortunately, policy makers' interest is well ahead of theory; we still have few serious empirically supported interpretations of the effects of specific policy measures on income distribution. As a result governments and aid agencies have moved ahead on the basis of inadequate analysis at best and presumption at worst.

The papers in this volume are an attempt to assess the distributional impact of a number of economic policies which have been pursued or seriously considered in Colombia. In part, we have focused on one country in order to provide a better base for quantitative comparisons of impact of different policies. In the absence of a comprehensive theory or model from which one can derive the efficacy of various policies in achieving given distributional objectives, it seems appropriate to study the effects of policies which have been tried. The already formidable complexities of such analysis are minimized if we concentrate on one country and compare policies pursued there.

We have chosen Colombia for this exercise for a number of reasons—aside from our own comparative advantage. First of all, a good deal is known about the distribution of income and how it has changed over time in Colombia. The evidence, to be sure, is not unequivocal but in comparison with what is known about income distribution in other LDCs the Colombian experience is relatively well documented. Second, Colombia is of interest both because of its very skewed income distribution and because of its early commitment to policies designed to promote a more equal distribution. Finally, Colombia is of particular interest because, despite two successive administrations which made distributional reform a specific target of their economic policies the evidence suggests that the distribution of income became even more unequal during this period.

The first chapter is a comprehensive and critical survey of the literature dealing with the evidence on the distribution of income in Colombia and its trends and the determinants of that distribution. The survey helps to place the papers in this volume in context and show how they relate to and build on previous work. Topics of the other papers in this volume have been selected because they involve variables which appear *a priori* to be important determinants of income distribution, because they involve variables which are relatively easy to manipulate by policy, or because they are policies which have been advocated or pursued by the Pastrana or Lopez administrations—the two governments which have most emphasized distributional goals.

The conclusions reached by the authors of these papers are discouraging for those development economists and policy advisers who anticipate fairly easy success in changing the distribution of income by public policy. It is evident, first of all, that distributional effects are seldom easy to predict; careful data collection and analysis are necessary in nearly every context. Secondly, the distributional results of some policies will remain a matter of speculation for quite some time. It appears that most equity oriented policies have, at best, only modest positive effects on the distribution of income, suggesting that to effect major change in that distribution would call for a coordinated attack on the problem. Some policies which were thought to have positive effects appear on closer analysis to increase inequality—or, as in the case of vigorous tax reform, not to be politically or administratively feasible. Finally, policies which do not have as an objective the improvement of distributional equity can, in fact, have important effects on income distribution. Thus, for example, the unanticipated high rate of inflation of recent years (reflecting primarily a lack of anti-inflation policy, rather than a deliberate attempt to raise prices) appears to have had a much greater (and negative) effect on income distribution than the combined effect of policies which specifically sought to generate greater equity. It is evident, therefore, that an effective attack on inequality should not begin with a distinction between one set of policies which are viewed as relevant from a distributional point of view and another set which are not.

All the above notwithstanding, the conclusions reached in the various chapters of this volume provide some grounds for optimism; a number of individual policy measures do have significant positive effects on equity, and their combined effect could be important. Though some would be expected to meet with strong political opposition, not all would. In short, a careless policy approach to distributional problems can not be expected to yield much if any fruit, but a serious, well planned one possibly could.

This volume is the outgrowth of work undertaken by the Program of Development Studies at Rice University. The Program was set up in 1970 as an interdisciplinary research group which, to date, has focused on the economic, political and social ramifications of the distribution of gains from growth in the LDCs. Initial support for the Program was provided by the Menil Foundation of Houston; this has been augmented by grants and contracts from NSF and USAID.

Most of the chapters in this volume were presented in draft form at a conference on Income Distribution and Policy in Colombia held at Rice University, May 2-4, 1975. Publication of this volume and several of the papers herein have been funded in part under Agency for International Development Contracts number AID/csd-3302 and AID/otr-C-1394. The views expressed in these papers reflect those of the individual authors and not necessarily those of the Agency.

We thank the authors of these papers for their cooperation in making this volume possible; Nancy Marcus Land for help and advice in moving from a raw manuscript to photo-ready copy; and Lois Thomas for her many contributions in the preparation, typing, and editing of the manuscript.

R. Albert Berry
Ronald Soligo

Economic Policy and Income Distribution in Colombia

Chapter 1

THE DISTRIBUTION OF INCOME IN COLOMBIA: AN OVERVIEW

R. Albert Berry
University of Toronto

Ronald Soligo
Rice University

1. INTRODUCTION

In Colombia, as in many other developing countries, there has been a heightened concern with inequality of the distribution of the material things in life. Severe income inequality places an obviously high premium on effective redistribution policy in Colombia. A substantial research effort has been generated both to learn more about that distribution and to isolate its major determinants for policy purposes. Despite these efforts, and Colombia has probably had more than most developing countries, our knowledge and understanding of distribution questions remains partial and inadequate to the task of confident policy making. Ironically, it appears that just as policy makers in Colombia began to concern themselves more explicity with income distribution, inequality became aggravated. Both the Pastrana administration (1970-74) and that of Lopez (1974-78) have designed and put into effect at least some policies whose objectives included improvements in income distribution. However, most of the empirical evidence suggests that the distribution deteriorated during the 1970s.

The main purpose of the chapters in this volume is to advance our understanding of the possible impact of various exogenous developments or policy tools on income distribution. This chapter attempts two complementary tasks: on the one hand, it reviews some of the descriptive evidence on income distribution in Colombia and its trends. Secondly, it reviews earlier studies dealing with the determinants of income distribution, to provide a better backdrop to the discussion of subsequent chapters and to show how they relate to prior work.

The study of income distribution may be conveniently catalogued into three steps. The first involves the measurement of inequality, including both the conceptual issues of what different indicators or sets of indicators are capable of measuring and the practical problems relating to data collection and use. A second is the study of the correlates of personal and/or family incomes, such as education, wealth, and occupation. Such studies are necessary to pave the way for the third and ultimately policy relevant type of study, involving the way in which changes in the structure of the economy or of government policy affect income distribution. To illustrate the relevance of each step consider the question of how an increase in public subsidies to higher education would affect distribution. The analyst might first decide that the relevant measure of inequality was the distribution of annual income (rather than of lifetime or monthly income). He would then face the difficulties involved in the accurate measurement of annual income of the members of the group in which he was interested, and of the existing relationship of income to level of education. Finally, a model of the economy designed to predict how a change in the relative supply of higher education would affect relative earnings for each person would be needed. Normally one would assume that an increase in the relative supply of higher education would lower its relative earnings, but the model would be required to predict by how much.

In this chapter we address each of these three areas. Although our ultimate interest is the prediction of how policy and/or structural change affects the distribution of welfare, the first two steps are necessary preludes.

2. THE MEASUREMENT OF INEQUALITY

Most persons interested in a country's income or consumption distribution see them as indicators of the welfare distribution. Such data provide an imperfect measure of well-being, both because other factors than access to material goods affect people's satisfaction and because satisfaction may be as much related to one's income (or consumption) relative to one's aspirations as to the absolute level of income (or consumption). Aspirations are obviously influenced by the levels achieved by other members of the community or society.

Since it is difficult (at least for economists) to evaluate the effect of an individual's relative income on his welfare, in practice no attempts to measure inequality have gone beyond the distribution of material consumption or the access thereto provided by income and wealth. The conceptual and methodological issues related to income distribution have thus revolved around the best way to quantify material well-being.

The most plausible indicators of the relative material well-being of a person are measures of lifetime consumption or potential lifetime consumption (e.g., actual consumption plus wealth at end of life). Potential consumption may be greater than actual consumption if the individual places a high enough value on risk aversion, on passing wealth on to the next generation, or on simply being wealthy. Clearly it would be inappropriate to consider a person poor if his wealth is high, even is his consumption is low. In this sense, then, potential consumption is the better measure of material welfare. The distribution of current income (whether by families, income earners, or persons) has, however, been the focus of most discussions. This emphasis has partly resulted from the central position of that variable in national accounting, and perhaps also from the fact that potential consumption is closely related to income.

Another conceptual matter relates to the treatment of public consumption, i.e., expenditures undertaken on people's behalf by government. In principle it is appropriate to add these to private expenditure to arrive at total expenditure, or to private disposable income to arrive at total income. This is not frequently attempted due to data and measurement problems and, in the case of true public goods, to more difficult conceptual problems.

Whatever variables are used to compare the material conditions of life for different people, the natural unit is the individual. But since individuals are grouped in families, whose members consume some items collectively and pool some or all of their income, much information on income and all information on consumption is collected at the level of the family. Very little is known about distribution of income and consumption within the family, so economists have normally opted for the assumption of an equal distribution, with equal amounts going either to each person or to each adult equivalent. When information on family size is not available, it may be unavoidable to talk in terms of unadjusted family income distribution. On other occasions data on income is available by earner and not by family; the direct information on welfare distribution provided is again less than for distribution by person (i.e., by family with information on family size).

As among (current) consumption, (current) income, and wealth distributions, practical factors greatly affect relative usefulness. Information on wealth is the hardest to obtain with a reasonable degree of accuracy, and fewer attempts have been made at the estimation of its distribution than for income and consumption. As between current income and current consumption, several considerations favor the latter. First, it is usually better measured than income. In many income and expenditure surveys, the estimated rate of savings is sometimes negative and usually well below that suggested by other types of information such as changes in the stock of financial and other assets. This implies that consumption is more fully recorded than income. Furthermore, income data from household surveys, when blown up to an estimate of total personal income (i.e., when multiplied by the ratio of population to the size of the sample), typically amounts to 50 to 80 percent of the national accounts estimate of the same variable when the latter is calculated on the basis of output data. Consumption is more likely to be 60-90 percent of the national accounts estimate.[1] Few people believe that national ac-

[1] Very little information exists on the magnitude of understatement by type of respondent. It may be hypothesized, however, that serious inaccuracies characterize the income reporting of independent workers (like farmers), as well as people with multiple sources of income, because of the complexity of the calculation needed to arrive at the true figure. In general, it seems probable that capital income will be less well recorded than labor income. There is no presumption that underreporting is similar across income levels, so it is quite probable that it leads to errors in the estimation of relative incomes.

counts tend to overestimate true values of the variables they seek to measure. A second advantage of the consumption variable is its greater stability. Income over a period from a week to four months, commonly chosen periods in surveys, may be a poor measure of annual income; on the other hand, consumption over those same short periods may give a better idea of annual consumption. This argument becomes stronger the longer the period in which one is conceptually interested. Young people and old people often consume above their current income levels, but in accord with their expected (in the case of the young) or actual (in the case of the old) average incomes over long periods. Consumption is often viewed as the best available proxy for "permanent" or "normal" income.

The problem of noncomparability of families or individuals at different stages in the life cycle is in a sense related to that of income instability. In a society where incomes are typically much lower for young people than for those in mid career, overlife distribution could be quite egalitarian, but at a point of time current income (and probably to a lesser extent current consumption) could be fairly unequal. The existence of income variability over the life cycle is an interesting aspect of an economy, but it is not directly relevant to most of the main questions of equity. To circumvent the problems it poses for cross-country or over-time comparisons of inequality, some analysts have measured inequality of people in the same age range (or families with household heads in the same age range).

Problems of comparisons across groups facing different prices are also serious. Income and consumption data are expressed in value terms, and comparisons of these values are only strictly accurate if the implicit prices for various individuals or groups are the same. As between rural and urban areas this is generally not the case, and to the extent that one price vector is, on balance, higher than the other, errors are introduced. This problem plagues both distribution analyses at a point of time and over time if, as is usually the case, the distribution of population between rural and urban changes over time.

At best, income, consumption, and wealth data provide only a partial picture of material well-being. It has sometimes been suggested that comparisons of the consumption of specific items (e.g., food, housing) may be good indicators of overall welfare. While they may be interesting indicators if data on total consumption are unavailable for example, they cannot be substitutes for the corresponding totals, since only these are really relevant if it is accepted that no social judgments on people's welfare should be based on the idea that a dollar obtained or used one way is different from a dollar obtained or used another way. (This presumption loses some of its merit, however, where such social problems as alcoholism of family head are prevalent.) There are, however, practical reasons to consider such specific indicators as housing conditions, education, and health to be relevant and helpful. Some may be easier to measure accurately than income or total consumption; some may reflect public expenditures and thus not be reflected in private income or consumption figures (e.g., education). Also, since most individual measures of inequality are still quite deficient relative to any standard of perfection, it is important to have as much information as possible, to enrich the detail of our picture of distribution and poverty and to provide internal consistency checks.

3. DEGREE AND PATTERNS OF INEQUALITY IN COLUMBIA

The pattern or shape of the income distribution (and in lesser degree the consumption distribution) has been analyzed in earlier studies and there is consensus on a number of its important characteristics. The major underlying determinants are a point of much disagreement and much less information, to which we return in section 5. All sources point to a high level of income inequality, whether one is referring to the distribution among households or among earners, the distribution of income or of consumption.[2] The more reliable of the available estimates show Gini coefficients in the range 0.50 to 0.55 or so, for both the distribution by earners and that by households; the top decile is typically reported to have 40 to nearly 50 percent of the income (or consumption) while the botom quintile is reported to have 2.5 to 5 percent. In Selowsky's particularly revealing 1974 survey, the Gini coefficient of the distribution among persons ranked by per capita family income was 0.50 (Table 1.1), being substantially higher (0.54) in the urban areas than in the rural areas (0.42).[3] The top decile had about 45 percent of in-

TABLE 1.1. Distribution of Income among Persons Ranked by Per Capita Household Income, 1974

Decile	Urban	Rural	Total
1	1.3	2.0	1.3
2	1.9	3.4	2.3
3	3.0	4.7	3.2
4	3.7	5.7	4.0
5	5.1	6.7	4.9
6	6.0	7.9	6.1
7	7.6	9.6	7.6
8	10.8	11.5	10.5
9	16.7	15.2	15.1
10	43.9	34.2	45.1
Top 5%	31.5	24.4	32.8
Gini Coefficient	0.54	0.42	0.50

Source: Interpolated on the basis of Selowsky, *op. cit.*, Table 13, p. 18. There are, as noted elsewhere, some anomalies in Selowsky's data, and he notes that little time was devoted to the income question in his survey.

[2] For a review of previous studies, see R. A. Berry, "Recent Trends in the Distribution of Income in Colombia: Possible Factors," 1978. (Manuscript.)

[3] Selowsky's is the only national survey used to produce a distribution in which households are ranked by per capita income or consumption, and is accordingly one of the most revealing sources with respect to the extent of inequality. There are, however, some anomalies in Selowsky's data, and he notes that little time was devoted to the income question in his survey. (See M. Selowsky, *Who Benefits from Government Expenditures?: A Case Study of Colombia* (Fairlawn, N. J.: Oxford Univ. Press, 1979.)

come, the top 5 percent about 33 percent, and the bottom quintile about 3.6. A comparison of these figures with the corresponding Gini coefficients of income distribution by households reveals a clear similarity with none of the three differing by more than 0.02. This suggests that the numerous surveys for which data have been presented only on the household distribution of income probably give a better idea of the degree of inequality than could have been presumed a priori. It is also reassuring that the various surveys giving distribution of income among households have generated Gini coefficients in the same general range.

The main conceptual criticism of income distribution figures (i.e., leaving aside the practical problem of accurate measurement) relates to the argument that inequality of current income is greater than that of current consumption, which in turn exceeds that of permanent income or consumption. Thus, for example, the inequality indicated in Selowsky's data would be an overestimate of the long-run inequality . However, data from the Centro de Estudios sobre Desarrollo Economico (CEDE) 1967/68 survey in the four largest cities, in which recording of both income and consumption appears to have been relatively good, show only a

TABLE 1.2. Income and Consumption Distribution, 1967-68 CEDE Study; Four Largest Cities

	Distribution of:						
Decile	Income among households ranked by income (1)		Consumption among households ranked by income (2)	Consumption among households ranked by consumption (3)		Consumption among people ranked by per capita consumption of family (estimate) (4)
1	1.9			2.3		1.8
2	3.0	8.8	12.3	3.6	10.5	2.4
3	3.9			4.6		3.5
4	4.7			5.5		4.4
5	5.8	17.5	21.6	6.5	19.7	6.0
6	7.0			7.7		7.2
7	8.5		9.6	9.0		8.0
8	10.8		11.3	11.5		11.0
9	16.0		15.0	15.3		15.7
10	38.4		30.1	33.7		40.1
Top 5%				22.2		27.4
Gini Coefficient	0.47			0.42		0.49

Sources: Col. 1 is from R. Prieto, *Estructura del Gasto y Distribucion del Ingreso Familiar en Cuatro Ciudades Colombianas,* Parte Primera (CEDE, Universidad de los Andes, 1971), p. 157. Col. 2 is from Berry, "Recent Trends in the Distribution of Income in Colombia: Possible Factors," 1978 (Manuscript), p. 27. Col. 3 is based on tabulations supplied by P. Musgrove of the Brookings Institution. Col. 4 is an adjustment of Col. 3 based on the difference between the distributions of income by households and by population, when in each case people are ranked by household income per capita.

TABLE 1.3. Gini Coefficients among Households by Age of Household Head, 1967/68 Bogotá and Medellin

Age of household head	Bogotá	Medellin
34 or less	0.45	0.49
35-49	0.43	0.50
50-64	0.54	0.50
65 or more	0.58	0.54
All ages	0.47	0.50

Source: R. Ferber, "Distribucion del Ingreso y Desigualdad de Ingresos en Algunas Areas Urbanas," *Ensayos ECIEL* (Estudios Conjuntos sobre Integracion Economica Latinoamericana), No. 3 (Agosto, 1976).

moderate difference in inequality of current income and of current consumption. For households the Gini coefficient for consumption was 0.42, as compared with 0.47 for income (Table 1.2). The share of the bottom decile of families in total consumption was only 2.3 percent compared with 1.9 percent for income. Column 4 of Table 1.2 presents a rough estimate of the distribution of persons by per capita consumption of the household, revealing a strikingly high Gini coefficient of 0.49.

There is less evidence on which to judge the relationship between current income or consumption and lifetime income or consumption. One relevant piece of evidence is the relationship between income or consumption inequality among those in specific age groups. Data from CEDE's 1967/68 four city sample show degrees of inequality not generally lower within cohorts defined by age of household head than for the universe, at least for the household distribution (Table 1.3).

Correlates of Income

Considerably more is known about the correlates of income by income earners than the correlates of income or consumption of households. A useful distinction among structural features which affect the incomes of at least some earners is between market imperfections and "other" features. The former are of particular interest since they are likely to lead to different incomes for persons with the same personal characteristics and thus are traceable and even measurable. For example, if as is often hypothesized less developed countries (LDCs) have "dual" labor markets, a person working in the protected "modern" sector will earn more than he would if he worked in the "traditional" sector.

Colombia has been relatively well studied in terms of most of the correlates of income for which data are readily available, such as age, experience, level of education, sex, geographic location (rural vs. urban and department) and some others as well. The results achieved to date may be summarized as follows.

(1) The best available predictor of a person's income level (especially his labor income) is his educational attainment; this variable explains a much higher percentage of variance than any other variable introduced thus far. In their analysis of the correlates of personal income (including non-labor income) based on a large sample from the 1973 population census, Fields and Schultz[4] found education, age, and sex to be the main available characteristics which would contribute to explaining the variance of income. The differentials for male employees are summarized in Table 1.4. The dominance of education is striking; among urban male employees, for example, the ratio of average income of those with higher education to that of those with no education varied between about 5 to 1 and about 12 to 1 according to age, for persons 20 or more. Although such differentials are presumably due in part to natural ability and to wealth (both of which are probably fairly closely correlated with education) it seems likely that even if these were held constant, very marked differentials would show up.

(2) After allowing for education (in four broad categories) and age, a substantial urban/rural income differential exists for men (see Table 1.4); data were not presented for women. It tends to be an increasing function of education and of age, except perhaps for persons with no education. For male employees, the gross differential (not normalized for age or education) is 3.12 to 1. For persons with no education it is 1.49 to 1. At the various educational levels it tends to be under 1.40 to 1 for persons less than 25, but it rapidly rises thereafter for all but the no-education group. The differentials are larger for employers.[5]

Allowing for a probable overstatement of the effect of rural vs. urban residence *per se* in these figures, it would appear that the income differential is small for employees under 25 and for most persons with no education, but substantial for most other groups.

When the rural/urban distinction is made (and education, age, and sex are allowed for) region is not a very important determinant of income, although the unadjusted income differentials among departments are fairly large. Part of what is measured as a rural/urban differential can also be expressed as interdepartmental or interregional differences, i.e., as statistical variables, the two are in part substitutes.

(3) The differential by sex, after allowing for age and education, is marked. The gross differential reported in the 1973 population census is about 2 to 1[6] (much greater than the 50 percent differential reported in the Departamento Administrativo Nacional de Estadistica (DANE) 1970 survey, which, however, did indicate a differential of 88 percent in urban areas and 47 percent in rural areas). Differences for employers tend to be much greater than for employees, possibly because a greater share of male employers' income is based on their capital than

[4] G. S. Fields and T. P. Schultz, "Sources of Income Variation in Colombia: Personal and Regional Effects," Yale Economic Growth Center Discussion Paper No. 262, June, 1977.

[5] See Fields and Schultz, *op. cit.*, p. 17.

[6] *Ibid.*, p. 18.

TABLE 1.4. Rural and Urban Mean Monthly Incomes by Age and Education, Male Employees 1973

Age	None		Primary		Secondary		Higher	
	Rural	Urban	Rural	Urban	Rural	Urban	Rural	Urban
10-19	400	412	377	513	632	835	–	1156
	(361)	(143)	(914)	(945)	(36)	(418)	–	(4)
20-24	485	634	492	820	923	1375	–	3054
	(291)	(118)	(722)	(923)	(47)	(783)	–	(99)
25-29	459	673	561	1020	1322	2046	8500	5236
	(202)	(84)	(499)	(798)	(41)	(684)	(2)	(161)
30-34	517	685	565	1181	1195	2595	3000	6590
	(184)	(94)	(401)	(733)	(17)	(415)	(2)	(159)
35-44	494	886	763	1343	1019	3309	–	9211
	(398)	(214)	(621)	(1258)	(14)	(525)	–	(136)
45-54	483	767	615	1397	2464	3766	8000	9551
	(274)	(196)	(392)	(771)	(7)	(235)	(1)	(54)
55+	426	623	560	1131	950	3206	1000	7601
	(268)	(160)	(252)	(377)	(4)	(76)	(1)	(28)
Total	463	688	543	1053	1060	2158	5333	6520
	(1978)	(1009)	(3801)	(5805)	(166)	(3136)	(6)	(641)

Source: Fields and Schultz, *op. cit.*, p. 16.

Figures in parentheses give the number of persons in the category. The total sample (from the 1973 population census) contained over 16,000 persons.

TABLE 1.5a. Ratio of Income of Persons in Age Bracket with Highest Average Income to That of Persons 20-24 Years, 1973[a]

Level of Education	Males	Females
Higher	3.94 (45-54)	1.87 (35-44)
Secondary	3.16 (55-64)	1.91 (55-64)
Primary	1.97 (45-54)	1.53 (45-54)
None	1.33 (45-54)	1.18 (45-54)

TABLE 1.5b. Ratio of Income of Men in Age Bracket with Highest Average Income to That of Men 20-24 Years, Rural and Urban, 1973

Level of Education	Rural	Urban
Higher	n. a.	3.26 (45-54)
Secondary	1.83 (35-44)	3.08 (55+)
Primary	1.68 (35-44)	1.85 (45-54)
None	1.21 (45-54)	1.60 (45-54)

[a]Age bracket having highest income indicated in parentheses.
Source: Fields and Schultz, *op. cit.*, p. 13.

in the case of female employers. For employees, the differentials are generally modest (say, a third or less) for persons below 25, and in fact seldom get above this level for persons with no or primary education. But for those with secondary and higher education the gap is more frequently 50-100 percent.

(4) Age is associated with income especially in the case of males, and more closely the higher the level of education. (Table 1.5.) The differentials are a little smaller when a rural vs. urban disaggregation is performed.

Part of these differentials are due to accumulation of capital over one's life span and part to the increase in labor incomes. It is interesting to note that the composition of income by source changes markedly over the life span. Thus, in the case of Bogotá (1967-68) the share of earned income coming from labor fell from about 73 percent for families whose heads were under 35 years to 52 percent for families whose heads were 50-64 and 38 percent for families whose heads were over 64 (Table 1.6).[7] For Medellin the corresponding figures would be 72 percent, 46 percent, and 14 percent.

To summarize thus far, easily measurable personal characteristics (education, age, sex, experience) typically explain (in the statistical sense) 30-40 percent of income variance among earners,[8] with education being the main contributor.

[7]Based on the assumption that half of self-employment income was from capital, and that the category "other" refers mainly to transfer and accidental incomes. If self-employment income were assumed to be two-thirds attributable to labor, these three figures would be 78 percent, 59 percent, and 40 percent.

[8]For a review of principal results of studies in Colombia, see G. Fields, "Analyzing Colombian Wage Structure," Studies in Employment and Rural Development, No. 46, Employment and Rural Development Division (Washington, D. C.: The World Bank, 1978).

TABLE 1.6. Source of Family Income by Age of Family Head
Bogotá and Medellin, 1967-68
(percent distribution)

Age of family head	Wages and salaries		Self-employment		Capital[a]		Other	
	Bogotá	Medellin	Bogotá	Medellin	Bogotá	Medellin	Bogotá	Medellin
34 or less	51.0	48.2	25.1	26.9	11.2	11.1	12.7	13.8
35-49	37.7	37.1	30.0	32.4	19.4	17.6	12.8	12.9
50-64	29.7	21.9	33.3	27.9	25.7	28.9	11.3	21.3
65 and up	21.9	3.2	10.0	15.9	39.2	59.8	28.9	21.1

[a]Includes imputed rent on owner occupied houses.
Source: Ferber, "Distribucion del Ingreso . . .," *op. cit.*, p. 98.

Since these variables remain highly significant in the presence of any others which have been introduced, and since economic considerations strongly suggest roles for these in income determination, it seems appropriate to treat them as core explanatory variables, and to measure the influence of other variables when these personal characteristics are held constant (i.e., also included in the analysis). Education and age appear to play much less important roles in rural areas. Fields reports that in these areas department is the principal explanatory variable for both employees and employers; education and age play minor roles. More specifically, of the 17.7 percent of the log variance explained for rural employees, 13.8 percent is explained by department, 1.7 percent by age, and 1.6 percent by education. Likewise, for rural employers, the respective figures are 27.3 percent (total), 23.7 percent (department), 0.7 percent (age), and 1.5 percent (education).[9]

Many structural variables such as sector of employment and size of firm are related to average income of persons, but their independent effects, after allowing for education, sex, etc., have not been studied. To the extent that they do have effects, these would usually be taken as reflections of one or another type of market imperfection. The most interesting findings to date along these lines are as follows.

(1) Among structural features often blamed for a significant amount of income inequality is the dualism, or perhaps better, the technological heterogeneity of the Colombian economy. Modernity is assumed to be related to some combination of size of establishment, nature of the product, and educational level of workers. Higher labor incomes are anticipated in this sector both because of higher productivity and because unions and labor legislation help to push wages up. Bourguignon has recently addressed this question, defining the modern sector as including all large production units of five or more employees, plus all individuals with a uni-

[9]Fields, "Analyzing...," *op. cit.*, p. 63.

versity education and all government employees.[10] While the gross income differential between the modern and traditional sectors was 1.86, most of it was related to educational and other characteristics likely to affect personal productivity. Bourguignon performed a wide range of tests providing some confidence in his conclusion that the typical modern-traditional differential (holding personal characteristics constant) is probably fairly low, e.g., under 20 percent.[11] If, as is plausible to assume, the modern sector selects workers of higher capacity, given education, experience, etc., then the true differential—holding ability constant—would be even less than Bourguignon's figures show. On the other hand, fringe benefits,which are higher in the modern sector, are seriously underreported. As Bourguignon notes, caution is called for since all the variables included in his analysis explain only 30-40 percent of the variance of log income; it could be that with a more complete specification of the income function and better data the modern-traditional differential could either disappear or become greater.

Based on these conclusions, it seems unlikely that the modern-traditional sort of distinction would explain more than a couple of percent of income variance in the country as a whole, when added to the other relevant variables included. There remains, of course, the possibility that such a market imperfection may in turn underlie some of the association of variables like education, age, and rural/urban with income. In that case, its true causal role as a determinant of the variance of income could be much greater. We suspect this is unlikely though, and that its true contribution is not more than, say, 5 percent.

(2) Some analyses have focused directly on one or more of the many factors which could help to explain the differential picked up by the modern-traditional distinction, including unionization, role of foreign firms which might have reasons for paying higher wages, and others. Tenjo's recent analysis of the effects of unionization[12] on the remuneration of paid workers in manufacturing in Bogotá and

[10] F. Bourguignon, "Pobriza y Dualism en el Sector Urbano de las Economias en Desarrollo: El Caso de Colombia, *Desarrollo y Sociedad*, Numero 1, 1979, p. 54. He used DANE's seven city income survey of 1974, and the delineation of the modern sector implied that 54.5 percent of earners were employed in it.

[11] Bourguignon used a log linear form with the following independent variables: a dummy for the modern sector, the wage rate per unit time worked, years of schooling, years of experience, years of experience squared, and in some equations an estimate of the share of income from capital (*ibid*., p. 63). Unlike many such analyses, Bourguignon's includes hours worked so his estimated coefficients assume a constant time worked. On average hours worked are a little lower in the traditional sector than in the modern sector (Bourguignon, *op. cit*., p. 45), perhaps by 6-7 percent. Thus, the differentials in income would be somewhat above those of wages, but still smaller than many discussions might suggest. It is the traditional sector self-employed who report lower hours worked than average; this may or may not reflect preferences.

[12] Jaime Tenjo, "Impacto de la Actividad Sindical Sobre Los Salarios: Un Analisis Econometrico," *Revista de Planeacion y Desarrollo*, Vol. VII, Numero 2 (Julio-Dec., 1975). Tenjo uses various measures of the degree of unionization of the three digit industries which are the units of observations in this analysis, and includes a measure of average output per blue collar worker and of "capacitacion" (measured by the ratio of non-blue collar workers to blue collar workers).

Medellin (1972) led him to conclude that company unions (the analysis was restricted to this type) could account for a total wage bill in manufacturing of 15 or 20 percent higher than it would otherwise have been; this implies a substantially greater differential between union and non-union workers, although the inability to include personal variables and to distinguish blue and white collar workers may have led to some overestimation.

In fact, studies which have attempted to analyze the impact of structural variables on wages, have systematically faced the problem of not being able to include personal variables or not being able to measure them precisely. In the former category is the study by Fields and Marulanda, who regressed average wage reported in two-digit branches of manufacturing, mining, services, commerce and government on a set of structural variables: plant size, capital intensity, share of foreign capital, labor productivity, and one variable related mainly to personal characteristics, the proportion of workers who are white collar.[13] In the four private sectors taken individually, the full set of variables explained 83 to 95 percent of the variance in average remuneration. When "percent of workers who are white collar" was omitted, the share of variance explained by the remaining "structural" variables was a substantial 56-91 percent. Whether this result suggests significant market imperfections depends on whether the workers "quality" or underlying productivity could be the dominant explanation for such intersectoral differences. The greater explanatory power of personal characteristics than variables related to type of technology and size and the failure of Bourguignon's study to identify a significant income differential between the modern and traditional sectors when relevant personal characteristics are included suggests that this may be the case. In the above analysis, labor productivity would certainly reflect personal characteristics at least in part, and various of the other variables could be statistically associated with personal characteristics even though not determined by them. So it remains to be seen whether such factors as firm size and capital intensity have significant independent effects on wages.

Most of our existing knowledge about the correlates of distribution relates mainly to the distribution of labor income; even when in principle the source of data includes all income, reporting of capital income is likely to be incomplete. As a result evidence on the distribution of wealth and of capital income remains rather sparse. Reporting appears to have been relatively good in CEDE's 1967/68 four city survey. On the basis of this data Musgrove notes that in Bogotá and Medellin capital income other than imputed rent accrues almost entirely to the top 20 percent of households, ranked by per capita income. Even including that imputed rent, the top quartile in terms of total income receives 60 percent of capital income in Bogotá and 73 percent in Medellin.[14] But income from inde-

[13] G. S. Fields and N. de Marulanda, "Intersectoral Wage Structure in Colombia," Yale Economic Growth Center Discussion Paper No. 251, August, 1976.

[14] P. Musgrove, *Consumer Behavior in Latin America: Income and Spending of Families in Ten Andean Cities* (Washington, D. C.: The Brookings Institution, 1978), Chapter 2.

pendent work is important in all quartiles (e.g., 24.7 percent of all income in Bogotá's bottom quartile and 20.2 percent in Medellin's) and one would have to disaggregate it into labor and capital income to know how much capital income the poor have.[15]

4. INCOME DISTRIBUTION TRENDS IN COLOMBIA

In addition to being important for its own sake, knowledge of how the degree of inequality is changing over time in a country may help us understand the determinants of that inequality. This section reviews briefly the evidence available on such trends in Colombia. In this context, it is important to emphasize the relative stability of many of the determinants of income distribution, such as the character of the social system, the distributions of education and wealth, and the sectoral structure of the economy.

In their study focusing on the three decades from the mid-thirties through the mid-sixties, Urrutia and Berry concluded that distribution had shown as apparent tendency towards greater inequality from the beginning of the period through the middle of the fifties and had then shown some improvement over the next decade. The distribution within agriculture, the largest single sector, appeared however to have worsened rather systematically over the thirty-year period, so that the overall improvement of distribution in the last decade corresponded to an improvement in nonagricultural distribution, complemented perhaps by the declining share of the agricultural labor force in the total. Within agriculture, the apparently worsening distribution was reflected in the stagnation of the average wage of agricultural workers while average income per capita in agriculture was rising rather rapidly.[16] The increase in demand for labor associated with the output growth was too small to exert upward pressure on the wage rate; small scale, labor-intensive farms saw a modest output growth while the relatively mechanized commercial production of such crops as rice and cotton expanded rapidly. The rapid increase in the use of machines was fostered by a positive government attitude and World Bank loans; its implications for income distribution are discussed by Thirsk in Chapter 8. The availability of credit, mainly to middle and large-scale farms, was expanded. Finally, the focus of research, whether by producers' organizations or by government stations, was on products disproportionately located on large farms.

One intriguing aspect of overall trends in distribution is the apparent improvement during a phase of relatively slow growth of output and even slower growth of income (mid-1950s to mid-1960s) and worsening under fast growth (1945 to

[15] See Junta del Acuerdo de Cartagena, *Grupo Andino: Distribucion de Ingresos y Estructura del Consumo* (Area Urbana), documento J/PR/68 (Lima, 15 March, 1976).

[16] It should be noted that the conclusions reached by Urrutia and Berry are tentative. Their results were derived by indirect methods, and their incomplete understanding with respect to family income sources leaves the results open to some question.

the mid-1950s). According to Urrutia-Berry,[17] for some of the low income categories absolute incomes fell or remained essentially constant under fast growth but advanced under slow growth. For example, agricultural workers, unskilled construction workers in Bogotá, and blue collar manufacturing workers all seemed to do better in the slow growth period than either the earlier or the recent fast growth period. The share of income accruing to human capital rose markedly during the fast growth period, but less rapidly (possibly it even declined) during the slow growth period, suggesting that rapid growth may have increased the concentration of labor income by disproportionately increasing the demand for scarce skills. Whether this is true depends, of course, on how human capital is distributed, a factor related to education but also to native ability and ability to learn on the job. Interestingly, the physical capital share was quite stable over the period 1950-70, with a slight downward trend; it showed no clear relationship with the rate of growth.

Evidence on Distributional Trends since the Mid-1960s

Concern with the issue of income distribution in Colombia is heightened by the considerable evidence suggesting increasing inequality during the fast growth period since the mid-1960s. While this worsening may be less than wage trend data suggest, and/or it could be a transitory result of the burst of inflation which occurred or the coffee bonanza, less optimistic interpretations are also possible (one of which relates to the effects of the drug boom), and the period warrants a very careful look.

One hint of a worsening distribution is a sharp decline in the share of income going to unskilled labor (defined here as the pure labor share). This share declined by at least 10 percent of net domestic income over 1967-76. (Such income is much more evenly distributed than that from human or physical capital.) Through 1969, the physical capital share remained about constant while that of human capital was rising.[18] The wage differential between white and blue collar workers widened, and the share of the labor force falling in the former category increased; both factors contributed to the increasing human capital share. Since, for the period 1970-75 the pure labor share fell sharply, and it is unlikely that the human capital share increased, it is clear that the share of physical capital rose significantly. The declining labor share during the early 1970s is reflected in the slow growth of most real wage series and an actual decline in construction and manufacturing. Agricultural wages have not been collected on a systematic basis since 1970, though Instituto Colombiano de Seguros Sociales (ICSS) data indicate a fall for them also. The coincidence of these declines with the step-up of inflation is noteworthy, and suggests the emergence of a price-wage gap.

For the decade 1965-75 as a whole, the wage data strongly suggest a worsening

[17] See Berry and Urrutia, *op. cit.*, Chapter 4.

[18] A. Berry, "Changing Income Distribution under Development: Colombia," *Review of Income and Wealth*, Income and Wealth Series 20, No. 3 (September, 1974).

of the relative position of the low-wage groups, the largest being the agricultural workers. While income per employed earner (all income–i.e., including that from capital) was rising at over 4 percent per year or 50 percent over the decade,[19] the labor income for agricultural workers stagnated while that of construction and personal service workers appears to have fallen. The better paid blue collar workers in factory manufacturing probably ended the decade at about the same real income as they began it. The decline in relative income was not limited to low paid workers, however. White collar employees in factory manufacturing gained rapidly over 1965-70, but suffered a loss of real income thereafter. Government employees at the national and departmental level appear to have achieved slight gains in the late 1960s, followed by losses in the 1970s.

In the face of lower or only moderately higher real wages in 1975 than in 1965 for the set of groups for which data are available[20] and a 50 percent increase in income per employed earner, it is evident that some subgroups have been losing their relative position rapidly, unless income from main job has been supplemented increasingly by capital income or income from second jobs. With respect to the 1970s, a key question is how the rapid increase in nonlabor income has been allocated. In this connection, there is considerable evidence pointing to an expansion of small scale activity in manufacturing and commerce over the period 1964 to the mid-1970s. But it remains to be seen who participated in this development and whether it was a defensive response to poor opportunities for paid employment and therefore not very lucrative or whether it provided relatively good earnings. Also of obvious relevance since the mid-1970s is the distribution of incomes from the coffee and drug bonanzas. As of 1975, coffee exports accounted directly for about five percent of GNP. This share expanded rapidly over the succeeding years to reach over eight percent at its peak. While income received in the drug (marijuana and cocaine) trade is unknown (because of its illegal nature), most estimates for the years since 1976 have fallen in the range of $400 million to one billion dollars per year. Thus, the share of GDP originating in this sector could be over five percent, or it could be as low as two-three percent. It is unlikely that the increase in coffee's share of GDP plus the drug share would together exceed ten percent; 5-8 percent would be a more likely range. While the way these "bonanza" incomes are distributed can obviously have some significance in determining overall distributions,[21] they would clearly not be major determinants,

[19] See Berry, "Recent Trends...," *op. cit.*, Table 9.

[20] Part of the negative impact of stagnant real wages by occupational categories is offset by a gradual shift of workers from lower to higher paying occupations, but there is no evidence to suggest that this offsets the effect of declining wages for specific occupations. A rough calculation suggests that over 1964-73 it might imply a 7 percent faster growth of average wage per wage earner than would occur were occupational structure unchanged, i.e., a little less than one percent per year.

[21] Coffee incomes have traditionally been less concentrated in Colombia than in some other countries, though still far from being reasonably equally distributed, and concentration appears to have been increasing in the last decade. Drug incomes are probably quite concentrated, but even if this is true, the already high share of the top 5% of earners in Colombia means that by most measures of inequality the drug income would not lead to much change.

comparable for example with the distribution of education. The tentative judgment, based on the above discussion, must be that inequity has increased during the 1970s, and possibly during the late 1960s as well.

The last decade has been one of rapid growth and structural change in Colombia; over 1965-75 the average growth of national income was 6.8 percent. There was considerable structural change as the share of agriculture et al. in output fell from 28.2 percent in 1965 to 24.1 percent in 1975, while the share in manufacturing rose (18.0 to 19.2 percent), as did that in real estate and financial services (2.9 to 4.6). The share of the population found in urban areas (centers of above 1,500 people) has risen from about 52.8 percent in 1964 to perhaps 65 percent in 1976. Considerable increases occurred in the share of persons reaching the secondary and higher levels of education. An export boom occurred in nontraditional items; in 1966 the ratio of exports to GNP (current prices) was 12.1 and in 1974 it was 15.1 percent. More recently, in the 1970s, there were coffee and drug bonanzas which greatly increased the available foreign exchange. As discussed in detail in Chapter 4, the 1970s have seen a dramatic step-up of inflation. The national income deflator rose from an average annual rate of 8.5 percent during 1966-70, to 17.6 percent over 1970-74; the national consumer price index for the blue collar workers rose at rates of 6.2 and 18.1 percent in the2 periods.

5. POLICY AND STRUCTURAL DETERMINANTS OF INCOME DISTRIBUTION

Most of the chapters in this volume deal with the distributional effects of various government policies. To place those chapters in better perspective, we review the more relevant previous studies on the policy determinants of Colombian income distribution, and their relation to the major findings of the chapters of this volume. The discussion is classified, somewhat arbitrarily, into the following policy areas: monetary and fiscal; education and training; trade and industrialization; agricultural and price policy; housing and urbanization; wages, labor market, and demographic; and the relevance of demand patterns for redistribution policies in general. The effects of any policy instrument on distribution will, naturally, be influenced by structural characteristics of the economy such as the distribution of wealth, access to education, and functioning of the labor market.

Several policy areas are of special interest, either because they involve variables which appear to be important determinants of income distribution, or because the policy tools can be manipulated relatively easily. In the former category is educational policy; the data presented in section 3 showed the power of educational level in explaining the variance of income among individuals. Fiscal policy falls in the latter group since it can redistribute so directly. Trade policy merits serious consideration because it can have clear and important effects on the economy and is relatively easy to manage.

Also of particular interest are those policies which recent Colombian governments have pursued with redistributional goals in mind. Of the Pastrana government's "four strategies,"[22] the emphasis on urban building was expected to accelerate the rate of growth *and* increase available employment for lower income groups. While the further expansion of minor exports (including international tourism) was not primarily motivated by its distributional implications, economic theory might suggest a positive impact. The third strategy, to increase rural productivity, would have distributional effects depending on how the objective was sought. Since the Pastrana government did not evolve a small farm policy, there was little reason to suppose that its productivity raising steps would improve distribution. The fourth strategy focused directly on improving distribution by making both taxes and expenditures more progressive.

The Lopez administration described its development plan as being designed to "achieve economic growth which would make possible massive creation of productive employment and would thereby especially benefit the poorer 50 percent of Colombians."[23] Major emphasis was placed on the tax reform (analyzed here in Chapter 2), on the slowing of inflation which was felt to hurt especially the poor (discussed in Chapter 4), and on changes in the monetary and fiscal system which would remove incentives to capital intensity and replace them where possible with incentives to the use of more labor. Along sectoral lines, integrated rural development was to receive special attention. And the National Food and Nutrition Plan was designed to benefit the poor in general. Equalization of educational opportunities, and especially the broadening of access and improvement of quality of education in rural areas was emphasized.

Research to date, including that reported in this volume, provides reasonable support for the hopes and expectations expressed in the last two Development Plans, i.e., it appears that most of the policies whose effects were expected to be positively redistributive were correctly evaluated. The deflation of hopes has been associated with the inability to implement those policies which in retrospect appear to have been most important from a distributional point of view (especially the control of inflation). The potential distributional benefits of some other policies may have been overestimated, especially relative to the damage which could come from inadequate performance in an area like inflation control.

Fiscal Policy

Defined in its broadest sense, fiscal management obviously has potentially important distributional implications. Public sector revenues have accounted for about 20 percent of national income in the 1970s, expenditures (including investment) a higher share. Potential distributional effects are large on both the tax and the expenditure sides of the budget. Appraising the effects of expenditure

[22] For a presentation, see Departamento de Planeacion Nacional, *Las Cuatro Estrategias* (Bogotá, Colombia: National Planning Department, 1972).

[23] Departamento Nacional de Planeacion, *Para Cerrar La Brecha: Plan de Desarrollo Social, Economico y Regional 1975-1978* (Bogotá: Banco de la Republica, 1975), p. VII.

involves evaluation of a very heterogeneous set of programs some of which are here considered separately, as with publicly financed education.

While the problems of measuring *overall* tax and expenditure incidence may be overwhelming, it is important to note that the incidence of some taxes and of some expenditures is less mysterious; accordingly, it is not difficult to alter a system so that the distributional impact is improved. To quote Bird and De Wulf, in their discussion of taxation and income distribution in Latin America:

> . . . probably few will disagree with the proposition that taxation in most Latin American countries appears to have done little to correct this initial inequality, both because of its relatively light burden in total in most countries, and, more specifically, because of the apparent regressive or proportional nature of its incidence. We, too, do not disagree with what we take to be the major message of this line of argument—that taxes have done and can do little to correct the distribution of incomes generated by the combination of imperfect markets and myriad interventionist policies that characterizes most Latin American countries. But we think the argument is both too optimistic in assuming that we know or can know what the burden of taxes is and, perhaps, although of this we are less certain, too pessimistic in ignoring the potential distributional effect of certain kinds of taxes in reducing the income, wealth, and power of the rich.[24]

For example, most wealth taxes and progressive income or consumption taxes have fairly predictable incidence.

The Tax System

Several useful studies of tax incidence have been undertaken in Colombia. The consensus is that even before the reforms of 1974-75, the system was at least somewhat progressive. McLure's estimate of incidence for 1970 (presented as Table 1.7) provides a good starting point for the discussion; it implies a degree of progressivity ranging from rather mild to fairly strong, depending on whether the corporation income tax was borne by foreigners, Colombian consumers, or Colombian shareholders, and whether coffee export duties were excluded from the analysis or included.[25]

Progressivity was found to result in large part from the personal income tax, but the liquor tax, the property taxes, and the luxury elements of the sales tax and customs duties contributed to it. Unfortunately, the results are sensitive to the incidence of the corporation income tax (with progressivity much greater if

[24] Richard Bird and Luc De Wulf, "Tax Incidence and Income Distribution in Latin America: A Critical Review of Empirical Studies," *IMF Staff Papers*, Vol. 20, 1973.

[25] C. E. McLure, Jr., "The Incidence of Colombian Taxes: 1970," *Economic Development and Cultural Change*., Vol. 24, No. 41 (October, 1975).

TABLE 1.7. Effective Rates of Taxation, All Taxes, All Households, 1970

Income Class (Pesos per year)	Direct Taxes a, c	Direct Taxes b	Indirect taxes	Total: All Taxes a, c	Total: All Taxes b
	Coffee Export Duties Included				
0-6,000	5.7	10.0	7.1	12.9	17.1
6,000-12,000	3.8	6.5	5.1	8.9	11.5
12,000-24,000	3.0	6.0	6.2	9.2	12.2
24,000-60,000	3.9	7.0	6.0	9.9	13.1
60,000-120,000	4.2	7.1	6.5	10.7	13.6
120,000-240,000:					
a	13.1	*	5.4	18.6	*
b	*	8.8	5.9	*	14.7
c	6.4	*	6.4	12.8	*
Over 240,000:					
a	29.3	*	7.0	36.2	*
b	*	21.9	8.0	*	29.9
c	22.5	*	9.4	31.9	*
Total:					
a	8.6	*	6.1	14.7	*
b	*	8.8	6.3	*	15.1
c	6.0	*	6.5	12.5	*
Over 120,000:					
a	19.2	*	6.0	25.2	*
b	*	13.6	6.6	*	19.2
c	12.1	*	7.5	19.6	*
	Coffee Export Duties Excluded				
0-6,000	0.1	4.6	7.6	7.6	12.1
6,000-12,000	0.3	3.0	5.3	5.5	8.2
12,000-24,000	0.5	3.5	6.3	6.8	9.9
24,000-60,000	1.5	4.7	6.2	7.7	10.9
60,000-120,000	2.2	5.1	6.6	8.8	11.7
120,000-240,000:					
a	11.5	*	5.5	17.0	*
b	*	7.0	6.0	*	12.9
c	4.3	*	6.6	10.9	*
Over 240,000:					
a	26.7	*	7.2	34.0	*
b	*	18.8	8.3	*	27.1
c	18.8	*	9.5	28.4	*
Total:					
a	6.2	*	6.3	12.5	*
b	*	6.4	6.5	*	12.8
c	3.5	*	6.7	10.1	*
Over 120,000:					
a	17.2	*	6.2	23.4	*
b	*	11.2	6.8	*	18.0
c	9.3	*	7.7	17.0	*

*Not applicable.

a: Corporation tax borne entirely by Colombian shareholders.

b: Corporation tax shifted entirely to Colombian consumers.

c: Corporation tax borne entirely by non-Colombians.

Source: McLure, *op. cit.*, p. 18.

it is assumed to fall on shareholders) and to whether the coffee export duty is treated as a tax or not. For example, the regressivity of incidence between the bottom two income categories distinguished in Table 1.7 and the lack of progressivity over the next few categories results from how coffee export duties, the indirect taxes and the corporation tax when it is assumed to fall on consumers are allocated. McLure assumed that indirect taxes and the shifted corporation tax fall on households according to their levels of consumption. But the low income urban families falling in the under 18,000 peso income brackets (nearly one-third of all households) had consumption about 14 percent above income, and the 7 percent with incomes under 9,000 pesos had consumption above income by about 25 percent.[26] Both the reordering of families by income per capita and the use of income measured over a longer period of time—which we consider appropriate—would tend to lower the relative burden of these taxes on the (now different) poorest families relative to the rest. The coffee duty, if one decides to include it, would also be less regressive (in its overall incidence) than McLure has assumed; he allocated it all to rural residents, whereas a considerable share is borne by well-off urban families owning coffee lands and some is probably borne by intermediaries. McLure also assumed that small coffee planters had no income from other sources, which is not in general the case. Probably the burden on the lowest income group is overestimated rather seriously.[27]

Imposing our judgment that the corporation tax is borne significantly by both shareholders and consumers and that the coffee tax has a more progressive incidence than estimated by McLure, and focusing on the incidence of the tax system when households are classified by long-run average (i.e., "permanent") per capita income or consumption, we conclude that progressivity is substantial and continuous across income levels. The burden might rise from 5-7 percent for the bottom decile to 20-25 percent for the top ones, probably in a fairly smooth way. If so, the redistributive impact of the system would remain considerable, with both the very rich and the very poor bearing a lower burden than indicated in Table 1.7.[28]

The tax reform initiated by the Lopez administration in 1974 and 1975 was, in Perry's words, "A political and economic event of special importance in the country, generating great international interest because of its potential for raising government revenue, and for increasing the equity and progressivity of the tax system."[29] Its indirect distributional effects were also expected to be considerable

[26] See A. Berry, *Resource Transfers between Agriculture and Non-agriculture in Colombia,* 1978, Chapter 3. (Mimeographed.)

[27] See the earlier version of McLure's paper, "The Incidence of Colombian Taxes, 1970," Program of Development Studies Discussion Paper No. 41, Rice University, 1973.

[28] This would be more in line with the more moderate progressivity of the earlier estimate by McLure for 1966. ("The Incidence of Taxation in Colombia," in *Fiscal Reform for Colombia,* ed. by R. A. Musgrave and M. Gillis (Cambridge, Mass.: Law School of Harvard University, 1971, Part 2, Chap. 1.)

[29] G. E. Perry, "Las Reformas Tributarias de 1974 y 1975 en Colombia," *Coyuntura Economica,* Vol. VII, No. 3 (November, 1977), p. 83.

as some of the spending programs highlighted in Lopez' plan *Para Cerrar la Brecha* were to be directed at the poorer segments of the population. Much serious deliberation underlay this reform, with the 1969 Musgrave tax mission being one important source of ideas. In Chapter 2 Gillis and McLure argue that from a technical point it was an excellent reform, whose potential for positive income redistribution rested mainly on:

(1) increased progressivity of the legal tax system, due to changes in income, sales and other taxes, and
(2) improved administrability.

They argue that the increase in the tax revenues of 1975 over 1974 may have fallen almost entirely on the top 20 percent of the income distribution, a very impressive distributional outcome indeed.[30] Tax revenues as a percent of GNP increased from 9.0 percent in 1974 to 10.5 percent in 1975.[31] Their major uncertainty with respect to the reform involved the questions of compliance and morality in tax administration. Taxpayer resistance was expected to rise as the implications of the reform came through to people. The ultimate question was, therefore, how much impact the reform would have after the system had moved back closer to a sort of "administrative equilibrium."

Some light can be shed on this issue by more recent studies. In 1976, central government tax revenues fell from 11.1 percent to 11.0 percent of national income, according to Perry's estimates; only the fortuitous increase in coffee taxes prevented a significant decline in the tax share of national income. The income tax (and complementary taxes) fell by 11 percent in real terms or from 5.31 percent of national income to 4.47 percent.

This decline was due in part to government back-pedalling and in part to increasing evasion. "At the end of 1975 a law was decreed which reduced the revenues from the tax by 8 percent in real terms; this law of 'tax relief,' diminished by 8 percent the tax rate on sociedades anonimas which represent nearly 90 percent of the effective tax base of sociedades, and arranged for annual modifications to the rates on individual taxpayers, moving the tax brackets up by 8 percent each year, as partial compensation for the effects of inflation, as well as authorizing other smaller benefits."[32] In 1975, taxpayers facing the presumptive income tax on 1974 income could not "tinker" with their "patrimony" since it

[30] Gillis and McLure, *op. cit.*, p. 65. This conclusion appears to be consistent with Perry's calculations based on a simulation analysis of a sample of returns for the tax year 1972. (See Perry, *op. cit.*, p. 110.)

[31] Perry's figures are a little higher, showing an increase from 9.2 percent of national income in 1974 to 11.1 percent in 1975. (See Perry, *op. cit.*, p. 86.) However, this is still well below the 11.8 percent achieved in 1970 and 1971. The income and complementary tax share (together with the inheritance and gift taxes which were integrated with it under the reform) rose from 4.18 to 5.38 percent, though part of this increase was "one shot" in nature, being due to an amnesty on interest on unpaid taxes, without which the increase would have been only to 5.22 (based on Perry, *op. cit.*, p. 92).

[32] Perry, *op. cit.*, p. 92.

had already been declared as of December, 1973; but thenceforward they could. They searched for and found weaknesses in the law. Evasion was facilitated by a strange feature of Colombian tax law, whereby if the government fails to challenge an individual's tax declaration within two years, it loses the chance to do so. The reform had indeed sought partial remedy for such loopholes, but the relevant articles were declared unconstitutional by the Supreme Court (because promulgated under the emergency powers). Proposals subsequently presented by the executive to Congress were much less satisfactory in their attack on these problems. An ambitious administrative reform, decreed in January, 1976, was delayed by the government's policy of austerity. Some branches of the government have, not surprisingly, been cool toward the whole set of reforms.[33]

More time will be required to judge the overall success of the tax reform, including its distributional impact. The latter is sensitive to the relative evasion of the income and complementary taxes by different groups which is not yet known. As of the end of 1976, it appeared that the reform had contributed to a sharp increase (over 1974-76) in the share of national income collected by the sales tax (1.24 percent to 2.19 percent–it was only 1.09 percent in 1973), whereas revenue from income and complementary taxes (including gift and inheritance taxes) increased only from 4.18 percent to 4.49 percent. The changes in sales tax incidence would thus have to be progressive for the reform to increase overall progressivity.[34] Finally, given the strong possibility that inflation has worsened income distribution in Colombia, the relationship between the tax reform and inflation takes on importance. The accelerating inflation of the early 1970s was mainly due to budgetary deficits which arose in the face of a declining tax share of national income (from 11.0 percent in 1970 to 9.2 percent in 1974); public expenditure did not increase as a share of national income at this time. The incoming Lopez administration (1974) did succeed in slowing inflation (from 27 percent in 1974 to 18 percent in 1975) with the aid of the increase in taxes. But at the end of 1975 expenditures increased again, and high coffee prices also contributed to inflationary pressures which led to an acceleration of price increases again in 1976 and 1977. One could argue that the inflation would have been somewhat worse without the tax reform.

Had the Lopez administration's fiscal hopes been met, the increased revenues made available by the reform would have permitted both fiscal balance and a substantial increase in expenditures directed towards the poor, i.e., the Integrated Rural Development Program, the Nutrition Plan, and other initiatives. Expenditures along these lines were not substantial until 1977; the government opted to finance them with foreign loans in order not to aggravate the domestic fiscal situation, and expenditures were delayed due to their inflationary implications.[35]

If the estimates of McLure/Gillis and Perry are correct, the tax reform of 1974

[33] Perry, *op. cit.*, p. 95.

[34] Perry is doubtful that these would have significant effects on the progressivity of the system (*op. cit.*, p. 103).

[35] Perry, *op. cit.*, p. 96.

would have transferred 1.5 to 2 percent of national income from the top few percent of earners (the top 5 percent, according to Perry) and would have lowered the Gini coefficient by .01, according to Perry's calculations. The redistributive effect of the pre-reform tax system, although considerable, was probably not enough to lower the Gini coefficient by more than .02 or .03.[36] Thus, if Perry's estimates of the effect of the 1974-75 reforms are accurate, they would significantly increase the redistributive effect of the tax system as measured by the Gini coefficient (e.g., by perhaps 50 percent, from about .02 to .03), a worthy goal but still necessarily a rather modest one.[37] If, as McLure and Gillis argue in Chapter 2 and as subsequent events have clearly indicated, the reform of 1974-75 was all and probably more than Colombia could aspire to administer, it is evident that the tax system cannot begin to handle the distribution problem by itself. It must be one of many avenues of attack. Administration is clearly as important as the legal tax system.

Public Expenditures

Berry-Urrutia have estimated the distribution of benefits from government expenditures as of 1966. When compared with the distribution of current income, these expenditures appear to be moderately to fairly strongly progressive; in particular, they increase the proportion of goods and services consumed by the poorest two deciles of the population[38] (see Table 1.8) even under the strong assumption that all government expenditures on general services benefited only the two richest deciles of the population. The expenditures which benefited these lower deciles most were on public health, education, and a variety of items included under "development expenditures"—by and large local expenditures. On a per capita basis the estimated benefits from public expenditure were substantially higher in the top decile than in the lower ones, nearly twice as high under the assumption that general services expenditures are distributed proportionately to

[36]The pretax distribution used by McLure before his adjustments for the corporation tax and retained earnings has a Gini coefficient of 0.534. The after tax distribution which would result from tax burdens ranging from 5 percent to 20 percent (we argue above [p. 21]that this is a reasonable guess of the range of tax burdens) across the income categories he uses (specifically 5, 6, 10, 15, 17, and 20 percent) would have a Gini of 0.516.

The household income distribution used by McLure, including his adjustments, has a pretax Gini coefficient of 0.65. Applying his calculated tax burdens corresponding to the case where coffee duties are excluded and the corporation tax falls on the shareholders generates an after tax Gini coefficient of 0.56. As discussed in the text, it is unlikely that the pretax Gini would be as high as 0.65, and therefore unlikely that the effect of the tax system is as progressive as indicated by McLure.

[37]The Gini coefficient is highly sensitive to the share of the top groups and is not the best indicator of inequality if one is more interested in the share of the bottom deciles. Nevertheless, the above conclusions would not appear to be very sensitive to the indicator chosen.

[38]Berry and Urrutia, *op. cit.*, p. 159.

others and over ten times as high on the strong assumption just cited. But since the distribution of current income is itself so unequal, the addition of a less unequally distributed set of public service benefits improves the overall distribution.

To the extent that the distribution of current income overestimates the inequality of longer run average (or "permanent") income, the redistributive impact of expenditures, like that of taxes, would almost certainly be less than indicated in Table 1.8, possibly considerably less. Estimates of the distribution of benefits from public expenditures are necessarily very crude at this point, and further work may lead to some considerable changes in the allocation of those benefits. But even with these two qualifications, we would guess that public expenditure did improve distribution as of 1966.[39]

Two recent studies of the distribution of benefits of certain public services tend to confirm this conclusion. Linn's study in this volume looks carefully at the impact of municipal expenditures and taxes in larger cities. His judgment is that, overall, the incidence of large city government budgets is quite progressive, due to the progressivity of public expenditures and public service prices. Local taxes increase or reduce overall progressivity depending on whether the property tax is assumed to be progressive or regressive. While the "best guess" benefits are 3.3 percent of the incomes of the lowest quintile, they are 0.7 percent of those for the highest quintile. Linn's figures suggest that the municipal government may be the most important level, in terms of benefits received, for the bottom two quintiles of the population of these larger cities. As Colombia becomes increasingly urbanized, the share of public expenditures carried out at the municipal level (mainly large cities) has increased. As of 1970 municipal entities (including the decentralized agencies providing services like water, electricity, etc.) probably accounted for one-third or more of total public expenditures.

Selowsky undertook a survey to measure directly the incidence of benefits from the public (national)[40] budget and to analyze the degree of subsidy involved for services which were not free to the user, focusing on those expenditures whose beneficiaries can be most accurately identified. Being based on survey data, his work provides the most accurate study of the distributional implications of government expenditures. In education and health, two major services whose subsidy component corresponded in 1974 to 2.2 and 0.7 percent respectively of

[39] A possibly important omission from the analysis reviewed here and most others is the failure to take account of the impact of government expenditures as a source of factor earnings, i.e., the focus is exclusively on the beneficiaries of the services produced. But government hires many people directly and indirectly (through the goods it purchases), with various distributional impacts. The average government employee earns a salary above the economy average (in 1970 about 50% above that average), so it might be argued that its effect is to worsen the distribution at least of labor incomes. But this would depend also on which services normally provided by the government would be provided in its absence by the private sector, and on many other rather complex considerations.

[40] It appears that expenditures of other levels of government are included when they go into the same programs as those of the national government, e.g., the National Health Service to which departmental governments make contributions. (Selowsky, *Who Benefits . . .*, p. 22.)

TABLE 1.8a. Distribution of Income after Taxes and All Transfers (1966 pesos)

Deciles of the Population	Pretax Income (Millions) (1)	Percentage of Total Personal Income		Public Expenditures Assigned to Users (Millions of pesos)					
		Before Taxes (2)	After Taxes (3)	Education and Culture (4)	Public Health (5)	Development Expenditures (6)	Public Works (7)	Agriculture (8)	Labor Expenditures (9)
Lowest	524.7	0.9	0.9	105.5	85.8	88.5	5.1	10.1	0.7
Second	1,107.6	1.9	1.9	105.5	85.7	47.6	42.3	27.3	1.3
Third	1,574.0	2.7	2.8	105.5	89.4	5.4	38.0	36.2	7.1
Fourth	2,040.4	3.5	3.7	141.5	89.2	6.3	43.5	26.4	6.4
Fifth	2,623.3	4.5	4.6	141.5	41.8	27.2	62.2	78.2	7.6
Sixth	3,206.3	5.5	5.6	170.9	12.7	70.0	52.1	20.0	32.5
Seventh	4,372.2	7.5	7.6	259.6	5.9	144.0	79.0	12.8	36.1
Eighth	5,829.6	10.0	10.3	297.2	–	106.3	84.2	19.6	40.9
Ninth	9,035.9	15.5	15.7	357.3	–	205.4	136.4	19.6	44.2
Second Highest 5%	7,578.5	13.0	12.9	166.8	–	205.4	141.8	9.2	50.5
Highest 5%	20,403.6	35.0	34.0	111.5	–	401.7	338.3	7.8	50.7
Total	58,296.1			1,962.8	452.3	1,307.8	1,023.9	267.2	278.0

TABLE 1.8b

	Expenditures on General Public Service[a]		Percentage of Total Expenditures		Income after Taxes plus Expenditures		Percentage of Personal Income after Taxes plus Expenditures	
	I	II	I	II	I	II	I	II
	(10)	(11)	(12)	(13)	(14)	(15)	(16)	(17)
	6.9	409.3	3.23	7.53	761.2	1,163.6	1.28	1.96
	11.4	413.8	3.48	7.73	1,289.1	1,691.5	2.18	2.86
	13.6	416.0	3.15	7.45	1,705.5	2,107.9	2.88	3.56
	11.1	413.5	3.45	7.75	2,151.6	2,554.0	3.63	4.31
	4.1	406.5	3.87	8.16	2,634.4	3,036.8	4.45	5.13
	–	402.4	4.14	8.43	3,183.2	3,585.6	5.37	6.05
	–	402.4	5.81	10.11	4,356.8	4,759.2	7.35	8.03
	–	402.3	5.92	10.21	5,695.8	6,098.1	9.61	10.29
	2,012.0	402.3	29.66	12.47	10,620.1	9,010.4	17.93	15.21
	1,005.9	201.2	16.88	8.28	7,991.0	7,186.3	13.49	12.13
	1,005.9	201.2	20.46	11.88	18,857.5	18,052.8	31.83	30.47
Total	4,070.9	4,070.9			59,246.2	59,246.2		

Note: I: It is assumed that with a few specific exceptions these costs are distributed between the richest two deciles of the population.
II: General public expenditures are assumed to benefit everyone in a similar way and are therefore distributed on an equal per capita basis.

[a] General public services includes expenditures of the Interior Ministry, Foreign Affairs, Justice, Defense, Police, Congress, Tax Collection, the Presidency, Planning, Statistics, the Civil Service, Government Procurement, Communications, and other services.

Source: Berry and Urrutia, *op. cit*., pp. 172-173.

TABLE 1.9. Annual Per Capita Subsidies Implicit in Public Expenditures on Education and Health, 1974, by Quintiles of Households

	Households Ranked by Per Capita Income Quintile					
	1	2	3	4	5	Total
Primary Education	190.0	182.0	155.0	123.0	59.0	148.0
Secondary Education	87.0	130.0	140.0	182.0	131.0	131.0
Higher Education	2.6	16.0	41.6	102.0	296.0	75.0
Total Education	279.6	327.4	336.0	406.0	486.0	354.0
Health	90.0	104.5	144.0	132.0	119.0	115.0
Education & Health	369.0	432.0	480.0	539.0	604.0	469.0
Subsidy as a percentage of households' income	24.5	14.5	10.3	7.0	2.5	6.6
Subsidy as a percentage of households' consumption (estimate)	17.1	11.1	8.4	6.5	3.0	

Source: Calculated from Selowsky, *Who Benefits . . .*, Table 1.7, pp. 24-25. The last row is calculated from the second to the last row and consumption/income ratios calculated on the basis of DANE.s 1970 household survey (EH 1) and assuming an overall consumption/income ratio of 0.95.

GNP, the subsidies went disproportionately to the higher income families, but they were a much greater share of income (or consumption) for the poorer families. Higher education is the only component of these services whose incidence is regressive (See Table 1.9). Among other categories studied, the benefits from the urban services (electricity, piped water, sewage and garbage collection) could not be estimated in so direct a fashion, but the data presented on access suggest a progressive effect on distribution, albeit less so than that of education and health due mainly to their being concentrated in urban areas. The same was true for attendance at SENA, and for educational fellowships. Caja Agraria loans had a strongly progressive effect.

To summarize, despite the need for many qualifications due to conceptual and statistical difficulties in the measurement of incidence, a strong case can be made that the separate and combined distributional impact of the two sides of the Colombian budget is progressive. It might lower the Gini coefficient by something on the order of 3 to 5 points.

Monetary and Financial Policy

Public policy in the monetary and financial areas affects distribution through two main avenues: (i) its effect through the credit system and the structure of the capital market on control of resources and thereby on factor incomes; and (ii) its effects via the rate of inflation.

The influence of public policy on the allocation and price of capital affects distribution in several ways. Its influence on which firms and industries can grow most easily directly affects the incomes of factors which are specific to or have a comparative advantage in those industries. When capital is made available at subsidized rates owners of capital benefit the most. Also the factor intensity of the industries can, by affecting the relative demands for various types of labor and capital, change the functional distribution of income. Finally, the incomes of savers are affected by the price at which capital is lent.

Though a start has recently been made on flow of funds analysis in Colombia, the financial structure has not yet been mapped out in a way which would permit a reasonably precise judgment as to how it affects income distribution. It is clear, however, that the "formal" financial system gives large firms greater access than small ones.[41] In so doing, it also favors capital intensity—given the strong association between size and capital intensity. The negative distributional effects of this bias are amplified when the funds supplied via the public sector are subsidized.

In terms also of relative returns to savers of various income levels, it appears that the financial system has a substantially regressive impact. In chapter 4, Berry's estimates of the real return on various financial assets indicate a negative return over 1967-74 for savings deposits, the only such asset apart from cash held by the poor, and a positive return for stocks, Unidad de Poder Adquisitivo Constante (UPAC) and some other assets held mainly by the higher income groups.

In summary, while the detailed information required to estimate the impact of the financial system on income distribution is not available, the generally accepted presumption that it is quite negative seems to be accurate. Some of this tendency is rather unavoidable, related to problems of economies of scale and problems of information in the financial system. The small saver has a problem getting the information needed to maximize the returns on his savings; banks have problems judging the credit worthiness of small borrowers and so on. Another contributing factor, however, is the tendency for the structure of the financial system and the operation of most of its component institutions to reflect the interests of the rich.

Judging from the magnitude of resource flows in the financial system, the terms on which these resources are lent can affect distribution importantly. In 1960 the ratio of financial assets (including money) to GNP was nearly 1.6.[42] If the average real return on these assets were 6 percent, income from financial assets would be equal to about 10 percent of GNP. Thus, the disposition of a sizable amount of purchasing power depends on how this system functions, suggesting that its potential distributive impact might be of a similar order of magnitude to that of the fiscal system.

Another way in which monetary and financial policy affects distribution is through its impact on the rate of inflation. The rapid inflation which occurred in

[41] The concentration of bank credit has been discussed by Urrutia and Berry, among others. (See Berry and Urrutia, *op. cit.*, pp. 208-213.)

[42] Banco de la Republica, *Analisis Preliminar de las Cuentas de Flujo de Fondos Financieros de la Economia Colombiana 1962-1969* (Bogotá: Banco de la Republica, 1971), p. 14.

the early 1970s is a new phenomenon for Colombia. As discussed in Chapter 4, its impact was considerable, with the lower income paid workers suffering mainly as a result of a wage price lag. By 1974 or 1975 their incomes were probably at least 10-15 percent lower than they otherwise would have been. Capital incomes of persons managing their own capital were correspondingly higher. Although the changing real values of assets resulting from the inflation may have been important, it appears that changes in the relationship between product prices and input prices (including the price of labor) have been the major redistributive mechanism.

Education

As discussed in section 3, variance in the level of education statistically explains as much as a quarter of the variance of reported income. This is a much greater share of income variance than can be explained by other easily measurable personal characteristics such as age, sex, years of work experience, rural vs. urban residence, and department of residence. This prominent and even dominant role played by the level of education places a high priority on our understanding its causal role as a determinant of income distribution. Studies of the rate of return to education in urban Colombia have estimated the highest social rates at the primary level, high rates at the secondary and vocational levels, and lower rates at the university level.[43] Private rates of return, however, are high at all levels because of substantial subsidies at each level. In the rural areas Haller's study indicated a reasonably high social rate of return and one which depended on the type of agriculture involved.[44] Overall, this evidence suggests that the effect of education on incomes is achieved at moderate to low social and private costs; low social costs imply a high gain in total national income per peso spent (by anyone) on education.

One cannot, of course, derive precise conclusions about education's role as a determinant of income distribution from its statistical explanatory power in regressions or analyses of variance, although when the latter is as powerful as observed here, the causal role is unlikely to be negligible. Two types of problems arise in the interpretation of such statistical analyses. The first involves the difficulty of including in the income function some relevant determinants. The standard regression to explain income includes, along with educational level, variables for sex, age, and years of work experience. Some analyses also include place of residence or work (rural vs. urban, state, etc.), occupation or sector, and some

[43] See, for example, the studies by Schultz and Selowsky. (T. Paul Schultz, *Returns to Education in Bogotá, Colombia*. Rand Memorandum RM-5645-RC/AID [Santa Monica, Calif.: Rand Corporation, 1968] M. Selowsky, "El Efecto del Desempleo y el Crecimiento sobre la Rentabilidad de la Inversion Educacional," *Revista de Planeacion y Dessarrollo* [Julio, 1969].)

[44] T. Haller, "Education and Rural Development in Colombia," Unpublished Ph.D. dissertation, Purdue University, 1972.

indicator of where the employer fits on the traditional-modern scale. Since these variables are not independent, exclusion of some may lead to biased estimates of the role of education. But even if this whole set is included, the true effect of education on income may be overestimated because of its positive correlation with other variables for which information is seldom available, in particular: (a) native ability; (b) socioeconomic background; (c) wealth, a major determinant of nonlabor income whose exclusion is important if the dependent variable is total rather than labor income alone.

The second problem in the prediction of the effect of changes in the distribution of education on the distribution of income revolves around the fact that cross section surveys permit only the estimation of income differentials associated with different levels of education at a point of time characterized by a given income structure and level of development, and given stocks of persons with the various levels of education. These differentials may give little guidance with respect to the changes in relative incomes which would result from changes in the relative amounts of different levels of education.

Two additional complexities in the relationship between the distribution of education and income distribution should be noted. When, as is the case of education, effects on the beneficiaries can be strong enough to markedly change their position in the distribution of income, one cannot assume that when the ratio of benefits (of the program) to income is higher for lower income groups, the distribution of income will be improved. Some beneficiaries will jump from the lower deciles to high ones, with no decrease in overall inequality of personal income necessarily resulting. What happens to the distribution of household incomes in such a case depends on the degree of income sharing within the family. Finally, changes in the distribution of education received by today's students would affect the distribution of income only gradually, as they enter the labor force. The full effects of a reorientation of policy would be felt only after several decades. So, although education may be a major determinant of income distribution, changes in educational policy may not be among the more hopeful ways to achieve greater equality in the short run.

In the light of these qualifications on the usefulness of existing statistical information, what can be said about the role of education as a cause of income inequality in Colombia? The answer still seems to be "a good deal." As of 1969, the "human capital" share of national income was estimated by Berry to be about one-third.[45] And a considerable portion of income variance is probably associated with the variance of education through its effect on labor incomes, perhaps 15-25 percent or so.[46] Capital incomes may also be substantially affected by educational level, so that the total impact of education could be quite large, indeed.

A few studies have focused on the direct income distributional impact of ed-

[45] Berry, "Changing Income Distribution...," *op. cit.*, p. 312.

[46] Based on the guess that 35-40 percent of income variance reflects the variance of labor (paid and imputed) income—somewhat higher than the guess mentioned in section 3 for the urban sector—and that a substantial part of this is due to differences in education.

ucation, including those of Berry-Urrutia, Jallade, and Fields.[47] Kugler's study in this volume also focuses on one important aspect of that question. Urrutia concluded that as of 1966 if the benefits of education were assumed to be equal to the costs, then public spending in this area tended on the whole to improve the size distribution of income by providing free services to less well-off families (see Table 1.8). The positive impact on distribution comes from primary education; public expenditures on higher education are likely to worsen it. In fact, with the high rates of return to education which appear to hold in Colombia, costs can be a quite substantial underestimate of benefits, especially at the primary and secondary levels, so the redistributive impact may be considerably greater than that implicit in the figures of Berry-Urrutia.

Both Jallade's work and Selowsky's recent survey-based estimates (see Table 1.9 above) confirm Berry-Urrutia's conclusion that the incidence of educational subsidies is strongly progressive, mainly, as Jallade noted, because higher income people tend to enroll their children in private schools.[48] Note that the progressive incidence of these expenditures is somewhat overestimated in Berry-Urrutia and Jallade, due to their use of household or personal income to rank families rather than a per capita consumption or income measure such as that used by Selowsky. But the results are not very sensitive to this methodological point.

The progressive incidence of public educational expenditures has changed somewhat over time. Between 1958 and 1970, the share of educational subsidies going to the poorest groups increased, as rural primary education reached a higher share of the population.[49] However, at the same time the share going to the top quarter of families may also have increased. A rough calculation suggests that the top quarter of families might have received about half of educational subsidies in 1958 and a little more in 1970. But their share of income is much higher than this, so the subsidies effect a greater percentage increase in incomes of poorer families than of the rich ones.

The difficult question of how changing relative supplies of various skills (determined partly by educational achievement) affect relative earnings for those skills remains a mystery, and means that the overall distributional implications of educational policy cannot be judged with much accuracy. In most countries, income differentials by educational level decrease over the course of develop-

[47] G. Fields, "Education and Economic Mobility in a Less Developed Country," Economic Growth Center Discussion Paper No. 237, Yale University, Revised Version 1976.

[48] Jallade's figures suggest that these subsidies varied from over 12 percent of the income of families earning less than 6000 pesos per year to less than one percent for those earning over 240,000 pesos. (J. P. Jallade, *Public Expenditures on Education and Income Distribution in Colombia*, World Bank Occasional Papers, No. 18 [Baltimore: Johns Hopkins Press, 1975], pp. 27-28, 40.) At the same time, in urban areas at least, subsidies per child were twice as high in middle income groups as for low income groups (p. 26).

[49] In 1958 probably 15 percent of all children (almost all of them in rural areas) did not enter primary and the ratio "children enrolled/population 6-10," was about 60-65 percent; in 1970, these figures were probably about 5 percent and 75 percent, respectively. Most non-attendees are in rural areas.

TABLE 1.10. Relative Incomes by Level of Education: Bogotá Male Income Recipients, 1963-66[a] and 1973
(Base: Primary School Income Level = 1.0)

Year	Age							
1963-66	10-19	20-24	25-29	30-34	35-44	45-54	55-64	65 & up
No education	0.74	0.49	0.50	0.51	0.53	0.49	n. a.	n. a.
Secondary	2.48	1.66	2.14	2.89	2.84	3.02	3.64[d]	n. a.
Higher[b]	4.33[c]	3.72	4.95	6.70	6.66	6.08	n. a.	n. a.
Higher/None	(5.88)	7.65	9.81	13.11	12.60	12.52	n. a.	n. a.
1973								
No education	0.65	0.83	0.70	0.69	0.62	0.56	0.61	0.53
Secondary	1.50	1.63	1.94	2.51	2.56	3.02	2.99	3.49
Higher	2.27	4.06	5.27	6.26	6.25	7.20	5.81	6.50
Higher/None	3.49	4.92	7.53	9.09	10.10	12.90	9.48	12.19

[a]Employees and independent workers. Employers are excluded. In the 1973 data they are included.

[b]Described as "university." The source does not indicate whether other forms of higher education are included or not.

[c]Only two observations.

[d]Data reported only for persons 55-59.

Sources: For 1963-66, M. Selowsky, *op. cit.*, Cuadro XX-A; for 1973, Fields and Schultz, *op. cit.*, pp. 71-72.

ment, reflecting at least in part the changes in relative supply. No thorough study of such trends has been undertaken in Colombia, though a comparison based on available data for Bogata males between 1963-66 and 1973 suggests a decline (Table 1.10). For specific age groups the differentials are generally lower in the latter year; the sources of data, unfortunately, are of different quality, so the result is less than definitive.

In all attempts to predict how income distribution would change under various educational policies, one of the major uncertainties has been the extent to which the positive observed relationship between income and education is due to the better contacts, pull, and knowledge of labor markets which characterize more educated people, advantages due in part to family connections. This is the issue addressed by Kugler in Chapter 5. He finds that the inclusion of variables relating to socioeconomic origin, and in particular "father's income" does indeed lower the amount of income variation which can be attributed to individuals' education and other personal characteristics, though the implicit rate of return to education falls by only 15 percent.[50] While variables relating to socioeconomic background are correlated with income, the correlations are generally smaller than those with individuals' personal characteristics, suggesting that the latter are indeed the

[50]Given the limited age range of the persons entering Kugler's sample, it remains to be seen whether this proportion would be about the same for the universe of income earners. (See Chapter 5.)

main determinants of labor income, and in particular that education is a key determinant.

Kugler's analysis is limited to those households in which at least two generations of income earners were living together, since the household survey on which it is based did not ask people about their socioeconomic origins. Fields has attempted to ascertain how general Kugler's results may be to all stages of an individual's working life, using CEDE's 1967 study of occupational and geographic mobility in four urban areas of Colombia.[51] Again, the socioeconomic background variables, in this case education and occupation of the parents, provide a weaker explanation of incomes than do the individuals' own characteristics. Unlike Kugler's study, which had information on father's income—the only significant antecedent variable in Kugler's study—this one does not. Parents' education is the only variable with both the right sign and a high level of significance.[52] When both individual characteristics and those of parents are included in the same regression, none of the parental variables have particularly significant effects. The unavailability of father's income in Fields' analysis reduces the strength of the conclusion that personal variables dominate socioeconomic background variables in explaining income levels for all age groups (recall that Kugler's analysis was essentially limited to quite young income earners), but it still constitutes support for that proposition.

Meanwhile, parental background is clearly an important determinant of children's education. Kugler finds income of the household head, parental education, father's occupation, and whether born in a rural or urban area to be quantitatively significant determinants. On the other hand, parents' occupation, individuals' migratory status, and sex show no statistically significant effect.

A potentially important determinant of the inequality in permanent income for a given cohort is the extent to which past inequalities are automatically transmitted to a new generation. If mobility is defined in terms of the frequency with which individuals can change their percentile location in the distribution of income (or in the distribution of some more basic indicator like wealth or prestige) then present inequality will depend on the degree of inequality in the past and the extent of "mobility." In a system with prefect equality of income distribution in the past (to take an extreme case), a rigid structure which precludes "mobility" in the above sense would contribute to the maintenance of that equality. At the other extreme, if the past distribution is highly unequal, and if there is imperfect correlation between income earning attributes of individuals and the wealth of their families, then mobility will help the system move toward equality. It seems a reasonable presumption that with Colombia's highly unequal distribution of income and wealth in the past, mobility so defined would contribute towards equality for the foreseeable future.

A number of studies bearing on this issue have been undertaken in Colombia and permit some tentative conclusions as to the extent to which existing mobility

[51] G. Fields, "Education and Economic Mobility...," *op. cit.*, p. 14.
[52] *Ibid.*, p. 17.

may lead to improvement of income distribution over time. This issue overlaps with or complements others previously considered in the sense that mobility involves the absence of noneconomic barriers to an economic determination of an individual's income.

There is, of course, little dispute that increasing education contributes to higher incomes for the labor force as a whole. For the most part, the children of high income parents get a lot of education and those of low income parents get little, but all groups of children get on average more education than their parents have. If mobility is defined in the sense of occupational or income gains in absolute terms, it is clear that education facilitates it. The more interesting question is whether education also leads to a considerable amount of "shifting" of relative positions in the income or socioeconomic scales, i.e., whether it facilitates mobility in the sense used here.

Fields has argued persuasively that, as between an open educational model (i.e., one which facilitates mobility), and a completely closed one, Colombia's system is roughly in the middle, but perhaps closer to the open end.[53] The conclusion is based on the fact that the correlation between parents' education and that of their children, while high, is far from perfect.[54] The conclusion that the system provides the avenue for some mobility, though it is obviously far from a levelling device, has been reached also by Urrutia, and in a more general context by Guillen.[55] Much of the dispute as to whether or not it promotes mobility has been of a semantic nature resulting from different definitions of a "significant" level of mobility.

International Economic Policy

International trade, exchange, and investment constitute one of the most significant areas of government policy, both because the way these issues are handled can clearly affect the rate and pattern of development and because implementation of policy is much easier than in many other areas (e.g., much of fiscal policy). Understanding the distributional effects of various trade policies is thus of great importance.

It has been suggested that in a country like Colombia the traditional trading patterns may have contributed to income equality since coffee is fairly labor-intensive and coffee revenues are rather widely distributed; coffee is more a small farm

[53] *Ibid.*, p. 34.
[54] *Ibid.*, p. 32.
[55] M. Urrutia, "La Educacion Como Factor de Movilidad Social," CEDE, Universidad de los Andes, Documento de Trabajo No. 12, Julio, 1974; F. Guillen M., *Raiz y Futuro de la Revolucion* (Bogotá: Ediciones Tercer Mundo, 1963). An opposing view has been presented by R. Parra in *Analisis de un Mito: La Educacion como Factor de la Movilidad Social en Colombia* (Bogotá: Universidad de los Andes, Departamento de Educacion, 1973).

crop in Colombia than are many primary product exports in other countries.[56]

This traditional trade pattern must be borne in mind when one considers the distributional impact of various types of trade restrictions. A commonly voiced proposition is that protectionist restrictions are likely to worsen distribution since the industries protected tend to be capital intensive and monopolistic or oligopolistic. Berry and Urrutia have noted that one characteristic of the period from the mid-1930s to the mid-1950s, during which income distribution appeared to have worsened, was extensive import substituting industrialization.[57]

The emphasis on promotion of new ("nontraditional") exports, which began to bear considerable fruit from the late 1960s on, has received considerable discussion as a growth strategy, with more limited attention having been directed to its distributional implications. If one accepts the proposition that import substitution usually worsens distribution, the development of new labor intensive exports is an attractive alternative. Table 1.11 compares factor proportions as between export oriented industries and import substituting ones for which data were available. The capital/labor ratio is 50 percent higher for the import substituting industries; labor productivity at Colombian prices is also on the order of 50 percent higher and both capital productivity and total factor productivity about the same. Average wage (not shown in Table 1.11) was about 30 percent higher in the import substitution industries. At world prices, labor productivity, capital productivity and total factor productivity are probably several times higher in the export industries.

Thoumi's recent study of the employment content of various types of manufactured goods throws further light on the distributional implications of trade in manufactured goods.[58] He classifies four digit industries into export oriented, non-traded, import competing, and nonimport competing according to the value of the ratio of imports minus exports to absorption in 1970. He finds the export-oriented industries to be much more labor-intensive, especially in blue collar labor, than the other categories (labor intensity is defined by the ratio of employment to value added) although their labor share is lower than for nonimport competing industries (See Table 1.12); no study has yet identified factor use in actual exports (as opposed to the two or four digit industries from which the exports come), or taken account of indirect effects. In their chapter in this volume, Berry and Diaz raise a number of such issues with respect to the income distribution effects of export promotion in the recent Colombian context. One important factor is the large size of the firms producing most of the new exports, a fact which creates a presumption that they are less labor-intensive than the average for the industries to which they belong and are not likely to create a large amount of

[56] See W. McGreevey, *An Economic History of Colombia* (Cambridge: Cambridge University Press, 1971), Chap. 9; and A. Berry, "Trade and Income Distribution over Time: Colombia." (Mimeographed.)

[57] Berry and Urrutia, *op. cit.*, Chapter 4.

[58] F. E. Thoumi, "Estrategias de Industrializacion, Empleo y Distribucion del Ingreso en Colombia," *Coyuntura Economica*, Vol. IX, No. 1 (April, 1979), pp. 119-142.

TABLE 1.11. A Comparison of Factor Productivities between Industries with Significant Exports and Industries of Important Recent Import Substitution, 1969

	Labor Productivity (Thousands of Pesos) (Col. Prices) (1a)	Labor Productivity (Thousands of Pesos) (World Prices) (1b)	Capital Productivity (Col. Prices) (2a)	Capital Productivity (World Prices) (2b)	Total Factor Productivity (Col. Prices) (3a)	Total Factor Productivity (World Prices) (3b)	Physical Capital/ Worker (Thousands of Pesos) (4)
Selected Recent Import Substitution Industries							
271 and 273 Pulp, Paper, Cardboard, and Cardboard Articles	107.6	80.0-95.0[a]	.342-.351	.266-.316[a]	1.07-1.09	1.03-1.25[a]	306.9-392.4
34 Basic Metals	80.0	3.2	.254	0.10	1.08	.038	312.6
37 Electrical Machinery	47.4	negative	.445	negative	1.16	negative	106.5
383 Vehicle Assembly	54.7	negative	.315-.365	negative	1.07-1.15	negative	150.0-174.0
311 Basic Chemicals	93.5		.176-.187		.94-.98		371.0-394.4
Above group	69.0	15.0-20.0[b]	.289-.302	.062-.103[c]	1.05-1.07	.284-.464[c]	231.3-240.6
Selected Industries with Significant Exports							
25 Wood	25.6	28.9	.353	.397	.99	1.17	72.6
253 Wood Sculpture, Carving, Toys	16.2		.526-.748		.98-1.07	1.18-1.20	21.6-30.7
272 Paper Articles	52.2		.515-.586		1.42-1.48		89.2-101.4
29 Leather	40.7	36.8	.409	.370	1.24	1.13	99.5
332 Glass	55.3		.559-.679		1.48-1.60		81.5-99.0
334 Cement	61.9		.153-.163		.68-.71		379.8-403.3
Above group	44.7	47.0[d]	.296-.315	.311-.331[d]	1.03-1.06	1.08-1.12[d]	141.7-151.1

[a]For industry 27, Hutcheson estimated effective protection of about 11%. Here we assume it to be 10-25% for the two subcategories considered, on the presumption that it is, if anything, lower in category 272.

[b]Precise value depends on how negative the value added per worker is for industries 37 and 383, and on the figures for 271/273 and for 311. If the first two were zero and the values for 311 and 271/3 were 50.0 and 95.0 respectively, then the average would be 23.8. If the first two were −10.0 and the others 40.0 and 80.0 respectively, the average would be 14.9.

[c]Estimates are consistent with those of column (1b).

[d]Assumes each three digit category included had the same world price/Colombian price ratio as the two digit industry of which it was a part.

Sources and Methodology: Output figures are from Banco de la Republica, *Cuentas Nacionales*; they are at market prices. Estimates of factor productivities at world prices are based primarily on Hutcheson's estimates of effective protection for manufacturing which, however, means factory manufacturing, in 1969. (See Thomas L. Hutcheson, "Incentives for Industrialization in Colombia" [unpublished Ph.D. dissertation, University of Michigan, 1973], p. 68.)

TABLE 1.12. Income Distribution and Employment in Non-traded, Export, Import-competing and Non-import Competing Manufacturing

Category of Manufactures	Total employment per million pesos of VA(*)	Blue-collar employment per million pesos of VA(*)	White-collar employment per million pesos of VA(*)	Ratio of white to blue-collar employment	Total labor remun. as percent of VA(*)	Blue plus white-collar remuneration as perc. VA(*)	Average labor remunera-tion	Direct plus indirect wages and salaries per peso VA(*)
Non-traded	10.9	7.7	2.6	.338	27.4	24.6	24,460	.307
Exports	29.1	23.9	3.6	.151	50.0	43.3	26,200	.576
Import-competing	15.5	11.0	3.2	.291	40.8	35.8	28,580	.523
Non-importing competing	21.7	16.3	3.8	.233	55.6	46.5	28,200	.643

(*) Value added.
Source: Thoumi, *op. cit.*, p. 141.

employment. Further, many of the large exporters are also important importers and producers of import substitutes, which complicates the analysis of the factor proportions and factor incomes associated with the exports.

No quantitative estimates have been made of the effects of trade policy on income distribution; clearly they depend on exactly what policies are being compared. But given trade's share of GDP and its indirect effects on economic structure, together with the great differences in factor proportions among tradeables (contrast coffee and petrochemicals), it seems clear that the difference between a policy oriented towards labor intensive exports and one oriented towards capital intensive import substitutes (to choose an arbitrary example) could be quite important for income distribution, ranking with fiscal policy, educational policy (in terms of long-run effects at any rate) and perhaps financial policy in its potency.

One export industry viewed as having considerable potential for employment generation is tourism. Both hotel construction and operation would appear to be very labor-intensive. However, as Roberts points out in Chapter 7, a closer look at the data suggests that in fact tourism is essentially capital-intensive; there are many other investment alternatives which would generate more employment per dollar invested. While marginal increases in the tourist industry, which would not require large investments in superstructure (hotels, restaurants) and infrastructure (airports, water supplies, and sewage systems), are much more labor intensive than discrete increases which do require such investments, the magnitude of employment increases resulting from marginal changes in tourism are too small to have any significant impact on all employment and income distribution.

Agricultural Policy

The distribution of income earned in agriculture is highly unequal in Colombia, a reflection of the very unequal distribution of land. Policy, meanwhile, has been mainly pro large farm, complementing the original inequality of land distribution[59] and contributing to an apparent worsening of the distribution of income generated in agriculture.

The implications of land distribution and of agrarian reform for income distribution are fairly straightforward and have been discussed by Sandoval and by Thirsk.[60] Clearly, a major redistribution of land could have a significant impact on overall income distribution, but given the decreasing share of agriculture in the economy, it would have to be a major one. A couple of decades ago or so, the opportunity to affect overall distribution by this means would have been greater.

[59]For an overview of agricultural policy and its effects on income distribution, see Berry and Urrutia, *op. cit.*, Chapter 11.

[60]C. E. de Sandoval, "Efectos de una Redistribucion de la Tierra Sobre la Distribucion del Ingreso Rural," Centro de Investigaciones para el Desarrollo (CID), Universidad Nacional de Colombia, *Documentos de Trabajo #2*, 1970, pp. 223-240; W. R. Thirsk, "The Distribution of Land Reform Benefits in Colombia," *Land Economics*, Vol. 52 (February, 1976).

Less evident are the implications of such policies as assistance in mechanization (i.e., tractorization) and price supports, the subjects of discussions by Thirsk in Chapters 8 and 9. For all crops considered in Chapter 9, increases in price would result in greater increases in expenditure than in earnings for low income groups and larger increments to earnings than to expenditures for the higher income groups. Taking into account the position of producers and consumers in the income distribution, he finds that most of the burden of price supports is borne by low income earners while most of the benefits are conferred on high income producers.

The simulations carried out in Chapter 8 point to the likelihood that subsidization of large scale mechanization also worsens income distribution, while its impact on national income is less clear.[61] The distributive effect could be substantial; one estimate implies that three percent of national income would be transferred to the top decile of earners from the rest of the economy.[62] The mechanism involved, a decrease in the price of capital to capital users, characterizes other sectors as well (e.g., parts of the manufacturing sector); so if an analysis were carried out to measure the impact of all such subsidized credit it would, as surmised in the discussion of financial policy above, probably imply a significant redistributive effect, e.g., one-tenth of the income of the top decile might be attributable to such subsidies.

Housing Policy

The central place given to urban building as part of the development strategy of the Pastrana government makes the distributional implications of such a policy of particular interest. In Chapter 10 Berry and Soligo conclude that the labor-intensive characteristics of urban building imply that the growth of that sector would be expected to improve income distribution in the short run, especially since a higher share of employees are unskilled blue collar workers than is true for most other urban sectors. These positive employment and distribution effects are not unambiguously demonstrated in the *ex post* data, however. Real wages in construction, as in all major sectors, were falling during the years 1972-74 when the plan was in full swing. Berry argues in Chapter 4 that those trends are probably attributable to the accelerating inflation of those years; still, the inflation makes it impossible to judge what impact the housing boom would have had on distribution under more normal conditions. Available data suggest there may have

[61] Many judgments about the desirability of farm mechanization are based on a comparison of post-mechanization large farm employment levels with those in the pre-mechanization era. If the output expansion effects dominate the labor substitution effects and large farm employment grows, mechanization is viewed favorably. The simulation results presented by Thirsk in Chapter 8, however, indicate strongly that this partial equilibrium view is an inadequate indicator of whether or not subsidized farm mechanization is labor saving within the whole economy.

[62] Chapter 8, p. 197.

been a slight reduction in unemployment during these years. While there is no strong reason to doubt that the distributive effects of this strategy were in the right direction (i.e., they were as planned), it appears that the size attained by the program even at its peak was not great enough to achieve a major distributional impact unless various indirect effects not discussed in Chapter 10 also had positive effects.

Bender argues in Chapter 11 that auto-construction, a type of housing activity not emphasized in the Pastrana government's strategy (which focused on commercial building) can also have important benefits for low income groups. The benefits of such activity for poorer families are not of a magnitude to substantially affect the Gini coefficient, though that measure is relatively insensitive to substantial percentage changes in the incomes of the poor. This type of housing solution, and its relationship to overall urban policy, clearly requires a deeper look. Unless a society is in a position to supply families with a better alternative, it appears to have real potential as an anti-poverty measure.

Demand Patterns and Income Distribution

The last decade has seen a renewed attention to the structure of demand as a determinant of income distribution. As Thirsk points out:

> The notion that there is a tight linkage between expenditures at various income levels and factor proportions has a long tradition in Latin America. It is closely associated with the structuralist school of economic development. According to one version of this school's line of thought, new industries that have been established in Latin America, cars in Brazil for example, provide incomes primarily for the rich who in turn use their incomes to purchase the products of the newly established industries. A corollary to this position is that the poor are employed in activities that sell their output mainly to the poor. If development follows this pattern in which the income and expenditure chain feeds on itself once it is put in motion, fiscal transfers may be a powerful instrument for alleviating any drift towards greater income concentration. Taxes imposed on the rich and transferred to the poor would augment the income of the poor by an amount larger than the sum that would be transferred.[63]

Much of the relevant discussion has focused on how the composition of final demand affects the demand for labor, but this may be viewed as one aspect of its impact on income distribution. The composition of final demand is affected, among other things, by government policy (government purchases, subsidies, and taxes) and by the distribution of income. The impact of income distribution

[63] W. R. Thirsk, "Income Distribution and the Composition of Demands: The Case of Colombia," *Journal of Development Studies* (in press).

through demand patterns and factor earnings back on income distribution is of particular interest here; the question is whether a policy measure (e.g., taxes/subsidies) or an exogenous shock which changes the distribution of income will be amplified or partially offset as a result of the effects of that initial change on the composition of demand. If the offset were strong, otherwise promising instruments to improve distribution could be less successful than hoped.

Most attempts to measure these secondary effects have concluded that they are relatively unimportant.[64] But most have suffered from serious methodological or data problems which could have biased the results strongly in this direction. The main problem, it appears, is the level of aggregation at which such tests have been carried out. Since factor proportions vary widely by firm size, a good deal of variation of factor proportions can be missed when aggregation is by product. The question, in other words, is whether there is within a given product category a systematic relationship between the income of purchasers and the income of the recipients of factor payments generated by the production of the item purchased.

Ballentine and Soligo and Thirsk have avoided some of the usual methodological problems in this sort of work, since their data base, a closed-input-output table developed by USAID and referring to 1968, provides data on both the uses and sources of income by products for different income groups. Unfortunately, lack of data forced the builders of the input-output table to make many guesses, so its quality is uncertain.[65]

Ballentine and Soligo tested for the final or general equilibrium effects of an exogenous change in income distribution in favor of the poor, including effects on the composition of output and thereby on factor earnings. The simulation analysis shows that changes in factor earnings are small compared to the initial tax and transfers and that the shift in factor earnings which does occur is not towards the poor (to reinforce the shift in disposable income), but towards the rich. Thus, with the distribution of earnings shifting toward the rich, the final impact of the exogenous redistribution toward the poor is partially offset. This tendency to offset is traced to the substantial share of the expenditures of the rich going to employ low income service workers.[66]

Thirsk has recently examined the importance of aggregation and the possibility

[64] The basic methodology involves the use of data on the consumption patterns of different income classes to determine how the composition of output would change given an arbitrary redistribution of disposable income. Sectoral capital-output and labor-output ratios are then used to calculate the effects of the income redistribution on factor demand, or data on the functional distribution of value-added are used to calculate the effects on the functional distribution of income in the aggregate. If the data on the distribution of value-added by income class are available for each producing sector, the change in output mix can be translated into the new distribution of factor earnings.

[65] J. G. Ballentine and R. Soligo, "Consumption and Earnings Patterns and Income Distribution," *Economic Development and Cultural Change*, Vol. 26, No. 4 (July, 1978), pp. 693-708.

[66] *Ibid.*, p. 18.

that there is a relationship between income of buyer and income of factor owner *within* sectors.[67] While assuming the same interindustry coefficients for each item of final consumption, he finds the results to be quite sensitive to intra-industry difference in factor proportions (due to differences in firm size) correlated to the income of consumers. Thus, until useful data on this question become available the possibility cannot be ruled out that the "second round" effects of an initial redistribution are such as to magnify the first round effects rather than to partially offset them.

Demographic Factors

Colombia's population grew very rapidly over most of the post-World War II period, reaching a peak of about 3 percent per year over the intercensal period 1951-64. Whatever other effect this growth may have had on distribution, its negative effect on the capital/labor ratio would be expected to depress wage rates and contribute to income inequality. More recently, population growth has decelerated substantially, a result both of falling birth rates [68] and of increased emigration (mainly to Venezuela and the U. S.). Labor force growth has also been slowed by the increasing average levels of education received by students.

After a decade or more of slowing labor force growth coupled with fast economic growth, there are indications that Colombia's traditional situation of surplus labor is coming to an end. Employers in many sectors cite the difficulty of recruiting workers more often than in the past. The effects of the onset of a relative labor scarcity, if indeed that is happening, have been disguised by the downward pressure of the 1970s inflation on real wages.[69] Recently real wages in several sectors have started to move up again; it remains to be seen how quickly they will regain and surpass the levels of the late 1960s.

The gradual character of demographic change makes it difficult to identify its effects on income distribution. But the major effect–for fast population growth to worsen distribution via its effect on the labor capital ratio–has probably played an important role in the maintenance of a high level of inequality in the past. If the current deceleration turns out to be a rapid one, it will probably have significant positive effects on distribution in the future. Other mechanisms which may link demographic trends to income distribution are not well understood, but are in our judgment unlikely to outweigh the effects of the changing labor capital ratio.

[67] Thirsk, *op. cit.*

[68] The extent to which conscious population policy has contributed to this decline has not been analyzed. Undoubtedly, it has played a role, but so have increasing incomes, education and urbanization.

[69] The fall in real wages may have stimulated labor demand and thereby hastened the arrival of labor scarcity.

Summary

Inequality of income and wealth distribution remains a major weakness of Colombian society. It has been highly unequal as far back as any judgment can be made, and has thus far shown no clear signs of secular improvement. However, improvement may occur in the next couple of decades, judging by certain trends now underway. Slowing labor force growth coupled with continued fast economic growth (as long as technological change is of a not too labor saving nature) may turn out to be the key phenomenon, by changing the relative earnings of labor and capital. Educational trends may lead to a more equal distribution of human capital.

While government policy in several areas could have important positive effects on distribution in principle, the evidence reviewed in this chapter gives grounds for caution, educational policy excepted. The fiscal and financial systems are cases in point. A relatively perfect capital market would probably lead to a substantially lower level of inequality (e.g., a Gini coefficient lower by more than 0.03); part of this gain could be brought about by a more general indexing of assets than now exists, but another part would require the difficult changes of financial structure needed to provide more equal treatment to the less powerful. Technically feasible changes to the tax and expenditure system could have strong distributional effects, but as the 1974-75 Tax Reform and its aftermath have shown, administrative and political feasibility are the more important constraints in this area. Redistribution through the budget is considerable now, but increasing it dramatically would be difficult.

The potential distributional effects of policy in most other areas appear to be less than for those just cited. Policy changes of the magnitude exemplified in the shift in trade policy towards export promotion, the emphasis on urban building in 1972-74, or the institution of agricultural price supports would not likely affect the Gini coefficient by more than 0.02 or 0.03, in our judgment.

The design and implementation of an income distributional policy will remain difficult for some time, both because few easy to effect policies are likely to have major impacts and because for many policies it is not yet even roughly clear how they would affect distribution. Lowering the Gini coefficient by, say, 0.10 or more would clearly require astute and well executed policy in a number of different areas. Previous governments have for the most part considered improvements in distribution to be secondary goals and/or have not been able to achieve their distributional objectives. Adequate technical knowledge to achieve some progress in this direction is available, but the political will and administrative capacity have not been. This is not to deny that many good policies with positive redistributional implications have been undertaken: general public primary education, health programs, family planning programs, and a progressive tax system have all been important. But, to date, the positive effects of these policies have been counterbalanced by powerful factors and policies working in the opposite direction. As noted above, two of the policies with the longest lasting effects–

educational expenditures and family planning—may become stronger positive factors in the future and may play a valuable role in bringing about the end to the condition of surplus low skilled labor. An equally or more important factor, however, will probably be the strong growth performance of the last decade, or more generally of the last several decades. In such a case, Colombia might be viewed *ex post* as a case where reasonable income inequality was only achieved through a process of growth—i.e., where the "expand the pie first, then worry about redistribution" approach was the one which brought results. Such a one-sided interpretation would, of course, be an oversimplification. The failure to achieve growth with redistribution at the stages of development through which Colombia has recently been passing creates no presumption that this combination of goals was technically difficult to achieve. But the experience with programs like the 1974-75 tax reform shows the political and administrative barriers. The fairly widespread distribution of the benefits of continued fast growth after labor surplus is terminated in such countries as Japan provides some optimism with respect to the fast growth approach. It may be that for the reasons cited marked improvement in distribution is very difficult to achieve politically prior to that point, and that it would not be desirable to compromise overall growth too much in pursuit of a difficult goal.

Chapter 2

THE 1974 COLOMBIAN TAX REFORM AND INCOME DISTRIBUTION*

Malcolm Gillis
Harvard University

Charles E. McLure, Jr.
National Bureau of Economic Research

1. INTRODUCTION

During the last four months of 1974 the government of Colombia introduced a major tax reform. Enacted under emergency powers provided by the Constitution, this reform covered the sales tax, export taxes and incentives, adjustments in import surcharges, and the tax treatment of governmental agencies, as well as the personal and company income taxes.[1] Generally speaking, the goals of the tax reform were (a) to increase the progressivity of the tax system, (b) to reduce the distorting effect the tax system had upon the allocation of resources, (c) to

*This paper is reproduced with the permission of the publisher from the *Journal of Development Economics* 5 (1978), pp. 233-258.

[1] It might reasonably be asked how a government that came into office on August 9 could, by the end of the emergency period on October 31, produce a reform package of such magnitude and complexity. The answer is that a small group of Colombian experts appointed by then President-elect Lopez Michelsen had been working in secret since May, analyzing alternatives for tax reform and drafting legislation. Beyond that, many of the reforms were solidly based on the proposals that the Musgrave Commission had made during its extensive 1968-69 examination of the Colombian fiscal system. Most of the experts who served on the Lopez task force had had experience on the staff of the Musgrave Commission or in follow-up analysis within the government or had been deeply involved in the public debate over the Musgrave proposals during the intervening half-dozen years. This experience and those debates enabled these experts to improve further upon the Musgrave proposals in many cases, and in others to go into questions not covered there–and to go from conceptual arguments to legislation in short order. Thus, the reforms were made quickly, but they were not ill-conceived.

promote economic stability, both by increasing revenue on a once-and-for-all basis and by enhancing the built-in response of the tax system to growth in national income, and (d) to simplify both administration and compliance, and in the process reduce evasion and increase yields. With a few exceptions, the new reforms go far in achieving all these objectives. In this paper we focus primarily upon distributional implications of various of the most important reforms.

In section 2 we set the stage for what follows by describing the prevailing distribution of income in Colombia and the likely incidence among income classes of taxes levied in 1970. Section 3 is devoted to a short outline of the tax reform. The evaluation of the reforms is contained in sections 4-6. That is, section 4 provides a qualitative evaluation of the distributional effects of the various components of the tax reform package, section 5 discusses the consequences of the judicial decisions that have nullified many of the gains that would have otherwise been made in tax administration, and section 6 presents results of crude attempts to quantify the distributional effects of the tax reform. The reforms are, for the most part, found to be progressive, though in most cases the increase in progressivity comes primarily from higher taxes on upper income groups, rather than from lower burdens on low-income groups. This is inevitably the case when reform is so heavily focused on the personal income tax, which is paid in important amounts by only the top 10-15 percent of households. The final section offers a few concluding remarks about the political feasibility of extensive tax reform in developing countries.

2. INCOME DISTRIBUTION AND TAX INCIDENCE

During the past decade nearly a half-dozen studies have been made of the distribution of income in Colombia.[2] While these studies have shown marked disparities in methodology, data sources, and the choice of whether to use individuals or households as the basis for the distribution estimates, they have produced a remarkably uniform picture of income inequality. It appears that the poorest two-thirds of families or individuals receive about one-quarter of personal income and that the most fortunate 10 percent receive some 40 to 50 percent of such income.[3] Inequality is greater, it appears, in rural areas than in the urban sector.[4]

The national pattern of income distribution just described would strike anyone familiar primarily with similar estimates for developed countries as exhibit-

[2]These studies are summarized in A. Berry and M. Urrutia, *Income Distribution in Colombia* (New Haven: Yale University Press, 1976), Chapter 2.

[3]See C. E. McLure, Jr., "The Incidence of Colombian Taxes: 1970," *Economic Development and Cultural Change*, Vol. 24 (October, 1975), 160-61. If corporate retained earnings, unshifted corporate taxes, and capital gains attributable to Colombian owners of corporate shares and other assets and export duties on coffee were included in the estimates, we could easily find that the top 10 percent of the distribution accounted for over one-half of income. See *ibid.*, pp. 162-65.

[4]Berry and Urrutia, *op. cit.*, pp. 31-36, 41-52. Note that absentee landlords were included in the rural distribution in Berry and Urrutia's analysis.

ing extreme inequality.[5] But even when compared with distributions in other developing countries, including those in Latin America, the Colombian distribution is found to be heavily skewed.[6] Quite simply, the distribution of income in Colombia may be almost as unequal as any in the world.[7]

The Colombian tax system contributes to the reduction of inequality in the distribution of income, but only at the top of the distribution. Indirect taxation shows little systematic deviation from proportionality. (See column d of Table 2.1.)[8] Colombia has a relatively advanced system of taxation in the sense that it relies more heavily on income taxes than do many developing countries.[9] But we can expect the corporation income tax to add little to the progressivity of Colombian taxation, since it is probably borne primarily by consumers or workers, to the extent that it is not exported to foreigners.[10] Thus virtually the only tax that contributes significantly to the progressivity of the Colombian tax system is the personal income tax.[11] It accounts for almost all of the difference between

[5]Berry and Urrutia, for example, *op. cit.*, p. 40, calculate the Colombian Gini coefficient to be 0.57 and cite estimates of Gini coefficients for the U.S. of 0.33 to 0.35. In developed countries the top decile of the distribution ordinarily accounts for about 30 percent of income.

[6]*Ibid.*

[7]One must qualify such statements because results of income distribution estimates may not be comparable due to differences in methodology, data and competence of analysts.

[8]Table 2.1 is drawn from McLure, *op. cit.*, pp. 170, 181, where incidence estimates based on three different assumptions about the incidence of the corporation income tax and two about the inclusion of coffee export duties are presented. Table 2.1 is based upon the assumptions (a) that coffee export duties should be treated like all other taxes, even though some revenues finance benefits for the coffee sector, and (b) that corporation income taxes are shifted to Colombian consumers. The first assumption, while it greatly affects the estimates of effective tax rates in the rural sector, has relatively little impact on the estimates for the entire nation. The assumption of forward shifting of the corporate tax, on the other hand, produces estimates of incidence patterns which are quite different from those based on the assumption of incidence entirely on Colombian shareholders, but not so different (except in level) from those based on assumed exporting of the tax to foreigners. Since forward shifting is not a standard assumption, it is defended below. Estimates of incidence under the most reasonable alternative assumptions of burden on labor and exporting to foreigners would not greatly alter the conclusions of Table 2.1.

[9]See R. J. Chelliah, H. J. Baas, and M. R. Kelly, "Tax Ratios and Tax Effort in Developing Countries, 1969-71," *IMF Staff Papers*, Vol. 22 (March, 1975), especially pp. 196-97

[10]While we would not assume that Colombia could export its corporate income tax to foreign consumers, partial exporting to foreigners occurs via the foreign tax credits available in many home countries of firms investing in Colombia. The argument that noncredited taxes are shifted to consumers is essentially that made in the next footnote for the property tax; international mobility of capital precludes the burden of the tax falling on shareholders.

[11]Property taxes probably do not have the markedly progressive effect assumed in McLure, *op. cit.*, pp. 170–71. In a nutshell, the reasoning is that capital is sufficiently mobile in and out of Colombia that investment would occur there only if a return equal to that available elsewhere were available; that is, if the tax could be shifted. For an extended discussion of this issue, see C. E. McLure, Jr., "The Relevance of the New View of the Incidence of the Property Tax in Less Developed Countries," in Roy W. Bahl, editor, *The Taxation of Urban Property in Less Developed Countries* (Madison: University of Wisconsin Press), 1978, pp. 51-76.

TABLE 2.1. Effective Rates of Taxation, All Households (Prior to the 1974 reform)

Annual household income (pesos)	Cumulative percentage of: Households (a)	Cumulative percentage of: Income (b)	Effective tax rates: Personal income tax (c)	Effective tax rates: Indirect Taxes and Corporate (d)	Effective tax rates: Subtotal, c and d (e)	Effective tax rates: Coffee export duties and property tax (f)	Effective tax rates: Total, all taxes (g)
0-6,000	19.0	1.9	0.0	11.3	11.3	5.8	17.1
6,000-12,000	39.2	7.8	0.2	7.7	7.9	3.7	11.5
12,000-24,000	64.1	21.8	0.3	9.2	9.5	2.7	12.2
24,000-60,000	87.0	48.7	1.2	9.1	10.3	2.7	13.1
60,000-120,000	95.8	71.8	1.9	9.4	11.3	2.4	13.6
120,000-240,000	99.2	89.7	2.6	8.9	11.5	3.2	14.7
Over 240,000	100.0	100.0	13.2	10.8	24.0	6.0	29.9
Total	–	–	2.7	9.3	12.8	3.2	15.1

Source: C. E. McLure, Jr., "The Incidence of Colombian Taxes: 1970," *Economic Development and Cultural Change*, Vol. 24 (October 1975), pp. 160-65, 170, 181, for assumption b, with coffee export duties included.

the effective rates of tax (tax as a percentage of income) paid by the top 4 percent of the population and those paid in lower income brackets. (Compare columns c and e of Table 2.1).[12]

Not only is the personal income tax the chief instrument of progressive taxation in Colombia; it is paid almost entirely by the upper income classes.[13] This being the case, it is inevitable that reform of the income tax affects primarily those at the upper end of the distribution and has little effect at the bottom. Tax reform in other areas can, of course, reduce burdens at the bottom of the distribution. But this seems rarely to be the objective of reform, perhaps because of recognition that it is difficult to provide more than minimal relief for poor persons by adjusting exemptions, rate structure, etc. of indirect taxes and that what gain is achieved is bought at the price of considerable complexity and deficiency of administration and compliance.[14] Rather, policy makers, including especially those in Colombia, seem to accept the dictum of Bird and De Wulf that, "if the principal aim of redistributive policy is to level up—to make the poor better off—the main role that the tax system has to play is . . . the limited and essentially negative one of not making them [the poor] poorer."[15] In so doing, they are perhaps recognizing that, in the words of the Musgrave report, " . . . it is difficult to bring about a major shift in tax burden or income distribution. The primary emphasis in any such effort must lie on the expenditure side of budget policy and on the overall strategy of development planning."[16]

[12]Coffee export duties (2.6 percent of income) and property taxes (0.6 percent of income) are combined in column f after the subtotal of other taxes because of uncertainty as to whether the first should be included on equal terms with other taxes and because property taxes probably should not be assumed to fall entirely on capitalists, as noted in the previous footnote. Omitting export duties and allocating property taxes in proportion to consumption or to land and labor would produce a pattern of effective rates similar to that shown in column e.

[13]Thus the top 4 percent of the distribution pays two-thirds of all personal income tax and the top 13 percent pays five-sixths. See the information in Table 2.1.

[14]An exception is the limitation of indirect taxes on food (and perhaps other necessities). Basic foodstuffs may be exempt in some countries as much because of the difficulties of collecting taxes on them as because of any conscious social policy. That cereal grains are often subject to import duties suggests that this is true. Moreover, hardly ever does anyone suggest that the regressive taxes on tobacco products and mass-consumed alcoholic beverages be reduced. For an exception, see C. E. McLure, Jr. and W. R. Thirsk, "The Inequity of Taxing Iniquity: A Plea for Reduced Sumptuary Taxes in Developing Countries," *Economic Development and Cultural Change*, Vol. 26 (April, 1978), pp. 487

[15]See R. M. Bird and L. De Wulf, "Tax Incidence and Income Distribution in Latin America: A Critical Review of Empirical Studies," *IMF Staff Papers*, Vol. 20 (November 1973), p. 673. For further discussion of this issue, see C. E. McLure, Jr., "Taxation and the Urban Poor In Developing Countries," *World Development*, Vol. 5 (March, 1977).

[16]R. A. Musgrave and M. Gillis, *Fiscal Reform for Colombia* (Cambridge, Mass.: Harvard Law School, 1971), p. 33. Estimates of the distributional impact of public expenditures in Colombia are summarized in Berry and Urrutia, *op. cit.*, Chapter 7. Such estimates have, however, been criticized strongly in L. De Wulf, "Fiscal Incidence Studies in Developing Countries: Survey and Critique," *IMF Staff Papers*, Vol. 22 (March 1975), pp. 61-131.

3. THE REFORM OUTLINED

Space constraints do not allow a full description of the many important provisions included in the recent reforms. But the most important can be summarized as follows:

A. Personal income and related taxes
   1. Revision of marginal tax rates under both the income tax and net wealth tax;
   2. Conversion of most income tax deductions and special exemptions to credits;
   3. Elimination of almost all exemptions for particular kinds of income and net wealth;
   4. Introduction of a presumption that income is at least 8 percent of the taxpayer's net wealth;
   5. Taxation as "occasional income" of such items as realized long-term capital gains, inheritances, gifts, and gambling receipts; and
   6. Improvements in administration.

B. Company income taxes
   1. Elimination of graduated rates on companies;
   2. Consolidation of the three previous classes of companies (corporations, limited-liability companies, and partnerships) into two classes, and abolition of a number of complementary income-based taxes, the combination of which often produced steeply progressive rates;
   3. Elimination of most exemptions and other tax incentives;
   4. Taxation of all capital gains as ordinary income;
   5. Replacement of many deductions by credits;
   6. Adoption of the presumption (for corporations only) that income is at least 8 percent of net wealth;
   7. Liberalization and clarification of existing depreciation allowances, while retaining historical cost as the basis for depreciation;
   8. Restriction of the use of percentage depletion for mineral assets;
   9. Introduction of loss carry-forward, primarily for corporations; and
   10. Inclusion of many state-owned enterprises in the income tax base.

C. Sales Taxation
   1. Increased emphasis upon the value-added method of implementation;
   2. Increased rates, especially on items judged to be consumed especially heavily by upper income groups, including personal and automotive services;
   3. An Andean Common Market variation of the Brussels Tariff Nomenclature (BTN) to specify rates for narrowly defined categories of commodities;
   4. Expansion of the category of previously exempt goods, especially food;
   5. Elimination of several important stamp taxes; and

6. Provision for increased sharing of revenues with subnational governments.

D. Foreign Trade Policies
   1. A slight increase in import surcharges;
   2. Subjection to import duties of the imports of government enterprises and decentralized agencies;
   3. A reduction in the coffee export tax; and
   4. Reduction in the rates at which certificates of tax credit (CATs) are paid on nontraditional exports.

These provisions–and others– are explained more fully and evaluated in the following sections.

4. EVALUATION OF THE 1974 REFORM

For the most part it is convenient to discuss the various income tax reforms without regard to whether they are found in the personal or company taxes. Similarly, we discuss taxation of government entities without regard for whether income taxes or tariffs are concerned. Finally, given the brief period that has elapsed since the reform was undertaken–and the consequent paucity of hard data for gauging changes in tax liability by income class–we can provide little more than qualitative judgments about the likely distributive effects of the reform. However, where possible we cite results of simulations of distributional effects, done in 1975 by the Ministry of Finance for several of the income tax components of the package.

The Individual Income Tax

1. Conversion of Deductions to Credits. Tax deductions and credits have the well-known characteristics that the value of a deduction, and therefore its stimulative effect, depends upon the marginal tax rate of the taxpayer, whereas the value of a credit is the same for everyone. Partly because of the distributional consequences of this difference, the Musgrave Commission proposed, and Colombia adopted in part, a system of vanishing deductions–deductions that would diminish as income rose above selected levels. But the consequences of vanishing deductions for both equity and neutrality are rather capricious, and experience in Colombia, albeit brief, has demonstrated that this device is complicated and particularly subject to erosion.

For these–or other–reasons, many allowances that were deductions or vanishing deductions under the old law were converted to credits in the 1974 reform. In particular, for individuals there is now (1) a personal credit of Col. $1,000 for the taxpayer (and for the spouse, in the case of a joint return) and a credit of Col. $500 for each additional dependent, (2) a "special" credit of the greater of $1,000 or the sum of 10 percent of medical expenses and expenses for primary and secondary education plus 20 percent of the first Col. $10,000 of rent and 5 percent of the excess over that, (3) in the case of joint returns, an additional special credit of Col. $1,000 for the spouse, (4) a credit of 20 percent of contributions (40 percent for corporations) to charity and governmental units (up to 10 percent of gross tax liability before credits), (5) a credit of 20 percent of the first Col. $40,000 of earnings received from savings accounts, dividends, and mutual funds by taxpayers with net wealth of no more than Col. $2,000,000, plus several other credits of less immediate interest. Other than deductions that are justified as costs of earning income, the only remaining deductions are for employee contributions to social security and private retirement funds, property taxes, and mortgage interest.

It is difficult to compare the distributional effects of the new law with those of the old, because many, but not all, of the old deductions were included in the vanishing formula. However, it seems that the change is likely to increase progressivity. First, the commonly applicable 20 percent credit is equivalent (in terms of tax savings) to a 100 percent deduction for someone in the 20 percent marginal tax bracket and worth more than a deduction to a taxpayer in a lower marginal tax bracket. Based on fragmentary information for 1968 and 1971, it appears that 50 percent or more of taxpayers may have paid marginal rates of less than 20 percent. At the other end of the scale, we might note that under the old law only one-half of certain deductions vanished, and at a rate of 20 percent of the excess of income over Col. $60,000. Therefore, taxpayers in marginal rate brackets above 40 percent could be no better off under the new regime than under the old. Thus, the shift from deductions to credits should increase progressivity, at least at the ends of the income distribution.

2. *Changes in Rate Structure.* It is difficult to compare the old and new rate structures under the individual income tax, due to the shift from deductions to credits. But it does appear that at least in the upper income levels progressivity has been increased. Similarly, the rate structure under the net wealth tax adds somewhat more to progressivity, due primarily to the increase in the exemption from Col. $20,000 to Col. $80,000 and the increase in the maximum rate from 1.5 to 2.0 percent.

Indicative of the distributional effects of the shift to tax credits and of rate adjustments under the income tax is Table 2.2 which presents the results of simulations of the new income tax law by the Ministry of Finance.[17] Column a shows that the modifications in tax rates and the shifts to credits, by themselves, would have freed the three lowest net income classes from virtually all income tax lia-

[17]The simulations are based on distributions of income and tax data for the income and complementary taxes for personal income taxpayers in taxable year 1973 (the relevant distributions for 1974 being unavailable). The simulations involved application of the post-reform income tax law to 1973 taxpayer liquidations. The revenue thus generated in each income class was then compared to actual tax collections, by each income class, for taxable year 1973. For complete citation, see Table 2.2.

TABLE 2.2. Implications of Some Key Aspects of the 1974 Tax Reform (Results of simulations comparing 1973 liabilities under pre-reform and post-reform income tax law)

Net income class (pesos)	Percentage change in income tax liabilities, by net income class, due to: Rate modifications and substitution of tax credits for deductions and exemptions (a)	*Plus*: effects of eliminating exemptions for capital income (b)
0-6,000	− 100	− 100
6-12,000	− 100	− 100
12-24,000	− 96	− 96
24-50,000	− 59	− 55
50-75,000	− 37	− 21
75-100,000	− 39	− 21
100-150,000	− 36	+ 15
150-200,000	− 26	+ 2
200-300,000	− 16	+ 25
300-400,000	− 6	+ 44
Over-400,000	+ 8	+ 186
Total	− 22	+ 41

Source: I. Obregon S. and G. Perry R. "Effectos Redistributivos de la Reforma Tributaria de 1975 en Colombia" (trabajo presentado ante el Seminario sobre Distribución de Ingresos Promovido por el Cede y el Banco Mundial), Bogota, June 1975, Tables B. 1-B. 6. See also *ibid*., footnote 1, p. 13, for a further description of methodology.

bility and would have reduced tax liabilities for all but the highest income class (Col. $400 thousand and above), but in declining proportion to income.

3. Exempt Income and Wealth. The old law exempted from taxation such items as interest on mortgages and government securities, monetary corrections on bank deposits of constant purchasing power (UPAC's), and income placed in so-called extraordinary reserves, and provided incentives for private electric companies and manufacturers and assemblers of automobiles. These exemptions were of benefit primarily to upper income groups and virtually none of them made sense as a matter of public policy; they had therefore generally been attacked by the Musgrave Commission. Thus, their elimination should be judged a positive step forward on grounds of resource allocation, revenue yield, and distribution. Similar statements could be made about exemptions for labor income, since they are not justifiable and probably benefit primarily workers in the top part of the income distribution. But the Constitution prevents using emergency powers to reduce gains made previously by labor. These exemptions are, of course, a suitable target for further reforms.

Running parallel to the exemptions under the income tax were a large number of exemptions under the net wealth tax. Virtually all of these—for such items as jewelry, books, works of art, government securities and mortgages, limited amounts of balances in savings accounts and shares in Colombian corporations, and investments in nonprofit enterprises, specified tax-exempt entities, assets yielding tax-exempt income, assets not capable of yielding income, and activities judged to be especially important for economic development—have been eliminated, leaving only a small number of relatively minor types of exempt wealth. Eliminating these exemptions should increase progressivity.

Data concerning the effects of elimination of exemptions for non-capital income and exemptions under the net wealth tax were not available. However, the Ministry of Finance did undertake simulations of the effect of abolition of exemptions for capital income. As Table 2.2 indicates, this measure was decidedly progressive in its distributional impact. Column b, which incorporates the effects of this change with those arising from rate modifications and the shift to tax credits, shows that the abolition of exemptions for capital income served to increase liabilities for all income classes save the three lowest (compare columns a and b), with the largest increases coming in the top two categories (Col. $300 thousand and above).

4. Presumptive Income. Due to the ease of hiding income, many wealthy Colombians, particularly those in agriculture, pay little or no income taxes. The presumptive income tax is, therefore, potentially a quite important component of the new tax law, especially so far as yield and equity are concerned. But the law provides several escape clauses—including natural disaster—through which the taxpayer can circumvent the tax. This is especially noteworthy since a similar law passed in 1973, but applicable only to agriculture, was rendered impotent by the declaration that the entire country was subject to natural disaster!

The measure clearly had a progressive impact, if presumptive tax liabilities are measured against net wealth. The aforementioned Ministry of Finance simulations of the 1974 reform on 1973 data shows that the presumptive tax led to substantial increases in income tax liabilities for all taxpayers with net wealth in excess of Col. $240 thousand.[18] For taxpayers in the bracket just above this amount, taxes under the new law were 2 percent higher than under the 1973 law. The differential rises steadily to 79 percent for taxpayers with net wealth of from Col. $2 million to Col. $3 million, and to 191 percent for taxpayers having between Col. $10 million and Col. $100 million in net wealth.

5. Irregular Income. Under the new law so-called irregular income of individuals is taxed in a way that provides for some averaging and some preferential treatment. Twenty percent of net irregular income is added to ordinary income. The marginal rate that would be applied to the sum is reduced by 10 percentage points and applied to all irregular income.

[18]See Obregon and Perry, *op. cit.*, Table III-B-5. The measure did not increase income taxes on net wealth brackets from zero to Col. $60 thousand, but substantially increased income taxes for those with net wealth between Col. $60 thousand and Col. $120 thousand. For this bracket, the absolute increase was small, but given the small amounts of taxes on these brackets under 1973 law, the percentage increase was substantial.

Though several other items are included in irregular income, the most important components of the tax base, especially from the distributional viewpoint, are long-term capital gains (gains on property held over two years) and 80 percent of net inheritances and gifts. Because the only capital gains that were formerly subject to any tax at all were those on real estate, and even gains on real estate other than owner-occupied housing are now taxed less favorably than before, the new tax on irregular income could add significantly to the progressivity of the tax system.

Unfortunately, the new law apparently does not provide for constructive realization of capital gains at death. This omission could both undermine the potential progressivity of the new law and increase the lock-in of investors who own appreciated assets. Finally, it should be noted that the inclusion of the asset in the base of the recipient's tax on irregular income or in the base of the inheritance tax does *not* substitute for constructive realization. The point is that taxation under the recipient's irregular income tax and the inheritance tax is based on asset values, not the change in asset value, as would be appropriate to measure the income of the donor. Moreover, the tax on constructively realized gains would be based on the marginal tax bracket of the donor, while the existing treatment of inheritances under the irregular income tax depends on the donee's marginal tax rate, which can be generally presumed to be lower.

For purposes of calculating future capital gains, taxpayers can revalue their assets to their market value as of the end of 1974 and by as much as 8 percent per year after that. These revaluations cannot be accumulated if not employed in a given year, and they must be used for purposes of the net wealth tax and the presumptive income tax–but apparently they need not be used for purposes of the *predial* (the local property tax) and they cannot be used for calculating depreciation for tax purposes.

Whether revaluation is attractive to the taxpayer depends upon (a) the taxpayer's marginal tax rates under the ordinary and irregular income taxes and the net wealth tax, (b) the extent to which the revaluation would be subject to the presumptive income tax, (c) the expected holding period, and (d) the taxpayer's discount rate. Because revaluation is less attractive the longer the asset is to be held, it may favor speculation, relative to productive investment. The distributional consequences of allowing revaluation are unclear, because in general taxpayers with high taxable incomes but low net wealth are favored. Finally, revaluation is least valuable for those for whom it would increase the presumptive income tax; that is, for those who are otherwise able to avoid or evade the ordinary income tax.

The Company Income Tax

1. Basic Taxation of Companies. Unification of the taxation of company income should have positive effects on income distribution, as well as its more obvious salutary effects on neutrality. Under the old law business forms were manipulated in order to minimize the total amount of tax that would be paid on a given flow of income. The result was, of course, complicated business structures and little revenue. It seems likely that the new unified rate structure will be less subject to manipulation. And the previous advantages of the use of the limited-liability form of organization have been reduced, relative to those attaching to the use of the corporate form. Since the earlier advantages accrued primarily to upper income groups, progressivity should be enhanced.[19] On the other hand, rates on corporations are somewhat lower in many cases than under the old regime, due to the elimination of many subsidiary taxes, and progressivity may have been reduced somewhat for that reason. But this change seems worthwhile, since these aggregate rates, which reached a maximum of 72 percent at the company level, may in many cases have done more to dull incentives and induce evasion than to raise revenue.

2. Depreciation and Depletion. The distributional effects of loosening regulations for depreciation allowances and tightening those for depletion depend upon the extent to which the benefits and burdens are captured by (or shifted to) consumers, rather than accruing to owners of firms utilizing the allowances. It seems reasonable to believe that competitive forces are sufficient that some, but not all, of the benefits and burdens accrue to consumers. If this is true, liberalizing depreciation allowances would benefit both industrialists–presumably upper income individuals–and consumers of manufactured goods. Earlier work on tax incidence in Colombia suggests that the consumer element of this tax reduction may be regressive at the bottom of the income scale (especially so far as poor rural families are concerned), but more or less proportionate above that. The reduction in the use of percentage depletion would have similar effects, but in the opposite direction. That is, there would be some unshifted burden on upper income owners and perhaps some burden on consumers of processed mineral products both produced and consumed within the country. This latter element would probably be somewhat more progressive in its incidence pattern than would the reduction of depreciation allowances, due to the heavy use of private automobiles by upper income groups. But these effects could easily be swamped by nontax and other nonfiscal mineral policies beyond the scope of this paper. Finally, we have no estimate of the likely amounts of revenue involved in the changes in either depreciation or depletion allowances. But it seems that on balance these reforms should be given positive marks for their resource allocation effects and that taken together they are more or less neutral from a distributional point of view. Similar comments apply to the liberalization of provisions for loss carry-forward.

3. Taxation of State Enterprises. Decree 1979 of September 19 provided for the taxation of the profits of state industrial and commerical enterprises on the

[19] Statements of this type are, to some extent, inconsistent with our previous suggestion that the corporation income tax might be borne by consumers, rather than shareholders. Whereas the business taxes might, on the average, be shifted to consumers, differentials above and below the average might affect profits.

same basis as those of private corporations and for the abolition of all customs exemptions enjoyed by government agencies, except for capital imports of public utilities, public health services, and the postal service. Subsequent modifications in the law served to dissipate most of these reforms, so far as customs duties are concerned, though the income tax provisions were allowed to stand essentially intact. The new law represents an important advance on the resource allocation front, though less of one than if the original provisions had not been modified. But it seems unlikely that these provisions have any significant effect on income distribution.

Sales Tax Reform

The modifications in the sales tax were intended to increase the yield (and perhaps the elasticity), to increase the progressivity (or reduce the regressivity), and to improve the administration of the tax. The increased use of the value-added technique should improve both administration and revenue performance, because historically there has been a substantial amount of "slack" in the administration of the tax, especially so far as firms allowed to purchase on a tax-exempt basis were concerned. To the extent that benefits of evasion have not been shared with consumers, improved administration should add somewhat to progressivity. Progressivity will also be enhanced somewhat by the increase in luxury rates from 25 percent to 35 percent and the inclusion of a number of income-elastic services in the tax base for the first time. On the other hand, the exemption of food has been substantially liberalized (from basically "unprocessed" food to almost all food) and the basic (generally applicable) rate has been raised from 5 to 15 percent. The taxation of capital goods at a rate of 6 percent, without any credit under the value added approach–intended to offset other policies that artificially cheapen capital in a labor-surplus economy– should also add marginally to progressivity, though much of this burden may be borne by consumers.

Use of the Brussels Tariff Nomenclature (BTN) to classify goods for purposes of the sales tax should facilitate collection of the portion of the tax that is levied on imports. But it will complicate the collection of taxes on domestic production, at least for a while. And in many instances it appears that the effort to "fine-tune" the tax by using different rates for slightly different products may result in discrimination between products that for some purposes are nearly perfect substitutes. Thus, this effort to improve administration may turn out to have been overzealous. On the other hand, little but good can come from the partial elimination of stamp taxes, many of which can only be characterized as "nuisance taxes." Finally, adoption of the BTN and elimination of several stamp taxes do not seem to have strong distributional implications.

The increased sharing of general sales tax revenues with subnational governments will probably have no great effect on the distribution of income, except to the extent that it increases the feasibility of subnational governments providing essential services to the poor within their jurisdiction. It is to be welcomed, given the dire fiscal straits in which many of those governments find themselves. And the total return to the department of consumption of the revenue collected from the 35 precent tax on the sales of the departmental liquor monopolies is to be applauded, for several reasons.

Other Measures

The increased surcharge on imports should not seriously affect the aftertax distribution of income. On the other hand, the reduction in the export tax on coffee will improve the urban-rural distribution of income and alter the size distributions for both the entire country and the rural sector. Finally, it is difficult to know, without further study, the distributional effects of the reduction in export incentives provided through the Certificado de Abono Tributario (CAT). But they are likely to be positive, since most workers (and, of course, most owners) in firms benefiting from CATs are probably relatively well-off. It should be remembered, however, that alterations in exchange rate and financial policies, increased export promotion, and improved techniques of freeing exports from sales taxes may leave producers in export industries little affected by the reductions in CATs.

One measure conspicuously absent from the list of 1974 reforms was rationalization of the mix of tax and exchange rate policies affecting petroleum products, particularly gasoline. Because of exchange rate subsidies, coupled with price controls on oil from old fields and low taxes per gallon of fuel, Colombian gasoline sold for a pump price of about U.S. $0.11 in late 1974. Even if one were willing—and able—to ignore the rapidly worsening problems of pollution and congestion in the largest Colombian cities, one could hardly imagine a worse energy policy for the late 1970's. Though the adverse results of this policy are pervasive, for our purpose we need only note that the subsidization of the consumption of gasoline benefited primarily upper-income groups, who own the vast majority of private automobiles, and that elimination of the subsidy would add to progressivity, especially if it could be combined with increased subsidization of urban bus transportation for the masses.

However, the government finally took steps, in August of 1975, to end the exchange rate subsidy, on a gradual basis. By May 1976 the exchange rate for petroleum had been unified with the "certificate" rate. Gasoline prices rose on this account, and because the taxes on fuel are ad valorem taxes, collections from this source began to rise as well. Maintenance of price controls on petroleum from older Colombian fields was retained, so that fuel prices in Colombia still do not approach their opportunity costs, but even so, the price of gasoline at the pump had risen to U.S. $0.187 by May 1976.[20] Elimination of this last vestige of an outdated energy policy would serve to increase significantly both revenues and the distributive impact of the tax system.

[20] *Revista del Banco de la República*, Bogotá, May 1976, p.3.

5. JUDICIAL AND ADMINISTRATIVE ASPECTS

Economists who undertake to assess the impact—distributive or otherwise—of a major policy change barely after the ink has dried on the enabling legislation or decrees do so at some peril. This is especially true in the case of tax reform, where successful implementation of administrative and procedural measures supportive of changes in tax structure is crucial if legislative intent is to be realized. The effects of given structural changes in a tax system depend not only upon the efficacy of the tools and procedures available to tax administrators, but also upon morality in tax collection and compliance. Neither the commitment to improved administration nor the climate for taxpayer compliance is easy to gauge under any circumstances, least of all following a reform involving major departures from past policy; the reciprocal interactions between structural tax reform and tax administration and compliance become evident only with the passage of time. The full effects of the Colombian reform were felt only in the second quarter of 1976, when taxpayers began filing income tax returns for 1975, the first complete year in which the income tax measures were operative.

The initial tax reforms announced in 1974 included a number of key changes in administrative procedures and practices for handling declaration and assessment of income which, had they been allowed to stand, would have vastly strengthened the hand of the tax administration in dealing with various of the ingenious techniques of evasion developed by Colombian taxpayers over more than a century of experience with the income tax. However, many of these procedural changes were quickly ruled invalid by the Supreme Court and the Council of State.[21]

Whether the climate for morality in tax administration and compliance has been altered since late 1974 is highly problematical. It is known that prior to the 1974 reform, administrator/taxpayer corruption was not uncommon.[22] In addition, it might be claimed that the full implications of taxpayer resistance to the reform may not show up until 1977-78 or beyond. A former tax official has observed that the 1974 reform, coming unexpectedly, caught taxpayers with their defenses down. By 1976, he argues, the initiative had returned to the taxpayers, who by then had had time to establish new or modified ways to evade or avoid taxes, within the limits established by those administrative changes that did survive into that year.[23]

[21] The most important of the procedural reforms and regulations ruled unconstitutional were those that circumscribed the scope for legal artifices to delay or escape tax entirely. These are outlined in L. J. Vasquez Caro and G. Palomeque, "Reforma Tributaria: Brechas entre Propósitos, Normas y Realidades," Tercer Seminario de Economía Colombiana, Universidad Externado de Colombia, Bogotá, May 1976, pp. 15-22.

[22] Vasquez and Palomeque estimate that in recent years, for every peso of "inducements" paid to tax assessors, the state lost 20 pesos in revenue. *Ibid.*, p. 29.

[23] *Ibid.*, p. 36.

While cognizant of the possible effects that adverse judicial rulings and deterioration in administration and compliance can have in thwarting the achievement of ambitious structural reform, the authors are not at all inclined to write off the Colombian reform as merely an interesting but futile exercise in sensible fiscal engineering. To do so would be to ignore the important implications of structural reform for administrative feasibility. Unless the reform somehow served to cause a marked retrogression in administrative capacity and compliance to levels well below that of the recent past, the comprehensive rationalization and simplification of Colombian tax law produced by the reform should itself have a significant positive impact on the efficiency with which taxes are administered in Colombia.

Beyond the issues raised above, another important factor complicates efforts to assess the distributive impact of this or any tax reform. As noted, the 1974 Colombian reform was explicitly geared to achieve allocative, stabilization (in this case, revenue) and administrative, as well as distributive, goals. Fiscal reform that affects any of the first three goals will almost certainly have distributional consequences quite apart from those of measures adopted primarily for redistributive purposes. In some instances these consequences will support distributive aims; in others they will not. The task of sorting out the effects on income distribution of allocative (or revenue or administrative) measures is no less difficult than that of identifying the allocative impact of measures primarily intended as redistributive instruments. But to some extent it is possible to reconcile distribution, allocation, revenue, and administration in the following ways.

First, virtually any reform which increases the administrative feasibility—and yield—of taxation has the potential of improving the lot of the poor, so long as a highly regressive tax is not involved. For one thing, if public funds are directed consciously toward providing services that benefit the poorest 50 percent of households, as was claimed to be the official policy of the Lopez Michelson government, a larger budget may be better for the poor than a smaller budget. Beyond that, if inflation is both inevitable in the absence of higher taxes or lower expenditures and more burdensome to the poor than to other groups, as has been asserted to be the case in Colombia, tighter tax administration will benefit especially the poor.

Finally, it seems reasonable to believe, but hard to demonstrate, that in general a tax reform which improves the allocation of resources, and therefore increases the real value of national output, is likely to improve the lot of the poor. This presumption is based upon the thought that tax policies that distort the allocation of resources did not just happen; more likely, they were enacted at the behest of taxpayers—often wealthy taxpayers. Since elimination of this kind of distortion can be expected to leave the preferentially treated taxpayer no better off than before, it probably benefits others, including the poor. But none of the points discussed in these two paragraphs should be pushed too far; nor are they the proper subject of this paper. Rather, suffice it to say that improved administration, increased yield (at least in the present context), and reduced distortion of resource allocation are, like increased progressivity (again given existing incidence patterns), acceptable goals in their own right.

6. INDICATIONS OF INITIAL IMPACT

How a particular tax reform affects income distribution depends on how it affects revenues, as well as structural features. In a world where all relevant elasticities (of demand and factor supply) are near zero, if it can be assumed (as in Colombia) that the reform did not significantly alter the tax burdens on lower income groups, it would not be inappropriate to begin assessment of the distributive impact of tax reform by focusing upon differences between pre-reform and post-reform tax collections from upper income groups.[24]

Whatever its ultimate distributive implications, the reform was clearly successful in augmenting government revenues in its first year of application (1975), even before the full effects of income tax reform were felt. Gross tax collections rose by nearly 47 percent over 1974 levels, and more importantly, net tax collections increased by nearly 51 percent (see Table 2.3).[25]

To be sure, a large part of the 1975 increase in revenues was not traceable to the reform as such, but to the built-in response of the tax system to changes in nominal income.[26] Indeed, a common assumption within the tax administration was that even in the absence of reform, the tax system would have generated 15 percent more (nominal) revenues in 1975 than in 1974.[27] But collections in 1975 far outpaced the growth in nominal GDP, which is estimated to have risen by 27.3 percent over 1974 levels.[28] Thus, the ex-post revenue elasticity of the tax system for 1975 was 1.71 on one view (gross collections) or 1.86 on another (net collec-

[24]Over time, as the relevant elasticities move from zero toward unity and beyond, effects of tax reform on factor supplies begin to take on a much more substantial significance and should not be ignored.

[25]The distinction between gross and net tax collections is important in Colombia. Gross taxes refer to the collections *inclusive* of taxes paid with various types of tax credit instruments used in Colombia since 1967. The most important of these has been the CAT (*Certificado de Abono Tributario*), an instrument issued to exporters of nontraditional products (typically equivalent to 15 percent of export value, prior to January, 1975). Nontaxable themselves, these instruments could then be used later to meet a variety of tax obligations, including those under the income tax and the sales tax. In 1973 and 1974, CAT payments amounted to 6.7 and 8.0 percent of total gross tax collection. With the changes introduced in the reform, the ratio of CATs to total taxes fell to 5.5 percent in 1975, and to not quite 1 percent in the first quarter of 1976.

[26]It might be argued that the sharp rise in coffee prices and export values beginning in July 1975 (following a disastrous freeze in Brazil) played a major role in the upsurge of tax collections for 1975. But closer inspection reveals that this was not the case. Revenues from coffee export taxes flow into a special exchange account of the Central Bank. Computations based on published Central Bank information indicate that revenues from coffee export taxes in 1975 were about Col. $300 million, or 26.7 percent above 1974 levels (*Revista del Banco de la República*, Bogotá, May 1976, pp. 3-4). Thus, the rate of growth in coffee export tax revenues in the special exchange account was about half that for total revenues in 1975.

[27]See for example Vasquez and Palomeque, *Ibid.*, p. 34.

[28]Based on Planeación figures showing 4.6 percent real growth and an increase of 21.7 percent in the implicit deflator for GDP.

TABLE 2.3. Colombia–Central Government Current Revenues, Gross Basis by type of revenue, inclusive of CAT, 1970-75 (millions of pesos)

Tax	1970	1971	1972	1973	1974	1975
I. Direct taxes	5,959	6,956	8,024	9,190	11,260	18,315
1. Income and complementary taxes[a]	5,624	6,492	7,624	8,778	10,725	18,063
2. Surcharge on property tax	13	24	23	28	30	34
3. Death and gift taxes	174	254	216	257	380	219
4. Cattle tax	149	176	159	137	125	–
II. Indirect taxes	5,885	7,375	8,581	11,596	16,035	22,172
1. Customs duties	2,242	2,670	2,909	3,706	4,849	5,410
2. Special exchange account	805	839	953	2,080	3,054	3,561
3. Earmarked customs surcharge[b]	298	320	342	452	805	1,594
4. Sales tax	1,078	1,670	2,019	2,449	3,945	7,758
5. Gasoline and diesel fuel taxes[c]	830	1,002	1,288	1,474	1,536	1,726
6. Special 5 percent tourism tax	25	28	31	43	59	77
7. Stamp taxes[d]	607	876	1,040	1,375	1,791	1,658
8. National sales tax on departmental liquors	–	–	–	–	–	390
III. Nontax revenues: interest and penalties	393	423	546	588	817	950
IV. Nontax revenues: contractual rents	161	206	270	324	365	382
Total current revenues (gross basis)	12,389	14,959	17,406	21,675	28,480	41,820
Total taxes paid by CATs	(424)	(543)	(1,103)	(1,456)	(2,283)	(2,318)

[a] Includes personal income and business taxes, withholding and advance payment of personal and business taxes, and the net wealth tax.

[b] Special surcharges on imports earmarked for export promotion and for the benefit of the coffee fund.

[c] Includes 10 percent tax on gasoline in addition to ad valorem rates for *Fondo Vial*.

[d] Taxes paid with tax credit certificate for exports and tourist development. CATs have been primarily used by exporters to pay income and complementary taxes, customs duties, and the sales tax.

Source: Dirección General de Impuestos Nacionales.

Note: Elements in columns may not add precisely to total due to rounding.

tions.[29] The significance of these figures can best be appreciated by examining ex-post revenue elasticities over the previous five-year span. Over that period, tax revenues barely grew as fast as nominal GDP (even with frequent changes in tax legislation designed to bolster revenues), as indicated by the overall coefficient of ex-post revenue elasticity, 1.01.[30] Further, revenue responsiveness to growth in GDP was highly variable over the period, with very low elasticity figures for 1972 and 1973 (0.80), and moderately high ones for 1970 and 1971 (1.28 and 1.17 respectively). But in no year did ex-post elasticities approach those recorded for 1975.

The surge in revenues in the first year following the 1974 reform had obvious consequences for the nation's tax ratio, historically one of the lowest in Latin America.[31] For the period 1969-74, the ratio of gross taxes to GDP declined steadily from 9.8 percent in 1970 to 9.0 percent by 1974. But in the first year following the reform, the tax ratio rose to 10.5 percent, an increase of 1.5 percentage points, or by about 17 percent. Despite all the shortcomings involved in using the tax ratio as an indicator of fiscal performance,[32] this increase is nevertheless of considerable significance; except in countries which, unlike Colombia, rely heavily on volatile taxes on natural resources (i.e., Zambia on copper and Indonesia on oil), such an increase in the tax ratio from one year to another is quite uncommon. Moreoever, there is (admittedly crude) basis for stating that, at least for 1975, virtually the entire increase may have arisen from increased taxes on the richest 20 percent of the income distribution.[33] The extent to which this shift on the tax side of the budget was (or could be) translated into a net transfer in favor of less advantaged members of Colombian society depends upon one's view of the incidence of public services in 1975, a question outside the scope of this paper.

7. CONCLUDING REMARKS

Though it is easy to find faults in the Colombian tax system, even after the massive tax reform of 1974, both the reform and the resulting tax system are impressive, in terms of equity, neutrality, and administrative feasibility.

[29] Ex-post revenue elasticities reflect not only the built-in response of the system to income growth, but effects of changes in tax legislation (base and rates) as well. An ex-ante elasticity coefficient would incorporate only the effects of built-in revenue growth. Given the frequency with which Colombian tax legislation has been altered since 1969, computation of historic ex-ante elasticity coefficients for this period would represent a nearly impossible task.

[30] Source: Revenue Reports of the Dirección General de Impuestos Nacionales, República de Colombia, and national income accounts information of the Departamento de Planeación Nacional.

[31] See Musgrave and Gillis, *op. cit.*, Chapter 3.

[32] *Ibid.*, Chapter 3, p. 23.

[33] The basis for this statement is given in the appendix.

The reforms of the income tax alone would rank the recent Colombian reform among the most ambitious and laudable ever, in either developed or developing countries. In terms of scope, basic conception, and objectives of neutrality and equity, these reforms are perhaps most nearly analogous to those proposed by the Carter Commission in Canada in the mid-1960's. But whereas the Carter proposals, called by several authorities a "landmark" in the history of fiscal reform, remain largely inoperative, the Colombian reforms, through the constitutional mechanism of emergency powers, have been enacted into law.

The nature of the reform and the way it was achieved must, however, leave the student of tax reform with mixed feelings. On the one hand, it is gratifying to learn that reform of this magnitude and excellence is possible in a democracy. On the other hand, it is a bit depressing to contemplate that the reform could be achieved only through the exercise of the extraordinary emergency powers provided in the Colombian Constitution. One must still wonder whether there is hope for meaningful tax reform in other democracies without resort to similar—and often unavailable—emergency provisions.

APPENDIX

The Share of 1975 GDP Taken from High-Income Recipients by the 1974 Tax Reform

We know from section 2 that the personal income tax is paid almost entirely by the upper income classes, with the top 13 percent paying five-sixths of the total. Given the configuration of the personal income tax element of the reform, it is fairly clear that the burden of any revenue increase arising from income tax reform would lie in the richest 10-15 percent of the distribution. Furthermore, the pattern of the changes in the sales tax was such that it would be difficult to argue (assuming forward shifting) that any significant proportion of the *increased burden* arose from the poorest 50-70 percent of the income distribution. Further, we know from section 6 that the historical ex-post elasticity of revenue growth with respect to GDP over the period 1969-74 was about unity. This information furnishes a crude basis for estimating the distributive impact of the 1974 reform, in broad macro terms.

If tax revenues had grown in 1975 at the same relative rate as in the five previous years (or in 1974, for that matter), they would have grown at about the same rate as nominal GDP. Thus, with total 1974 revenues of Col. $28,480 million (see Table 2.3), and nominal growth of GDP of 27.3 percent in 1975, it would not have been unreasonable to have expected revenues to reach roughly Col. $36,255 million in 1975, even in the absence of the 1974 reform. But, revenues actually grew by nearly 47 percent, to Col. $41,820 million (see Table 2.3), or by Col. $5,565 million more than they would have with the historical GDP elasticity of near unity.

Collections from two tax categories grew substantially faster than nominal GDP. Together, the income and wealth taxes and the sales tax accounted for well over 100 percent of 1975 revenue growth in excess of the 1975 rate of growth of GDP. That is, these two taxes generated Col. $7,147 million (of which income taxes were Col. $4,410 million and sales taxes Col. $2,737 million) in addition to the 27.3 percent revenue growth that might have been expected on the basis of past performance.[34] Since the entire tax system in 1975 generated only Col. $5,565 million over and above that expected had revenue growth just matched the rate of growth of GDP, the excess growth in income and sales taxes may on this crude basis be said to represent 128 percent of the additional revenues flowing from reform, or at least the entire increase of 1.5 percentage points in the overall tax ratio.

If the reform measures had been confined to the *personal* income and wealth taxes, it would appear legitimate to assume that 100 percent of the excess growth in income tax revenues came from the top quintile, if not the top decile, of the income distribution. And it would also appear reasonable to assume that at least 80 percent (Col. $2,190) of the growth in sales tax revenues attributable to reform arose from the top quintile. On this basis, it may be said that 119 percent (Col. $6,600) of the revenue growth from reform was due to increased income and sales taxes on the top quintile, or again, at least the entire increase in the tax ratio.

But the figure of 119 percent just calculated would probably overstate the redistributive impact of the reform, since the income tax data in Table 2.3 do not separate personal income and wealth taxes from similar taxes imposed on companies. (Recall that we have argued that the latter taxes may add little to progressivity.) Previous studies found that the corporation income tax typically accounts for about half of total revenues from total income and complementary taxes.[35] If this relationship also held in 1975, then growth in personal income tax revenues could not have accounted for much more than *half* of the Col. $4,410 million mentioned above, and reform of the personal income tax and the sales tax together generated only an additional Col. $4,395 million (Col. $2,205 million and

[34]Income tax revenues amounted to Col. $10,725 million in 1974. At a rate of growth of 27.3 percent, 1975 income taxes would have reached Col. $13,653 million. But the actual total for 1975 was Col. $18,063 million. Thus, the income tax *reform* could itself have increased revenues by Col. $4,410 million. Sales tax revenues for 1974 were Col. $3,945 million. At a rate of growth of 27.3 percent, they would have risen to Col. $5,021 in 1975. But actual 1975 revenues reached Col. $7,758 million. Thus, sales tax reform may have produced as much as an additional $2,737 million in revenues in 1975.

[35]See McLure, *op. cit.*, and Musgrave and Gillis, *op. cit.*, Table 11-1. It is, of course, quite possible, given the nature of the reforms, that more than half of the extraordinary growth occurred in the personal income tax.

Col. $2,190 million respectively) in excess of that expected with a unitary revenue elasticity. Even so, this is still 79 percent (Col. $4,395 million vs. Col. $5,565 million) of the total increase in tax collections, over and above the 27.3 percent rate of GDP growth. Moreover, if we allocate even half the excess growth in corporate income tax (Col. $1,103) to consumers in the top 20 percent of the income distribution, the total taxes attributable to this group rises to Col. $5,498, or about 99 percent of the growth in revenues not explained by historical trends.[36]

If separate revenue elasticities are used for each of the two taxes, instead of the global figure of one, the results are only slightly different from those indicated above. For the period 1969-74, the historical ex-post revenue elasticity for the income tax was 0.91, while that for the sales tax was 1.46. If 1975 income tax revenues had grown at the same rate, relative to nominal income, as in the past, they would have reached about Col. $13,389 million in 1975, half of which (i.e. Col. $6,695 million) would have been personal income tax collections. But personal income tax revenues in 1975 actually reached Col. $9,032 million (one-half of total income tax collections). Thus the reform could have yielded as much as an additional Col. $2,337 million in personal income tax revenues. Similarly, if 1975 sales tax revenues had grown at the same rate as was implicit in the ex-post elasticity of 1.46 for 1969-1974, then 1975 revenues from the tax would have reached Col. $5,517 million. Sales tax revenues actually amounted to Col. $7,758 million in 1975. Thus, adjustment in the sales tax in the 1974 reform could have brought in an additional Col. $2,241 million for 1975, of which 80 percent, or Col. $1,793, might be attributed to the top decile. Therefore, on this alternative basis, the personal income tax and the sales tax reform measures may have accounted for a combined increase of Col. $4,130 million in taxes on the richest 20 percent of households. Adding again half the excess growth in the corporate tax, we have a total of Col. $5,299 arising from the tax reform and attributable to the top quintile.

Again, since the overall tax system generated (in 1975) only Col. $5,565 million over and above that expected had revenue growth just matched GDP growth, then reform of personal income and sales taxes accounted for 74 percent of total revenue growth from the entire reform package. Of greater relevance, once the share of the richest 20 percent in increased corporate taxes is added, this figure climbs to 95 percent and we see that the reform may have shifted a minimum of 1.43 percentage points of GDP (0.95 x 1.5) away from the top quintile of the distribution.

[36]The figures in McLure, *op. cit.*, suggest that if the corporation income tax is shifted to consumers in the long run, those in the top 13 percent of the income distribution pay roughly half of it. In the short run, the percentage paid by the top 20 percent is probably even higher, even though allowance must be made for some short-run shifting to nonresident owners of capital and foreign governments.

Chapter 3

THE DISTRIBUTIVE EFFECTS OF LOCAL GOVERNMENT FINANCES IN COLOMBIA: A REVIEW OF THE EVIDENCE

Johannes F. Linn*
The World Bank

1. INTRODUCTION

Local public finances have in the past received more attention in Colombia than has generally been the case in developing countries.[1] However, most authors have considered the distributive impact of local government activities only in passing

*In preparing this paper the author has benefited from extensive comments by Hernando Acevedo, Roy W. Bahl, Albert Berry, Richard M. Bird, Orville F. Grimes, Douglas Keare, Charles E. McLure, Jr., and Jacob Meerman. He also acknowledges gratefully the assistance of many Colombian officials at the national and local level, who helped in assembling the information on which this paper is based. Responsibility for any errors of conception or fact remain with the author. Moreover, the views expressed are those of the author and not necessarily those of the World Bank.

[1]See R. M. Bird, *Taxation and Development: Lessons from the Colombian Experience* (Cambridge, Mass.: Harvard University Press, 1970), Chap. 5; L. Currie, *Una Politica Urbana para los Paises en Desarrollo* (Bogotá, D.E.: Ediciones Tercer Mundo, 1965), Chap. 10; S. M. Hey, "A Study of Municipal Public Finances in Bogotá, D. E., Medellin and Cali, Colombia" (Unpublished Ph.D. dissertation, Johns Hopkins University, 1970); A. Kalnins, *Estudio del Impuesto Predial y Complementarios del Distrito Especial de Bogotá, 1950-1962* (Bogotá, D. E.: Departamento Administrativo de Planeacion Distrital, 1962); R. A. Musgrave and M. Gillis, eds., *Fiscal Reform for Colombia* (Cambridge, Mass.: International Tax Program, Harvard Law School, 1971), Chap. 14, 16-18; D. Netzer, "Some Aspects of Local Government Finance in Colombia," Economic Development Report No. 51 (Cambridge, Mass.: Development Advisory Service, Harvard University, 1967); Republic of Colombia, The World Bank-United Nations Development Program (IBRD-UNDP), "Fiscal Studies," in *Bogotá, Urban Development Study Phase II* (Bogotá, D. E., 1973) (referred to below as *Phase II Report*); M. C. Taylor, *et al.*, *Fiscal Survey of Colombia* (Baltimore: The Johns Hopkins Press, 1965), Chap. 7, 10.

if at all.[2] Two main reasons are likely to explain this neglect: first, the importance of local government in the overall public sector activities and thus the distributive impact of local finances, is generally underestimated. One of the objectives of this paper is to demonstrate that, particularly in urban areas, local government accounts for a significant proportion of public sector responsibilities, and that the potential for redistribution through the local public sector should not be neglected. A second reason for the apparent reluctance to deal with the distributive effects of local finances may rest with methodological reservations.[3]

The conventional theory of fiscal decentralization holds that central government authorities have a comparative advantage in pursuing the goal of income redistribution and therefore that concern with the distributive effect of local public finances is inappropriate.[4] But one may counter this view on various levels: first, the conventional wisdom is based on a number of assumptions, such as perfect information and perfect mobility of the factors of production, of industrial and commercial activities, and of residential location, which would ensure a movement of factors and activities sufficient to offset local government initiatives in pursuing a particular target of redistribution. While these assumptions may have some justification in highly industrialized countries such as the U. S., they are less appropriate for most developing countries like Colombia, where a high degree of regionalization, and a continuing lack of communication result in significant barriers to mobility and information flows. Second, national policy concerned with distribution can direct local fiscal instruments by setting nationwide standards which guide their use in the appropriate direction. In Colombia, the national pricing policy for local public services is a prime example of this approach. Finally, in a country where all policy instruments, including national fiscal policy, remain extremely imperfect and limited tools for reaching a given target of redistribution, the policy makers will want to be able to utilize all available instruments, even those which may be relatively weak, provided their beneficial distributional effects are not more than offset by efficiency losses.

The purpose of this paper is therefore to focus explicitly on the distributive impacts of local government finances in Colombia by conducting a comprehensive

[2] In the *Phase II Report, op. cit.*, an attempt was made to estimate the incidence of local taxes in Bogotá, D. E. In the context of a comprehensive tax incidence study of Colombia by C. E. McLure, Jr. the incidence of local taxes was analyzed along with other higher level taxes. (See C. E. McLure, Jr., "The Incidence of Colombian Taxes, 1970," *Economic Development and Cultural Change*, Vol. 24 (October, 1975), pp. 155-183.) This is also the case for the tax incidence analysis in Taylor, *op. cit.* The incidence of local public expenditures was analyzed jointly with that of all public sector spending in M. Urrutia-Montoya and C. E. de Sandoval, "Politica Fiscal y Distribucion del Ingreso en Colombia," *Revista del Banco de la Republica*, Vol. 44 (July, 1971), pp. 1072-87.

[3] A further constraint, and possibly the binding one, may have been that factual evidence on local government activity has been very sparse, and that only a case study approach or surveys conducted on a large scale can provide meaningful insights into the operations of local governments in developing countries.

[4] See e.g., R. Musgrave and P. B. Musgrave, *Public Finance in Theory and Practice* (New York: McGraw-Hill, 1973), p. 606.

review of the scattered and frequently unpublished evidence on this issue. The remainder of the paper is organized in six sections: Section 2 highlights the institutional framework of local government, in order to clarify the linkages between local authorities and other decision makers in the public and private sectors. Section 3 demonstrates the relative importance of local government in Colombia. Section 4 reviews the evidence on the incidence of local taxation and expenditure. Section 5 presents an initial attempt to analyze the distributive effects of pricing policies for user-charge financed public services, which provide a major and rapidly growing share of local fiscal capacity. Section 6 focuses on the issue of access to local public services by different income groups. Finally, section 7 pulls together the results and conclusions of the paper in assessing the policy implications of the preceding discussion. Throughout the paper most attention is given to local government in urban areas, since it is in the urban sector that local government contributes most to public sector activities and where as a result its potential for affecting the distribution of income is most significant.

2. THE INSTITUTIONAL FRAMEWORK OF LOCAL GOVERNMENT

As a first step in the analysis of local government finance[5] in Colombia it is necessary to describe briefly the institutional framework in which the public authorities operate at the local level. Three sets of agents act, and to some degree interact, in municipal government: the *municipal administration*, which is the local executive branch, is headed by the mayor; the mayor is appointed by the governor of the department (state), who in turn is an appointee of the President of the Republic. The executive branch of local government is thus a creation of, and to a large degree dependent on higher level authorities.[6] Second, the *municipal council*, which is the legislative branch of local government, is popularly elected. The autonomous (decentralized) local *public enterprises*, which are the main agents in providing local public services especially in larger cities, are only to a very limited extent under the control of either the mayor or the municipal council, and therefore can, and frequently do, act independently of outside administrative or political control. Attempts by the executive branches in some of the major cities (e.g., Bogotá and Cali) to centralize administrative decision making in the hands of the mayor through the creation of planning offices with com-

[5]The definition of "local government" is here restricted to the municipal level; the departmental (state) level is treated only in passing. Note that in Colombia municipalities are the only administrative form of local government, and therefore cover urban as well as rural areas of the country.

[6]This did not rule out conflicts between the local and the higher level executive branches in the past, especially since under the constitutional rules of the National Front parity had to be maintained in the appointment of governors between the two major parties, and the mayor of each departmental capital cannot be drawn from the party to which the departmental governor belongs.

prehensive statutory powers have thus far failed to produce a unified local government planning and decision making process.

The political pressures operating on the local authorities include those by the local elite, the local electorate, local and regional industrial and commercial interests, and the national government. The municipal council responds primarily to the first three of these sets of pressures; the mayor in addition has to consider regional and national influences; while the local public enterprises are strongly influenced by central government, in addition to various local pressures. The latter may be made effective through the mayor and the municipal council in their (limited) control function over the activities of the local enterprises.

Given these public agents at the local level and the numerous pressures to which they are subjected, it is not surprising that on balance the distributional impact of local government activities tends to be very diverse in different localities of Colombia. For instance, while it appears that in Cali local government has responded to local pressures towards socially progressive policies and appears aware of the distributive impacts of its activities, the local public sector in Cartagena in the past seems to have been characterized by an absence of such awareness. Moreover, the fact that numerous agencies operate with very different objective functions explains the often contradictory results of local government decision making. A striking example may be observed in Cartagena, where the rate structures of the two most important municipal taxes show strongly regressive characteristics, while the tariffs for water supply and sewerage services are strongly progressive.[7]

The most important force which tends to level differences in local fiscal management between various localities is the influence of the national government. While it does not exert direct control over the budgeting process at the subnational level, it limits the revenue authority of local public agencies.[8] In the field of taxation national legislation has delegated only two major taxes to local government, the property tax and the industry and commerce tax.[9] All other major tax instruments, in particular the income and wealth taxes, the corporation tax, and the sales tax are exclusively reserved for the national government.[10] The rate structure for local taxes is generally limited by national legislation. Moreover, public service pricing at all levels of government is regulated by the National Tarriff Board, a branch of the National Planning Department, which has to approve the tariffs for all public services. Mainly as a result of the influence of the Board, the tariff *structure* is quite uniform for the major public

[7] J. F. Linn, "Urban Public Finances in Developing Countries: Case Study of Cartagena, Colombia," Urban and Regional Report No. 77-1, The Work Bank, 1975. (Mimeographed.)

[8] The central government also shares responsibility in the provision of some local public services, generally through its decentralized agencies. This is the case particularly in smaller towns and rural communities.

[9] With the exception of Bogotá and Medellín, the tax base for the property tax is appraised by a national agency, the Geographic Institute "Agustín Codazzi." National legislation has also set maximum rates for property taxation.

[10] A share of the sales tax is distributed to local government.

services throughout the country, although the tariff levels differ.[11] The National Planning Department further has to approve all foreign and most domestic borrowing by public agencies, including those at the local level.[12] Finally, central government grants, especially those for public utility construction programs and for education and health may be used to exert central government leverage over local government decision making.

In summary, the national government limits local government activities through the constraints placed on revenue sources, and acts as a unifying leveling force particularly in the area of public service provision and pricing. But local government in Colombia remains functionally fragmented and subject to numerous pressures which operate differentially on the various local agents. As a result, cities may be expected to differ widely as regards the distributional impact of their activities and in their concern for it. Furthermore, within each city *prima facie* contradictory distributive choices are frequently made.

3. THE CONTRIBUTION OF LOCAL GOVERNMENT TO TAXATION AND PUBLIC EXPENDITURE

Before turning to an analysis of the evidence of distributive impacts of local government fiscal actions, the contribution of the local public sector to the overall fiscal structure needs to be reviewed, in order to assess the importance of local government in financing and providing public services, relative to other levels of government.

Beginning with taxation, Table 3.1 shows the shares of the three levels of government (national, departmental, and municipal) in the total tax burden for the country as a whole, as well as an estimate of these shares for three major Colombian cities.[13] For the nation as a whole the share of subnational tax burden amounts to some 20 percent, of which municipal governments contribute a little less than half. In the case of Bogotá, where municipal and departmental tax authority is combined, almost 22 percent of the tax burden is accounted for by District taxes. For the other two cities the municipal governments impose a larger burden than the departmental authorities. Since this is the reverse of the national pattern for all municipalities combined, municipal taxes in the urban sector are likely to be more important than the departmental taxes, while the opposite holds for the rural sector.

The importance of the municipal revenue structure is further emphasized

[11] For a detailed description of the pricing principles entertained by the Board and the tariff structure, see Section 5 below.

[12] See National Planning Department, "Crédito Públi Interno," Documento DNP-998-UDRU-DEDM, December 10, 1972; and "Disposiciones Legales sobre la Cóntratacion de Crédito Externo," Documento DAP-126-GPE, August 28, 1968.

[13] For a discussion of the assumptions underlying these estimates and their resulting limitations, see the Appendix.

TABLE 3.1. Percentage Distribution of Revenue Burden by Level of Government, 1970

	All Municipalities		Bogotá	Cali	Cartagena
	Taxes	Total Current Revenues	Taxes	Taxes	Taxes
National	79.4	75.8	78.3	78.3	77.1
Departmental	11.7	9.0	–	10.1	9.3
Municipal	8.9	15.2	21.7	11.6	13.6
Total	100.0	100.0	100.0	100.0	100.0

Source: Taxes: Appendix Table A-1; Current Revenues: International Bank for Reconstructional and Development (IBRD), *Economic Position and Prospects of Colombia,* Report No. 696-Co, Vol. I, Table 5.4.

when considering all current local revenue sources. Approximately 25 percent of all current revenues of the public sector were collected by subnational governments in 1970, and municipal authorities accounted for almost two-thirds of this (Table 3.1). These data also indicate that non-tax revenues, consisting mostly of user charges, make an important contribution particularly at the municipal level.

The importance of local government in total public sector activity is further highlighted when looking at public sector expenditures. Despite a relatively slow growth rate in overall municipal spending between 1970 and 1973, the share of municipal governments in 1973 in total public sector spending was 17 percent (Table 3.2). In the major cities the share of local government was considerably higher, and is estimated to have reached almost 50 percent in Bogotá and Cali.

A further breakdown of municipal spending (not shown in Table 3.2 indicates, first, that for all municipalities the expenditures of decentralized agencies accounted for over 80 percent of total municipal expenditure in 1973 and that

TABLE 3.2. Distribution of Expenditure by Level of Government[1]

	All Municipalities[a]		Bogotá[b]	Cali[b]	Cartagena[b]
	Percent Distrib. 1973	Growth Rate[2] 1970-73	Percentage Distribution 1972	1975[3]	1972
National Government	71.0	21.2	50.1	44.5	68.4
Central Gov't.	(32.4)	(20.5)	(23.1)	(20.1)	(31.5)
Nat'l Decentralized Agencies	(38.6)	(22.1)	(27.0)	(24.4)	(36.9)
Departmental Gov't[4]	11.6	22.0	–	6.7	8.5
Municipal Gov't.[4]	17.4	18.6	49.9	48.8	23.0
Total	100.0	20.8	100.0	100.0	100.0

[1] Net of intergovernmental transfers.
[2] Average annual compound growth rate, in nominal terms.
[3] Budget figures.
[4] Including decentralized agencies at the departmental and municipal levels, respectively.

Sources: [a] IBRD, *op. cit.*
[b] Appendix Table A-2.

TABLE 3.3. Local Public Sector Responsibility for Urban Services

Functions	Bogotá[a]	Cali[a]	Cartagena[a]	All Municipalities[b] (1)	(2)	(3)
Water	P	P	P	79	(137)	57.7
Sewerage	P	P	P	79	(137)	57.7
Electricity	P	P	–	24	(144)	16.7
Telephones (Local)	P	P	P	55	(62)	88.7
Roads and Bridges	P	P	P	S		
Street Lighting	P	P	–	24	(144)	16.7
Refuse Collection	P	P	P	P		
Parks and Recreation	P	P	P	P		
Fire Protection	P	P	P	P		
Markets and Abattoirs	P	P	P	P		
Cemeteries	P	P	P	P		
Transportation	S	N	N	N		
Law Enforcement	S	N	N	N		
Education						
Primary	P	N	N	N		
Secondary	P	N	N	N		
Health	S	S	–	N		
Social Welfare	P	S	–	N		
Housing	S	S	–	N		

Notes: P: Primary Responsibility
S: Secondary Responsibility
N: Negligible Responsibility
[1]Number of cities where local government has primary responsibility for the service.
[2]Total number of cities covered.
[3]Percentage of cities where local government has primary responsibility for the service.
Sources: [a]Based on author's observation during field visits.
[b]Arvids Kalnins, *Entidades Descentralizadas Territoriales de Colombia,* Presidencia de la República de Colombia, Bogotá, D. E., 1974.

they have grown at an annual rate of about 30 percent between 1970 and 1973.[14] Since these agencies are largely financed by user charges it is clear that a study of the distributive effects of local government will have to consider explicitly the incidence of public service prices.

A further dimension of the issue of local government participation in total public sector activity may be explored by looking at the distribution of responsibility for the main public service functions which are carried out in the urban sector. Table 3.3 shows the degree of involvement of local agencies in the provision of these services in a number of cities. In Bogotá, city authorities have primary responsibility for virtually all functions, but local government involvement declines for intermediate and smaller cities, especially as regards social services. However, even in the medium and smaller cities local government generally retains responsibility for water and sewerage, and for a number of the

[14]Dirrección General del Presupesto, "Análisis de los Presupuestos Consolidados del Sector Público 1970-73," 1975. (Mimeographed.)

minor public services, such as refuse collection, fire protection, markets, cemeteries, etc., and is secondarily involved in a number of the other services.

The preceding discussion of local revenues and expenditures in the overall public finance setting of Colombia suggests that it is desirable to investigate in greater detail the distributive effects of local taxation, of local expenditures, and of the provision and pricing of local public services. The following three sections will discuss each of these issues in turn on the basis of the empirical evidence presently available and will suggest directions for future research.

4. THE INCIDENCE OF LOCAL TAXES AND EXPENDITURES

This section reviews some conventional estimates of the incidence of local taxes and expenditures in Colombia. These studies have not considered the incidence of user charges or of user-charge financed public expenditures, which may have important distributive effects, as sections 5 and 6 below attempt to show. However, traditional tax and expenditure incidence studies remain of considerable importance and are therefore subjected to a thorough analysis in the present section.

Tax Incidence

Two recent estimates of the incidence of local taxes in Colombia are available: in his nationwide study of Colombian tax incidence McLure has considered the two main local taxes, the property tax and the industry and commerce tax.[15] Further, in Phase II of the Bogotá Urban Development Study an analysis of the incidence of local taxes in Bogotá was made.[16] Incidence studies are notoriously difficult to compare,[17] but for the purpose of this paper a presentation of the results and of the likely causes for differences between the two studies will be instructive in conveying a broad impression of the probable incidence of local taxes, and of the critical analytical issues requiring further study. Since the property tax is the most important local tax, and the most controversial as regards the distribution of its burden, this section will concentrate on the incidence of property taxation, while reviewing the remaining taxes only briefly.

[15] C. E. McLure, Jr., *op. cit.* Earlier tax incidence studies are also found in Musgrave and Gillis, *op. cit.*, and Taylor, *op. cit.*

[16] Phase II Study, *op. cit.*

[17] See C. E. McLure, Jr., "Taxation and the Urban Poor in Developing Countries," IBRD *Staff Working Paper No. 222*, December, 1975, for a discussion of these difficulties. Unfortunately, the Phase II Study does not offer enough detail on estimation procedures to assess the differences between its results and those of McLure, except as regards the shifting assumptions discussed further below.

TABLE 3.4. Estimates of the Incidence of the Urban Property Tax, 1970

Income Class (Col. $ p. a.)	Percentage of All urban households[a]	Property Tax/Income Ratio		
		Phase II[b]		
		Money Income	Total Income	McLure[a]
0- 12,000	14.7	1.01	0.85	0.1
12,000- 24,000	30.2	0.82	0.73	0.1
24,000- 36,000	17.5	0.77	0.70	0.1[1]
36,000- 60,000	16.8	0.83	0.77	0.3[1]
60,000-174,000	17.7	0.68	0.65	0.5-0.6[1]
174,000 and over	3.1	0.61	0.58	1.7-2.3[1]
Average		0.76	0.66	0.6-0.7[1]

[1] Average of ratios for income subclasses, weighted by the share of income in each class.
Sources: [a]Charles E. McLure, Jr., "The Incidence . . . ," *op. cit.*
[b]Phase II Study, *op. cit.*

The Property Tax.[18] McLure found the property tax[19] to be strongly progressive in middle and upper income brackets, while the Bogotá Phase II Study found it highly regressive, especially when measured relative to monetary and not total family income (see Table 3.4)[20] This difference is largely explained by the differing shifting assumptions employed, and is thus illustrative of the difficulties encountered in measuring and comparing tax incidence. McLure assumes that, in the case of residential properties, the tax is borne by capital owners, and in the case of commercial and industrial properties by the firms' shareholders, who are assumed to have incomes above Col. $120,000 per annum. In contrast, the Phase II Study assumes that the tax is shifted fully to occupants in the case of residential properties, and to consumers in the case of commercial and industrial properties. These contrary sets of shifting assumptions reflect extreme versions of the conflicting views of the "new" and the "traditional" approaches to the analysis of property tax incidence.[21]

On the assumption that factors are fixed in supply and perfectly mobile within a country, and that markets are perfectly competitive, the new view concludes that a uniform nation-wide property tax will be borne by all owners of land and capital. And since the ownership of these factors tends to be more highly con-

[18] For a more detailed discussion of the incidence of property taxation, see J. F. Linn, "The Incidence of Urban Property Taxation in Developing Countries," World Bank *Staff Working Paper No. 264*, Washington, D. C., 1977.

[19] Including the valorization tax. The incidence of this tax is discussed separately below.

[20] Property tax incidence estimates in the earlier two incidence studies cited above fall between these two extremes.

[21] For a brief review of the controversy see Helen F. Ladd, "The Role of the Property Tax: A Reassessment." in *Broad-Based Taxes: New Options and Sources*, ed. by R. A. Musgrave (Baltimore: Johns Hopkins Press, 1973), pp. 39-86.

TABLE 3.5. Statutory and Effective Property Tax Rates in Three Colombian Cities (percentage)

	Bogotá		Cali		Cartagena	
Statutory Rate[a]	1.52	(1972)[b]	1.42	(1973)[b]	0.84-1.75[c]	(1972)
Effective Average Rate on Assessed Value[d]	0.57	(1972)	0.45	(1973)	1.04	(1972)
Effective Average Rate	0.58	(1969)	n. a.		0.82	(1969)
on Est. Market value[e]	0.49	(1972)	0.20	(1973)	0.55	(1972)

[a]Improved urban properties; the base consists of the capital value of land and improvements.

[b]Including rates charged by Regional Development Corporation (CAR in Bogotá, CVC in Cali).

[c]Graduated so that the statutory rate declines as one moves from low to high property value classes.

[d]Computed as the ratio of property tax revenues to assessed property value.

[e]Computed as the ratio of property tax revenues to estimated market value of properties.

Source: Data collected by the author.

centrated than income, the property tax is taken to be progressive.[22] The new view also recognizes that property tax rates do not apply uniformly for all types of land and capital, and that rates may differ between and within jurisdictions. It allows that these differentials will induce factor and commodity movements, and therefore price, or "excise" effects so that part of the property tax may be shifted either to labor, to land, or to consumers. However, most analysts have judged it extremely difficult, if not impossible, to determine the net incidence of these excise effects on a country-wide basis,[23] and in fact most incidence studies consider only the impact of the average property tax rate.[24]

In the case of Colombia these excise effects are likely to be of some importance, since business inventories and most machinery are excluded from the property tax base; since exemptions of private and public lands are substantial,[25] and since effective tax rates vary between jurisdictions (see Table 3.5) and within jurisdictions. The regional rate differences are partly due to differences in the legal rates, which are determined by local jurisdictions subject to uniform upper limits set by national legislation. But more importantly, differences in collection performance and assessment ratios account for the differences in effective

[22]See H. Aaron, "A New View of Property Tax Incidence," *American Economic Review*, Vol. 64, No. 2 (May, 1974), pp. 212-231 for a concise exposition of this view, and for references to the original contributions by Harberger and Mieszkowski. See also H. Aaron, *Who Pays the Property Tax? A New View* (Washington, D. C.: The Brookings Institution, 1975).

[23]Aaron, "A New View of Property Tax Incidence," p. 218; and Dick Netzer, "The Property Tax: Discussion," *American Economic Review*, Vol. 64, No. 2 (May, 1974), p. 231.

[24]E.g., C. E. McLure, Jr., "Incidence of Colombian Taxes, 1970,"; and J. A. Pechman and B. A. Okner, *Who Bears the Tax Burden*? (Washington, D. C.: The Brookings Institution, 1974).

[25]In 1969, 12.8 percent of all assessed urban property value was exempted from property taxation.

property rates.[26] The excise effects cannot be assessed in the absence of detailed information on relative capital intensities of taxed versus nontaxed activities, on the elasticities of factor substitution and commodity demand, and on the degree and nature of correlation between effective property tax rates and regional per capita incomes. Based on a review of the available evidence, a recent study of property tax incidence in Colombia has shown that the excise effects are likely to increase the progressivity of the property tax estimated previously using the "new view" assumptions.[27]

More damaging to the new view of property tax incidence, particularly in a country like Colombia, is the lack of justification for the assumptions of complete inelasticity of factor supplies and perfect competition in the rental and commodity markets. In a small country with substantial foreign investment and access to foreign capital markets, capital cannot be assumed to be in fixed supply, even in the short run.[28] Furthermore, in the rapidly expanding cities of Colombia urban land cannot be assumed to be in fixed supply, especially in the longer run, since the rate of conversion of low-taxed rural land into highly taxed urban land[29] is likely to be affected at the margin by changes in the property tax differential.[30] As a result, the property tax in Colombia is almost certainly less progressive than a strict application of the new view would indicate. This conclusion is further strengthened by the observation that as in most developing countries rental and commodity markets are far from perfect.[31] Thus, at least

[26]The intrajurisdictional variations result from differential tax rates applying to urban and rural properties respectively; and from wide differentials in the effective assessment ratios, given the fact that in most larger Colombian cities reassessments proceed sequentially by areas within the city, rather than covering the whole urban area each time.

[27]See Linn, "Urban Property Taxation."

[28]Proponents of the new view have recognized the possibility of long-run flexibility of capital supply through a variable savings ratio, but the importance of international capital mobility has generally been neglected. Two recent exceptions are McLure, "Taxation and Urban Poor," and R. M. Bird, "The Incidence of the Property Tax: Old Wine in New Bottles," paper presented to Symposium on Property Taxation, sponsored by the Ministry of State for Urban Affairs, Toronto, February 17, 1976, p. 17.

[29]In Bogotá, D. E., rural land is taxed at a rate of 0.695 percent while residential urban land is taxed at a rate of 1.520 percent in nominal terms.

[30]For a general statement of this proposition, see P. Mieszkowski, "The Property Tax: An Excise Tax or a Profits Tax," *Journal of Public Economics*, Vol. 1 (April, 1972), pp. 73-96. See also R. M. Bird, *Taxing Agricultural Land in Developing Countries* (Cambridge, Mass.: Harvard University Press, 1974), pp. 167-68 for a discussion of the flexibility of rural land supply.

[31]On the imperfections in the housing markets of less developed countries, see O. F. Grimes, Jr., *Housing for Low Income Urban Families* (Baltimore: The Johns Hopkins University Press, 1976), where it is stated that rent payments implying rates of return on capital of 30 to 100 percent per annum have been observed for low income families in many less developed countries (LDCs). The figures are illustrative of the often huge quasi-rents evident in housing markets of LDCs. For a discussion of the effects of market imperfections on property tax incidence, see R. A. Musgrave, "Is a Property Tax on Housing Progressive?" *American Economic Review*, Vol. 64, No. 2 (May, 1974).

a part of the property tax is likely to be passed on to renters and consumers which also would tend to lessen the progressivity of the property tax.

Despite these limitations of incidence estimates based on the new view, one would err in the opposite direction in accepting the traditional view and incidence estimates based thereon. Land and capital, while not entirely fixed in supply, are not likely to be available in perfectly elastic supply to the country as a whole, as is assumed under the traditional approach. In the case of land, the marginal costs of expansion at the urban periphery are certainly rising in the short run, and possibly even in the long run, as cities expand into areas which are more inaccessible and more difficult and costly to service.[32] In the case of foreign capital, the well-known pattern of rising costs of foreign borrowing which has been observed for other developing countries is certain to apply also to Colombia. Furthermore, while market imperfections as a result of monopoly power exist, they are not likely to be so pervasive as to allow the extreme traditional shifting assumption. Finally, the Phase II Study results were based on current income, not permanent income estimates. Consideration of permanent income would tend to make the incidence of the property tax less regressive, since the permanent income elasticity of demand for housing can be assumed to be higher than the current income elasticity, and probably in the neighborhood of unity.[33] As a result one would have to conclude that the incidence of property taxation on residential property would tend to be much less regressive than estimated in the Phase II Study. Indeed, a detailed analysis of property tax incidence for residential properties in Cali, using the "traditional" assumptions, has shown that the tax is likely to be neutral, if not slightly progressive.[34] The regressive impact of the tax on industrial and commercial properties may remain important, but as Bird has pointed out full forward shifting is not likely "owing to the different relative importance of taxed structures in the production of various goods and services."[35] This may be of particular importance in a country like Colombia, where a substantial portion of commercial and service activity in the informal, low-income sector is likely to be carried on outside (taxed) premises or where property in low-income neighborhoods is underassessed (or the tax on it is undercollected).[36]

The most appealing way of resolving the apparent conflict between the traditional and the new view of property tax incidence was suggested by Bird, who observed that "the traditional view deals, in effect, with the incidence of a tax in a particular locality; the new view, on the other hand, focuses on the inci-

[32] Casual observation of the geographic conditions of cities like Bogotá, Cali, and Cartagena would confirm this view.

[33] Evidence on housing demand elasticities for LDCs is scant; see Grimes, *op. cit.*, for some data which appear to suggest that the current income elasticity is generally in the neighborhood of unity or slightly below.

[34] See Linn, "Urban Property Taxation."

[35] R. M. Bird, "Who Pays the Property Tax?" *Policy Paper No. 12*, Institute for Policy Analysis, University of Toronto (October, 1975), p. 13.

[36] I am indebted to J. C. English for this point.

dence of the tax in the country as a whole."[37] This results from the realization that the chief "traditional" assumption (elastic factor supplies) is more nearly met in the case where an individual jurisdiction changes its property tax rate, while the chief "new" assumption (fixed factor supply) is more appropriate for an entire country. Therefore, those estimates that are based on "traditional" assumptions, such as the Phase II Report and other similar studies are more nearly correct in predicting the incidence of a change in the property tax rate which is restricted to a particular jurisdiction, such as Bogotá, while McLure's "new view" estimate is more appropriate for the analysis of the property tax incidence on a country-wide basis. Given the caveats previously introduced in the discussion of each "view," and the incidence estimates for Cali cited above, one may conclude that the expected incidence of a property tax change in a particular jurisdiction in Colombia is likely to be approximately neutral. In contrast, the expected incidence of a property tax change on a nation-wide basis, such as was planned under a recently proposed law for education finance, would probably be progressive, with neutrality representing a lower bound.

The Valorization Tax. Another municipal tax, which is related to property taxation and which has become of growing importance in Colombia, particularly in the larger cities, is the valorization tax, a special assessment levy designed to recoup the cost of public infrastructure projects.[38] The distributive impact of this tax is likely to differ from that of the property tax, since it is linked directly to the costs, and indirectly to the benefits, of a public project. Somewhat superficially, Rhoads and Bird have concluded that the valorization program tends to be neutral in its incidence, "for all tax payers would receive benefits equal to or greater than the payment."[39] Doebele, Grimes, and Linn have given some greater attention to the distributive effects of valorization by considering in qualitative terms the improved access of low income groups to employment and housing; the payments systems; the force sale of property; premature subdivision; and other effects. They conclude that, at least for Bogotá, redistribution is a small and mixed bag.[40] Unfortunately, neither of these two studies provides a comprehensive and quantitative analysis of the incidence of valorization programs.

[37] Bird, "Old Wine in New Bottles," p. 13.

[38] An early description and analysis of the valorization system is found in W. G. Rhoads, and R. M. Bird, "The Valorization Tax in Colombia; An Example for Other Developing Countries?" in *Land and Building Taxes: Their Effect on Economic Development*, ed. by A.P. Becker (Madison, Wisc.: University of Wisconsin Press, 1969). For more recent and more detailed reviews of the valorization system, see W. A. Doebele, O. F. Grimes, and J. F. Linn, "Participation of Beneficiaries in Financing Urban Services: Valorization Charges in Bogotá, Colombia," *Land Economics*, Vol. 55, No. 1 (Feb. 1979).

[39] Rhoads and Bird, *op. cit.*, p. 236.

[40] Doebele, Grimes, and Linn, *op. cit.*, pp. 86-88.

A comprehensive approach to this question would have to start from the realization that the incidence of a valorization program depends on whether it is complementary with, or whether it substitutes for, other revenue sources and expenditure programs. Four cases may be distinguished. First, the valorization program may be complementary both on the revenue and on the expenditure side, in the sense that it raises additional financial resources over and above what would have been raised without it, and that it generates investment projects in addition to those which would have been carried out without it. The program would then be regressive, neutral, or progressive depending on whether the net benefit of the program is distributed more or less equally than the existing income distribution. Second, the valorization program may generate additional resources which are used to carry out projects that would otherwise have been carried out from general resources. The distributive effect of the additional expenditures which are financed from the general resources that are thus freed by the program, may offset or reinforce the distributive impact of the net benefit generated by the valorization program. Third, if valorization revenues substitute for general resources which would have been raised in the absence of the program, and if on the expenditure side the projects that are thus financed by valorization would have been undertaken anyway, then the program is progressive or regressive depending on whether the supplanted revenue source was more or less progressive than the valorization tax itself. Finally, if valorization revenues again substitute for other revenues, and lead at the same time to an expenditure program which is biased more or less heavily in favor of high income groups than would have been the case otherwise, then the incidence of the program depends on the relative incidence effect of the displaced revenue sources and expenditure programs.

This brief and incomplete review of possible incidence effects of a valorization scheme reveals the complexity of analysis required of a comprehensive approach to the problem. Unfortunately there exists virtually no evidence on the crucial issue of the complementary or substitutive effects of the Colombian valorization program. On the basis of rather scant evidence, Rhoads and Bird inferred that on the revenue side the valorization program has been complementary.[41] While this may be true in the short run, it is less clear that in the long run valorization taxes are complementary to other revenue sources. To the extent to which they appropriate part of the betterment value of public works, they reduce the growth in the property tax base and revenues.[42] Given the lack of a well defined theoretical framework and the lack of empirical information, a quantitiative approximation of the incidence of valorization programs in

[41] Rhoads and Bird, *op. cit.*, p. 217.

[42] One may, however, argue that without valorization programs the infrastructure expenditures which lead to land value increments could never have been generated in the first place, since in the absence of a satisfactory municipal bond market, municipalities would not have been able to raise the necessary resources.

Colombia is not feasible, but this remains without doubt one of the more challenging areas for further research.[43]

Other Local Taxes. Turning then to the industry and commerce tax one finds that its rate structure and base varies even more between cities than is the case for the property tax.[44] The industry and commerce tax is assessed on commercial and industrial assets, on the value of sales, or on other indicators of industrial and commercial capacity (horse power of machinery installed, rental value, etc.)[45] To the extent that the tax is levied on assets or rental value similar arguments apply concerning its incidence as in the case of the property tax. In particular, it is probably not correct to assume full forward shifting as is done in the estimates by McLure and those of the Phase II Study (see Table 3.6). As a result, the industry and commerce tax is probably less regressive than estimated in both studies.

Colombian municipalities further impose numerous minor taxes and stamp duties. Their revenue potential and distributional impact is negligible, with the exception of the municipal vehicle tax, which appears to combine salutory efficiency and distributive effects with a considerable revenue potential.[46] An estimate of the distributive impact of this tax in Bogotá, D. E. (Table 3.6) shows it to be highly progressive especially in the income classes above Col. $60,000. So far, the tax has not been utilized by Colombian municipalities to any major extent,[47] which may be explained on two grounds. First, and most important, national import tariffs on motor vehicles are very high; as a result, local governments may feel themselves politically unable to add further to the domestic prices of automobiles. Second, problems of administration were encountered, especially in Bogotá, where it is suspected that a substantial proportion of motor vehicles are registered in municipalities surrounding the Special District, since lower rates apply there.

[43]McLure in his "Colombian Taxes" includes the valorization tax with the property taxes. This is only justified if in fact the valorization tax is a substitute for the property tax and the same expenditure program is followed with, as without the tax. And even then it would be more appropriate to apply the analysis of the "old view" on property tax incidence, rather than the "new view," since valorization programs are in use only in relatively few cities.

[44]This is largely due to the fact that this tax is entirely under local jurisdiction, in contrast to the property tax.

[45]Where the tax is levied on rental value, it amounts to an additional tax on real estate in commercial and industrial use, although the valuation of the base is likely to differ from the assessment of properties in the local cadastre.

[46]See for example J. F. Linn, "Automotive Taxation in the Cities of Developing Countries," *Nagarlok* (India), Vol. IX, No. 1 (January-March, 1979).

[47]For the departmental capitals in Colombia budgeted revenues under the heading of "Circulacion y Transito" amounted to only 4.5 percent of local tax revenues in 1973. In Bogotá, the vehicle tax contributed 5.1 percent to District Tax Revenues in 1972; and in Cartagena its contribution amounted to 2.1 percent, according to data collected by the author.

TABLE 3.6. Estimated Rates of Municipal and Departmental Taxes, 1970[a]

Income Household	Municipal Taxes						
	Property Tax		Ind. and Comm. Tax		Vehicle Tax	Sub-total	
(Col. $ p.s.)	Phase II	McLure[b]	Phase II	McLure	Phase II	Phase II	McLure[c]
0- 12,000	0.85	0.01	0.25	0.40	0.02	1.12	0.41
12,000- 24,000	0.73	0.01	0.29	0.30	0.03	1.05	0.31
24,000- 36,000	0.70	0.01	0.27	0.30	0.03	1.00	0.31
36,000- 60,000	0.77	0.03	0.24	0.30	0.02	1.03	0.33
60,000-174,000	0.65	0.5-0.6	0.21	0.30	0.05	0.91	0.80-0.90
174,000 and over	0.58	1.7-2.3	0.15	0.30	0.13	0.86	2.00-2.60
Average	0.66	0.6-0.7	0.21	0.30	0.08	0.95	0.9-1.0

Household Income	Departmental and District Taxes						Total[e]	
	Alcoholic Bev.		Tobacco Taxes		Sub-total[d]			
(Col. $ p.s.)	Phase II	McLure	Phase II	McLure	PhaseII	McLure	Phase II	McLure
0- 12,000	0.12	0.10	0.15	0.64	0.28	1.30	1.40	1.71
12,000- 24,000	2.21	1.30	0.21	0.80	2.30	2.40	3.35	2.71
24,000- 36,000	1.72	1.20	0.23	0.40	1.92	1.80	2.92	2.11
36,000- 60,000	1.97	1.20	0.16	0.40	2.16	1.80	3.19	2.13
60,000-174,000	0.16	1.00[f]	0.12	0.30[f]	0.39	1.40[f]	1.30	2.20-2.30
174,000 and over	0.15	0.20[f]	0.07	0.30[f]	0.40	0.60[f]	1.26	2.60-3.20
Average	0.75	0.80	0.14	0.60	0.93	1.70	1.88	2.60-2.70

[a]Phase II estimates apply to Bogotá, D. E. (total income); McLure estimates apply to the urban sector.
[b]Includes valorization.
[c]Includes only the property and the industry and commerce taxes.
[d]Includes departmental sales and gasoline taxes.
[e]Sum of municipal and departmental sub-totals.
[f]Interpolated by approximation since different boundaries for income classes are used.

Source: Phase II, *op. cit.*; Charles E. McLure, Jr., "The Incidence of Colombian Taxes, 1970," *Economic Development and Cultural Change* (October, 1975).

TABLE 3.7. Estimated Rates of Municipal and Departmental Taxes, 1970, assuming Neutral Property Tax Incidence[a]

Income Group (Col. $ p. a.)	Property tax	Municipal taxes[b]	Total Municipal and departmental[b]
0- 12,000	0.7	1.1 (13.8)	2.4 (30.0)
12,000- 24,000	0.7	1.0 (10.0)	3.4 (34.0)
24,000- 36,000	0.7	1.0 (9.4)	2.8 (26.4)
36,000- 60,000	0.7	1.0 (8.8)	2.8 (24.8)
60,000-174,000	0.7	1.0 (8.4)	2.4 (20.2)
174,000 and over	0.7	1.0 (4.6)	1.6 (7.3)
Average	0.7	1.0 (7.5)	2.7 (20.3)

[a]Using McLure's average property tax rate and all other incidence estimates.

[b]Figures in parentheses show the tax rates as percentages of the total tax burden for each income bracket, on the basis of McLure's national tax incidence study (assuming that the corporation tax is shifted to consumers).

Source: Table 3.6, and McLure, "Colombian Taxes, 1970."

Summary of Local Tax Incidence. The incidence of the sum of municipal taxes is strongly dependent on the incidence of the property tax. If the regressivity found in the Phase II Report is assumed, then the municipal tax system (in Bogotá) in clearly regressive; with the assumption that the owners of land and capital bear the tax the urban municipal tax system is lightly regressive in the lower income ranges, and then turns strongly progressive in the high income ranges. As was argued earlier the true incidence of the property tax probably falls between these two extremes. Assuming this tax is distributionally neutral, then the incidence pattern of municipal taxes is also approximately neutral (see Table 3.7). Assessing the weight of these tax burdens by income class in the overall burden of national taxes one finds from McLure's national incidence estimate that municipal taxes account for the highest proportion of total tax burden in the lowest income bracket (13.8 percent), but that their share declines for the higher income brackets (Table 3.7).

Since the Special District of Bogotá combines municipal and departmental taxing authority, the incidence of departmental taxes must also briefly be discussed. These taxes, which are predominantly sumptuary taxes levied on alcoholic beverages (especially beer) and tobacco, show a strongly regressive pattern with the exception of the very lowest income group (see Table 3.6).[48] As a result, the overall incidence of taxes of subnational governments in Colombia is found to be strongly regressive on the basis of Phase II estimates for Bogotá, D. E., and approximately neutral on the basis of McLure's study. Assuming a neutral property tax, the overall incidence of taxes levied by the subnational authorities is regressive (see Table 3.7). The share of subnational taxes in total tax burden is some thirty percent in the lower income ranges, while it amounts to less than ten percent in the highest income range (see Table 3.7). By implication, a broadly

[48]For a discussion of the faults of sumptuary taxes, see Charles E. McLure, Jr. and Wayne R. Thirsk, "The Inequity of Taxing Iniquity: A Plea for Reduced Sumptuary Taxes in Developing Countries," *Economic Development and Cultural Change*, Vol. 26, No. 3 (April, 1978).

based attempt to aid the urban poor through a reduction of the tax burden would do well to consider in some detail a reform of the subnational tax system aimed towards replacing regressive taxes by progressive, or at least neutral revenue instruments. But in any case, local tax reform in Bogotá should aim at preventing further increases in reliance on the beer tax, which has been one of the most rapidly growing revenue sources for the District in recent years, and as a result of which the incidence of local taxes in Bogotá has probably significantly worsened.

The Incidence of Local Public Expenditure

While interest in tax incidence has a long history in Colombia as elsewhere, the incidence of public spending has only recently become a field of investigation for public finance experts. In Colombia, an attempt at estimating the incidence of public expenditure was made by Urrutia and Sandoval.[49] Under what the authors regarded as their most appropriate set of assumptions, they found that the redistributive impact of expenditures is very progressive in the lower eight population deciles, but turns regressive for the last two deciles.[50] The data also permit a breakdown of expenditures by level of government. For municipal expenditures an essentially similar pattern of incidence is found (see Table 3.8), although the average ratio of municipal to total public expenditures is highest for the lowest four deciles (10.5 percent), and lowest for the next four deciles (5.6 percent). But the conventional analysis of expenditure incidence in this and similar studies is based on very tenuous assumptions, which seriously limit the meaningfulness of such estimates.[51] The chief problems are the difficulty of measuring benefits rather than costs of public expenditure on a global scale, the problems of assessing the changes in factor and commodity prices associated with public expenditures, and the impossibility of assigning benefits from some public goods. A further problem results from the fact that as in the case of tax incidence studies all those services which are financed from user charges are not included in the analysis. But, as section 6 of this paper tries to establish, access to these services varies among income groups and this may be an important determinant of the distribution of benefits from public sector activities.

[49] Urrutia and Sandoval, *op. cit.*

[50] This reversal in incidence is due to the assumption that such general public expenditures as defense, justice, police, general administration, planning, etc. benefit virtually exclusively the highest two deciles.

[51] For a discussion of the analytical barriers to benefit and expenditure incidence, see C. E. McLure, Jr., "On the Theory and Methodology of Estimating Benefit and Expenditure Incidence," Paper presented at a Workshop on "Income Distribution and Its Role in Development," Program of Development Studies, Rice University, April 26, 1974.

TABLE 3.8. Estimated Incidence of Municipal Expenditures in Colombia, 1966

Population Percentile	Municipal Expenditures as % of Personal Income	Municipal Expenditures as % of Total Public Expenditures
0- 10	4.6	8.0
10- 20	2.2	7.6
20- 30	3.3	17.6
30- 40	1.4	8.9
40- 50	0.8	5.8
50- 60	0.8	6.6
60- 70	0.6	4.8
70- 80	0.5	5.2
80- 90	2.7	8.8
90- 95	1.6	7.7
95-100	0.6	6.4

Source: Computed from Urrutia and Sandoval, *op. cit.* Tables 14 and 15.

5. THE INCIDENCE OF USER CHARGES FOR URBAN PUBLIC SERVICES

Studies of the incidence of public sector activity have generally not examined the distributive effects of user charges. This neglect appears to be based on the assumption that user charge financed public services do not generate significant financial transfers and have mostly private good characteristics. Therefore, user charges are treated like payments for goods and services provided by the private sector, and are not incorporated into public sector incidence studies. However, recent work on public service pricing in the U. S. and Colombia has begun to consider explicitly the distributive impact of user charges, since it was recognized that even in the absence of financial transfers pricing practices may result in implicit taxes and subsidies which can effectively redistribute income.[52]

In Colombia an analysis of the distributive effects of public service prices is particularly important since national policy explicitly employs user charges as a tool for redistribution. Furthermore, the share of self-financed activities in total public spending has rapidly increased in recent years, particularly at the local level, where they have traditionally been the most important expenditure cate-

[52] See for instance M. S. Feldstein, "Distributional Equity and the Optimal Structure of Public Prices," *The American Economic Review*, Vol. 62 (March, 1972), pp. 32-36; S. A. Hanke and R. D. Davis, "Demand Management through Responsive Pricing," *Journal of the American Water Works Association*, Vol. 63 (September, 1971), pp. 555-60; P. B. Downing, "The Distributional Impact of User Charges," Paper presented at the Southern Economic Association Meetings, November 14, 1974, Atlanta, Georgia; M. I. Gutierrez de Gomez, "Politica Tarifaria y Distribucion de Ingresos," Colombian National Planning Department, 1975. (Mimeographed.)

gory (see pp. 74 ff. above).[53] This section examines first the national policy on user charges; next, the possible definitions of cross-subsidization and their usefulness in measuring the incidence of user charges; finally, as a basis for further research it suggests a more general approach to measuring the incidence of public service provision and pricing.

National Pricing Policy for Public Services in Colombia

As mentioned previously, the National Tariff Board must approve all changes in public service charges, and it has used this authority to introduce two main principles into general practice in the pricing of public services throughout the country.[54]

The first criterion is that the average tariff[55] for a service should equal the long run average cost of production and distribution, including a "reasonable" rate of return to capital. In principle this rules out any financial transfers between different public services. However, in practice such cross-financing is recognized to occur and apparently little pressure is exerted by the Board to remove it. Thus, the first criterion in practice has been amended to require the average tariff to be set at a level where an "acceptable" degree of cross-subsidization between individual services is achieved.[56] Furthermore, in the case of water and sewerage charges, the policy of financial self-sufficiency is reduced to require systems in small towns and rural areas to cover only operating costs through user charges. The main reason for these deviations from the principle of long-run average cost pricing is related to the second criterion, which postulates that the income distribution should be improved through the public service pricing system. This aim is pursued by linking tariffs progressively to assessed property values (water, sewerage, telephones), and/or to the volume of consumption (water and sewerage, electricity); by allowing cross-financing between services (e.g., water and sewerage revenues have subsidized markets and slaughter house operations in Cartagena in the past);[57] by setting tariffs at higher rates for com-

[53] The share of self-financed activities is here approximated by the share of the expenditure of the decentralized agencies in total public spending.

[54] Strictly speaking, the Board only sets maximum rates, which do not necessarily have to be applied in full. For instance, a survey by the Board of Water charges in 1973 revealed that of 19 public water supply companies 9 had tariffs below the levels approved by the Board.

[55] The terms "user charge," "service price," or "service tariff" are used interchangeably in this study.

[56] One might argue that this criterion is so flexible as to be quite meaningless; however, the presumption is that long run average cost is to be covered for each individual service unless good cause can be shown why this should not be the case.

[57] J. F. Linn, "Urban Public Finances."

mercial and industrial users, than for residential subscribers,[58] and by subsidizing public services in rural areas.

The water tariff, which is required by the National Tariff Board and generally in use throughout the country, is an example of the application of this criterion. For residential users a certain minimum quantity of water ("cupo") is sold to consumers for a lump sum charge ("cargo fijo"), which is graduated progressively according to assessed property value classes. For consumption above the "cupo," an excess consumption charge is levied per unit of additional quantity consumed; this charge is generally uniform across property value classes, but rises in blocks with increased consumption. In addition, higher rates may apply for industrial and commercial users. Recently the Tariff Board has considered abandoning the link between property values and water charges in favor of an exclusive reliance of rising block rates for residential users. The reason for this is that although some redistribution is achieved under the present system (see below), the property assessments are felt to be frequently so out of date and uneven that serious horizontal inequities are introduced into the pricing structure.

The structure of public service charges, especially for public utilities, has been increasingly unified across the country, but the actual level and degree of progression varies considerably between cities, due to differences in the relationship between assessed values and market values, different demand and cost conditions, and different political settings.[59]

The Board has not developed explicit principles for connection fees and installation charges. As a result, the structure and level of these fees varies widely between cities: in some cases they are linked to assessed property values in addition to a charge covering installation costs (Bogotá, Cartagena). In others only a nominal charge below actual cost is imposed (Cali).[60]

Two further contrasting practices should be mentioned: first, the National Tariff Board requires that all changes in assessed property values be submitted for its approval before they can be taken as a basis of public service tariffs. Therefore property value rolls are updated for public service pricing purposes only when the tariffs are changed, and even then not necessarily. This eliminates

[58]The reason given for this practice is that industrial and commercial users have a higher ability to pay. This does not recognize the problem of (hidden) incidence, which would have to be investigated before it can be presumed that higher tariffs to industrial and commercial users lead to redistribution. In the extreme case of a brewery, for example, a large proportion of the higher tariff may be passed on to predominantly low-income consumers of beer. Another reason for charging particularly industrial consumers higher water and sewer rates could be the higher social costs associated with industrial effluents. However, this argument does not appear in the Board's reasoning.

[59]In 1973 average water and sewer rates combined varied between Col. \$0.96/m^3 in Cucuta and Col. \$2.09 in Barranquilla, according to a survey by the Tariff Board.

[60]The potential importance of capital charges in determining the ability of low income consumers to hook up to the service, and the trade-off between subsidies among existing users and subsidies between actual users and potential users does not appear to have been considered explicitly by the Board.

automatic adjustments in user charges which would result from increases in assessed values, and which could serve to maintain the real value of the user charges in an inflationary environment. Second, in 1972 the National Tariff Board approved automatic monthly increases in the excess consumption charge for water supply in Cali,[61] and recently followed suit for Medellin. While these automatic monthly increases are not directly linked to inflation rates they provide at least some regular adjustment. Since excess consumption is probably a greater proportion of total consumption for higher tariff categories (higher income groups) than for lower tariff categories (lower income groups) these automatic increases can be assumed to make the tariff structure more progressive.

Public Service Pricing and the Incidence of Subsidies[62]

Given the growing importance of user-charge financed public services in Colombia and the government's avowed intention of achieving income redistribution through public service pricing, an estimate of the distributive effect of user charges is desirable. One approach would be to measure the tariffs paid by each income group as a proportion of its income. This represents a simple extension of the tax incidence measurement, but it neglects the fact that, in contrast to taxes, the service charges are paid in direct exchange for a service provided by the public sector. To account for this particular aspect of user charges, one can instead attempt to measure the subsidies which are implicitly provided to some consumers and the implicit taxes paid by others, as a result of the existing public service prices. But these subsidies (taxes)[63] must be defined as the deviation from some norm, and it is far from clear which norm, or base price, is appropriate. This section will briefly outline those alternative definitions of subsidies which have in the past been suggested for the measurement of the incidence of public service prices, and it will review the evidence for the magnitude of such subsidies in Colombia.

The simplest approach to measuring subsidies associated with public service pricing–and the only one which has been tried so far in Colombia–defines the subsidy (S_i) per unit of the service consumed by individual or group i as the difference between the average tariff (AT) for all users of a particular service, and the actual price (P_i) paid by consumer (group) i:

$$S_i = AT - P_i \tag{1}$$

[61] In February, 1975, the increase ranged from 1.5 percent per month for the lowest block rate to 1.2 percent per month for the highest block rate.

[62] In developing the analytical approach used in this Section, I benefited from extensive discussions with C. E. McLure, who has considerably helped to sharpen the subsidy concepts reviewed here.

[63] When referring to subsidies in the following paragraphs, taxes (negative subsidies) are by implication also covered.

This definition of subsidy is based on a norm of equity in a narrow sense, since it presumes that without subsidies every user would pay the same price. It does not allow for the fact that differential benefits may accrue to different consumers; that differential costs may have to be incurred by the public service agency on behalf of different consumers; and that costs may be imposed on or benefits derived by society in general as a result of the consumption of and payment for the service, e.g., through financial transfers to or from the public agency providing the service.

A second definition of subsidies, which amends some of the shortcomings of the first, measures the subsidy as the difference between the long run average cost (AC) of the system as a whole and the price paid by an individual:

$$S'_i = AC - P_i \tag{2}$$

This definition considers as the norm the average cost incurred by the public service agency and society on behalf of all users,[64] on the supposition that in the absence of distributive considerations the users of a service as a group ought to contribute equally to making the public service operation self-sufficient and sustainable (or replicable), without imposing financial or economic burdens on the rest of society. A further refinement of this definition of subsidy considers the average cost incurred on behalf of an individual consumer or group i (AC_i), instead of the aggregate average system costs:

$$S''_i = AC_i - P_i \tag{2a}$$

This subsidy definition presumes as the basic norm that the charges to every customer (group) should cover total cost of providing the service to this particular individual, i.e., everybody should pay his way, except of course for distributive considerations. This norm thus links a criterion of equity with the objective of fiscal and financial prudence in public utility management.

Third, one can define a subsidy as the difference between the marginal cost incurred in providing the service to the individual consumer or group i (MC_i) and the price actually paid for the service:

$$S'''_i = MC_i - P_i \tag{3}$$

The norm in this case is the price which would lead to an efficient, Pareto-optimal allocation of resources, and the unit subsidy is measured as the deviation from this norm.[65]

Finally, G. R. Faulhaber has recently suggested yet a different norm relative to which subsidies can be defined.[66] On the basis of a game theoretic analysis he

[64] Including external costs imposed on society as a result of the service.

[65] The cost concept is strictly speaking short-run marginal cost, since it is not clear how long-run marginal cost pricing would, in general, lead to Pareto-optimality, when investments are lumpy, as is typically the case for most public utilities.

[66] G. R. Faulhaber, "Cross-Subsidization: Pricing in Public Enterprises," *American Economic Review*, Vol. 65, No. 5 (December, 1975), pp. 966-77.

proposes that the norm be whether or not under the given pricing structure any consumer, or coalition of consumers, would benefit from seeking a supply of the commodity or service independently of the public enterprise, e.g., by obtaining water from individual wells, rather than from the piped water supply system. Under this norm, if any individual (or group) has an incentive to leave the enterprise, then the pricing structure is not "subsidy-free." The problem with this definition is that it does not allow a measurement of subsidies, since there may exist an infinite number of prices which are "subsidy-free" or none at all. More fundamentally, while Faulhaber defines a "subsidy-free" price, he does not appear to define a subsidy itself, which is of course crucial if one wants to arrive at a quantitative measurement of the distributive effects of pricing policies.

To demonstrate the first three alternative definitions of subsidy, a very crude and preliminary estimate of these concepts of cross-subsidy was made for water supply and sewerage services in Cali, where it appears that the average cost of providing services is higher in the predominantly low income part of the city as compared with the high income areas.[67] Marginal costs are approximately the same for both areas. Some transfers occur from water and sewerage account to the general account of the municipal government.[68] In addition, as is generally the case in Colombia, tariffs are structured progressively. The resulting estimates for the alternative subsidy concepts are graphed in Figure 3.1, where the S, S″, and S‴ curves represent the subsidies as defined in equations (1), (2a) and (3) above. The basic pattern of progressivity is determined by the tariff structure since the S″ and S‴ curves (which reflect the difference between the marginal and average costs respectively on the one hand, and the water tariff on the other) do not deviate substantially from the S curve (which shows the difference between the average tariff and the tariff for each tariff category). The S‴ curve lies above the S curve throughout, since the uniform marginal cost lies above the average tariff, and therefore the subsidy to low income consumers is higher (and the implicit tax on high income consumers lower) when marginal cost is taken as the baseline for comparison.[69] When average cost for each consumer group is taken as the baseline (S″), the progressivity of the tariff structure is increased for the upper tariff categories, since average cost is below marginal cost for these groups, but remains equal to marginal cost for the low income groups.[70] As a result of defining subsidies with respect to average cost, the total range of the subsidies is increased by about 14 percent over the range

[67]See the Appendix for further details. The data on costs, tariffs, consumption and income are approximations in this first estimate. Research is currently proceeding which will refine the data base.

[68]These take the form of free services to municipal offices, and a 4 percent tax on gross service revenues levied by the municipal administration.

[69]It is here assumed that the tariff categories (low, medium-low, etc.) approximately overlap with income categories (low, medium-low, etc.).

[70]The average cost concept used here is short-run average cost. If instead long-run average cost were taken, the entire S″ curve would shift upward.

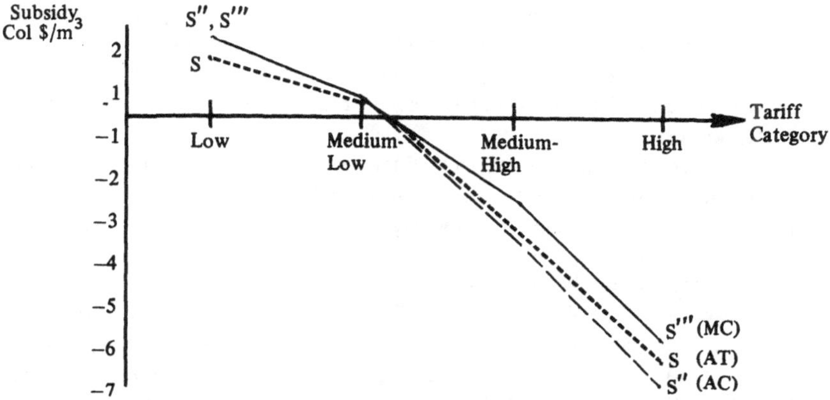

Figure 3.1. Cali: Cross subsidies between tariff categories of water and sewerage services.

of subsidies when marginal cost is taken as the base. Larger impacts may well occur when a less aggregative approach is taken in analyzing the subsidy issue.

The extent to which these definitions of subsidies lead to different results for incidence estimation depends on the degree to which costs differ systematically between service areas; on the degree to which marginal and average cost differ from each other for each consumer (group); on the size of financial transfers into, or out of, a particular service; and finally on the existence of externalities associated with the provision of the service. If there are no transfers or externalities, and if marginal costs are constant and equal throughout the service area (or uncorrelated with incomes), then all three definitions lead to the same measure of subsidy.[71] In Colombia there is evidence that at least for some services in some cities a systematic negative correlation between service costs and income levels exists. The reason for this correlation may be found in the determinants of residential land use: low income groups generally settle in areas where land values are low due to the difficulty of access and/or the poor physical qualities of land (e.g., swamps and marshes in Cartagena and Cali, steep mountain side in Bogotá and Cali); moreover, as the late-comers to urban development, low-income groups are forced to live (often in squatter settlements) at the periphery where land values are still low.[72] In each of these cases service costs[73] are likely to be higher in the low-income as compared with high-income

[71] In the model of perfect competition and equal costs all three definitions lead also to identical results, since then $MC_j = AC_i = AT = P_i$.

[72] The patterns here described need not be universal even within Colombia; a lot of basic research on the correlation between land use, service costs, and household income needs to be conducted before these observations can be generalized. For some evidence in Bogotá, see G. Vernez, "Pirate Settlements, Housing Construction by Incremental Development and Low Income Housing Policies in Bogotá, Colombia," The New York City-Rand Institute, New York, 1973, p. 57. (Mimeographed.)

[73] Especially capital costs; but even operating costs can be affected by differences in location, due to the need for extra pumping or higher maintenance requirements.

areas. The degree to which marginal cost deviates from average cost depends on the service, and on city-specific conditions. But at least in the case of water production there can be little doubt that long-run marginal costs increase as the growth in demand requires that water be obtained from increasingly remote or costly sources.

Moreover, implicit and explicit financial transfers between services occur frequently: first, cross-financing between different services occurs as, e.g., in Cartagena between water and sewerage services on the one hand, and public markets and slaughter services on the other. Second, transfers between user-charge financed public services and the general account of local government take place; e.g., in Cali 4 percent of all gross revenues of the local public utility company are transferred to general account; in Cartagena, a municipal tax is levied on local telephone users; in Bogotá earmarked local taxes are used to finance partially the District Valorization Office (now called the Urban Development Institute) and the District Public Service Enterprise (EDIS). Third, cross-financing occurs between local public service users and the national taxpayers. Those transfers take the form of national grants to the local public service agencies which are mainly directed to water and sewerage programs, and to health and education;[74] or of nationally provided credits which are generally awarded at rates below the prevailing private market rates and the opportunity cost of capital. Table 3.3 compares the actual average tariff for water and sewerage services to the average long-run unit costs[75] in 1974. It reveals the wide range of subsidies to water and sewerage beneficiaries, as well as the importance of these subsidies on the average, which would tend to put a significant wedge between the subsidy defined on the basis of the average tariff and the other subsidy measurements which are based on costs.

Addressing then the question of which of the three subsidy definitions are preferable in the measurement of incidence of public service prices, there can be little doubt that, if an overall incidence measure is sought, the cost measures provide a more comprehensive picture of the full incidence of charges, since they do not neglect the existence of implicit or explicit transfers to public service users from the users of other services or from local or national taxpayers. The choice between the subsidy measures based on the different cost concepts depends on what norm, average or marginal cost pricing, is favored by the policy maker in the absence of distributional considerations.[76] However, offsetting this conceptual advantage of the subsidy definitions based on costs, is the overriding

[74] To the extent that these are provided to account for externalities affecting the whole country as a result of the particular services one may not want to call the transfers cross-subsidies.

[75] Defined as the sum of operating costs, depreciation, and an 8 percent return of net fixed assets (revalued at reproduction cost).

[76] The economist is likely to stress the efficiency norm as the point of departure in measuring subsidies, while the utility manager, banker, and possibly the ubiquitous man-in-the-street would regard the self-sufficiency norm of average cost pricing as financially sound and equitable.

TABLE 3.9. Shortfall of Actual Average Tariff from Average Long-Run Cost of Water and Sewerage Services in Nine Colombian Cities, 1974

City	Actual Average tariff[a]	Long-Run Cost[b]	Percentage Shortfall of actual tariff from long-run average cost
	(Col. $/m)	(Col. $/m)	
Bogotá	1.84	3.60	49.9
Medellin	1.40	1.79	21.8
Cali	2.16	3.06	29.4
Barranquilla	2.53	3.32	23.8
Cartagena	1.95	4.44	56.1
Cucuta	1.40	2.82	50.4
Armenia	1.54	2.19	29.7
Neiva	1.38	1.45	4.8
Tulua	1.30	2.30	43.5
Average			34.4

[a]Total revenue from sale of water (including sewer surcharge) divided by quantity sold.
[b]Sum of operating costs plus depreciation plus 8 percent of revalued net fixed assets, divided by quantity sold.
Source: National Tariff Board of Colombia.

consideration of practicality in nationwide studies of incidence. The fact that the subsidy measure based on average tariffs requires no cost information nor any knowledge about who bears the transfers to the public service agencies makes the estimation of this subsidy concept considerably easier.

An Estimate of Subsidies in Urban Public Utility Pricing

A study of the incidence of public service charges in Colombia has been undertaken by Gutierrez de Gomez.[77] The services included in this study are residential water supply and sewerage, electricity, garbage collection and local telephone services. Four cities were covered (Bogotá, Barranquilla, Cali and Medellin), using city specific household income and expenditure data from a DANE survey for 1970, and applying the tariff structures for 1974. On the basis of some very strong assumptions[78] it was possible to compute for ten population groups the subsidy as the deviation of actual from average tariff for each service. Table 3.10 summarizes the results for the four cities considered, by expressing the subsidy (tax) for each population decile as a fraction of income in that decile; it also

[77]M. I. Gutierrez de Gomez, *op. cit.*

[78]Most importantly, it was assumed, first, that the market value of properties may be calculated from real or imputed rental expenditure; and second, that these market values correspond to assessed property values. Neither of these two assumptions is likely to be close to actual fact. Finally, it was assumed that the charge for garbage collection, which takes the form of a property tax surcharge, is actually borne by the occupant, not the owner, a rather extreme hypothesis (see above, pp. 17 ff.).

TABLE 3.10. Public Service Subsidies (Taxes) as Percentage of Income by Population Group, and Change in Gini-Coefficients, in Four Cities, 1974[a]

Population decile	Bogotá	Barranquilla	Cali	Medellin
0- 10	0.18	–	0.20	1.3
10- 20	0.40	0.12	1.90	1.6
20- 30	0.34	0.92	1.50	3.1
30- 40	1.95	0.61	1.40	3.7
40- 50	1.47	0.26	1.10	2.4
50- 60	1.18	0.22	0.80	1.9
60- 70	0.70	(0.02)	(0.03)	1.5
70- 80	0.24	(0.44)	(0.07)	1.2
80- 90	(0.42)	(0.56)	(0.30)	(0.5)
90-100	(1.24)	(0.66)	(1.50)	(0.7)
Gini-coefficient of income distribution				
without charges	0.5103	1.4145	0.4308	0.4593
with charges	0.5070	0.4129	0.4261	0.4533

[a]Figures without parentheses are subsidies; those with parentheses are taxes (negative subsidies).
Source: M. I. Gutierrez de Gomez, *op. cit.*, Annex Table 4-7, 11.

shows the Gini coefficient before and after taking into account the impact of the implicit subsidies and taxes on the income distribution of each city. With the exception of the lowest income groups, where lack of access to some or all of the services prevents the possibility of providing subsidies through the pricing system, the pattern is generally progressive, with higher subsidies in the lower-middle income groups, declining for the middle income groups, and turning negative in the highest income groups. In Bogotá and Medellin the top two deciles, in Barranquilla and Cali the top four deciles subsidize the remaining income groups. The income distribution impact is largest in Cali and Medellin as reflected in the larger range of relative subsidies and taxes there than in Bogotá and Barranquilla and in the fact that the Gini-coefficient is reduced most in these two cities after considering service charges. While the changes in the Gini-coefficient do not appear to be large, it must be remembered that the absence of progressivity in the very lowest income groups reduces the impact of the progressive pricing scheme considerably. It should also be noted that the size of the impact relative to the distributive effect of local taxes (see Table 3.7) is considerable, particularly for the lower-middle income groups. For instance, in the case of Medellin the implicit subsidy expressed as a proportion of income for the fourth percentile of the population (3.7 percent) exceeds the average municipal and departmental tax burden on urban households in Colombia at approximately the same percentile (3.4 percent).

Finally, this investigation established that the redistributive impact of electricity charges is generally most important relative to the other services, since coverage is highest for electricity service and since expenditures for this service occupy the largest share in household expenditures among all public services. These factors combine to give the progressive electricity rates the highest weights. Water and sewerage service charges take second place, followed by garbage collection taxes. The least significant influence is exerted by telephone service charges, since the coverage of this service is very limited and charges are generally not very progressive.

Some Further Issues in Public Service Pricing

While the results of the study cited in the preceding paragraphs are suggestive of the possible scope and implications of user charges for income redistribution, the approach appears of only limited usefulness due to its narrow analytical base and the empirical difficulties mentioned above. Although the two alternative definitions of subsidy which explicitly consider service costs may remedy some of the methodological problems, they only worsen the empirical ones. Moreover, even these conceptual approaches do not explicitly incorporate benefit considerations.

One way to allow for public service benefits would be to apply the methodology used in the analysis of incidence of public sector activity which is financed from tax revenues. For each income group the incidence of benefits and charges could be assessed separately or jointly in determining the incidence of the particular activity. In mathematical terms:

where NB_i is the net benefit to individual (group) i, B_i is the gross benefit to individual (group) i, T_i is the total charge paid by individual (group i) for the service, and Y_i is the income of individual (group) i.

This definition of user charge incidence differs fundamentally from the subsidy measures previously discussed (equations [1] to [3] above) in that it does not compare the incidence of charges to any particular pricing norm, and in particular makes no reference to the costs of the providing the service to individual (group) i. In fact, equation (4) identifies the pure and complete distributional impact of service pricing without accounting for the efficiency costs associated with it. For an optimal pricing decision, this is clearly not sufficient. The costs of providing the service must also be allowed for.

No attempt is made here to develop a full model of optimal pricing which would allow for the distributional objective. It would be necessary to weight differentially the costs and benefits, depending on who bears them or to whom they accrue in the private and/or public sector. In this the simple definitions of cross-subsidies explored in the previous section are generally of little use, because they provide a measure of comparison between unweighted costs and benefits. This conclusion further confirms the earlier finding that the usefulness of defining and measuring cross-subsidies is very narrowly limited by the purpose to which these concepts and measurements are put. In general one may expect that any particular definition of cross-subsidy, including the one which measures the deviation of actual tariffs from the efficient price, will only tell a very small part of the whole story about the impact of the pricing structure.

Furthermore, for pricing policy the crucial question to be asked is probably not what are total costs and benefits associated with any particular price, but rather, what are the effects of a change in social costs and benefits associated with a change in the structure of user charges. This is analogous to the recent recognition by some public finance experts concerned with tax incidence that what matters is not the overall incidence of the entire existing tax system, but rather the distributive effect of particular changes in the tax system which are feasible given the institutional and political context of a country.[79]

One avenue of progress in research may be expected to consist of the estimation of demand functions for services in a first effort to determine the degree of excess burden caused by deviation from the efficient price. A recent estimate of short-run price elasticities for water supply in Cartagena[80] showed that low income groups tend to have a demand elasticity close to zero (0.25) while high income groups have a demand elasticity close to unity (0.75). If this estimate is borne out also for long-run elasticities, then it would appear that the excess burden from deviations from the marginal cost price results mainly from the reduction in consumption among high income groups. Low income consumers will change their consumption pattern only little in response to cross-subsidies.

However, there is an added implication to this estimate of differential demand elasticities, which relates to the trade-off between cross-subsidizing existing low income users and increasing access to the service by those groups presently not yet served. Given the relatively high elasticity of demand for high income consumers an increase in the tariff for these consumers will lead only to a relatively small increase in revenues which may be used to cross-subsidize either the other low-income consumers or those who are not yet served, by extending the distribution system at subsidized capital charges. In order to finance a significant extension of the access to public services it may be necessary to reduce the subsidy on the low income groups already connected to the service, since only this would provide the needed revenue expansion. Once access is universal (or near universal as in Cali for water supply) a higher degree of cross-subsidization between existing users can again be aimed for.

Finally, while the main issue covered in this paper concerns questions of vertical equity and distribution, a discussion of pricing systems should also consider the issue of horizontal equity. It is in this context that the use of property value

[79] See McLure, "Taxation and the Urban Poor," and references cited there. I am indebted to C. E. McLure, Jr. for pointing out to me this analogy.

[80] By K. Rinkskog for The World Bank.

assessments as a basis for discriminatory pricing will have its most serious drawbacks, unless the assessment practicies are such that significant horizontal inequities can be prevented. Evidence collected in Bogotá, Cartagena, and Cali indicates that the cadastral property value base has serious deficiencies in this respect, and that as a result a progressively structured tariff schedule may result in entirely spurious, unintended distributive effects.

6. ACCESS TO PUBLIC SERVICES

Concern about the incidence of taxation and public spending has a considerable history in Colombia, as elsewhere, as was shown in Section 4. In contrast to most other countries, user charges for public services have also become an important element of public income redistribution policy in Colombia. However, little attention has generally been given to a measurement of the distributive effects of differential access to public services between income groups, or to an analysis of the causes of these differentials. The central theme of this section is that access to public services, particularly in the urban sector, is an important determinant of the degree to which different income groups benefit from public expenditures. There is evidence to suggest that access to public services, such as water supply, sanitation, electricity, education, and health provides substantial consumers' surpluses (benefits in excess of costs to the consumer), which may well exceed the net gains derived from higher levels of quantity and/or quality of the service, once the individual has gained access.[81]

In Colombia, where redistribution through public service charges is an objective of national policy, the importance of access to the public services by low income groups is further heightened, since the poor can benefit from subsidized user charges only when they consume the services, i.e., have access to them. Table 3.10 above shows very clearly how the lack of access reduces the subsidies to the lowest income groups in four Colombian cities.

Overall figures on the availability of public services in Colombia are scant, but there can be little doubt that sizable portions of the urban population do not have any or only very limited access to such public services as in-house water

[81] Although a quantitative proof of this hypothesis is not feasible at present, various sources of evidence may be cited. First, the unit price paid for public services is frequently much lower than the price for the private substitute. For instance, according to local public utility officials in Cali, the price of a cubic meter of water supplied by private hawkers in low income areas without access to the public system is approximately Col. $35, while those with access to the public system pay approximately Col. $1. Second, the value of paved roads is demonstrated by the fact that in Cali even some of the lowest income neighborhoods actively solicit valorization works and actually collect partial payments of the tax in advance to ensure that the Valorization Office initiates the work. Third, the importance of access to education facilities is demonstrated by the conclusions of recent migration studies that, next to the availability of employment opportunities, access to educational opportunities was found to be an important motivation for the migrants.

and electricity supply, sanitary sewage and solid waste disposal, education and health services. Table 3.11 shows that the average proportion of population not served by public water supply in 21 major cities of Colombia was 25 percent in 1974, without systematic variation across city size. As regards sewerage services, about 30 percent of the population in the four largest cities was without sanitary sewerage services during the same year, while 60 percent in the medium-size cities, and 43 percent in the smaller cities were without that service.

Evidence on the distribution of access to public services by income groups is even harder to come by. One possible approach is to analyze the spatial distribution of services in an urban area.[82] The correlation between the proportion of the population served in each neighborhood (barrio), or between the number of service facilities per family on the one hand, and average family income in the neighborhood on the other hand was investigated in Bogotá and Cartagena to establish whether there is a systematic relationship between access to public services and the level of income. In Bogotá, sample data for sixty neighborhoods covering the entire city show that for the most important urban services there exists a significant correlation between average family income and access to services. In Cartagena the average service levels in seventeen low income neighborhoods were first compared with the average service levels for the city as a whole. A lower percentage of households was found to have access to urban public services in the lower income areas than throughout the city. And even among the low income neighborhoods there is a significant positive correlation between income levels and access to some services.[83]

It is worth pointing out in this context that the provision of paved roads can be of central importance in some parts of Colombia, where during the rainy season unpaved streets become virtually impassable for motor vehicles and thus inhibit or prevent the provision of other urban services, such as public transportation, garbage disposal and street cleaning, police and fire protection, and maintenance of the water supply, telephone and electricity distribution systems.[84]

More evidence needs to be accumulated on the distribution of public services to strengthen these conclusions and an attempt at quantifying the welfare gains derived from access to a particular public service must be made.[85] But one may speculate about the reason for the positive correlation between incomes and access to public services. First and most obviously the ability to pay for the capital

[82]This is true at least for Colombia and many Latin American cities, where neighborhoods tend to be relatively homogenous with respect to socioeconomic characteristics. Elsewhere, as e.g., in India, greater interspersal of different socioeconomic groups may make this approach more difficult.

[83]Linn, "Urban Public Finances."

[84]In Cali a sample of 55 neighborhoods without paved roads had an average family income of about 40 percent of average family income in Cali in 1974. Officials there confirmed the fact that during the rainy season public services are very difficult, if not impossible to provide in these neighborhoods.

[85]For an important step in this direction see Marcelo Selowsky, *Who Benefits from Government Expenditure*? (New York: Oxford University Press, 1979).

TABLE 3.11. Percent of Population Served by Water and Sewerage Services in 21 Major Colombia Cities, 1974

City	Population Index[a]	Percent of Population Served by Sanitary Sewerage System[b]	Percent of Population Served by Sanitary Sewerage System[b]
Bogotá	100.0	70.9 (1.7)	70.2 (1.8)
Medellín	36.9	80.4 (−3.8)	77.8 (−1.2)
Cali	31.3	87.5 (−0.7)	81.0 (−3.2)
Barranquilla	22.7	67.7 (−4.0)	54.0 (−1.9)
Average[c]		75.1	71.5
Cartagena	12.3	55.6 (2.9)	19.9 (−2.1)
Bucaramanga	11.3	89.6 (n.a.)	– (n.a.)
Cúcuta	7.5	82.5 (1.3)	66.0 (1.0)
Manizales	6.7	74.6 (0.1)	69.6 (−4.3)
Ibagué	6.2	78.3 (n.a.)	59.3 (n.a.)
Armenia	4.5	89.2 (2.3)	87.9 (3.3)
Santa Marta	4.4	64.3 (−0.5)	37.1 (1.8)
Average[c]		75.3	40.3
Neiva	3.6	86.0 (0.9)	80.5 (3.3)
Valledupar	3.4	44.9 (−1.3)	10.3 (−1.4)
Monteria	3.1	68.3 (−5.8)	14.0 (0.4)
Tuluá	3.0	76.8 (−1.5)	69.5 (0.0)
Popayán	2.6	94.6 (n.a.)	90.4 (n.a.)
Sincelejo	2.6	46.4 (0.3)	28.3 (−1.0)
Cartago	2.4	86.9 (29.7)	79.9 (26.8)
Tunja	1.7	95.6 (n.a.)	78.8 (n.a.)
Sogamoso	1.7	93.3 (n.a.)	82.5 (n.a.)
Duitama	1.2	85.3 (n.a.)	82.2 (n.a.)
Average[c]		75.2	57.3

[a]Population of Bogotá, 1973: 3,043,863 = 100.0%; based on 1973 DANE census figures, and cited in the source.

[b]Figures in brackets show changes between 1973 and 1974 in the population covered (in percentage points).

[c]Averages weighted by population.

Source: Junta Nacional de Tarifas, "Resultados de la Información Basica Anual Sobre los Servicios de Acueducto y Alcantarillado de las Principales Ciudades del País, 1974," Documento JNT-279-UNIF, September 1975 Annex Tables 1 and 7.

and distribution costs of public services is lowest for the lowest income groups, particularly since imperfect capital markets operate against lower income groups in their ability to raise money to pay installation fees and related expenses. This problem is aggravated by the fact that in some Colombian cities high connection and installation fees are charged to new subscribers, including those from low income areas, although, once on the system, they are cross-subsidized by higher income users. In Bogotá, for example, monthly quotas for water connection and installation fees payable over 42 months are estimated to amount to between 9 and 12 percent of the average low income family's monthly earnings.[86]

The demand for access to services may, therefore, be limited by the inability of low income groups to pay the high connection charges. Furthermore, there is evidence that for some services higher capital and/or distribution costs are incurred in providing the services to low income areas as compared with high income areas.[87] And since in Colombia user charges for some of the public services, especially water and sewerage, are usually progressively graduated (lower unit prices for the low income groups and higher unit prices for the high income groups), rising costs and falling revenues per unit of production result from an expansion of the service to low income areas, posing potential financial problems for the public service agency.

Finally, there is always the possibility of political bias in the allocation of scarce public resources to higher income groups. The degree to which this factor plays a role is obviously difficult to assess, but it is likely to contribute in some cases to the failure of local government to provide services to the lower income groups.

In summary, available data show that the poor in at least two Colombian cities have significantly less access to public services than the better-off families. Given the crucial importance of access, this may be taken as evidence that lower income groups benefit less from the provision of public services, at least in absolute terms, than the higher income groups.[88] Among the causes for this condition are the lower income groups' inability to pay for the services, particularly for the capital charges; the higher costs of providing the service to the poor income neighborhoods; the fiscal constraints on the public authorities given the cross-subsidization among existing users; and possibly political biases. The policy implications of this analysis are that increased access to public services ought to be emphasized, rather than cross-subsidies between users, as long as a sizable portion of the low-income population are not served. This would imply, first, that capital charges ought to be spread over larger time periods for low-income groups than is frequently the practice in Colombia. Second, that cross-subsidization, if desired, should focus on capital, rather than current costs and charges, in order to maximize access by the poor. Current charges, even where based on cost, usually do not amount to more than one or two percent of monthly household income, while capital charges, as noted above, may amount to as much as 12 percent of family income for water supply alone even when spread over extended periods. Finally, the investment policy of public services should be directed at giving as

[86]Empresa de Acueducto y Alcantarillado de Bogotá, D. E., *Estudio Economico-Financiero* (Bogotá, June, 1975).

[87]See, e.g., Vernez, *op. cit.*, p. 7.

[88]Whether this amounts to a regressive benefit incidence of public services cannot be determined on the basis of the available data, since one would have to estimate the sum of all welfare gains derived from public services for each income group and then compare the ratio of the sum of welfare gains to income for various income groups in order to determine the incidence of all public services combined.

much attention to extending the distribution capacity, as is traditionally paid to extending the productive capacity of the system. This holds not only for public utility services, but also for such services as health and education, where proximity and location may be important factors determining the use of existing facilities by low-income groups.

7. CONCLUSIONS

Local government plays an important role in the provision and financing of public services in Colombia. Its contribution is most significant in the large cities, and least in the rural municipalities. But, due to the nature of the political process of local government and administration in Colombia, a wide degree of diversity exists between jurisdictions as regards the distributive impact of the local public sector. Therefore, it is difficult to derive country-wide estimates of the incidence of local government activity.

In considering the individual components of this activity, these difficulties were found to be further aggravated by methodological and empirical problems inherent in attempting to estimate the distributive effects of local taxation, local expenditure, and public service pricing. The primary conclusion for future research directions in all three of these areas was, therefore, to emphasize the need for further case-study work at the project or city level, which, once available in sufficient numbers, may permit an interpolation of conclusions to local governments in the entire country. Given these very serious caveats not much credence can be given to any overall statement on the incidence of local public activity. However, for the curious, Table 3.12 summarizes in very approximate terms what evidence has been carried together in this paper. From this it would appear that, overall, the incidence of local government is very progressive, due to the progressivity of public expenditure and public service prices. Local taxes increase or reduce overall progressivity depending on whether the property tax is assumed to be progressive or regressive. The fact that the lowest population quintile derives a net benefit relative to its income which is smaller than that of the next quintile is largely explained by the lack of access to user-charge financed services. These results confirm the view that local government plays an important role in the redistribution of income, and they further indicate the importance of access to public services in bringing the benefits of redistribution to the very poor. Further substantive conclusions, as well as directions for policy and further research, may be derived from a review of the individual areas of local government action.

The *incidence of municipal taxes* in Colombia is likely to be about neutral across income classes. When departmental taxes are added, the incidence of all subnational taxation was found to be quite regressive, partially offsetting the progressivity of central government taxation. Subnational taxes account for up to one-third of the total tax burden on lower income groups in Colombia. Among

TABLE 3.12. Summary of Estimated Local Government Incidence in Urban Areas[1]

Population percentile	Municipal Taxes[a] with property tax			Municipal expenditure[b]	Public Service pricing subsidies[c]	Total with property tax with property tax assumed		
	Regressive	Neutral	Progressive			Regressive	Neutral	Progressive
0- 10	(1.2)	(1.1)	(0.4)	3.0	0.3	2.1	2.2	2.9
20- 40	(1.1)	(1.0)	(0.3)	2.5	1.3	2.7	2.8	3.5
40- 60	(1.0)	(1.0)	(0.3)	0.8	1.3	1.1	1.1	1.8
60- 80	(1.0)	(1.0)	(0.3)	0.5	0.4	(0.1)	(0.1)	0.6
80-100	(0.9)	(1.0)	(1.6)	1.5	(0.8)	(0.2)	(0.3)	(0.9)

[1]Expressed as percentage of income; interpolated for quintiles. Figures in brackets are net taxes, figures without brackets net financial benefits (subsidies).

Sources: [a]Tables 6 and 7.
[b]Table 8.
[c]Table 10, Bogotá.

municipal taxes the property tax is the most important, and analytically also the most controversial, as regards is incidence. This paper has argued that neither the extreme conventional approach to property tax incidence nor the extreme new view is likely to be acceptable for estimation purposes in Colombia. As a result, it was postulated that an intermediate incidence result approximating neutrality is most appropriate. Given this conclusion, it may be argued that an increased reliance on property taxation would probably leave the income distribution in Colombia unaffected, although that judgment may have to be modified according to whether this policy is pursued on a nationwide scale or only in a particular municipality, and according to whether it is achieved by rate changes or improvements in assessment and collection practices. In contrast, the other major source of local tax revenue, the industry and commerce tax, as most generally applied is likely to be mildly regressive. Since, in addition, this tax has undesirable efficiency implications as presently administered in most cities, reliance on it should be reduced as far as possible in any attempt at local fiscal reforms. Similarly, the strongly regressive nature of departmental sumptuary taxes suggests that reliance on these taxes should be reduced as increases in other revenue sources will permit.

The incidence of local government expenditure cannot be ascertained with any degree of confidence given present data. A very rough estimate appears to indicate a progressive distribution; however, the quantitative results are closely correlated with dubious incidence assumptions.

One of the areas of national policy where the distributive goal has been pursued most actively is the pricing of *user-charge financed public services*. These services are frequently under local control, particularly in the larger urban areas, and contribute a large and growing share to local public sector resources and spending: progressively structured tariff schedules are in force for most of these services, and although a comprehensive judgment on the distributive impact of user charges in Colombia is not possible for analytical and empirical reasons, very tentative estimates for the four largest cities indicate that the magnitude of cross-subsidies between users of particular services is significant, approaching that of the tax burden of municipal and departmental taxes combined for some income groups. One of the prime analytical problems remains the question of how the distributive impact of pricing is to be measured, particularly if one has no way of measuring adequately the benefits associated with the consumption of a service. Alternative definitions of subsidy were reviewed and all were found deficient either in analytical or in empirical aspects. In any case, it was concluded that to be feasible a correct approach must restrict itself, at least initially, to a study of distributive effects in a case study context, where it is possible to specify carefully the demand and cost conditions under which the service is provided. Furthermore, it was argued that the analysis should focus on changes of tariff structures and the associated changes in the distribution of net benefits, rather than trying to establish the overall system costs and benefits for any particular pricing system. This approach not only facilitates considerably the estimation procedures, but also is more relevant in the policy context, where the cost structure of the existing production and distribution system is affected only at the margin by tariff changes.

Finally, this paper focused on the distributive effects of unequal *access to public services* across income groups. Scattered quantitative evidence confirms the general observation that low income groups tend not to have access to public services. As a result they do not receive the threshold benefits associated with access to public services, which is likely to bias the incidence of public expenditure towards the regressive side. It also has the effect of preventing the lowest income groups from benefiting from the progressive structure of public service pricing in Colombia. Given the probable importance of access to public services in determining the real income of the poor, it is imperative that research be directed at quantifying the benefits associated with access as well as analyzing the causes for lack of access. In turn, policy should aim at minimizing the barriers to access, such as that resulting from overly heavy emphasis on expanding productive capacity at the expense of distribution facilities; or as resulting from prohibitively high connection charges, which prevent potential low income consumers from connecting to the service given their limited ability to pay, and their lack of access to capital markets.

APPENDIX

Tax Burden by Level of Government

Methodological and data constraints prevent a direct comparison of tax burdens imposed by different levels of government within a particular municipality. The approach chosen here instead (Table A-1) compares the tax-income ratios for each level of government, where each ratio is defined such that tax collections by a particular level of government are divided by the income in its jurisdiction. This assumes that higher levels of government impose a burden in a particular municipality equal to the average tax burden in their respective jurisdiction. This approach is based on the presumption that particularly for national government taxes income is an appropriate proxy for the government's "tax handle."

Distribution of Public Expenditure by Level of Government

As with taxation methodological and data limitations make difficult a direct analysis of the shares in total public expenditures by government level in particular metropolitan areas. Only for the case of Cali has a direct estimation approach been used. For the two other cities it was assumed that higher level government expenditures may be assigned to a particular locality by assuming that the share of the expenditure going to the locality is proportional to the population of the city relative to the population of the country; or in other words, per capita spend-

TABLE A.1. Tax-Income Ratios by Level of Government, 1970

	All Municipalities[a]	Bogotá[b]	Cali[b] (Valle)	Cartagena[b] (Bolivar)
National Government Per Capita Tax Revenues (Col. $)	544.5	544.5	544.5	544.5
National Per Capita Income (Col. $)	5,030	5,030	5,030	5,030
National Government Tax Ratio (%)	10.8	10.8	10.8	10.8
Departmental Per Capita Tax Revenue (Col. $)	81.7	–	86.8	56.9
Departmental Per Capita Income (Col. $)	5,030	–	6,137[1]	4,500
Departmental Tax Ratio (%)	1.6	–	1.4[1]	1.3
Municipal Per Capita Tax Revenue (Col. $)	61.7	214.0	102.9	94.8
Municipal Per Capita Income (Col. $)	5,030	7,028	6,471[1]	5,000
Municipal Tax Ratio (%)	1.2	3.0	1.6[1]	1.9
Departmental plus Municipal Tax Ratio (%)	2.8	3.0	3.0[1]	3.2
(as Percentage of Total Tax Ratio)	(20.6)	(21.7)	(21.7[1])	(22.9)

[1] The income data for the Dept. of Valle and for Cali are probably too high relative to those of Bogotá and Cartagena. As a result the tax ratios are lower than will be the case otherwise.

Source: [a] Direccion General del Presupuesto, *Boletin*, No. 64 (December, 1973).
[b] Data collected by the author from city accounts.

ing by the central government in the country as a whole is taken as a proxy for central government spending per capita in a particular location (Table A-2). To the extent that higher per capita spending is directed at urban as against rural areas, the proportion of national spending in the cities considered is understated. In Cali, the direct estimate of national and departmental spending in the city actually results in a higher municipal share than the estimate on the basis of the simplifying assumptions made for the other two cities. This is in part explained by the fact that the direct estimation procedure may not have been able to catch all high level government spending. It may furthermore reflect the rapid expansion in municipal spending which has taken place in Cali since 1969.

It is worth pointing out that the two sets of assumptions employed respectively in estimating tax burdens and expenditure shares by level of government for individual cities jointly imply that the national and departmental governments follow a fiscal policy which is progressive overall, since national government taxes are allocated proportional to income, but national spending proportional to population. This is in line with the results from the overall incidence study of Urrutia and Sandoval (see page 86 above) where it was found that indeed the overall fiscal system in Colombia redistributes income mainly as a result of progressive expenditure policies. This result is also confirmed by a recent preliminary investigation conducted in the National Planning Department, which appears to indicate that national tax and expenditure policy is such as to lead to net transfers from high income to low income departments.

Cali: Cross-Subsidies between Users of Water and Sewerage Services

A very crude preliminary estimate of the three alternative types of cross-subsidies was attempted for water and sewerage users in Cali. This estimate will be refined in future research, but the initial results can be viewed as a useful first step.

For present purposes the main feature of the provision of water supply and sewerage services in Cali is the division into a high and a low level (i.e., low altitude) system. The average cost of operation is high in the low-level area, and low in the high-level area.[89] The high level production capacity is exhausted and cannot be further extended due to source limitations. Therefore, all additional demand for water in the high level area has to be met by extending low-level production. It appears reasonable to assume that the low-level plant operates under constant cost conditions. Therefore, marginal cost, which is the same for both areas, also equals average cost in the low-level area. However, average cost in the high level area is below marginal cost. Moreover, socioeconomic evidence indicates that the high income groups live mainly in the low-level area.

[89] This is due mainly to the need for pumping and more treatment of water from the low-level source, while no pumping and little treatment is necessary for the water from the high-level source. Gravity disposal of sewerage in the high-level area also reduces operation costs there, in contrast to the need for pumping of sewage in the low-level area.

TABLE A.2. Estimated Per Capita Expenditures of National,Departmental and Local Public Sector Agencies in Bogotá, Cali, and Cartagena[1]

	Bogotá		Cali (1975)[a]		Cali (1969)		Cartagena (1972)	
	Indirect Estimation[2]		Direct Estimation[3]		Indirect Estimation[2]		Indirect Estimation[2]	
	Col. $	Percent	Col. $	Percent	Col. $	Percent	Col. $	Percent
National Government[b]	1,314	50.1	2,169	44.5	871	49.0	1,314	68.4
Central Gov't	(605)	(23.1)	(980)	(20.1)	(412)[c]	(22.9)	(605)	(31.5)
Decentralized Agencies	(709)	(27.0)	(1,189)	(24.4)	(469)	(26.1)	(709)	(36.9)
Departmental Government[b]	–	–	326	6.7	192	10.7	164	8.5
Municipal Government[c]	1,309	49.9	2,378	48.8	724	40.3	441	23.0
Total	2,623	100.0	4,870	100.0	1,797	100.0	1,919	100.0

[1] Transfers are netted out.

[2] National and departmental expenditures in the city are assumed to equal average per capita spending in the country and department, respectively.

[3] Estimated from actual spending figures, obtained from national and departmental agencies in Cali.

Sources: [a] World Bank research mission estimates by Richard M. Bird, based on agency budgets.

[b] Direccion General del Presupuesto, *Boletin*, No. 64 (December, 1973) (with exception of the column entitled "Cali [1975]").

[c] Data collected by the author from city accounts.

TABLE A.3. Cali: Preliminary Estimate of Cross-Subsidies between Different User Groups of Water and Sewerage Services, 1974
(Negative Values in Brackets)

Tariff category	Consumption[a] (m^3/month)	Tariff[b] (T) (Col.$/$m^3$/mo.)	Marginal Cost[c] (MC) (Col.$/$m^3$/mo.)	Average Cost[d] (AC) (Col.$/$m^3$/mo.)	Average Tariff[e] (AT) (Col.$/$m^3$/mo.)	Subsidy (Col.$/$m^3$/mo.) MC-T	Subsidy (Col.$/$m^3$/mo.) AC-T	Subsidy (Col.$/$m^3$/mo.) AT-T
Low	30	0.24	2.56	2.56	2.19	2.32	2.32	1.95
Med.-Low	35	1.60	2.56	2.56	2.19	0.96	0.96	0.59
Med.-High	40	4.88	2.56	1.46	2.19	(2.42)	(3.42)	(2.69)
High	45	8.32	2.56	1.46	2.19	(5.76)	(6.86)	(6.13)

[a] Assumed consumption pattern.

[b] Computed as the average price per m^3, by adding the fixed charge for the "cupo" and the excess consumption charge.

[c] Estimated operational and maintenance cost for the low-level service area including depreciation, where constant costs are assumed. This probably overestimates short-run marginal costs since not all operational and maintenance costs vary with consumption.

[d] Estimated operation cost for the high- and low-level areas, respectively.

[e] Total water and sewerage revenues divided by the quantity of water consumed.

This basic information together with general cost and tariff data for Cali and a number of assumptions concerning the relation between incomes, tariff categories, and consumption patterns, led to a very preliminary estimate of cross-subsidies between different tariff categories (and, by assumption, income groups) for alternative definitions of the concept of cross-subsidies (see Table A-3 and Figure 3.1 in main text).

Currently ongoing research attempts to refine the data for consumption, tariffs, incomes and costs on the basis of a more detailed demand analysis at the household and neighborhood level, and a careful review of the cost structure by sub-areas and for water supply and sewerage services separately.

Chapter 4

THE EFFECTS OF INFLATION ON INCOME DISTRIBUTION IN COLOMBIA: SOME HYPOTHESES AND A FRAMEWORK FOR ANALYSIS

R. Albert Berry
University of Toronto

1. INTRODUCTION

Among the phenomena which have produced shockwaves in the Colombian economy during the last decade or so, the post-1970 inflation is one of the most prominent. During the first half of the 1970s real wages fell or stagnated for important groups despite a rapidly increasing average real per capita income for the nation as a whole. This combination of events suggests a worsening of the income distribution.[1] The coincidental timing of the inflation and the real wage declines raises the hypothesis that the inflation has been responsible for the declines, and the related question of whether, if this is the case, they will be arrested or reversed as the rate of price increase returns to more normal levels? This paper is an attempt to shed some light on these questions.

Inflation has been favored as a deliberate policy of redistribution by some groups on the grounds that it redistributes from creditors to debtors. More often, perhaps, it is castigated for its negative effects on persons with fixed nominal incomes, often assumed to be relatively poor. These and other effects are considered below. In the Colombian context, inflation has not been the result of a specific policy decision to increase prices, but rather of the low priority given to its control relative to other objectives of the government. In the early 1970s there were inflationary pressures in the world economy but Colombia, with its free but managed exchange rate, was in a good position to largely insulate itself from them,

[1] Attempts to judge distribution trends are difficult, and there are enough ambiguities in the evidence to preclude definitive conclusions. For a fuller discussion, see A. Berry, "Recent Trends in the Distribution of Income in Colombia: Possible Factors," 1977. (Mimeographed.)

A major source of the inflation was the budgetary deficit which resulted from a marked decline in the share of current government revenues in the national income. Whereas in 1971 the ratio of current government revenues (minus interest on the public debt) to Gross Domestic Product (GDP) at market prices was 17 percent, by 1974 it had fallen to 14.7 percent. Public sector saving fell from 5.9 percent of GDP in 1970 to a low of 3.7 percent in 1973 and an average of 4.1 percent over 1973-75. Although public sector expenditures were not rising at an inordinate rate during these years, the very low elasticity of real current revenues to real output growth contributed importantly to the inflation.

A second important source, beginning in 1972, was the dramatic increase in export prices and revenues. These contributed to inflation by increasing the monetary base; imports were not increased rapidly enough to prevent price increases. Between 1971 and 1975 the national accounts peso price index of exports rose by 216 percent while that of imports rose 178 percent, and that of GDP by 115 percent. Whereas the deficit on current account had averaged 38 percent of current income from the rest of the world over 1969-71, it averaged only 15 percent of a rapidly increasing level of current income from the rest of the world during 1972-74.

Both of the above factors imply a demand pull type of inflation. While cost increases doubtlessly played a role in the propagation of inflationary impulses, it is not plausible to argue that they were the major causal factor.

The primary direct mechanisms by which inflation affects pretax income distribution are through its effects on real wages and through its effects on the prices and returns to the various assets and obligations held by individuals (or families) at different income and wealth levels. Inflation may also alter the relative tax burden on different groups, altering the relationship between the after-tax and before-tax distributions. There are many less direct effects of inflation, as for example through its effect on the rate or type of growth; under inflation the benefits may be distributed differently from those of a noninflationary growth process. Among the innumerable indirect effects which are possible, only those most likely to be relevant are considered below.

In appraising the effects of inflation one may also consider whether it was caused by policies which themselves had distributional effects. If a rapid expansion of government spending on the poor were to cause inflation, it may be more relevant to consider the distributional effects of the inflation producing policy, including both the direct effects and those operating through the inflation than to focus only on the latter. The likelihood that a given increase in public spending or reduction in taxes may trigger an inflation is a key consideration in the prediction of its distributional effects. Hence, the double importance of judging how inflation affects distribution.

There are many reasons to believe that the effects of a continuous and, therefore, generally anticipated inflation on the real values of economic variables would be different from those of an unanticipated one, usually synonomous with an acceleration of the rate of price increase. Under some conditions in theory an anticipated inflation would have little effect on real variables, although in a developing country like Colombia with many market imperfections even a fully predicted and stable level of inflation may have significant distributional effects. When inflation is above 5 percent, the rate is seldom stable for long; hence discussions of the impact of "inflation" on output, distribution, or whatever, are usually discussions of changes in the rate of inflation. Since the rate of price increase is not the same in all sectors, relative prices change during the course of an inflationary period; thus, food prices may rise quickly when the rate of increase of the general price index is accelerating while rents may lag, but in the subsequent deceleration the opposite may be true. These changes in relative prices may be important for an analysis of the income distribution effects of inflation, since persons at different income levels purchase different bundles of goods.

If an unanticipated increase in the rate of inflation worsened distribution and an unanticipated decrease improved it, a burst of rapid inflation followed by a return to the normal level (to which the system has become accustomed) might affect distribution as indicated in Figure 4.1a; i.e., in the same direction but with some lag. The total impact is different at different points of time and must be described accordingly; after the cycle has been completed, distribution might be better (as shown in the figure) or worse—this being a matter requiring demonstration. If inflation accelerates to a new level and stays there, distribution might at first worsen, then move back towards its initial state as the new level of inflation becomes better and better anticipated, though it would not necessarily move right back to that initial state.[2] Figure 4.1b illustrates such a sequence. Again, whether the increase in inflation leaves distribution better or worse in the long run is a matter for investigation.

2. AN OVERVIEW OF THE EVIDENCE IN COLOMBIA

The main evidence which suggests that the rapid inflation of the early 1970s led to a significant worsening in Colombia's income distribution includes the following facts:

(a) For the first time since systematic national accounts have been produced for Colombia (1945), the figures indicate a sharp decline in the paid labor share of national income between 1971 and 1974. Underlying this were declines in real wages of most, if not all, major occupational categories.

(b) These years witnessed the acceleration of consumer prices from about 11 percent in 1971 to nearly 25 percent in 1974. The national price index for blue

[2]Several factors may help to prevent this. First, there may always be some money illusion, some interest rate ceilings, or other institutional factors which prevent variables taking on the same real values under inflation as in its absence. Second, since money cannot have a positive nominal return, its real return must be affected by the inflation. Finally, the distributional effects during the period of transition to the new stable rate of inflation are likely to affect the distribution of wealth which will in turn affect the distribution of income in subsequent periods.

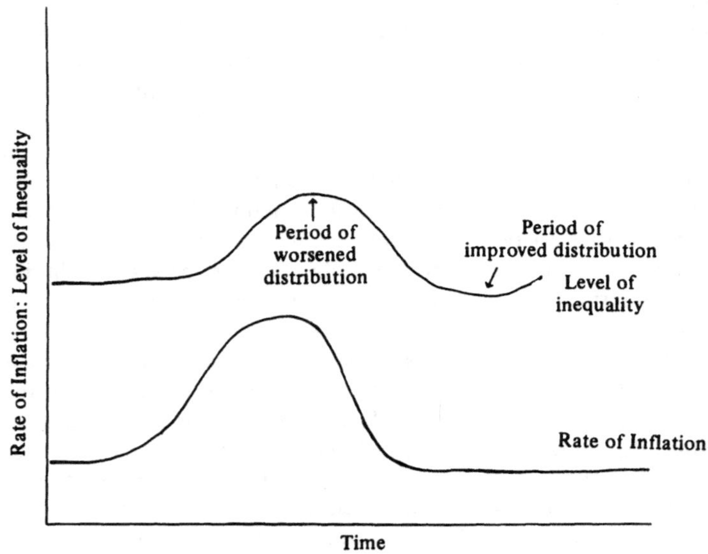

Figure 4.1a.

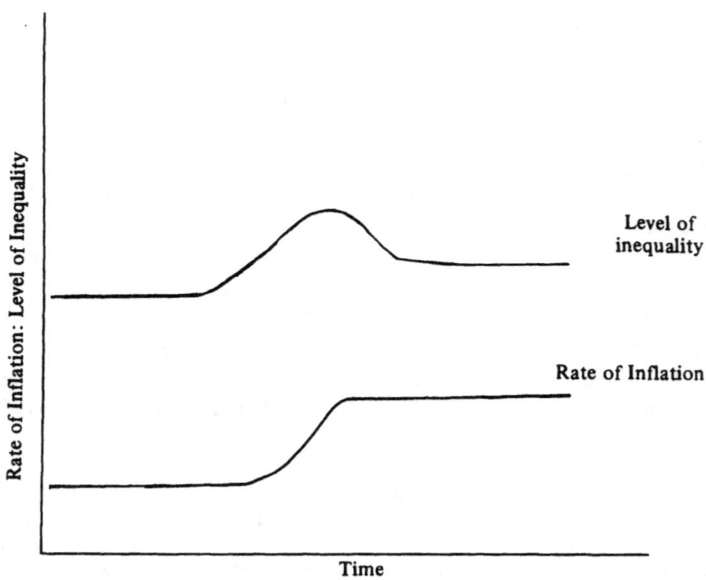

Figure 4.1b.

collar workers rose at a rate of 7.2 percent during 1966-70 and 18.1 percent during 1970-74. As Table 4.1 shows, the acceleration was rather gradual from 1970 to the peak in 1974, with only modest slowdown since then (and a renewed acceleration in early 1977, not shown here).

(c) Considerable evidence supports the proposition that most low income families have little capital income (except for imputed rent on their house when they own it) so that a lowering of labor income means for most poor families a lowering of total income.

Although the rate of inflation fell a little in 1975 and 1976 from its peak level in 1974, there is no evidence of a recovery by low income workers of the relative income positions they had in 1970.[3] It remains to be seen whether a further lowering of the inflation rate would have that effect.

A declining labor share is indicated in Table 4.2, which shows the paid labor share in the economy, in nonagriculture and in a number of specific sectors, as estimated in the national accounts. These figures are based on the necessarily incomplete wage and employment data used by the national accounts division of the Banco de la Republica. Though there are reasons to suspect that the downward trend shown in these figures may have been exaggerated,[4] it seems unlikely that it did not occur at all. The declines in agriculture, manufacturing, and commerce are particularly noteworthy.

Between 1971 and 1974 real wages fell for all occupational categories for which data are available, with the possible exception of agricultural workers. The trends are summarized in Table 4.3, including a comparison with the period 1966-71 which had been characterized by relative price stability. Although the data are not all consistent, they do suggest a marked difference between the two periods, and a sharp decline for each group relative to average income per capita in the economy during 1971-74. Average labor income per worker probably did not fall

TABLE 4.1. Inflation Rates, 1967-76: Annual Increase in the Cost of Living[a]

	Blue Collar Index	White Collar Index
1965	7.1	8.7
1966	16.7	16.8
1967	8.1	8.9
1968	7.4	7.6
1969	6.9	7.0
1970	6.7	7.3
1971	11.8	10.9
1972	13.8	13.2
1973	21.9	19.7
1974	25.3	23.3
1975	23.6	21.8
1976	20.2	21.0

[a] Figures refer to the increase in prices between the year cited and the previous one.
Source: Banco de la Republica, *Revista del Banco de la Republica*, various issues.

[3] Agricultural workers may be an exception. See Table 4.3.
[4] See the discussion on p. 119.

TABLE 4.2. Paid Labor Share of Value Added at Factor Cost, by Sector, 1965-1975

	Agriculture	Manufacturing	Construction	Commerce	Personal services	Nonagriculture	Total
1965	34.3	38.1	74.4	18.3	49.0	41.3	39.2
1966	32.3	37.8	75.6	18.3	50.1	42.4	39.4
1967	32.6	38.9	77.4	18.3	47.8	43.8	40.4
1968	30.2	40.1	78.1	21.5	47.7	43.6	39.5
1969	31.3	39.9	81.1	21.7	58.6	45.4	41.1
1970	30.1	41.8	80.6	18.9	58.0	45.4	41.2
1971	29.7	40.8	78.7	18.6	59.6	45.9	41.5
1972	27.1	40.2	75.7	16.2	58.2	44.5	40.0
1973	23.9	35.2	73.7	14.0	61.7	42.9	37.6
1974	25.5	30.4	73.9	11.9	63.6	40.5	36.3
1975	25.5	30.4	75.0	11.8	62.9	41.0	36.5

Source: Banco de la Republica, *Cuentas Nacionales*.

TABLE 4.3. Real Wage Movements of Selected Groups, 1966-71 and 1971-74

	1966-71	1971-74	Other Period
Agricultural			
paid workers	–4	–16.2[a]	–5.3[a] (1971-75)
			+15.6 (1970 to 1st quarter 1976)
Manufacturing			
paid workers	15.2	–4.4	–3.2 (1971-75)
Blue Collar	12.4	–7	
White Collar	12.3	–9	
Construction workers			
Bogotá			
Four largest cities	–6.0	–4[a] to –12	
Transport and			
communication workers		–10.1[a]	
Commerce workers		–9.9[a]	
Service workers		–2[a] to +1[a]	

[a] Based on data from Instituto Colombiano de Seguros Sociales (ICSS).

Note: Various sources have been used in the estimation of these trends; for a fuller description see the source. The most reliable and conceptually appropriate figures are those for manufacturing, based mainly on Departamento Administrativo Nacional de Estadistica (DANE) wage bill data, and taking account of fringe benefits. Most of the series are based on ICSS, and will show downward biased trends if the ratio of fringe benefits to basic wages was rising, since the former are not taken into account. The data for agricultural workers are particularly troublesome; the DANE series provides the evidence up to 1970 and was reinitiated in 1976, but it is not yet clear whether the old and new series are comparable; ICSS data are available since 1969.

Source: Data presented in Berry, "Recent Trends," *op. cit.*

as fast for all workers taken together as for specific occupational groups, since there is a gradual shift from lower income jobs to higher income ones. But this latter effect, estimated to be the equivalent of a one percent per year wage increase over 1967-75, could not offset the downward trends in the individual wage series.[5]

With labor income falling and average incomes rising, the capital share was evidently increasing. Most capital income accrues to high income persons so only if its distribution became significantly less unequal at this time could one conclude that the distribution of current income did not worsen over 1971-74. While this possibility cannot be ruled out on the basis of existing evidence, it seems unlikely.[6]

When inflation reflects a booming economy and a rapid growth in real aggregate demand, it is expected in developed countries to lower unemployment rates (whereas stabilization policies do the opposite). In the substantially different

[5] Berry, "Recent Trends," *op. cit.*

[6] The evidence reviewed in Berry, "Recent Trends," *op. cit.*, is inconclusive with respect to whether there has been a shift away from paid employment in the manufacturing and commerce sectors, sectors which would have to be the source of much new capital income for low income persons had the distribution of capital income in fact improved. It seems unlikely that the distribution of income from financial assets would have improved markedly during the early 1970s.

TABLE 4.4. Unemployment Rates, by City[a]

Reference area	1967	1968	1969	1970	1971	1972	1974	1975	1976
Four largest cities	14.1						12.3	11.4	11.2
Bogotá	13.1	11.5	9.6	13.1 (7.9)[b]	8.9	6.9	10.5	9.2	9.7
Medellin	12.7						13.2	14.1	13.3
Cali	14.9	14.9					12.3	10.9	12.6
Barranquilla	18.4						17.8	14.7	12.1

[a] Figures are averages of all observations in that city in the year, ranging from one to four depending on the city and the year.

[b] CEDE figure.

[c] Figures for the four cities weighted by their 1964 populations.

Sources: Figures for 1967-69 are based mainly on CEDE surveys. They are reported, among other places, in *Towards Full Employment* (Geneva: International Labor Office (ILO), 1970), pp. 362-63. Figures for subsequent years are based on DANE surveys, reported periodically in DANE's *Boletin Mensual de Estadistica* and Fedesarrollo's *Coyuntura Economica*.

context of a developing country like Colombia, there is little reason to expect this result, both because a lack of aggregate demand is seldom a problem in the first place, and also because open unemployment seems to be more the result of events on the supply side of the labor market (including rural-urban migration) than events on the demand side. An increase in demand will raise prices with no predictable effect on employment or unemployment.[7] If demand pressure does contribute to an increased demand for labor, it may show up in the form of upward pressure on wages, decreased unemployment or neither, depending on the characteristics of labor supply.

The available unemployment figures provide no evidence that the high levels of inflation alleviated employment problems (Table 4.4). There is no noticeable trend in the rates since 1970, though they are now lower than in the high year of 1967, the first year when many cities were analyzed. If anything, the data suggest an increase in unemployment as the inflation accelerated to its peak in 1974. Interestingly, it did not rise in the "recession" year of 1975. Relief of employment difficulties might in any case be more likely reflected in increased participation rates, but the partial information available suggests no such effect.

3. MECHANISMS LINKING INFLATION TO DISTRIBUTION

In this section we take a closer look at the relationship between the acceleration of inflation in 1972-74 and the falling labor share of national income and declining

[7] Cost push inflation factors can, of course, play a role in developing country inflation; labor costs and import prices are often cited. These mechanisms are not normally important unless the labor movement is very strong or international trade is unusually important; certainly they cannot account for inflation rates of 20 percent or higher. It seems safe to assume that the factors which changed as Colombia's rate of inflation moved from its low levels of the late 1960s to over 20 percent in the 1970s were primarily on the demand side.

wage rates for many groups of workers. We also consider other mechanisms whereby inflation might have affected distribution.

A. The Inflation-Real Wage Link

Over the longer run the relationship between inflation and the labor share has been rather close. There has been an inverse relation between the direction of change of these two variables in virtually every year since 1953. Allowing for the time trend in the paid labor share, the relationship for the period 1951-75 is as follows:

$$PLS = 35.58 - 0.16\dot{P} + 0.37T \qquad R^2 = 0.71$$
$$(46.13 \quad (-2.56) \quad (6.44)$$

Where PLS is the paid labor share expressed in percent; $\dot{P}$ is the change in the GDP deflator, defined with base 1958 = 100; T is the time trend, and the t statistics are shown in parentheses. The equation implies that for each additional ten percentage points in the annual rate of inflation, the paid labor share will be lower by about 1.6 percent. Other variations of equation (1) (not shown) suggest something closer to 1.0 percent, but all indicate that the effect in question is substantial. In an analysis of the relationship between inflation and real wages, Urrutia and Tenjo have regressed the rate of change of real wages in manufacturing on changes of employment and changes in the cost of living, finding real wages positively related to the former and negatively to the latter, in the period 1958-74; they used separate equations for blue and white collar workers.[8] Since one would expect lags to complicate the relationship, the "goodness of fit" in both Equation 1 and in the Tenjo/Urrutia regressions (2) and (3) is somewhat surprising.

$$\dot{W} = f\left(\dot{E}, \frac{1}{\dot{P}}\right) \text{ obreros} \qquad \dot{W} = -0.16 + 0.58\dot{E} + 0.014\,\frac{1}{\dot{P}} \quad (2)$$
$$(3.78) \quad (7.00)$$
$$R^2 = 0.77$$
$$D.W. = 1.94$$

$$\dot{W} = f\left(\dot{E}, \frac{1}{\dot{P}}\right) \text{ empleados} \qquad \dot{W} = 0.16 + 0.31\dot{E} + 0.016\,\frac{1}{\dot{P}} \quad (3)$$
$$(1.40) \quad (4.71)$$
$$R^2 = 0.57$$
$$D.W. = 2.02$$

Where $\dot{W}$ is rate of change of the real wage rate in manufacturing; $\dot{E}$ is the rate of change in the level of employment in manufacturing; P is the rate of change in DANE's cost of living index for blue collar workers (equation 2) and white collar workers (Equation 3) and t statistics are shown in the parentheses.

[8] M. Urrutia and J. Tenjo, "Politica de Estabilizacion y Distribucion del Ingreso en Colombia," *Coyuntura Economica*, Vol. VI, No. 4 (December, 1976), pp. 140-48.

Before reading too much into the decline in real wages which has accompanied the recent inflation, one must consider whether there have been some offsetting benefits for the lower income groups such as increased or improved employment. Increases in paid employment should in principle have shown up in the paid labor share, but such information is not available on a continuing basis so the national accounts division must use extrapolations of past trends. Within manufacturing, the growth of employment in the factory sector (nearly all hired workers) does appear to have accelerated in the 1970s. After increasing at an annual rate of 3.5 percent in the late 1960s (1964-70) it increased at about 6.5 percent per year over 1970-74. Comparable data are not available for other sectors, though DANE's household surveys suggest if anything a decrease in the share of workers who are paid a wage or salary. A comparison of data on sector of activity from the 1964 and 1973 population censuses and the 1970 Household Survey suggests a marked decline in the share of the labor force in agriculture, and increases especially in manufacturing and finance. If these shifts have been accelerated by declining real wages, the distributional impact of the latter phenomenon is again complicated.

Falling real wages could contribute to greater employment if some real wage rates had for various institutional reasons come to be above their equilibrium levels and could fall only when there was an increase in prices. This proposition would be especially plausible if there were persuasive evidence that institutional factors such as minimum wages and unions had been able to raise the wages of certain subsets of workers well above their equilibria. While a few studies have addressed this issue in Colombia there is, as yet, no consensus.[9]

It is, of course, possible that the temporal coincidence of falling real wages and accelerating inflation in the 1970s was in part spurious. Wage gains in the late 1960s decreased for several groups, including construction workers in Bogotá, and blue collar workers in the manufacturing sector.[10] The period saw a continued mechanization of agriculture, which along with other events contributed to a further decline in the labor share in that sector. There may have been some concentration of land holding between the 1960 and 1970-71 agricultural censuses. The economy's rapid growth since the mid-1960s has been accompanied by expanding export earnings and foreign credit, so as to permit a continuously increasing flow of imports. Possibly the rapid increase in the capital stock during this decade, and the associated technological change, has had a substantial dampening effect on the demand for labor. In short, one cannot discount the possibility that

[9]Tenjo's recent analysis of the effects of unionization in the remuneration of paid workers in manufacturing in Bogotá and Medellin (1972) led him to conclude that a company union (the analysis was restricted to this type) could account for a total wage bill of 15 or 20 percent higher than it would otherwise have been. In the nature of the calculation, this implies a substantially greater differential between union workers and others, although methodological problems may have led to some overestimation. (J. Tenjo G., "Impacto de la Actividad Sindical Sobre Los Salarios; Un Analisis Econometrico," *Revista de Planeacion y Desarrollo*, Vol. VII, No. 2 [Julio-Dec., 1975], p. 131.)

[10]See Berry, "Recent Trends...," *op. cit.*, Table 8. Construction wages appear to have fallen over 1965-70 while the blue collar manufacturing workers gained at 2.9% per year as compared with 4.8% over 1956-66.

underlying changes in the economy have been working to widen the gap between the average product of labor in the economy and the marginal product (and therefore the earnings) of various groups of workers in sectors like agriculture and construction. These factors may have been especially dominant in the early 1970s, or the inflation may have facilitated the emergence of their natural results in the form of lowered real wages for the groups in question.

B. Relative Price Increases for Different Income Groups

In the inflation of the early 1970s, food prices led the increases; as a result the cost of living index rose faster for blue collar than for white collar workers. The price index probably rose faster for poorer families in general than for those who are better-off. For example, as of 1970, the poorest quartile of families in the seven cities used in the calculation of the cost of living series spent over 60 percent of their total expenditures on food.[11] Over 1971-75, while the white collar index was rising by 104 percent, the blue collar role by 115 percent and a series with a 60 percent weight for food would have risen by about 119 percent. For the poorest urban families and a good number of rural ones, the increase would be larger, up to 125 percent. Between the poorest and the richest deciles, the difference in price increase was probably 25-30 percent; thus, if monetary incomes of the two groups had risen at the same rates, and the rich had an increase in real income of 10 percent, the poorest decile would have suffered a decline of up to 4 percent. Given the slower increase of monetary incomes of the poor, the rise in food prices clearly increased income inequality, at least as between rich and poor families which buy their food.[12] Households which produce food, by the same token, should gain; some intermediaries may also have gained, though this is less certain. Since the poorest agricultural families (paid workers with little or no land) produce less food than they consume they, along with poor urban families, are the main losers from high food prices.

C. Changes in the Distribution of Current Net Income from Capital and Transfers; Capital Gains and Losses

No detailed description has as yet been presented of the composition of assets and liabilities of Colombian families by income levels. There is some direct evidence on the distribution of capital incomes and some extrapolations can be made from the evidence for other countries, both on distribution of capital incomes and distribution of wealth by types.

In terms of the impact of inflation, it is convenient to distinguish four broad

[11] For a discussion of sources, see the longer version of this paper, available from the author.

[12] This result emerges strongly in Chapter 9, Thirsk's study on "Income Distribution Consequences of Agricultural Price Supports in Colombia."

categories of capital, i.e., money, property rented out for money (including financial assets), business capital yielding profits, and property whose consumption services are used by the owner. Money yields no income but suffers capital losses depending simply on the rate of inflation. Many types of property income (including capital gains or losses) may be negatively affected by lags very similar to those affecting some wage rates. Depending on the frequency of contract, institutional limits (e.g., interest rate ceilings) and other factors, some assets do better than others; on average, however, property income falls under inflationary conditions. When both property income and labor income are negatively affected by inflation, the residual, i.e., business income or profits, must increase.[13] In general, few persons towards the bottom of the income distribution have much income falling in the categories whose relative size increases in an inflation.

The Colombian evidence appears consistent with that of the U. S. and elsewhere in suggesting that real income from rented property and financial assets is negatively affected by inflation unless there is indexing. Rental incomes lag substantially. Between 1971 and 1974 the share of net rental income on housing fell from 5.7 to 4.5 percent of GDP at factor cost. Between 1971 and 1975, while the overall cost of living indices were rising by 115 percent and 104 percent for blue and white collar workers, respectively, the housing component was rising by only 78 percent and 76 percent, respectively–i.e., the real rental price was falling by a rather dramatic 24-30 percent over these years.

Most real interest rates fell sharply during these years, so the holders of money and bonds lost; the real interest flows decreased and the real value of the assets decreased. The exception was the Unidad de Poder Adquisitivo Constante (UPAC), introduced in 1972 and bearing a fixed real return of 5 percent. This asset quickly became an important component of portfolios and reduced the loss to holders of financial assets during the years from 1972. The return to stocks fared no better than that of most other financial assets; the real return in the early 1970s was well below the levels reached in the 1960s. One study of the stocks of 13 major companies (including several banks) found the weighted average return to the current stock price ranged between 12.9 and 18.2 percent over 1961-1970.[14] Taking account jointly of stock appreciation and dividends, Junguito and Jaramillo found an annual real return of about one percent for these companies over 1961-62 to 1965-66, during which period inflation averaged 14.1 percent per year, and 23 percent per year over 1966-67 to 1969-70, with inflation averaging only 17 percent. Over

[13]For assets whose services are used by the owners (e.g., houses), a change in the price of the service affects them one way as owners, another way as users. Such assets can be largely neglected in discussing the effects of inflation since the two effects cancel out. For self-employed persons, changes in the relative earnings from labor and capital are partially cancelled out; if the imputed wage rate goes down, the imputed return to capital goes up.

[14]See R. Junguito and J. Carlos Jaramillo, "Determinantes Economicos del Comportamiento Bursatil Colombiano," in Banco de la Republica, *El Mercado de Capitales en Colombia* (Bogotá: Banco de la Republica, 1971), p. 335. In these calculations, the yield is defined to include the effect of subscriptions (where the stock is sold by the company below its current market price).

the decade, the real return averaged 10.2 percent.[15] While the inflation was doubtless responsible for only a part of this difference in real returns between the subperiods, the suggestion is that the real return is quite price elastic at least in the short run. In the period 1971-74, the real return to stocks has been negative (see Table 4.5).

Nominal rates of return on a number of financial assets were raised in the early 1970s, softening the impact of the inflation. Thus, the real return on savings deposits fell moderately from -3.2 percent over 1967-70 to -8.1 percent in 1971-74. By 1975, with the nominal effective rate up to 17.0 percent, the real rate was about zero. All other major assets had positive real rates over 1967-70 (see Table 4.5), and a rough estimate of the weighted average return on these assets is 9.0 percent or higher.[16] Most assets apart from stocks saw their real rates suffer by a little more than those of savings deposits during the years 1971-74, while the return of stocks fell much more sharply. The average return on the portfolio of assets other than savings deposits was about -3.2 percent if the atypically bad year for stocks (1971) is excluded and -5.7 percent if it is included.[17] In short, the assets held by lower income savers were still yielding less than those of the better off, but the gap appears to have been narrowed by the inflation so that now both groups were losing in real terms. Inclusion of money balances decreases the real returns to financial assets in each period and widens the gap between rich and poor; it also increases the likelihood that the inflation would contribute to the size of the gap. For an income group with the same ratio of cash to income as all families (i.e., around 0.10 in the early 1970s) an inflation of 25 percent would lower real income by 2.5 percent. In fact, the cash/income ratio is undoubtedly a decreasing function of income over much of the range,[18] and there are fairly low income groups (though it is not clear just how low) with cash/income ratios well above 0.10. It may be that the very poorest in Colombia have ratios below this, and have virtually no financial assets of any kind. In the next income ranges, where families keep fairly high cash/income ratios and have some savings deposits, the average return to all financial assets is very low, and losses as a share of income are in normal times greatest. For a family with one-third of its financial assets in savings deposits and two-thirds in cash, the real return would have been -6.1 percent in 1967-70 and -15.0 percent in 1971-74. The top quartile of families probably have most of the better paying assets; if cash constituted 10 percent of their

[15] Based on *ibid.*, p. 337. Figures presented by Schlesinger and Ruiz, based on the indices calculated by the Bolsa de Bogotá, imply an average real return of under 5 percent for 1962-70. (D. Schlesinger R. and A. Ruiz H., "Algunos Aspectos Especificos del Mercado de Capitales Colombiano: Tasas de Interes y Exenciones Impositivas," *Revista del Banco de la Republica* (Mayo 1975), p. 12.

[16] Because of the atypically high returns to stocks in this period, the lower average for 1966-70 was used in estimating a rate of 9.0%. With the actual return to stocks over 1967-70, it would be 12.4%.

[17] The cyclical character of stock prices makes it dangerous to assume that any short period provides "typical" measures of yields, and complicates any guesses as to the impact of inflation on real returns.

[18] In the U.S. this is true over most of the income range.

TABLE 4.5. Effect of Inflation on Rates of Return of Various Financial Assets

	1967-70		1971-74		1975	
	Effective interest rate	Real effective interest rate	Effective interest rate	Real effective interest rate	Effective interest rate	Real effective interest rate
Savings deposits[a]	4.1	–3.2	8.6	–8.1	17.0	–0.5
BCH Cedulas	10.7	3.0	13.4	–4.2	15.3	–1.9
Government bonds (economic development class B)	11.4	3.6	14.5	–3.3	16.8	–0.6
UPAC[b]	–	–	24.5	3.4	25.4	6.7
Stocks[c]	25.2	16.4	9.6	–7.6	n.a.	n.a.
	[21.1]	[11.6]	(15.3)	(–4.1)		

( ) Excluding 1971.
[ ] Including 1966.

Note: Rates are unweighted averages of the rates for the years cited.

a) Term deposits had similar effective rates except over 1969-71 when they yielded 3% more than savings deposits. But they are relatively much less important.

b) Unweighted averages of returns to "cuentas" and "certificados;" data refer to 1972 and on.

c) Unweighted average of financial and industrial stocks.

Sources and Methodology: Data on effective interest rates is taken from Daniel Schlesinger R. and Alvaro Ruiz H., "Algunos Aspectos Especificos del Mercado de Capitales Colombiano: Tasas de Interes y Exenciones Impositivas," *Revista del Banco de la Republica* (Mayo, 1975), p. 12. The inflation rates used to calculate real interest rates are those of the white collar cost of living index from December to December.

portfolio and savings deposits another 10 percent, their average real return would have been 8.2 percent in 1967-70,[19] and -5.9 percent in 1971-74.[20] Inclusion of cash in the calculations emphasizes the substantial losses for most income groups under inflation; interestingly, though, the estimated decline in real return due to inflation remains greater for richer than for poorer families, given the above assumptions.

Meanwhile, business income was affected in a positive direction by the inflation. Both business and property income are relatively concentrated. Which is more concentrated in families with high lifetime incomes is not entirely clear; when families are not distinguished by age, property income is somewhat more concentrated than business income in the U. S. If the pattern in Colombia is similar, then some groups of well-off families will suffer from the inflation while others will benefit. But the better-off families as a group will benefit considerably. A rough quantification is attempted below.[21]

D. The Distributional Impact of Lowered Real Debt

The effect of inflation on debtors doubtless varies by income level, both because the debt/income and debt/net wealth ratios vary with income and because the inflation affects real interest rates differently for different income groups. Low income persons usually borrow in the informal credit market, and nominal rates are likely to rise substantially under inflationary conditions, so borrowers may not gain much if at all. (Intrafamily credit may be an exception to this tendency.) But real interest on formal sector credit usually falls markedly. This increases the demand for it, which may further squeeze out less well connected borrowers. Data on debt positions of families or persons by income level are not available in Colombia. Rough estimates of the distribution of agricultural credit of the Caja Agraria by patrimony of farmer, and of the banking system by gross

[19] Assuming the return for stocks corresponding to 1966-70.

[20] Assuming the return for stocks corresponding to 1972-74.

[21] Note that transfer income is not a major source of revenue for Colombian families, if available statistics are reasonably accurate. The national accounts imply that transfers (mainly from government, with smaller amounts from abroad) accounted for something under 3% of family income (2.86% in 1970 and 2.70% in 1975). Public transfers (mainly social security) appear to have no overall effect on the concentration of income in Bogotá and Medellin. (Based on the Estudios Conjuntos Sobre Integracion Economica Latino Americana (ECIEL) analyses of CEDE's family budget surveys of 1967–68.) For the country as a whole they probably worsen it somewhat, since they do not reach a significant share of the rural poor. Private transfers do improve income distribution in Bogotá and Medellin, and may well do so for the country as a whole.

The impact of inflation on real public sector transfers is generally negative, since the flows are not indexed for inflation. A decrease in real transfers to the public because of inflation would work mainly against the middle income groups which benefit from social security. The effect of inflation on private transfers can only be guessed at until more is known about the sources.

assets of borrower (whether person or firm) leave little doubt that it is concentrated in the upper income groups.[22] Data on requests for Banco Central Hipotecaria loans show the same pattern; the great majority of loans go to families in the top decile of the income distribution.[23]

As of 1969, liabilities to formal sector financial institutions or to the government were perhaps 22-25 percent of family income [24] and about 36-42 percent of family's financial assets.[25] The average real interst rate paid was probably 4-5 percent. By 1974, authorized interest rates had risen but the real rate had fallen substantially, to an average of perhaps – 10 percent. Most of the gains from these subsidized interest rates accrue to upper income groups, though whether debt holding is more concentrated than financial asset holding is not clear. In total, the direct gains from the decrease in real interest paid are less than the losses families suffer from the lower returns to financial assets held.[26]

E. Effects on Revenue of the Public Sector and Its Implications

Another important effect of inflation in Colombia has been to decrease the real revenue of the public sector and to decrease the progressivity (or increase the regressivity) of the tax system. With taxable labor incomes subject to withholding and capital incomes not, a substantial inequity is introduced. Between 1970 and 1974, the withholding of income tax on labor income rose from 9.1 to 19.2 percent of total income tax revenues. While inflation may theoretically raise the income tax share of personal income, in practice the opposite tends to occur for several reasons including (1) the lag between accrual of the income and payment of tax (except where withholding is applied) during which the real value of the tax payment falls; and (2) the increase in the share of income going to capital, which lowers tax receipts and further increases the lag between accrual and tax payment.[27]

The share of personal income paid in direct taxes (excluding contributions to social security) fell abruptly to 2.62 percent in 1972 from 3.38 percent the previous year and remained well below the level of the late 1960s until the tax reform of 1974 began to have an effect in 1975. The share had increased over 1967-71, presumably reflecting a situation of rapid income growth, relative price stability,

[22] A. Berry and M. Urrutia, *Income Distribution in Colombia* (New Haven: Yale University Press, 1976), p. 234 and p. 210.

[23] *Ibid.*, p. 219.

[24] See the longer version of this paper (available from the author), p. 61.

[25] See the longer version of this paper, Table A-7.

[26] Since, if we assume the value of credit to be unaffected by the real interest rate, then there must be a gainer for every loser, this statement implies that the government and companies must have gained. According to how their gains are ultimately distributed to families, the statement would have to be altered to take account of the indirect effects of the changes in real interest rates.

[27] I am indebted to G. Perry for these observations, in connection with an earlier version of this paper.

and some improvements in collection procedures. With real incomes still rising rapidly over 1972-74, a further increase would have been expected; the inflation was one of the factors which held these tax revenues perhaps a quarter below what might have been expected.[28] Meanwhile direct taxes on companies as a share of GDP fell by about the same proportion.

The benefits of lowered company taxes probably accrue mainly, though at one remove, to the owners of the capital. And since personal income tax is progressive in Colombia,[29] a reduction worsens after tax distribution.

F. A Comparison of the Mechanisms whereby Inflation Affects Income Distribution in Colombia

Inflation has certain fairly predictable effects on the real incomes of specific groups; other of its effects may vary considerably from country to country. For the lower income groups in Colombia whose income is largely from the labor services they render, it seems likely that the main source of loss over the first half of the 1970s was the fall in real wages. Judging the effect of the inflation on those wages involves difficult identification problems, so estimates have a considerable range of error. For higher income groups, the other effects discussed above take on more importance.

Table 4.6 presents illustrative estimates of how the inflation of 1971-74 may have affected selected ideal types of families, each having income from financial assets in addition to one of the following sources: work, rental property, and business management. In fact, real world families do not fit neatly into these categories, so the impact of inflation is some combination of the effects cited here. But the generally close relation between total income and income source means that the figures give some idea of how various deciles are affected by the inflation. Each estimate is based on a good deal of guesswork. The figure for property owners who rent out their capital is the least meaningful since it is subject to large fluctuations, and since our estimate is weakest for this group.

Overall, the data suggest that the inflation caused significant losses to all groups except persons with business incomes; the higher real return to capital was not translated into higher real returns on financial assets. For the lower income groups the wage lag is the main source of loss. For the white collar category, the decreased returns on financial assets may be as important or more so; but all conclusions about financial assets must be taken with a grain of salt since stock market behavior, which is in any case erratic, was the determining factor in the losses calculated. Since the inflationary period analyzed, 1971-74, corresponded to the introduction of the UPAC, the influence of its positive return on the aver-

[28]Over 1969-71, the share of personal income paid in direct taxes averaged 3.13%, and over 1972-74, 2.63%. A plausible expectation for the latter period would have been about 3.50%.

[29]See C. McLure, Jr., "The Incidence of Taxation in Colombia, 1970," *Economic Development and Cultural Change,* Vol. 24, No. 1 (1975).

TABLE 4.6. Illustrative Estimates (expressed as percentage changes) of the Short Run Average Annual Impact of Inflation on the Real Income of Selected Ideal Types of Families, 1971-74

Type of effect	Blue Collar Worker: Poor[a]	Blue Collar Worker: Moderate[c]	White Collar[e] worker	Property Owner who rents out his capital[g]	Proprietor who manages his capital[i]
Wage lag	–4 to –6[b]	–4 to –6[b]	–4 to –6[b]	–	–
Relative price movements	–1.5	0	0	0	+
Change in returns to financial assets	–0.9	–1.3	–6.2	–62.2[h]	–
Change in returns to managed capital	0	0	0	0	7.3[j]
Change in cost of debt	0	+0.1[d]	2.4[f]	2.4[f]	
Change in real tax payments	0	0	1.25	1.25	1.0
Total	–6.4 to –8.4	–5.2 to 7.2	–6.6 to 8.6	–58.6	8.3

[a] Assumed to be an unskilled worker, e.g., in agriculture or construction. Spends 75% of total expenditures on food, i.e., well above the proportion assumed in the market basket of blue collar workers used in constructing the blue collar cost of living index. The only financial asset is cash, equal to 5% of income. Cost of debt assumed unaffected by the inflation. Pays no direct taxes.

[b] Based roughly on Table 4.3 and the presumption that in the absence of inflation real wages would have been about stable or increasing slightly. These figures show a larger loss than would occur in the first year of the accelerated inflation and a lower one that would be true after 3 years.

[c] Better paid worker, e.g., semiskilled or skilled in manufacturing. Market basket corresponds to that used in construction of the blue collar cost of living price index. Has a cash/income of 0.10 and savings deposits equal to 0.05 of income. Has consumer credit equal to 0.02 of income. Pays direct taxes of 1% of income.

[d] Real cost assumed to fall by 5%.

[e] Market basket corresponds to that of the white collar price index. Cash is 0.10 of income, savings deposits 0.05 and other financial assets (among which the composition is the same as for all families–clearly an oversimplification) .40. (In 1972 the average for all families was 0.44.) Direct taxes are 5% of income.

We neglect the fact that for this group the holding of financial assets normally provides a modest share of total income; i.e., the calculations of income loss or gain use wage income as the denominator.

[f] Assumes the ratio of debt to income is 0.30 and that the real cost falls by 8%. Much of the debt would be related to housing and in the 1970s the introduction of UPAC raised the real cost for many families, so this may overstate the gains.

[g] Income is assumed to be 60% from rental of property and 40% from interest and dividends. The return to housing is assumed to have been 5% lower over this period due to the inflation; by 1974 the relative price was 10% below the 1971 level. Cash is assumed to be 6% of income. Direct taxes are 5% of income.

[h] The dramatic decline results from the fact that, with capital losses taken into account, this group gets negative income from financial assets over this period. With income from financial assets a high share of total income to start with, the losses are high in relation to original income. If housing and land prices rise, the loww could be offset, of course.

[i] Have income exclusively from managed capital. Pay 4% of income in taxes.

[j] The percent increase in the share of family income from work or capital accruing to proprietors was 7.3% as between 1969-70 and 1971-74 (by the end of the period it was greater). (Based on Banco de la Republica, *Cuentas Nacionales.*)

age return to financial assets was not yet strong. By the end of this period, the effect on property owners renting out their capital would be much less bad than for the period as a whole.

6. REVIEW OF CONCLUSIONS

Despite the many ambiguities in the above analysis, the case seems strong that the rapid inflation of the early 1970s worsened Colombia's income distribution. The key mechanism was a wage price lag. The beneficiaries were persons with business incomes; recipients of rental, interest and dividend income may have lost as badly as or worse than workers. After-tax distribution probably worsened more than before-tax distribution as revenues from the main source of progressivity in the tax structure, the income tax, declined relative to income.

An important factor in the initial acceleration of inflation was the declining share of current government revenue in national income, with expenditures remaining relatively constant. If the government deficit could be viewed as benefiting the poor, the joint impact of the inflation itself and the factors which caused it might be less negative. But unless the distribution of the benefits of government expenditures shifted towards the poor at this time, no such argument could be countenanced. Rather, the decrease in the tax burden would suggest that the distributional impact of the public budget may have worsened. Leaving the government aside, the main feature of the period was, clearly, the shift of income from labor to capital.

As discussed in section 1, a satisfactory treatment requires that the impact of inflation on distribution be viewed in dynamic terms. The data discussed in section 5 suggest a significant worsening of distribution during the acceleration phase. It now remains to be seen whether or in what sense these shifts were transitory. Will inequality return roughtly to its 1970 level with the end of the acceleration phase? Would it return to that level only if inflation were brought again below 10 percent? Has the distribution of wealth been affected in such a way as to imply a permanent negative effect of this inflation on distribution, even after the inflation ends? Or has the inflation brought about structural changes which will improve distribution in the long run? Not even this last alternative can be ruled out with confidence on the basis of our current fragmentary understanding of the factors at work.

Chapter 5

THE INFLUENCE OF EDUCATION ON LABOR INCOMES: THE COLOMBIAN CASE

Bernardo Kugler*

Corporacion Centro Regional de Poblacion
Bogotá, Colombia

1. INTRODUCTION

One aspect of socioeconomic policy that has received much attention from politicians, social reformers and technicians has been that of education. Such prominence has arisen from concern with human rights, equality of opportunity and lately, economic development. In Colombia, education objectives are to be found in the Constitution and in development plans and the topic has been the subject of studies in the field of the economics of education.

The economic literature contains many studies concerned with the relationship between income, its distribution, and education. It has been observed that countries with high income levels show higher educational levels and also a lower dispersion in their income distribution; at the personal level the observation is that individuals with greater education tend also to have higher incomes.

*This article is based on research financed by the Corporacion para el Fomento de las Investigaciones Economicas (CORP). The author wishes to thank R. Hertford, G. Perry and A. Reyes for their interest and comments; the Departamento Administrativo Nacional de Estadistica (DANE), A. Velasquez, A. Pachon, E. Behrents and R. Plata for their help in making possible the use and processing of data and A. Rodriquez for his help in the preparation of government expenditures data. The responsibility of this work rests with the author. This paper has been translated from the original in Spanish by Maria Teresa Méndez.

Based on these observations and the theory of human capital, the role of education as a productive input and its influence on the income levels of individuals and on economic development in general have been studied.[1] It is argued that education generates greater labor productivity and therefore higher labor income for its recipients; thus, if higher levels of education are generalized in a society it will be characterized by greater productivity and higher per capita incomes. Clearly this represents a desirable goal within the development process and points to education as a means to promote social equality.

In what follows the theory sketched above is tested against empirical material for Colombia; education is treated as a capital good and an internal rate of return calculated. Labor is classified by educational level and the benefits from education are measured by the difference in incomes between individuals with one educational level and those with another.

Several rate of return studies have been done for Colombia's urban sector following the above methodology,[3] though with a few slight variations. A common assumption in these studies is that wage differentials are explained by differences in education, age, sex, and (sometimes) experience. The results show high social rates of return to primary and secondary education and a relatively low social return to university education.

Recent studies have analyzed the effects of education for income distribution as well.[4] Since education is a productive factor, an unequal distribution of education will *ceteris paribus* lead to an unequal distribution of income.[5] In the Colombian case Urrutia and Sandoval conclude that "Probably the most efficient policy instrument that can be used to counterbalance the effects of family envi-

[1]G. S. Becker, *Human Capital* (New York: Columbia University Press, 1964); and "Human Capital and the Personal Distribution of Income," Waytinsky Lecture 1, University of Michigan, 1967; J. Mincer, "The Distribution of Labor Incomes," *Journal of Economic Literature*, Vol. VIII, No. 4 (December, 1970).

[2]One would also describe it as dynamic with stationary expectations. One way to make the model dynamic would be to take into account future "group wage" changes due to changes in the number of persons in the group, that is, due to changes in the composition of the labor supply.

[3]T. P. Schultz, "Returns to Education in Bogotá," Rand Corporation, RM5645 RC/AID, 1969; C.R.S. Dougherty, "Optimal Allocation of Investment in Education," *Economic Development Report* No. 129, (Cambridge, Mass., Harvard University Advisory Service, 1968) 1968; M. Selowsky, "El efecto del desempleo y el crecimiento sobre la rentabilidad de la inversion educacional," *Revista de Planeacion y Desarrollo*, Volumen I (Julio, 1969).

[4]G. S. Becker, "Human Capital," *op. cit.* (1967); J. Mincer, *op. cit.*

[5]On the other hand, a greater average educational level does not necessarily result in a greater concentration of the income distribution. For example, Chiswick and Mincer find that "a unitary increase in the schooling level increases the inequality by 0.113 points." (B. R. Chiswick and J. Mincer, "Time Series Changes in Personal Income Inequality," *Journal of Political Economy*, Vol. 80 [May-June, 1972], pp. 34-67.) Cordova finds that in Colombia's urban sector income distribution is more unequal among people with secondary education than among those with only primary education. (P. Cordova, "La Distribución de Ingresos en Colombia," *Boletin Mensual de Estadistica*, No. 237 (April, 1971), p. 80.

ronment and inherited wealth on the income distribution is that of free public education."[6]

In most of the studies mentioned above a great deal of attention has been given to the effects of education on other variables (especially income) and relatively little to the way in which the educational level of individuals is determined, i.e., the educational level of individuals is taken as given for the purposes of the analysis. In what follows some implications of this approach are briefly discussed, the convenience of treating both questions jointly is shown and a scheme to do so is proposed. Section 3 describes the sampling method employed as well as the variables used in the analysis; the determinants of education are discussed in section 4 and those of income in section 5. Section 6 summarizes our general conclusions.

2. FACTORS AFFECTING THE EDUCATIONAL LEVEL OF INDIVIDUALS AND THE EFFECTS OF THIS LEVEL ON THEIR INCOMES

Traditionally, studies attempting to measure the effects of education on income have made labor income (y_i) a function of education (e_i), age (A_i), and sex (S_i).

$$y_i = g(e_i, A_i, S_i)$$

It is known that omission of variables that have a positive influence on income and are positively correlated with education will introduce a positive bias in the coefficient of the latter.[7] A discussion of such omitted variables is undertaken below. It is also possible to overestimate the effect of the distribution of education on the distribution of labor income. In the presence of other determinants of income (o) one can write

$$y = \alpha + \beta e + \gamma o$$

Using σ for variances and covariances[8]

$$\sigma_y^2 = \beta^2 \sigma_e^2 + \gamma^2 \sigma_o^2 + 2\beta\gamma\sigma_{eo}$$

[6] M. Urrutia and C. E. de Sandoval, "Distribución de la Educacion y Distribucion del Ingreso," Centro de Investgaciones para el Desarrollo (CID), Universidad Nacional, 1971 (Mimeographed).

[7] See, for example, D. J. Aigner, *Basic Econometrics* (Englewood Cliffs, N.J.: Prentice Hall, 1971).

[8] Under certain circumstances the variance is an adequate indicator of the dispersion of economic variables. (See J. Aitchison and J.A.C. Brown, *The Log Normal Distribution* [Cambridge, Cambridge University Press, 1964]; A. B. Atkinson, "On the Measurement of Inequality," *Journal of Economic Theory*, Vol. 2 [1970], pp. 244-63.)

If σ_o^2 and ρ_{eo} (the correlation coefficient between education and the "other" variables) are constant, a change in σ_e^2 leads to a change in σ_{eo} so that:[9]

$$\frac{\partial \sigma_y^2}{\partial \sigma_e^2} = \beta^2 + 2\beta\gamma \frac{\partial \sigma_{eo}}{\partial \sigma_e^2}$$

When no relevant variables have been omitted and $\sigma_{eo} = 0$, then unequivocally,

$$\frac{\partial \sigma_y^2}{\partial \sigma_e^2} = \beta^2$$

When relevant variables have been omitted the effect of a change in σ^2 is overestimated. Furthermore, if $\sigma_{eo} \neq 0$, it is not possible to know whether the change in σ^2 is due to the change in e or to the change in o.

The results attained in theoretical exercises under dynamic assumptions have highlighted the importance of taking into consideration other determinants of labor income. Following neoclassical growth models Stiglitz assumes that wealth is distributed on a class basis; he arrives at the total of capital available to the economy by addition of the wealth held by the different classes; this allows him to treat factor owners explicity and consider their income distribution. Given his assumptions, including homogeneous labor, a linear savings function and the remuneration of factors according to their marginal productivity, both the income and the wealth distributions tend to equality in the long run. Kugler[10] found that when he changed the assumption of labor homogeneity, admitted productivity differentials due to different educational levels, incorporated a linear savings function for human capital, and left the other assumptions as in the Stiglitz model, there was no longer any tendency towards equalization in either distribution. This difference in results suggests that if a more equitable income distribution is an objective, one way of attaining it is to determine one of the distributions (i.e., either income or wealth) outside the competitive system, achieving its equalization by some non-market method, and let the market equalize the other distribution. This idea has led many people to think that more uniform access to education is a powerful means to increase equality in the income distribution. However, if access is not completely uniform, this conclusion is not obvious and the issue requires detailed study.[11] If there are more than two productive factors, the equalization of ownership of only one of them may result in very partial

[9] $$\frac{\partial \sigma_{eo}}{\partial \sigma_e^2} = \frac{\rho \sigma_o}{2\sigma_e}$$

[10] B. Kugler, "Economic Growth and Individual Income Distributions," University of Minnesota, 1971. (Mimeographed.)

[11] Stiglitz, for instance, shows that if there are two kinds of workers with sufficiently different productivities, in the long run those with higher productivity will be the only owners of wealth and the others will consume all of their income. (See J. E. Stiglitz, "Distribution of Income and Wealth among Individuals," *Econometrica*, Vol. 37, No. 3 [July, 1969], pp. 368-81.)

equalization of income (contrary to what was originally expected), according to the degree of interdependence that persists between the equalized factor and the other productive factors of the economy.

The other determinants of labor income traditionally omitted in this type of analysis are largely those hidden from view by the assumptions of homogeneity and competition; however, these factors may play important roles. The information, accessibility, adaptability, and forecasting ability of a person with respect to the market influences the degree to which the person can take advantage of opportunities. Such variables seem to be positively correlated with education. Looking back on the life of a person there is a series of antecedents that influence not only the individual's attitude towards education but his attitude to other markets to which he relates.

The basic working hypothesis in this paper is that to analyze the role of education as a means of social mobility and a determinant of labor incomes and their distribution, it is necessary to consider the possibility that an individual's socioeconomic background influences his labor income not only indirectly through the level of education he attains but also directly through the factors mentioned above. In other words, socioeconomic background and environment not only influence the quantity of education a person receives and through it one's labor income, but also help to determine one's access and adaptability to occupations high in the job hierarchy; these are their direct effects on labor income. The correlation among the above mentioned variables can be found and their causal relationships analyzed when the data are available over a period of time; however, cause-effect relationships between the variables at a given point in time can only be guessed at—the limitations of the statistical methods must be emphasized.

To formalize, then, an individual's educational level depends on the available funds he (or his family) has to spend on his education. In Colombia public funds are not available to finance the whole of an individual's education; partial public financing can be represented by an indicator showing government education expenditure per student, as explained in Section 3 below. The inadequacy of public financing coupled with the difficulty in obtaining private loans for educational purposes (an imperfection in the capital market) results in the family's provision of funds to finance at least transportation, books, and sometimes fees; the net cost of this education to the family thus includes these outlays plus the student's opportunity cost. Private financing clearly depends on availability of funds. It also depends on the attitude of parents towards education, which is likely to be related to such correlates as their social position, educational level, occupational level, and geographic origin (urban, rural) as well as their income. Beliefs about how much education a child should receive may depend on whether it is a boy or a girl.

Income, meanwhile, depends on an individual's level of education and on experience but presumably also on his natural abilities, his preschool formation and, more generally, on his view of society and of his position in it. For example, if it is true that in general the jobs done by people with high educational levels require analytic capacity and initiative, it can be expected that as between two individuals with identical formal education and experience the one that grew up in an atmosphere where analysis and initiative were rewarded will achieve a higher income than one whose development occurred in an environment where questioning was forbidden and submission was the rule. A different sort of link between income and family background follows from the fact that information on certain types of jobs and access to them depend on that background. To take such relationships into account, we include the education and occupation of parents as well as geographic origin as explanatory variables.

Our objective is to quantify the above relationships through equations of the form:

$$Q = H(X)$$
$$Y = G(Q, X, P)$$

where Q = quantity of education acquired, X = a socioeconomic background vector, including urban-rural origin, sex and parental income, occupation and education, Y = labor income, and P = experience.

The first equation expresses the relation between the quantity of education acquired and the socioeconomic background of the family. The second expresses the relationships between the traditional set of explanatory variables and labor income. Even though the correlations that exist amongst these independent variables make it difficult to isolate their individual effects on income, it is possible to find the upper and lower limits of such partial effects, and to make some further conjectures about them.

3. THE SAMPLE AND THE VARIABLES

The ideal unit of observation for this study would be persons who had finished their education and for whom the relevant direct information as well as information on family background was available. Given the data available, the need for this latter type of information restricts our analysis to children who still live with their parents; for such persons, all of the necessary data is available in DANE's *Encuesta Nacional de Hogares-Etapa 5*, which is basically a sample of the municipal seats in late 1971. Individuals older than 16 years who had been out of school longer than four years were excluded to avoid a bias in the sample towards children who continue to live with their parents for an atypically long period. Finally, only persons with positive incomes are included.

The resulting sample size is 607 persons for whom data are available on sex, age, place of residence, place of birth, length of residence at present location, urban-rural origin, educational level, highest grade passed in school, occupation and income; with respect to the individual's parents data are available on age, education, income and home ownership. Income is classified into labor income, profit income, income in kind and other income; it includes fringe benefits when relevant.

The variables used and a brief description of how they were obtained is as follows:

Educational variables: Q_h, the individual's years of education; E_f, E_m years of education of the fathers and mothers, respectively; the data on the latter two correspond to the last school year passed by each of the parents.

Income variables: Y_h, monthly monetary income of the individual in pesos; Y_f, monthly income of the head of the household (father or mother), including income from any source. Income data are expressed in logarithmic form. Income reported is that of the preceding month, but an attempt has been made to approximate the concept of permanent income; Y_f has been adjusted by age and homeownership; a subsequent adjustment making use of data on hours worked, desired hours of work, and "normal" working hours produced income figures which did not appear to be significantly better and were therefore not used. Mother's income and total family income did not increase the explanatory power of the equations enough to justify their inclusion instead of the variable "income of household head."

Occupational variables: 0_f^1, 0_f^2, 0_f^3 are binary variables that describe the father's occupation; 0_m refers to the mother's occupation. The original occupational data in the Encuesta is presented according to the United Nations' three-digit breakdown; for this study a reclassification of father's occupation was made into four categories, i.e., unskilled workers (0), specialized workers (1), white collar workers (2), and professionals, executives and owners (3). Superscripts correspond to this classification. Thus, the coefficient of the variable 0_f^1 would show the effect on a person's income of being in category (1) rather than in category (0). In the case of the mother's occupation not enough cases were found in groups (2) and (3) so the breakdown consists of only two groups: housewives and women who participate in the labor force, the latter designated by 0_m. The variable that shows the person's origin (rural-urban) refers to place of birth; R denotes rural origin. With respect to the sex variable, S refers to women.

Besides socioeconomic background, government expenditure on education was introduced as a determinant of educational level. The Encuesta data on department of residence, length of residence and department of birth plus data on the age of the individual helped in locating the person's department of residence during their school years. Figures on yearly departmental and municipal expenditures on education were computed, as well as the number of persons in the 5-14 age bracket by department and by year. An indicator of public expenditures on education per person of school age, i.e., an index of the accessibility of public education by department and by age was obtained by using the figures mentioned above and assuming that central government expenditures on education per department are proportional to the total expenditure on education in each department; for a given person the index of accessibility to public education (GG) was calculated by dividing the average number of years of school for the appropriate department into the public expenditures on education. This variable is expressed in pesos per person.

The experience of the individual, E_x, was calculated on basis of age and educational level: i.e., E_x = Age - Years in School - 7.

4. THE DETERMINANTS OF EDUCATION

In order to analyze the extent to which family background influences the years of education a child gets, a regression was run between the years of education of the individual and his/her father's income, parents' occupation and education, region of origin, sex and public expenditure on education per person. The results are shown in Table 5.1; the set of independent variables used explained 76 percent of the variance in the schooling of individuals; this is quite satisfactory in a cross section sample. The results are significant at the 99 percent confidence level. The regression and correlation coefficients are not significantly different when the variable GG is excluded. The only non-significant variable is 0_f^3 . The signs of the variables are as expected except in the case of government expenditures, and perhaps sex.

The regression results imply the following with respect to the effect of the independent variables on education of the individual. The elasticity of education with respect to income of household head seems low ($0.63/Q_h$); there is, of course, a positive correlation between parental income and other explanatory variables. Calculating the elasticity using the coefficient of a simple regression (not shown) of education vs. the father's income ($2.27/Q_h$) might be closer to the general concept of income elasticity. The partial effect of the father's income is such that a doubling implies slightly less than an additional half year of education ($0.63 \ln 2 = 0.43$) whereas if all other variables maintained their normal relation with income a doubling of the income would result on average in one and one-half more years of education for the child.

With other variables held constant, the children of skilled workers have on average 0.8 years more of education than the children of unskilled workers; the children of white collar workers have 1.48 more years than the latter and 0.68 more than the former. The occupational group including professionals and owners is not significantly different from that of untrained workers; this is due to the fact that business owners were included indiscriminately in this category and thus an important part of it consists of small owners and independent workers which in a more rigorous classification by skill would not belong in this top group. With respect to the mother's occupation, the children of women whose main activity was housework had on average 0.53 more years of education than the children of those who worked outside the home. It should be noted that 29 percent of mothers belong to the labor force and of these, only 6 percent fall within the upper occupational groups as defined earlier. This indicates that most mothers in the labor force enter it because of necessity, a fact confirmed by the negative correlation between the mothers' participation in the labor force and the other variables measuring socioeconomic status.

The effects of parents' education are quire interesting; that of the mother's education is quite important and that of the father's education reasonably so. An additional year of father's education implies 0.22 more years for the child and an additional year of mother's education implies 0.40 more years for the

TABLE 5.1. Regression Explaining Level of Education Received (Q_h)

Independent Variable (Symbols defined in text)	$\log Y_f$	0_f^1	0_f^2	0_f^3	0_m	E_f	E_m	R	S	GG
Coefficient	0.63	0.80	1.48	NS	−0.53	0.22	0.40	−1.40	0.27	−0.04
T statistic	4.13	2.91	3.97	0.61	−2.27	4.79	7.65	−5.53	2.86	−5.58

$R^2 = 0.76$

Degrees of freedom = 596

F Statistic 82.79

NS: Variable not significantly different from 0 at 95% level of confidence.

child. These figures, however, quite possibly underestimate the real effect. A simple regression against the father's education yields a coefficient of 0.70; with the mother's, 0.87. The regression against both variables yields a correlation coefficient of 0.68 with regression coefficients of 0.40 and 0.57 respectively; this last result indicates that if all other variables were allowed to change with parents' education, an individual each of whose parents had one more year of education than the parents of another would have on average 0.97 (0.40 + 0.57) more years of education than the second. In such a system the (absolute) differences in education would not change intergenerationally.

An individual's place of birth (rural, urban) is another highly significant variable. Other variables held constant, an individual not born in a municipal seat has, on average, 1.4 years less education than one born in an urban area; this confirms the precariousness of educational conditions in the rural areas which in their turn generate cultural barriers difficult to surpass even after migration. Being female implies an additional 0.27 years of education; this is not surprising in view of the fact that relatively more women than men attend and complete primary education and that 80 percent of people have primary education or less.

A measure of public expenditure on education was included in the analysis on the presumption that it has some impact on the educational achievement of individuals; we also hoped to learn something about the distribution of such expenditure. Even in the worst of cases, the effect of such expenditure should be positive, even if small; the results obtained here, then, indicate that the measure used is not an appropriate one. Possibly central government expenditure by regions is not proportional to the region's own expenditures, or possibly private expenditure is such that it complements public expenditures. The latter possibility is suggested by the fact that enrollment in private institutions has been increasing more than in public ones in recent years.

The separation of the various effects mentioned above may tend to disguise the total impact of socioeconomic background, since many of the variables included are highly correlated with one another; thus, for example a person who was born in the rural area, whose father is an untrained worker with a monthly income of 400 pesos (the minimum wage in 1970) and whose parents both had primary eduction would have on average 8 years less of education than a person born in the city with a white collar father whose monthly income is 2,400 pesos and whose parents both had secondary education (5 or 6 years more education than the former). It is interesting also to study the distribution of years of education of parents and children:

	Mean Years of education	Standard deviation	Coefficient of variation
Child	4.11	3.78	0.74
Father	3.29	3.24	0.98
Mother	2.83	2.71	0.96
Average for parents	3.06	2.70	0.88

The increase in the standard deviation from parents to children indicates greater absolute differences in years of education among the children than among their parents, though the lower coefficient of variation implies smaller relative differences; this is the result of a general increase in education: an average of 2 years more for the children vis-à-vis their parents.

In summary, the generation entering the labor force shows significant variance in educational level, based substantially on differences in the socioeconomic status of the families of the individuals. Even though there may have been some intergenerational improvement in the relative distribution of education along with the increase in average educational level, the absolute differences have not only persisted but have increased. Accordingly, one cannot say on the basis of this evidence that education has been an important means of social mobility in the Colombian urban sector, and even less so in the country as a whole.

5. THE INFLUENCE OF EDUCATION ON INCOME

As has been indicated above, the central aim of this study is to ascertain the influence of a person's education on his income, independently of his socioeconomic background. Given the close correlation between socioeconomic background and education (as reported in section 4) it is naturally difficult to distinguish their separate effects on income. In general, studies of the return to education have included experience and sex as other important determinants of income. The usual methodology first finds upper limits to the share of the income dispersion which is explained by each variable (or group of variables) and then finds what are, given a correct specification of the model, corresponding lower limits. The standard deviation of the logarithm of income is used as an indicator of the dispersion of incomes; it has the advantage of defining the Gini coefficient when the income distribution is lognormal. The upper limits to the contribution of an independent variable to income variation is given by the R^2 between the variable and the logarithm of income. The lower limit is defined by the difference between the R^2 when all the explanatory variables are included and that when the variable or variables under analysis are excluded.

The R^2 of a simple regression of the log of income with some of the explanatory variables are as follows:

Years of education (Q_h)	0.666
Log of the father's income ($\log Y_f$)	0.487
Years of education of the father (E_f)	0.438
Years of education of the mother (E_m)	0.451
Rural origin (R)	0.347

Since the father's occupational category is described by the three variables 0_f^1, 0_f^2, and 0_f^3, we have computed the multiple correlation coefficient of these variables with respect to the income of the individual: 0.356.

These figures give the upper limit to the part of the dispersion of the person's income explained by the variable; thus, education might be responsible for up to 66.6 percent and the father's income up to 48.7 percent of the variation of people's incomes.

In order to find the lower limits for the effects of the explanatory variables the regressions shown in Table 5.2 were run. In these regressions the logarithm of the income of the individual is expressed as a function of contemporary variables like years of education, experience, sex, and/or socioeconomic background variables like father's income, years of education and occupation of both parents, and origin (rural vs. urban).

All the regressions are significant at a confidence level of 0.99. Regression 1 indicates that the set of socioeconomic factors explains up to 58.1 percent of the variance of income. The effects of the significant variables, assuming all others constant, are as follows: a 100 percent difference between fathers' incomes implies a 20 percent difference in the children's incomes; the child of a white collar worker has, on average, an income 30 percent greater than the child of an untrained worker;[12] someone born in a rural area has an income 27 percent lower than someone born in a municipal seat; and a difference of 5 years of education on the part of the mother is associated with a 20 percent difference in the child's income.

According to Regression 2 up to 70.3 percent of income dispersion can be explained by variations in the education and experience levels of individuals. The partial regression coefficients imply that 4 years of additional education result in 100 percent more income; the same income differential results from a 5 year difference in experience. Following Chiswick and Mincer's suggestion in interpreting coefficients of education and experience as their rates of return such rates are 16.9 percent per year of education and 14.5 percent per year of experience; these values are in line with results of other studies done for Colombia.

Regression 3 includes the variables of the previous two regressions; as was to be expected, due to the positive correlation among the explanatory variables all the coefficients are lower than those reported above. Thus, the rate of return on education implicit in this regression is 14.6 percent per year of education (a reduction of 15 percent with respect to Regression 2), although this variable has the highest level of confidence of all the variables. The coefficient of the experience variable also falls. Socioeconomic factors are no longer significant with the exception of the father's income and the individual's origin (rural vs. urban); the income elasticity of the father's income decreases from 0.2 in Regression 1 to 0.116. Assuming that all relevant variables were included in the complete model, the difference between the correlation coefficient for this regression (0.719) and that of Regression 1 (0.581) indicates that the set of contemporary variables explains

[12] Given a semilogarithmic function, the regression coefficients express the percentages of change in income generated by small changes in the explanatory variables. When the changes in the explanatory variables are sizable, the percentage changes are greater as a result of which the values that appear are lower limits.

TABLE 5.2. Determinants of Income

Regression 1: Socioeconomic Background Variables Only

Variable	log Y_f	0_f^1	0_f^2	0_f^3	0_m	E_f	E_m	R
Coefficient	0.20	NS	0.30	NS	−0.16	0.01	0.04	−0.27
t Statistic	5.26	0.16	3.18	−0.25	2.66	1.67	3.29	4.30

$R^2 = 0.581$
Degree of freedom = 598
F statistic = 38.11
NS: Variable not significantly different from 0 at 95% level of confidence.

Regression 2: Personal Characteristics Only

Variable	Q_h	E_x	S
Coefficient	0.169	0.145	NS
t Statistic	22.61	7.71	−0.56

$R^2 = 0.703$
Degrees of freedom = 603
F Statistic = 196.41
NS: Variable not significantly different from 0 at 95% level of confidence.

Regression 3: Socioeconomic Background and Personal Variables

Variable	Q_h	E_x	S	log Y_f	0_f^1	0_f^2	0_f^3	0_m	E_f	E_m	R
Coefficient	0.146	0.128	NS	0.116	NS	NS	NS	NS	NS	NS	−0.103
t Statistic	14.92	6.90	−0.70	3.51	−1.40	1.21	−0.28	−1.47	−0.81	−0.09	0.86

$R^2 = 0.719$
Degrees of freedom = 595
F Statistic = 57.74
NS: Variable not significantly different from 0 at 95% level of confidence.

Regression 4: Personal Variables and Father's Income

Variable	Q_h	E_x	S	log Y_f
Coefficient	0.151	0.135	NS	0.127
t Statistic	17.79	7.22	−0.89	4.28

$R^2 = 0.714$
Degrees of freedom = 602
F Statistic = 156.12
NS: Variable not significantly different from 0 at 95% level of confidence.

at least 13.8 percent of the standard deviation of the log of income; for education the percentage is also 13.8 percent. Comparing Regressions 3 and 2 implies a lower limit for the explanatory role of the socioeconomic factors of 1.6 percent of total variance of the log of income.

Regression 4 was run to ascertain the effects of exclusion of nonsignificant socioeconomic factors; R^2 decreases slightly by 0.005. The R^2 adjusted for degrees of freedom has the same value of 0.712 for regressions 3 and 4, but since the methodology used in the calculation of lower limits can be justified only if no variables are omitted in the regression it was decided to keep the "complete system" of Regression 3.

An example can illustrate the potential effects that changes in the educational system or in the socioeconomic structure might have upon the distribution of labor incomes. For instance, if the parental socioeconomic structure did not change but the educational system turned out a generation of individuals each having identical educational levels, that generation would have a distribution of labor incomes with a standard deviation between 13.8 percent and 70.3 percent lower than the present one.[13]

6. CONCLUSIONS

Because the educational level attained by individuals is closely linked to their socioeconomic background, it was not possible to distinguish clearly between the effects of education and socioeconomic background on the labor income of individuals; it is clear, however, that education plays an important role, and that socioeconomic background may also, although to a lesser extent. Previous calculations of the rate of return on education in Colombia have probably overestimated it by about 15 percent as a result of the omission of the direct effects of socioeconomic background.

At an individual level, education is without doubt a factor in increasing the private productivity and therefore the potential earnings of people. There is, however, no definite evidence permitting this assertion with respect to social productivity. For example, it is not possible to conclude from the evidence used above that if the Colombian labor force as a whole had a greater educational level (*ceteris paribus*) it would have also a greater general productivity and the country would have a higher national income.

[13] Under the assumption that in fact new entrants can get jobs that pay the incomes corresponding to these hypothetical educational levels.

Chapter 6

THE NEW COLOMBIAN EXPORTS: POSSIBLE EFFECTS ON THE DISTRIBUTION OF INCOME

R. Albert Berry
University of Toronto

Carlos Diaz-Alejandro
Yale University
Economic Growth Center

Several factors lend importance to the question of the impact of Colombia's new exports on her income distribution. It was David Ricardo, discoverer of the principal of comparative advantage, who postulated that income distribution is the principal concern of political economy. In the Latin American context, many observers have tended to link the characteristics of the old traditional exports with a regressive income distribution, so it is natural to consider the impact which a change in the export structure may have on that distribution. Finally, enthusiasm over the new export boom in some Asian countries, such as South Korea and Taiwan, has induced some authors to suggest that those exports are accompanied by (and have caused) not only greater efficiency and growth, but also an improvement in the distribution of income. It is interesting to speculate on whether a similar result should be expected under Latin conditions.

What is included under "new exports"? For many countries, characterized in the past by situations approximating mono export, it is not difficult to define nontraditional exports.[1] In Colombia, for example, such exports could include

[1] In other Latin countries, with more diversified traditional export patterns, the quality of "new" may be rather difficult to apply with exactitude. Such is the case of the Argentine Republic. There may also be problems of aggregation at the regional level: an export which is new for one country may be traditional for another. An analysis for the region as a whole would have to take this factor into account, especially when the Latin American participation in world trade in that product is high.

everything but coffee and petroleum. Note that this definition includes agricultural exports, minerals, and manufactures. One could also include new services (such as tourism, remittances of workers abroad, etc.); these, nevertheless, will be left aside in this study since in the Colombian case they still do not loom very large. It seems in general somewhat artificial and misleading to divide new exports into some which are "truly" new (often considered to be the manufactures) and others which inspire less enthusiasm.

In this study we will be concerned, principally, with the distribution of income, i.e., with the shares of total income received by various groups; nevertheless, we will make some observations on the possible effects of the new exports on the absolute level of the income of the less favored groups. We will not enter in great detail into the exact measurement of distribution and the possible ambiguities of the various indices which attempt to summarize the degree of income concentration. The period under discussion is the medium and long-run, when the economy has more or less adjusted to the situation created by the greater growth of the new exports.

The study is organized as follows: first, we consider what the positive theories of international trade say about relationship between income distribution and larger or smaller involvement in international trade. The postulated greater or smaller involvement can be conceived as being induced by the manipulation of some instrument of trade policy with a general impact–for example, an ad valorem tax on all the imports which could vary between zero and 200 percent. Subsequently, we consider the various theories on the relationship between involvement in international trade and the rate of economic growth, and what those relationships imply for the income distribution. Few countries have in fact manipulated the degree of their involvement in international trade by one general instrument of commercial policy. Accordingly, we consider briefly what can be said *a priori* about the ways in which the relation between involvement in trade and income distribution is modified by the nature of the policy instruments utilized to achieve that level of involvement; some Colombian experiences are discussed in this context.

Next, we review the principal aspects of the evolution of the Colombian economy during 1967-74, discussing in particular the characteristics of the new manufactured, agricultural and mining exports. Without attempting a complete analysis or a general equilibrium model with all the possible interactions, we quantify some characteristics of the new exports which appear to affect income distribution, and cite important gaps in the existing information. The study closes with some tentative conclusions and other considerations relevant to the theme.

POSITIVE TRADE THEORIES AND THEIR IMPLICATIONS WITH RESPECT TO INCOME DISTRIBUTION

What little the positive trade theories tell us about the redistributive effects attendant on greater or lesser involvement in international trade is related to the functional distribution of income between those who earn labor income and those who earn capital income. The influence on family distribution, on the bottom half of the income distribution, or on regional distribution lie outside the usual analysis.

The more orthodox theories introduce the redistributive effects of trade by comparing the demand for factors corresponding to a high level of international trade with the demand corresponding to a lower level; the extreme cases are free trade and autarchy. Since the usual simple theories presuppose full employment of all factors of production under both conditions and a perfectly inelastic supply of them, as well as perfect mobility of factors within the country and perfect competition in market structures, the redistributive effects depend on how the level of international trade affects the real earnings of the factors, presumed to be of given fixed quantities.

The aforesaid describes the most popular versions of the Hecksher-Ohlin-Samuelson model (HOS); before going further into this model it is perhaps convenient to remember Ricardo's model (or models). The sources of comparative advantage in the simplest Ricardian model are not precisely specified: they are the "atmosphere" or the "context" which determines why some sectors are more productive than others, and in differing degrees from country to country. In the transition from autarchy to international trade in such a situation, who benefits? In the model–illustrated by Ricardo in numerical examples–and in which there is full employment of labor, the only factor explicitly taken into account, the answer is not obvious; it depends on the degree of appropriability of "atmosphere" which causes the high productivity in the export sector relative to other sectors in the economy. Other parts of the Ricardian study are more explicit with respect to who can benefit from freer foreign trade. In the context of the English social structure of the day, with landlords, workers and capitalists, and supposing also that the production of food is characterized by comparative disadvantage in England, Ricardo concluded that a lowering of the tariff on food would lead to a redistribution from landlords to capitalists, and that the real wage of workers would remain constant.

In a world with two goods, two sectors, and two countries, the HOS model permits the conclusion that an increase in international trade will worsen not only the relative earnings of the scarce factor but its absolute real income as well.[2] In other words, the abundant factor captures all of the increase in national income resulting from the greater specialization, plus a redistribution from the scarce factor. If the distribution of the abundant factor among families is less concentrated than that of the scarce factor (as could be the case if the abundant factor is labor and the scarce factor is capital) the redistribution will tend to be egalitarian. This appears to be the model used by those who believe that the increased trade of Taiwan and South Korea has led or will lead not only to greater

[2] Assuming that the domestic price of the imported good falls (or that the price of the exported good rises) when the economy is opened to trade.

efficiency and growth but also to an improvement in income distribution.[3] At the same time, what might be called the Argentine-Australian version of this model, with land as the abundant factor concentrated in a few families and labor as the scarce and widely distributed factor, could lead to the opposite conclusion with respect to the redistributive effects of an expansion of international trade.

It is known that when the number of goods and factors increases, even though equally, the clear results of the Stolper-Samuelson theorem presented in the previous paragraph lose their precision. In other words, in a model which distinguishes various types of exportable and importable goods along with the important category of nontradables, and includes land, capital, and skilled or unskilled labor as factors, the distributive implications of an expansion of international trade cannot be deduced *a priori* without more information than is summarized in the model. In this expanded model, an expansion of trade leads not only to the expansion of the export sector with respect to the domestic sector which produces importables, but can also lead to a contraction of production of nontraded goods, to the benefit of the tradables as a group. It may be conjectured that, while the export sector cannot intensively use the same factors of production in the two countries of the HOS model, this is compatible with the amplified model; and there is a certain plausibility to the assumption that in both countries the production of nontradables uses unskilled labor intensively.

When the country which is being analyzed with the HOS model is neither India nor the United States, there is the possibility that its trade with one group of countries involves a different input structure than that corresponding to the rest of its trade. In the Latin American case, for example, where interzone trade is now taking on quantitative importance especially for the nontraditional exports, it may be expected *a priori* that such trade uses factors in different proportions from that of the new exports directed outside the region. It then becomes difficult to establish with certainty if such a phenomenon, which as we see later can be shown to exist in the Colombian case, is the result of spontaneous and nondistorted market forces, or if it is due also in part to the trade policies of the region. This being as it may, the fact that a large share of new Colombian exports are directed to countries with similar resource endowments suggests that the effect of that trade on the structure of demand for factors will not be very different from the effect of a greater emphasis on import substitution at the Colombian level.

Beginning with Leontiff's discussion of his paradox, there have been serious doubts as to how much of the structure of world trade can be explained by

[3] The recent literature relating to less developed countries' trade expansion to employment and distribution includes: John C. H. Fei and Gustav Ranis, "A Model of Growth and Employment in the Open Dualistic Economy: The Cases of Korea and Taiwan," *Journal of Development Studies*, Vol. II, No. 2 (January, 1975); H. F. Lydall, *Trade and Employment* (Geneva: International Labor Office, 1975); "Export Oriented Industrialization: A Contribution to Solving Employment Problems in Developing Countries," papers by William G. Tyler and Lutz Hoffman; S. E. Tan in *The International Division of Labor: Problems and Perspectives*, edited by Herbert Giersch, 1974.

the HOS model. Some analysts prefer to modify the assumptions of the model in order to make it more compatible with empirical reality. Thus, for example, it may be supposed that production functions are not identical in all countries, differing perhaps in the absolute level of efficiency. Such a return to the Ricardian "atmosphere" context implies that a country will tend to export those goods in which its total factor productivity is greatest. Once again, the question arises as to who captures the returns to that beneficent atmosphere. Also, since that export sector is likely to be characterized by high labor productivity, its expansion could imply a limited increase in the demand for labor.

There are, naturally, many ways to introduce variations into the basic HOS model, including distortions and rigidities in the markets for goods and factors, which can be the result of government policy or of intrinsic weaknesses in those markets. Rather than following that route, which reminds one a little of ptolmaic astronomy and its epicycles, other positive theories have been proposed to explain the structure of international trade. Their implications for income distribution are, in general, less worked out than those of the HOS model.

Product cycle theory, elaborated by Seev Hirsch and Raymond Vernon, implies that developing countries have comparative advantage in manufactured goods whose technological processes are already standardized, or characterized by a low rate of technological change or slow design changes. Such goods may be capital intensive (glass, cement, steel) or labor intensive, particularly in semiskilled labor (lathes, boilers). The postulated comparative advantage on the production side can be seen to be strengthened by additional comparative advantage in the international commercialization of these products, since their standardization makes it less difficult to avoid the networks of international marketing controls by companies from the industrialized countries. The consequences for income distribution of a trade based on the exportation of standardized products are not discernable *a priori*; all that can be said is that excluding technological rents is unimportant.

The theory developed by Linder adduces that a country exports those manufactured products consumed on a large scale in the internal market, and that it exports to other countries whose demand patterns are similar to its own. An active trade between the Andean countries in refrigerators, washing machines, and other "middle class goods" with a certain differentiation would be compatible with this theory. Obviously, the demand for inputs generated by Linder-type exports will not be substantially different from those of domestic consumption patterns.

In contrast with the HOS theory, the vent for surplus theory which had its origin with Adam Smith and was redeveloped by Myint, does not assume full employment of internal factors under conditions of autarchy. On the contrary, it implies that the major function of exports is to mobilize resources which would otherwise remain unutilized or badly utilized. The opening of trade can thus generate enormous quasi-rents for those resources which under circumstances of lesser involvement in world markets would have very low opportunity costs. Those resources can be more or less homogeneous, in contrast with the factor "land" in HOS models. Who controls the resources will control a large part of the benefits resulting from the exports. Although traditionally it has been considered that this theory refers to natural resources, a more favorable interpretation with respect to its effects on the distribution of income could point to the surplus of unskilled labor as the superabundant resource which will find its utilization increased by foreign demand. Nevertheless, historically the resistance of the importing countries has been greater against goods which incorporate this last type of surplus than against those which embody natural resources, and even without such resistance it would be difficult to find ways to channel a high share of the surplus of unskilled labor towards export goods.

The channeling agent who transforms the surplus of internal resources to exports has often been a foreign company. In extreme cases, the operation converts itself into an enclave, whose demand for national inputs, apart from the resource in excess supply, is minimal. Historical cases of enclaves are associated with mining and agricultural activities, although modern versions can be found in the free zones of Taiwan or the frontier manufacturing of maquila in Mexico.

TRADE, GROWTH, AND DISTRIBUTION

Numerous theoretical frameworks, especially those related to HOS, are available to analyze the impact of an exogenously generated growth on the structure of international trade. However, there are few models in that tradition which attempt to analyze the effect on the rate of growth of greater or lesser involvement in trade. The "triangles" of static theory can be applied to more dynamic situations, but the magnitudes are generally disconcertingly low. The conceptualization of historical experience, especially those based on the countries with extensive open spaces in the nineteenth century, tend to depend on one or another version of the "vent for surplus" theory. One such version, known as the staple product thesis, argues that the characteristics of the production function of the main export good will not only determine the strength of the positive impulses which will be transmitted from exports to growth, but will also determine the political and social characteristics of that growth, including the distribution of income.

Although the staple thesis has a certain explanatory power in Colombian economic history before the Second World War, the increasing diversification of the economy has gradually reduced this. A two gap model, with a dominant foreign trade gap, appears to be the most valid conceptualization of the relationship between commerce and growth in the postwar Colombian economy. A greater inflow of foreign exchange according to this model brings faster growth in all sectors of the economy, in contrast with the HOS model where a growth of exports is accompanied by a diminution of the import substituting sector. In other words, the two gap model supposes, as does the vent for surplus model, that a relative closing of the economy causes a fall in the degree of utilization of resources, not just changes in their real remunerations.

An increased rate of growth generated by a greater flow of foreign exchange, by increasing the demand for labor can diminish structural unemployment (open or disguised). It seems plausible to hope that this may improve the distribution of income though it cannot be taken for granted. It may also be true that faster growth generates fiscal resources which can be utilized in public programs of a redistributive nature.

The positive effects on employment which arise from faster overall growth may be partially compensated by greater imports of machinery and equipment, especially on the part of small and medium businesses which in a regime of quite restricted imports generally face higher effective prices for the purchases of foreign capital goods. The large firms, whose access to import licenses is easier but still limited when there is a shortage of reserves, can also take advantage of the greater import facilities created by an increase in exports to re-equip and modernize their plants. Those which participate in the export push typically argue that such modernization is indispensable in order to maintain a competitive position in foreign markets, and reinforce their requests for imports with foreign credits received in part or supported in part by their demonstrated capacity to earn foreign exchange. Employment and income of certain artisan sectors and agriculture can suffer in absolute terms due to the mechanization facilitated by a greater inflow of foreign exchange. Tractorization, for example, can lead not only to the unemployment of unskilled rural labor, but also to pressures to increase size of already large farms.

The growth induced by a large expansion of exports may have a Schumpeterian flavor, in which case there will exist strong demand for the scarce entrepreneurial and professional resources and unskilled labor, leading to the creation of important quasi-rents which principally benefit the three upper deciles of the income distribution.

ENTRY INTO FOREIGN MARKETS, POLICY INSTRUMENTS, AND THE DISTRIBUTION OF INCOME

The agnosticism which may be derived from a review of the various theories on the distributive impact of a greater involvement in trade is reinforced by consideration of the distributive effects associated with many of the tools which a government has to induce and control that increase. The redistributive effects of greater Colombian exports of sugar, to give an extreme example, will be different from the effect which a greater export of Cuban sugar would have. We have already mentioned the import controls which typically accompany a situation of low trade and scarcity of foreign exchange, and its discriminatory incidence between large and small firms.[4] It is known that such controls, in contrast with

[4] The discriminatory effect can be documented in the Colombian case, see Chapter 6 of C. Diaz-Alejandro, *Foreign Trade Regimes and Economic Development: Colombia* (New York: National Bureau of Economic Research, 1976).

a uniform tariff which implies the same degree of restriction across the board, generates monopolistic profits distributed erratically (from an economic point of view). While in an HOS model for example, a greater restriction, achieved by means of a general tariff increase, can lead to an increase or diminution in the profit rate of all activities in the economy, the institutional reality of controls creates notable dispersions in the profit rate, depending on the degree of monopoly which the system generates. A greater openness of the economy can lead to a dismantling of the most extreme protection and to a reduction in the most exorbitant profit rates, with positive effects (although perhaps not dramatic ones) on the distribution of income.

Just as import substitutions can be pushed by means of selective and ad hoc policies on a sectoral or even a firm-by-firm basis, so can the new exports be. Although the dangers that such methods imply for efficient allocation of resources and the existence of quasi-rents and administrative irregularities on the export side are not strictly symmetrical with those of import substitution, the danger does exist. Here the key categories appear to be not the methods of export promotion as contrasted with those directed at stimulating import substitution, but the use of general as opposed to particular and ad hoc incentives. The complexity and variety of incentives can be an additional factor to be considered in this type of analysis.

In the Colombian case the tools of inducing new exports have been more general and homogeneous than those which stimulated import substitution. Contraband of imports and exports, although it exists and continues, has tended to diminish. In some cases there were "fictitious exports" which took advantage of the differential between the effective exchange rate for exports of goods (including the general subsidy, the certificate of tax rebate) and that corresponding to entrance of unregistered foreign exchange, which was less.

The use of fiscal and credit incentives for the new exports, even when it uses simple and general systems, will have different distributive effects to those which would result from equivalent incentives in value but generated by a higher exchange rate. The exact incidence will depend on the sources of funds used to subsidize the exports, which can include a reduction of other expenditures of the government, income taxes, etc. When the funds come from an *ad valorem* uniform tariff on all imports in order to finance a subsidy, also uniform and at the same level for all exports, the incidence would be identical to that of a higher exchange rate.

THE COLOMBIAN CASE DURING 1967-1974: SOME KEY CHARACTERISTICS

Between 1967 and 1972 Colombian nontraditional exports, measured in current dollars, grew at a rate of nearly 15 percent annually. Between 1972 and 1974 registered exports doubled.[5] These spectacular statistics reflect in part important increases in the dollar prices of Colombia's minor exports, as well as a certain rechanneling of the contraband to neighboring countries and elsewhere into the legal and registered channels. Some of the new exports also incorporate strong doses of foreign inputs, thus exaggerating the flows of foreign trade. But, although quantum indices are not yet available for all of Colombia's new exports, it is obvious that the fundamental explanation for the accelerated growth of nontraditional Colombian exports lies in the vigorous business response to the package of incentives which Colombia has been applying, especially from 1967. In 1974, the nontraditional exports reached more than half the value of total exports; in 1968 they had been less than a third of the total.

The new Colombian exports cover a wide variety of products. During the first semester of 1975, four basic products (cotton, sugar, bananas, and tobacco) constituted about 30 percent of the nontraditional exports; for 1968-70 the corresponding figure was 38 percent. Manufactured goods (branches, CUCI #3–excluding petroleum, 5, 6, 7 and 9) represented a quarter of the new exports, a decline in their share from the 1968-70 level. The rest of the nontraditional exports are composed mainly of raw materials and of agricultural goods.

The increasing diversification is reflected in the number of CUCI categories at the three digit level in which Colombia has had exports in excess of one million dollars (current prices). The number of such categories (excluding coffee and crude petroleum) has been: 9 in 1960; 16 in 1964; 28 in 1968; 33 in 1970 and 45 in 1972.

In is obvious that a fundamental source of Colombia's revealed comparative advantage, thanks to the promotion policy, is the country's richness in natural resources, a richness which had been disguised by the overwhelming productivity of coffee. The explanation for the manufactured exports is less clear. Such exports include, among other products, cement, cotton textiles, liquid ammonium, and herbicides. In some cases, such as in that of corrugated paper boxes, manufactured exports are clearly complementary to some other export (in this case, bananas). In others, manufactured exports incorporate as inputs a high proportion of exportable raw materials, as in the case of cotton textiles. The explanation for the export of goods like cement appears to depend in good measure on advantages of geographic location, cost of transport, and so on. It would be imprudent to try to attribute the expansion of manufactured exports to one source of comparative advantage. Also, as we see later, the characteristics of these exports differ according to their geographic destination.

The relaxation in balance of payments, achieved in good measure by the development of nontraditional exports, has been accompanied during 1967-74 by an acceleration in the rate of overall growth and in that of capital formation.

[5] For the period before 1973 the principal source of data cited in this study is the book mentioned in the previous footnote. For more recent years, we rely on figures, many of them preliminary, of the Instituto de Comercio Exterior de Colombia (INCOMEX).

The gross domestic product (GDP), which during 1956-67 expanded at an annual rate of 4.6 percent, has since 1967 grown at more than 6 percent per year. The expansion has been general, including all the important branches of agricultural production and manufacturing. Available data do not permit one to establish with precision what has happened in terms of income distribution, but there are indications that during the most recent period there have been regressive tendencies in that respect.

It is difficult with available data for macroeconomic analysis to shed greater light on the distributive impact of the new exports. It is desirable to go into detail with respect to the microeconomic characteristics of such exports, which can suggest the possible direction and magnitude of the redistributive impact.

MANUFACTURED EXPORTS: SECTORS, PARTICIPANTS, AND DESTINATION. SOME METHODOLOGICAL PROBLEMS

As has been seen above, the theories of international trade use as basic analytical categories the various sectors of production, and assume identical production functions within each sector but different functions between sectors. A frequently noted characteristic of Colombian industry is the great contrast between the large, medium, and small firms of the same sector (at least at a two digit level of aggregation) in terms of their labor productivity, which presumably reflects different factor proportions or different levels of efficiency or scale economies. Thus, it is important to examine not only the sectoral origin of the manufactured exports, but also the size of firm which produces them. Ideally, it would be interesting to compare the direct and indirect resource utilization of exporting firms with firms which are on the import substitution frontier, that is, those producing goods most similar to imports which would be candidates for substitution had the new exports not been developed. Here we must note a curious fact: with great frequency the large firms which export are also active in the import substitution area and even on the frontier of that process. It is rare, indeed, to find an exporting company which dedicates itself totally to sales abroad. Under these circumstances it is problemmatic not only to use averages taken from an input-output table by industrial sector, which may or may not reflect the reality of the exporting and import substituting firms, but even to use firm input averages, since ideally it would be desirable to distinguish within the firm's accounting how it assigns costs (especially fixed costs) among the various branches of production.

It can be documented that Colombia's industrial exports have been concentrated in a relatively small number of firms, at least in their initial state. Thus, 24 firms contributed 62 percent of the industrial exports (excluding sugar) in 1970. Of these companies, 10 were foreign owned; by themselves they accounted for 27 percent of the industrial exports of that year. Though these firms were the largest exporters, for the group as a whole imports exceeded exports. Their average size was far above the average for industry as a whole.

In a study carried out the by Banco de la Republica in 1971 and limited to firms with at least some foreign capital, in seven of eight industrial sectors analyzed firms which exported were much larger than those which did not. While the average for all exporting firms was 314 workers, for nonexporters it was 135 workers. Of all exports made by the firms included in the study, 57 percent corresponded to those of 200 workers and up.[6]

In summary, it can be said that a good part of Colombia's industrial exports come from large firms which, be they of national or foreign ownership, tend to use capital, skilled labor, and imports in greater proportions than does industry as a whole, and probably in proportions not too dissimilar from those used by the firms on the frontier of import substitution, excluding perhaps some extreme cases.

The impact of the new exports on the composition of input demand depends not only on the industrial sector from which they originate and the entrepreneur who undertakes them, but also on their geographic destination. Colombia's new manufacturing exports to LAFTA show, for 1970, the clear tendency to be more intensive in the use of capital and imported inputs than those destined for the rest of the world. A strong presence of foreign firms in exports to LAFTA is also notable.

It may be argued that not only the phenomenon of concentration of new exports in relatively large firms, but also the differential utilization of inputs according to geographic destination may be due to erroneous trade policy, or may characterize only the earlier phases of the export promotion process. It is true that in the policy package designed to give incentives to new exports there have been some biases in favor of large firms and of exports which are intensive in imported inputs and capital. For example, the Vallejo Plan (the principal drawback system in Colombia) imposes requirements whose fulfillment is difficult for small and medium sized firms. The compelementation agreements with LAFTA have been limited to industries of high capital intensity. Even when erroneous trade policies have been overcome, their legacy may be a biased industrial structure which generates a type of export designed to take advantage of excess capacity at least during the first stages of the new process.

The information and experience in Colombia does not permit a complete evaluation of these arguments, which would imply a greater optimism on the longer run income distribution impact of the new exports. Up to now, though, there is no evidence of a tendency towards deconcentration of manufactured exports, nor of an increase in the relative importance of items which are more intensive in unskilled labor. The final influence of the Andean group and LAFTA on Colombia's manufactured exports also remains to be seen. Few businessmen have shown interest in becoming completely specialized in the foreign market; a prudent diversification between the relatively captive internal market and a

[6] The study is entitled "Exportaciones Manufacturados por empresas con inversion extranjera directa," Julio, 1973 (Mimeographed).

foreign one which absorbs varying excesses sold, if necessary, at marginal cost appears to be the ideal of the industrial businessman at the moment.

NEW AGRICULTURAL AND MINING EXPORTS

The information on inputs used by these new exports, as well as on the size of the productive units involved, is even more deficient than that corresponding to manufactured exports. Nevertheless, there remains the general impression that on average the new agricultural exports use less labor per unit of value added than the major traditional export, coffee. Further, it would appear that land utilized in this last crop is more equally distributed among producers than that used in the production of cotton, sugar, and beef cattle, to give some examples. Possible mineral exports, such as coal and nickel, require large investments per worker employed, including infrastructural needs. It is predicted that these operations will be undertaken jointly by the state and foreign capital.

It is necessary to emphasize, nevertheless, the great heterogeneity of the exports, and the probable dispersion and differences which exist in their cost and ownership structures. Activities like production of carnations and vegetables for export, as well as the production of emeralds, appear to be closer to coffee than to cotton in their implicit demand for labor.

It may be supposed that the expansion of new agricultural exports will induce a reallocation of land from crops for nontraded goods to those used to produce traded goods, thus transmitting the relative price increases generated by the greater involvement in trade to all agricultural goods. It is also logical to presume that the market basket of the lower income groups has a greater weight of agricultural products, particularly those which in Colombia are relatively nontradable, such as potatoes and yucca. This situation will naturally generate regressive pressures on the distribution of income, which can reach quantitatively important dimensions.

As has already been indicated, expansion of exportable crops with large utilization of land and a high degree of mechanization tends to physically displace small producers from their plots, not always via equitable arrangements. The contribution of these large units to exports and their apparent efficiency are arguments brandished with great effectiveness against plans to achieve a more equitable distribution of agrarian poverty.

The characteristics of the internal and external trade of the new agriculturally exported goods plays also an important role in the distribution (national and international) of income derived directly from those exports. But on this matter available information is almost nil.

SOME FINAL CONSIDERATIONS

Not only theory but institutional details appear to suggest the same conclusions: there is no clear and unequivocal relation between foreign trade policies and the distribution of income. In the Colombian case a healthy number of positive effects may be cataloged, and negative ones as well; available information does not permit any trustworthy conclusions as to the net balance. The impression, nevertheless, would appear to be that the balance, whether it be positive or negative, would not alter Colombia's income distribution a great deal. This impression is reinforced on considering the fraction of gross national product which would be potentially influenced by foreign trade policies—in other words, the maximum and minimum limits which would be realistic to expect Colombia's economic openness or autarchy to reach. As of 1974, Colombia's minor exports were about 7 percent of GDP; domestic value added in the production of those exports was perhaps about 6 percent spread among the various sectors of the economy (manufacturing, agriculture, commerce, etc.). The combination of factor inputs involved in the production of 6 percent of GDP is unlikely to be so atypical as to change the relative demands for the various inputs in the aggregate. While the ratio of domestic value added in new exports to GDP might with a more pro-export policy range up to 12-15 percent, it would still seem unrealistic to expect a great impact on distribution, unless the existence of such exports had a substantial general effect by some channel such as a reduction in monopoly profits through increased competition. In any case, our earlier discussion gives no grounds for expecting the distributional effect to be positive in Colombia.

Few, or no one, has suggested that the principal contribution of foreign trade policy be the improvement of income distribution; and some have specifically cautioned against high expectations for its distributional effects, e.g. Donald Keesing, "Income Distribution from Outward-Looking Development Policies," *Pakistan Development Review*, Vol. XIII, No. 2 (Summer, 1974). Our tentative conclusion should therefore not be interpreted as a criticism of export promotion, whose success in raising the rate of growth of the Colombian economy is undeniable. It is rare to find a situation where a single policy can advance the system dramatically in terms of several disparate goals, and it is dangerous to use such a hope in order to sell some policy suggestion.

The world recession of 1974-75 has tested the solidity and resistance of the new Colombian exports. According to preliminary data, nontraditional exports will be maintained in 1975 at levels approximating those reached in 1974, measured in current dollars. It is interesting to note, nevertheless, that this overall behavior appears to be accompanied by a substantial fall in manufactured exports, made up by other nontraditional exports.[7]

Finally, two interesting themes related to our discussion (and which have generally been ignored) may be briefly mentioned. One is the question of the distributive effects of the international financial relationships which accompany a greater trade openness towards the exterior, including not only direct investment but also the entrance and exit of foreign financial capital. The second inverts the question raised in this study, and considers the possible effects on nontraditional exports of an internal redistribution policy.

[7] Estimates of FEDESARROLLO, *Coyuntura Economica* Vol. 6 (April, 1976), p. 93.

Chapter 7

EMPLOYMENT AND DISTRIBUTION EFFECTS OF TOURISM

David L. Roberts
Rice University

Colombia's 1971 Development Plan states that the importance of tourism "may be measured by reference to three economic indicators: generation of foreign exchange and its influence on the balance of payments, generation of employment and its importance for regional development, and lastly the redistribution of income as a balancing factor in development."[1] The present and potential importance of tourism in Colombia's economy calls for an extensive examination, including both theoretical and empirical analyses to comprehend its impact. This paper attempts to establish a framework for this analysis and to use the available data to understand some aspects of the impact of tourism on regional incomes, employment, and income distribution. The first section discusses a conceptual framework for analyzing tourism in the general case. Several important distinctions among sources of tourist income and of investments in tourism, short- and long-run effects of tourism, and possible roles of the state in promoting tourism are noted. The second section assembles the available data to take a general look at the tourism industry and potential tourist resources in Colombia and to estimate the economic effects of tourism on the three economic indicators mentioned in the 1971 development plan. A final section offers some tentative conclusions.

1. A CONCEPTUAL FRAMEWORK

It is useful to begin with some stylized facts. Tourism is a regional industry, concentrated in areas possessing interesting historical or natural resources, which are often located in depressed regions of the country; these resources are com-

[1] Departamento Nacional de Planeación, *Plan de Desarrollo: Turismo*, 1971, p. iii (author's translation).

bined with domestic and foreign inputs of fixed capital (e.g., hotels, restaurants, airports), skilled and unskilled labor and intermediate goods (liquor, food) to produce a flow of tourist services. Outputs are generally consumed by nonlocals who may be either nationals from other regions or foreigners. Purchases by nationals affect regional incomes; purchases by foreigners also provide foreign exchange. Expenditures by tourists accrue to foreign and domestic property owners, workers and governments, and thus influence the factor and size distribution of incomes. Incomes are affected during both the construction and use phases of tourist operations. Growth of the industry is financed by private and public funds attracted from domestic or foreign sources. Growth may occur incrementally, largely utilizing existing infrastructure, or may require large investments in new roads, airports, water treatment plants, even towns to house workers in the industry. Expenditures by tourists might have multiplier effects on other sectors of the regional or national economy. The actual employment and distributive effects of tourism, therefore, depend on at least five considerations:

- i the types of capital (public or private, fixed or working, foreign or domestic) used to expand tourism,
- ii the breakdown of tourists between domestic and foreign,
- iii the source of financing (domestic or foreign),
- iv the regional structure of tourism employment, and
- v multiplier effects of tourist expenditures.

Results may also differ between the short and the longer run.

The distinctions among the kinds of capital required to finance an expansion of the tourist industry are quite important. It is sufficient to analyze three overlapping distinctions: incremental vs. discrete, superstructure vs. infrastructure,[2] and private vs. public investments. Investments are incremental if they involve relatively small demands on the existing infrastructure. The construction of an additional hotel in a large city or in an established tourist area does not require large investments in social overhead capital (infrastructure). If already existing infrastructure exhibits increasing returns to scale, additional tourists lower the long-run marginal costs of providing these goods. This argument applies to airports and roads which have been built with excess capacity, so that increased tourism implies that the demand curve for these goods shifts out toward the point of minimum long-run average costs. Conversely, if infrastructure is already operating beyond the point of minimum costs (as is often the case in developing countries) diseconomies will result.

Tourism projects may be termed discrete if they require large investments in

[2]In this paper, "superstructure" refers to facilities used directly and exclusively by the tourist; "infrastructure" refers to social overhead capital used by the industry which also benefits local residents and businesses. For example, hotels, restaurants and roads or airports used exclusively or almost exclusively for tourism are superstructure while regional airports or fresh-water supplies shared by the region are included in infrastructure. In practice, superstructure is usually privately owned and financed; infrastructure is always public.

social overhead capital. This investment in infrastructure can radically change the employment and capital intensity characteristics of tourism. As a rough example, if a project requires investments in infrastructure equal and in addition to the investment in superstructure, and if both investments have the same service life, then the capital investment per unit of output (e.g., per hotel room) has doubled, although the employment required to operate the project has increased very little (since social overhead capital typically requires few laborers to operate).

The fact that tourism generates employment during both the construction and use phases of the investment adds complexity to the measurement of its employment and distributive effects. The labor-capital ratio of a steady state tourist industry, with a constant amount of depreciated infrastructure and superstructure replaced each year, would be appropriately defined as the sum of the amount of employment generated per dollar expended on construction divided by the length of life of the project plus the employment generated in the use phase, i.e.:

$$SS_{L/K} = \left(\frac{L_c}{N} + L_o\right)/K \tag{1}$$

where $SS_{L/K}$ is the steady-state/capital ratio, L_c is labor employed in the construction phase, N is the lifetime of the project, L_o is labor employed in the output phase, and K is the total infrastructure and superstructure cost of the project. However, when large-scale discrete investments to raise the total capital stock in tourism are contemplated, the labor/capital ratio corresponding to the steady-state does not provide the necessary information. Employment and L/K will vary over time. For planning purposes it is desirable to be able, nevertheless, to compare projects' employment creation capacities on the basis of single numbers; such a number must take account of employment created in the early construction phases and that generated later during the operations phase. Equation 2 suggests a time-discounted approach:

$$TD_{L/K} = \left\{ \sum_{i=1}^{N} L_i(1 + r)^{-i}/N \right\} /K \tag{2}$$

where L_i is the employment generated either in construction or operation in the ith period, and r is the appropriate social discount rate. This measure explicitly introduces time into the decision function. The discount rate reflects society's preference for present over future employment creation. If planners expect the labor market to be tighter in the future, they would presumably choose a positive discount rate.

Another important distinction is that between domestic and foreign tourism. Since the consumption benefits of tourism accrue to middle-and upper-income families, public expenditures to develop domestic tourism are justifiable on distributional grounds only if the distribution of gains to factors of production has a sufficiently positive effect on overall distribution to counterbalance these benefit effects. In the case of foreign tourism, we are not interested in the distribution of benefit effects since these affect only foreigners. Similarly, the diversion of consumption expenditures by foreigners from other sectors to tourism will affect only that foreign economy;[3] since we are interested in the Colombian economy, we need not worry about these matters. On the other hand, if domestic tourism increases, other sectors within Colombia will be affected, with consequent employment and distributive reverberations.

To finance a vacation a family must reduce its purchases of other goods and services, thus reducing output and employment in other sectors. The demand shifts induce shifts of both labor and investment into the tourist industry and region. Assuming that the patterns of expenditures of persons do not depend on the sector in which they earn their income, the full effects of a demand shift are predictable from its direct effects. For example, if vacationing families forego restaurant meals, maid services, durable goods purchases, and so on, in order to finance their vacation, the capital-output and labor-output ratios in each foregone activity weighted by the appropriate proportion of foregone expenditures in the vacationer's budget yield measures which are comparable with the additions to employment and income in the tourist region. Whether total demand for labor increases is not obvious; vacationers will forego those goods and services which have a high cross-elasticity with tourism and it is possible that these goods have higher labor-capital ratios than tourism.

Two other points related to domestic tourism are germane. First, domestic tourists consume a different product than do foreign tourists. They generally bring fairly large families, consume meals in their rooms or in inexpensive restaurants and do not share the beaches and other tourist facilities with foreigners. The services they purchase may or may not be more labor-intensive than those favored by foreign tourists. Since their peak vacation periods largely coincide with foreign vacations, domestic tourism cannot be expected to be concentrated during slack periods of foreign tourist demand; so provision of domestic tourist facilities is not complementary with foreign tourism in this sense. If the provision of luxury facilities for foreigners induced many wealthy domestic families to take their vacations at home, its foreign exchange impact could be comparable to that of foreign tourism. But the motivation of the large number of wealthy domestic families who go abroad for holidays is often to purchase clothes and durable goods to bring home, so they may be unwilling to forego their trips abroad.

Second, any inducement to domestic tourism is likely to affect the level and timing of private saving. A rightward shift in the supply of tourism services could lead to either an increase or decrease in the expenditure on this item (depending on whether price elasticity of demand is less or greater than one) and could affect long-term savings either way. It may also affect the level of short-term (e.g., seasonal) savings. The major portion of vacations must be financed from previous savings or by obtaining credit. Some families finance vacations by accumulating a fund throughout the year, thus increasing the rate of personal saving.

[3] Exchange rate changes resulting from changes in the flow of foreign tourism would affect the Colombian economy; however, since they would probably be of small magnitude they may safely be neglected.

For example, if a family dedicates 5 percent of its income to a vacation, the average level of this savings fund over the course of the year is about 2.5 percent of the year's income. Other families divert funds from the purchase of durable goods or other items which require a larger accumulation of funds before the expenditure is made; their average savings over the course of the year will be lowered. Finally, many families finance a substantial portion of their vacations with credit, which reduces personal savings. Which of these tendencies dominates is an empirical question on which we have as yet no information.

The source of finance for tourism projects is another issue of concern. If the industry is financed domestically, or if foreign funds would have entered the country regardless of the presence of a given project, then the project's benefits must be compared with the potential productivity (and distributional effects) of the resources in the uses to which they would otherwise be put. When foreign funds which would not otherwise have been available are used, there is a net addition to resources available to be paid for by a net outflow of profit and interest remittances in the future, calling for a more complex comparison between benefits and costs. Demand for labor will be increased during the construction phase and decreased as profits are remitted. In addition, there could be dynamic effects whereby, for example, foreign investment might raise productive capacity so that its net effect on future as well as current national income would be positive. In this context it is necessary also to consider any effects which the use of foreign capital may have on the capital intensity of the investment.[4]

The expansion of tourism can, clearly, have an effect on the regional structure of employment. Potential tourist areas often suffer severe underemployment.[5] Whether tourism can substantially alleviate this problem depends on how well the available unemployed labor meshes with the structure of employment in tourism. The total employment created by even a large tourist project will tend to be small relative to underemployment in the tourist region.[6] A large propor-

[4]This issue has no clear answer yet in the sectors where it has been researched (mainly manufacturing).

[5]For example, in Barranquilla the unemployment rate was estimated at 16.0% (Dec., 1966), 18.4% (Oct. 1967), 15.4% (Nov., 1971), 12.6% (Sept.-Oct., 1972), 19.3% (June, 1974). Only in 1976 has it ever been recorded as low as 11%. In Sept.-Oct., 1972, the rate in Cartagena was measured as 16.8%. Other major cities, meanwhile, tend to have lower rates, frequently in the range 8-12% and tending to average not far from 10%. (See, for example, DANE, *Boletin Mensual de Estadistica* #300, Julio 1976, p. 300.)

[6]For example, the large tourism project envisioned for the north coast of Colombia would provide an estimated 20,500 jobs in 1990 (Corporación Nacional de Turismo, *Action Plan for Tourism Projects in the Caribbean Coast of Colombia and San Andres Islands*, Vol. II [Bogotá, July 1972, p. 67]). This represents about two percent of total regional employment in 1970 and a small fraction of the expected increase in both employment and underemployment between 1970 and 1990. (The ILO projects five million new jobs must be created to reduce unemployment in Colombia to 5% by 1985. See International Labor Office, *Towards Full Employment: A Programme for Colombia* [Geneva: ILO, 1970].) An empirical estimate of the opportunity cost of increasing regional employment through tourism is presented in section 2. Many of the jobs in the tourist industry will not benefit unemployed or underemployed persons in the region.

tion of the permanent jobs in the tourist industry require skilled, bilingual persons who may be either foreigners or migrants from other regions. The seasonal nature of tourism implies that many persons will only be employed for part of the year. They may be students from the more developed regions, local urban inhabitants, or rural dwellers attracted from agriculture. Further, since the tourist season generally coincides with the peak agricultural season, the opportunity for combining agricultural and tourist activities would be small and the result could be a decrease in average year-round agricultural underemployment accompanied by an increase in open unemployment in the tourist area during the off-season.

The indirect impact of tourist expenditures on employment and incomes has been the subject of some controversy. However, second (and subsequent) round increases in output can be expected only if there is excess capacity in industries experiencing an increase in demand.

Where excess productive capacity does not exist, these Keynesian "multiplier effects" do not occur. Any secondary increase in output usually requires a concomitant increase in investment, which presumably implies that investment in some other sector will decrease. The final effect of an investment in tourism on employment depends on the relative capital-labor ratios between tourism and the industries which are stimulated by the growth of tourism as compared with the sectors where investments are decreased. It is quite possible that tourist expenditures may increase the demand for products like beef or milk, both of which are more capital-intensive in production than most agricultural products, and which must be kept in capital-intensive refrigerated storerooms. Nor will expenditures of tourism employees necessarily increase secondary employment. If the marginal propensity to import and consume capital-intensive goods of these employees is greater than the economy-wide average, total employment will tend to fall. Due to these shifts in investments it seems possible that the "tourism employment multiplier" could be negative for the national economy, although it probably would be positive for the tourism region itself.[7]

These theoretical considerations suggest that the influence of the tourism industry on employment, incomes and foreign exchange may depend very much upon the type of tourism. Large projects, financed domestically, requiring major infrastructure and/or superstructure investments, and attracting tourists who tend to purchase import and capital-intensive goods may be an expensive method of encouraging regional development.

[7]The controversy over the importance of the tourism multiplier was opened in the Zinder Report (Zinder and Associates, *The Future of Tourism in the Eastern Caribbean*, May 1969) and continued in K. Levitt and C. Iqbal, "Income Effects of Tourist Spending; Mystification Multiplied, A Critical Comment on the Zinder Report," *Social and Economic Studies* (September, 1970); and J. Bryden and N. Faber, "Multipliers and the Tourism Multiplier," *Social and Economic Studies* (December, 1970).

2. THE COLOMBIAN TOURISM INDUSTRY

This section marshalls the available evidence on the actual and potential structure of Colombian tourism to serve two purposes: to give the reader a "feel" for the magnitudes of various aspects of tourism in Colombia, and to present empirical data relevant for the theoretical issues addressed in the preceding section. Due to the normal data limitations, part of the evidence presented is impressionistic; still, some interesting results emerge.

Colombian tourism is a fairly large and rapidly growing industry. The two basic estimates of the level of foreign tourism, prepared by the Banco de la República and the Corporación Nacional de Turismo (CNT), diverge widely with respect to the annual number, expenditures, and growth rate of tourists; but both imply that tourism is a significant and increasing export industry. The CNT counts the number of tourist cards issued, overestimating the actual number of tourists by the number of businessmen and others who choose to travel under a tourist visa. In 1969, the CNT increased its estimate of average expenditures per tourist from U.S. $20 to U.S. $30 per day, and of the average length of stay from 5 to 7 days. Since the real exchange rate did not change at that time, the reason for these adjustments is not apparent. In any case, the rule of thumb approach is necessarily arbitrary, reflecting the lack of information about variations in the composition of demand. On the other hand, the Banco applies a fixed coefficient (about 50 percent) to the estimate of total foreign visitors supplied by DANE (the Central Statistical Agency) to estimate the number of tourists. To estimate tourist expenditures the Banco applies a differential measure by country of origin, averaging $28.50 (U. S. 1974 prices) per day for a five-day stay. This figure agrees with the independent estimate obtained by the Arthur D. Little and Integral Consultants in their study of tourism in the Colombian Caribbean.[8]

Table 7.1 presents both sets of estimates, together with a compromise which combines the CNT's estimate of the number of foreign tourists, arbitrarily reduced by 10 percent to reflect the overestimate of tourists, with the Banco's estimate of expenditure per foreign tourist and length of stay. The compromise estimate indicates that foreign tourist expenditures grew at an average rate of 16.5 percent per year, that expenditures increased at a significantly faster absolute rate in the late 1960s, and that this tourism is subject to considerable cyclic variation. The variation coincides with changes in the state of the U. S. economy. Since tourism is a luxury good, this procyclic variation, which has continued into the 1970s, is not surprising. These data are not by themselves sufficient to predict future trends in tourism. It may meet capacity constraints, tastes may change, the high growth rate may reflect the small base of 1960, etc. Still, it appears that even in the absence of strong governmental promotion, foreign tourism is a growth industry.

[8] Corporación Nacional de Turismo, *Action Plan, op. cit.*

TABLE 7.1

Year	No. of Tourists			Tourist Expenditures			Percent change of tourist expenditures (compromise estimate)
	CNT	BANCO	Compromise	CNT	BANCO (U.S. $1000s)	Compromise	
1960	42,735	47,872	38,462	3,419	7,985	5,480	
1961	54,329	51,772	48,896	3,346	8,580	6,968	27
1962	70,218	36,878	63,196	5,617	6,064	9,005	29
1963	78,936	45,462	71,042	6,315	7,546	10,123	12
1964	77,337	44,841	69,603	9,667	7,436	9,918	−2
1965	79,196	53,437	71,276	9,900	8,889	10,157	2
1966	93,744	65,468	84,370	11,718	10,890	12,023	18
1967	106,095	71,555	98,186	22,280	11,882	13,992	16
1968	139,429	94,761	125,486	29,280	18,623	17,882	28
1969	142,585	90,100	128,327	29,943	17,670	18,286	2
1970	161,668	96,600	145,501	33,950	18,976	20,733	13
1971	197,503		177,753	41,476		25,330	22

Source: Fedesarrollo, Coyuntura Economica, Vol. II, No. 4, p. 128, Table X-1.

Although yearly estimates of tourist arrivals are unavailable for the recent period, tourism in Colombia, as in other countries, continues to vary. Although private investors in luxury hotels may be expected to assess the risks of their investments and absorb the losses of a fall in demand, large tourist projects involving social infrastructure investments imply that some risks will be borne by the public sector. As an example, the large-scale tourism project projected for Cartegena and Santa Marta involved an expenditure of over U.S. $65 million of government funds for the period 1972-77, representing 66 percent of total investments in Caribbean Coast tourism.[9]

Neither tourists nor the outputs of the tourist industry are homogeneous. North Americans (32 percent of foreign tourists in 1970) are typically individuals and couples preferring luxury or first-class accomodations. In contrast Central and South Americans (52 percent) usually travel in family groups and seek modest accomodations, as do Europeans (14 percent).[10] Thus, if a recession occurs in North America, it is difficult to utilize the expensive hotels for other tourists.

One of the major costs of tourism is for transportation to and from the vacation area. Colombia is disadvantaged in this respect since most other Caribbean locales are located significantly closer to North America. The minimum round-trip airfare to Colombia is roughly 25 percent above the fare to Jamaica, Mexico, or Puerto Rico.[11] Since the demand for tourism appears to be price elastic,[12] Colombia must offer tourists facilities at considerably lower prices. Since discrete investments in tourism require large infrastructure and superstructure investments, and since the real cost of capital in Colombia may well be greater than that of other Caribbean countries,[13] it may be difficult for Colombia to achieve real costs as low as those competitors; the main cost advantage is in the currently lower wage rates.

A reasonable estimate of the direct effects of tourist expenditures on the demand for labor and on factor incomes would require three types of information. First, knowledge of the types of expenditures by the typical foreign or domestic tourist. This information could be combined with capital/output ratios for each type of good or service to yield the investment required to support each

[9]Due to the availability of the Arthur D. Little study of the Costa Atlantica project many of the examples and estimates refer to this area. The results are intended to have wider applicability.

[10]Corporación Nacional de Turismo, *Action Plan*, Vol. III. Ch. XIII.

[11]Colombia's relative disadvantage continues to the present time (1979) despite increased discounting and price rates competition by Caribbean airlines.

[12]An IMF study estimates the price elasticity of European tourism by North Americans as about −2.6. See Jacques R. Artar, "An Econometric Analysis of European Travel," IMF *Staff Papers*, XIX, 3 (November, 1972), pp. 570-614.

[13]It is difficult to find reliable estimates of comparative capital costs. Casual empiricism indicates that countries such as Venezuela, and probably Puerto Rico and Mexico, with their relatively high per capita incomes and wage rates, have lower opportunity costs of capital than Colombia.

dollar of tourist expenditure. Finally, knowledge of capital/labor ratios for each spending category would indicate the employment associated with a dollar of expenditure, according to the simple relationship: labor per dollar of spending equals the capital/output ratio times the labor/capital ratio, each category weighted by its share in total expenditures. These estimates would then have to be contrasted with comparable figures for the alternative uses of the capital in question. Unfortunately, not all of the necessary data for this calculation are available. In fact, neither the composition of expenditures nor the capital-output ratios for all components of tourist expenditures can be directly calculated. Therefore, this paper offers a series of surrogate computations, intended to shed some qualitative light on the issues.

To begin, assume that the distribution of foreign tourists' expenditures in Colombia is similar to that estimated by the World Bank for the Ixtapa project in Mexico: accomodation–34 percent; food and beverages–27 percent; entertainment–10 percent; local transport–10 percent; other purchases–12 percent; miscellaneous–7 percent.[14] There is no reason to suppose that the expenditure pattern in Colombia departs dramatically from these figures. Thus, since accommodation and food represent both the bulk of expenditures and the primary use of capital and labor employed in the industry, it is important to examine these sectors with some care.

Table 7.2 presents estimates of the demand for labor services generated by investments in each component of tourist expenditures and some alternative investment categories. The information requires a number of clarifying remarks. "Variant 1" is based on equation 1 in the previous section, the steady-state model. "Variant 2" is based on equation 2, the time discounted approach. Since the "proper" discount factor is unknown, two possibilities are offered–10 percent and 15 percent. Both capital expenditures and labor services are discounted at the same rate.[15] Variant 2 is projected over an arbitrary thirty-year horizon. The impact of employment generated farther in the future is negligible when discounted to the present. No repair costs or working capital requirements are included; in effect all assets have a thirty-year one-horse-shay life span. Variant 1 presents the flow of man-years per year and Variant 2 the discounted stock of man-years over a thirty-year period; thus, the numbers are not directly comparable. At any rate, only comparisons among row entries are necessary.

Despite the cited data problems the figures suggest some interesting possibilities. By the steady-state method of weighting the employment effects, large investments in either superstructure or superstructure plus infrastructure appear to demand less labor services than equal investments in manufacturing. The contrast between cottage manufacturing and superstructure plus infrastructure is especially

[14] International Bank for Reconstruction and Development, *The Zihuatenejo Project, Mexico* (1971), Annex 1, p. 9. Document for internal circulation.

[15] Capital expenditures are assumed to occur over a ten-year construction phase. The distribution of these expenditures over time are assumed to be the same as those given in the *Action Plan*.

TABLE 7.2. Labor-Capital Ratios: Demand for Labor Services (Man-years) Generated by U. S. $1,000,000 Investment

	Superstructure[1]	Superstructure plus infra-structrue[1]	Food[1] and beverages[2]
Variant 1 (steady-state)	192	108	663
Variant 2 (discounted at 10%)	3852	1772	6349
Variant 2 (discounted at 15%)	3103	1269	4386

	Local transportation[2]	Manufactures[2]	Services[2]
Variant 1	113	230	461
Variant 2 (10%)	1082	2202	4415
Variant 2 (15%)	748	1522	3050

	Manufacturing[3]				
	Factory	Cottage shop	Total	Food[3]	Economy-wide[3]
Variant 1	127	1698	328	128	292
Variant 2 (10%)	1216	16,260	3141	1220	2796
Variant 2 (15%)	840	11,234	2170	847	1932

[1] Weighted average of projected three phases of the Costa Atlantica development. *Source:* Corporación Nacional de Turismo, *Action Plan for Colombian Tourism Projects*, Vol. I, Table II-3; Vol. III, Table XII-6. For Variant 2 both labor services and capital investments are discounted at the same (10% or 15%) discount rate. Estimates include fixed capital investments only; they include both operating and construction employment. One-third of construction employment is assumed applicable to superstructure. Assumed exchange rate 21 pesos per dollar.

[2] *Source: Aspectos Cuantitativos del Plan de Desarrollo*, Tables II-2 and II-8. Includes direct and indirect labor service and fixed capital requirements. Food and Beverages weights food 80%, beverages 20%. Assumed exchange rate: 17.5 pesos per dollar.

[3] *Source*: A. Berry, "Trade and Income Distribution Over Time: Colombia" (Mimeo, 1969).

Notes: The first two columns are derived from the *Action Plan* report. The superstructure entries are based on direct and indirect investment and employment in hotels, restaurants and other tourist facilities, without including any infrastructure investments. Employment included some persons operating infrastructure, such as airport employees, since these were not disaggregated in the available data. They also assign one-third of the total persons employed in construction to superstructure construction. Underlying data did not distinguish employment in superstructure from infrastructure employment (e.g., airport employees). This biases the labor content of superstructure upward. The exclusion of working capital also biases these estimates upwards.

The next four columns are obtained from *Aspectos Cuantitativos del Plan de Desarrollo.* These data reflect average rather than marginal capital-output and labor-output ratios. Incremental capital-output ratios are presumably higher, due to the greater capital intensity of new projects, perhaps especially in manufacturing. On the other hand, new projects may use both labor and capital more efficiently, with unclear results for labor-capital ratios. Further, since the data do not include labor employed in the associated construction and capital goods industries, while including direct and indirect fixed capital, they underestimate total employment. Since these biases are offsetting in sign, although of unknown magnitude, we may assume them to be roughly comparable to the information on tourist facilities. The columns headed "Food," "Manufactuirng," and "Economy-wide" are taken from Berry, *op. cit.*, in which his methodology is discussed. The discrepancy between his "Total Manufacturing" and the "Manufactures" of the *Aspectos Cuantitativos* probably reflects the virtual exclusion of cottage-shop manufacturing from the latter's estimates.

striking. However, by either time-discounted measure the conclusion is not so strong. Using the 15 percent discount rate, which heavily weights construction employment, manufacturing appears to provide significantly more employment than the large tourism projects included under superstructure plus infrastructure, despite the omission of construction employment from the manufacturing calculations.[16] On the other hand, the discounted figures indicate that investment only in superstructure demands more labor services than manufacturing and about the same as services.

The other components of tourist expenditures such as transportation and factory manufactures (e.g., souvenirs), with the exception of food and beverages, provide less employment per dollar invested than the economy-wide average. This suggests that capital invested in the ancillary activities of tourism will tend to provide less employment than in an alternative use. Of course, this does not mean that these investments will not positively affect regional employment. This depends on the alternative use of the capital, whether within the region or outside.

Labor-services/capital ratios illuminate only one aspect of the employment impact of tourist investment. A further important question relates to the labor-services demanded by tourist expenditures, that is, the labor/output ratio. The labor services/capital ratio indicates the relative effectiveness of tourism in generating employment. If this ratio is sufficiently high, the government should encourage investments in the sector. The labor services/output ratio serves as an index of the expected growth of employment in the industry. A higher than average labor/output ratio indicates that, even in the absence of special governmental consideration, as tourism expands it will absorb an increasing fraction of regional employment. By applying projected growth rates of demand to the labor/output ratio, the potential of tourism for reducing regional unemployment may be estimated.

In principle the labor/output ratio for tourism can be computed by estimating the labor-services/output ratio of each component of tourist expenditures and obtaining an overall measure as an average of each component weighted by its share in total expenditures. Regrettably a reasonable estimate of this ratio is even more difficult to obtain than the labor services/capital ratio. However, in view of the importance of this measure it is worthwhile to make a reasonable attempt to estimate it in the best available fashion.

Table 7.3 summarizes the results of this exercise. To begin, assume that the composition of expenditures in Colombia is the same as that calculated for the Ixtapa project in Mexico previously mentioned. The remaining problem is to estimate the labor-output ratio for each component. For most components the *Aspectos Cuantitativos* volume provides estimates of labor/output ratios, although

[16]Note that the capital intensity of manufacturing depends greatly on whether small "cottage shop" activities are included. When they are, physical capital/worker appears to be a little below the economy-wide average (as of 1969). When only the factory sector (defined here as plants with five or more workers) is included, the K/L ratio is a little over twice that of the economy as a whole.

TABLE 7.3. Labor Services Demanded per (U.S.) $1,000,000 of Tourist Expenditures

Category	% of Tourist expenditures	Labor Services/ output	Capital/ output	Labor/ capital
Food (L)[1]	.27	382		
Food and Beverages (H)[2,3]	.27	520.9		
Accommodation (H)	.34	1599.3	8.33[6]	192[8]
Accommodation (L)	.34	540.1	5.00[7]	108[8]
Local Transport[2]	.10	207.0		
Entertainment[2,4]	.10	605.3		
Other Purchases[2,5]	.12	207.0		
Miscellaneous[2,4]	.10	605.3		
Tourist Expenditures[9] (H)	1.00	846		
Tourist Expenditures[9] (L)	1.00	453		
Mass Consumption Goods[10]		469		
Cottage Shop Mfg.[1]		2966		
Whole Economy[1]		946		

[1] *Source:* A. Berry, "Trade and Income Distribution," Table 1.

[2] *Source: Aspectos Cuantitativos del Plan de Desarrollo (op. cit.)* Table II-2. Converting pesos to dollars at 16.5:1.

[3] Weighting Food–80%, Beverages–20%. Assuming no food is imported.

[4] Using the labor-output entry for services as a proxy.

[5] Using "manufacturas diversas" as a proxy.

[6] Using the Jimenez estimate for housing services as a proxy.

[7] Assuming that a net pre-tax return on capital of 20% implies a capital-output ratio of 5.

[8] *Source:* Table 7.2.

[9] Combining the Labor-services/output ratios of column 2 with the weights of Column 1.

[10] "Mass Consumption Goods" is defined by *Aspectos Cuantitativos* (p. 16) as an unweighted average of the sectors of agriculture, food, beverages, tobacco, clothing, furniture, publishing, housing and urban services. This method implicitly weights furniture, publishing, and tobacco as over 30% of consumer demand. These sectors are not labor-intensive. Thus, the category is biased downward.

these estimates are subject to biases analogous to those previously mentioned (see Table 7.3: Notes) concerning its labor-services/capital ratios. For example, due to the greater import and capital-content of processed food and beverages consumed by tourists, we would expect the economy-wide averages in the *Aspectos Cuantitativos* to overestimate the labor services/output ratio of tourists' consumption. By contrast, the entry for "Food" obtained from the Berry paper is derived from the national accounts estimate of factory processed food and is, therefore, lower. The other estimates obtained from the *Aspectos Cuantitativos* have similar biases. Nevertheless, they do provide a rough index.

The major obstacle is the estimation of the labor-services/output ratio for accommodation. This is the major component of tourist expenditures and the component for which the least reliable estimates are available. No direct labor-services/output ratio is presented in the *Action Plan* study. Table 7.3 adopts the solution of multiplying the labor/capital ratios of Table 7.2 times a reasonable guess of the capital/output ratio for accommodation. Two approximations are provided. Version 1, the high guess, applies a capital/output ratio for housing services in

Colombia supplied by Jiminez (8.33).[17] This estimate, combined with the superstructure only labor-services/capital ratio, indicates a quite high labor services/output ratio. On the other hand, the capital-services/output ratio in tourist accommodations may be lower than that in housing. The low estimate arbitrarily assumes a capital/output ratio of 5.0 and combines this with the lower superstructure plus infrastructure labor-services/capital ratio. Perhaps the truth lies somewhere between these estimates.

Table 7.3 presents two estimates of the weighted labor services/output ratio in order to represent the extremes of reasonable possibilities. According to the low estimate tourism provides somewhat less employment than either the category "mass consumption goods" of the *Aspectos Cuantitativos*, or the "whole economy" of A. Berry. The high estimate exceeds the "mass consumption goods" estimate but remains less than the "whole economy" figures. Cottage shop manufacturing is clearly more labor-intensive (in this present sense) than tourism. It is reasonable to conclude that tourist expenditures are fairly labor-intensive but not extraordinarily so.

Assuming that the higher the labor/capital ratio of a sector, the more likely its expansion is to improve income distribution, we must conclude that the available data leaves this an open question in the case of tourism. It appears that some types of tourism might be beneficial and other types harmful in this respect. When regional considerations are taken into account, specifically when it is recognized that average wages are lower in the Atlantic Coast than, for example, in the major industrial centers of Colombia, the distributional impact of tourism may be expected to be more positive than would otherwise be the case.

3. CONCLUSIONS

Despite the weakness of the available data on the Colombian tourism industry, some tentative conclusions emerge from the theoretical and empirical survey. Since this paper confines itself to the employment, regional, and income distribution aspects of tourism, it does not offer grounds to support or reject tourism promotion on allocational or balance-of-payments grounds; however, there is no immediately apparent reason why tourism merits government finance or subsidization for either of these reasons. Also, as previously noted, it is probably not correct to claim any "multiplier" indirect employment effects for tourism since additional employment normally requires additional capital investments. Thus, this paper bases its conclusions on regional or total direct employment effects of tourism.

Tourism is an important and growing export industry. However, comparing optimistic estimates of potential employment in this sector with reasonable esti-

[17]G. Jimenez, "The Capital, Labor and Import Content of Urban Consumption Patterns in Colombia" (Unpublished M. A. dissertation, Rice University, 1972).

mates of the growth in the labor force, it appears unlikely that the tourism industry can absorb a large fraction of the increased labor force even in those regions which are especially suited to it.

The empirical analysis suggests that investment in tourism is essentially capital-intensive in nature, in the sense that this type of investment creates less employment than investment in many alternatives. Investment in large tourist projects requiring both superstructure and infrasturcture appears to generate less than half the demand for labor services as the economy-wide average; investments requiring only superstructure demand less labor than manufacturing. The contrast is especially striking between tourism and such activities as cottage shop manufacturing (Table 7.2). When employment in the present is weighted more heavily than future employment (Variant 2) tourism appears somewhat more favorable. Thus, investment in tourism superstructure provides sufficient employment in the present (particularly during construction) to reverse the steady-state ranking between superstructure and either manufactures or the economy-wide average. Even when infrastructure investments are included, the comparison between tourism and factory manufacturing improves when present employment is weighted more heavily than future employment.[18] We may conclude that when capital is diverted from such activities as food production, the general category of services or perhaps some areas of manufacturing, net employment in the economy, although not necessarily in the tourism region, will decline. The major portion of the net decline will occur in the future, after the construction phase is completed.

Table 7.2 demonstrates some differences between incremental and discrete tourism. By definition, incremental expansion requires little infrastructure investment. The first two columns indicate that projects using existing infrastructure may generate twice the demand for labor services as those requiring new infrastructure investments. Additionally, it may be surmised that investments in smaller, less luxurious hotels which require less capital per room would provide more employment per unit of capital invested.[19] Thus, investments in incremental tourist projects may be desirable to reduce some regional unemployment.

Foreign finance of tourism could have desirable employment effects. If, for example, half of total investments come from abroad and if those funds would not otherwise be available, the employment per unit of domestic capital invested would double. Of course, the contribution of tourism to foreign exchange should be considered as well. Foreign finance of foreign tourism offers a better means of increasing employment in the tourist region without reducing total employment in the economy than domestic finance of domestic tourism since neither

[18] As previously noted, only the superstructure and superstructure plus infrastructure entries include employment in construction. Therefore, even these mild successes for tourism could be reversed if the construction employment effects of other sectors were measured.

[19] The *Action Plan* (*op. cit.*) states that Five Star (luxury) hotels require twice as much investment per room ($[Col.] 488,000) as Three Star (moderate) hotels ($[Col.] 241,500). W. Elkan supports this view in "The Relations between Tourism and Employment in Kenya and Tanzania," *Journal of Development Studies*, Vol. 11, (January, 1975).

the capital nor the demand is diverted from other domestic regions.

The effects of increased domestic tourism remain somewhat unclear. The results depend on the unknown cross-elasticity between tourism and other activities. Table 7.3 indicates that, at best, increased tourism doe not provide significantly more employment than a general expansion of the economy. However, increased domestic tourism probably will increase total employment in the tourist region, at some risk of reducing total employment in the economy. Given the degree of unemployment in these regions and the skill structure of employment in tourism, it is unlikely that either domestic or foreign tourism will significantly reduce regional unemployment.

In summary, this paper predicts that two types of tourism do not have favorable overall employment and income distribution effects: promotion of domestic tourism and large-scale projects largely financed with domestic government or private capital. Two other types are more likely to have desirable outcomes, particularly on regional employment: small-scale, incremental investments, and projects which are largely financed by foreign capital which would otherwise not be available (and which do not promote investments of a more capital-intensive nature than would domestic capital). In all cases, it is important to distinguish the short run, where labor-intensive construction activities (especially on superstructure) may be quite employment creating, from the longer run where the capital intensity of the industry shows up. The desirability of tourist development could be substantially affected by the trade-off between employment creation now and later. In final conclusion, the hypothesis that government promotion of tourism may have an adverse impact on the distribution of incomes and employment in the national economy without significantly improving regional incomes in the tourist areas cannot be rejected.

Chapter 8

A GENERAL EQUILIBRIUM ANALYSIS OF THE EFFECTS OF SUBSIDIZED FARM MECHANIZATION ON OUTPUT AND INCOME DISTRIBUTION IN COLOMBIA[1]

Wayne R. Thirsk
University of Waterloo

1. INTRODUCTION

The consequences of introducing developed country farm machinery into less developed countries have been the subject of much recent debate.[2] Points of view frequently differ according to the relative importance attached to the output-expanding and the factor substitution effects of mechanization. Almost all of the discussion, however, has focused on the adjustments which occur at the micro level of the individual farm or, at best, the region. From observations at this level of analysis, attempts have been made to infer the output, income distribution and employment impacts of mechanization for the entire economy. Such leaps from the micro to the macro context are usually unconvincing because of the strong and implausible *ceteris paribus* conditions that must be imposed. This study takes the opposite tack. At the cost of suppressing some micro detail, it tries to free the analysis of farm mechanization from the prison of partial equilibrium by examining the issue in a general equilibrium context.

When importation of an alien and advanced technology has been viewed from the perspective of the whole economy, judgments on its desirability have been

[1] I wish to express my appreciation to R. A. Berry, R. Evenson, and C. E. McLure, Jr. for their helpful comments on earlier versions of this paper. Remaining errors, of course, are the responsibility of the author.

[2] Machine size is an important dimension in this debate. In several Asian countries, including Japan and Taiwan, small machines have been adopted by small scale farmers. The issues raised by this process are quite different from those arising in countries like Colombia where large machines are imported from developed countries and imply capital-intensive technologies.

usually negative; its effects on employment, income distribution, and sometimes total output, are invariably argued to be harmful. Behind these pessimistic views is the observation that the factor proportions associated with such mechanization seldom match the resource endowment of poor countries. In North America, farm mechanization was spurred by labor shortage and a rising price of labor compared to capital. In Latin America, in India-Pakistan, and in many other LDCs the adoption of mechanized practices has been encouraged by governments' ambitions for the country to be more "modern" that typically result in policies which *reduce* the price of capital relative to labor. In either case, however, mechanization is seen as a rational farmer response to relative factor price changes and the desire to lower costs of production.

This common macroeconomic assessment may, however, be wide of the mark because of its implicit assumption that factor markets would function well in the absence of mechanization, i.e., that the below equilibrium price of capital prompting greater mechanization is the only major distortion in the economy. Where factor markets are initially distorted, mechanization could conceivably lessen the degree of initial distortion and have beneficial effects even on employment and income distribution. We attempt to overcome this defect in the standard approach by employing a general equilibrium analysis of the Colombian experience which includes a more appropriate modelling of the initial conditions for that country.

The question posed is the following: how has government policy, which has reduced the cost of capital used in large farm crop production, altered the structure of relative prices in the economy and thereby affected the distribution of income and the allocation of resources? Satisfactory answers to this question depend on our ability to understand how the land, labor and capital markets perform. Restrictions on factor mobility are particularly important. Prior to mechanization, land and labor appear to have been severely misallocated. Widely differing factor proportions between large and small crop farms are highly suggestive of the importance of these factor market distortions. For all types of crop production small farms use many times more labor per hectare than larger farms.[3]

Constraints on factor use are prevalent in Colombia and account for the persistence of the enormous disparity in factor proportions by farm size. Institutional impediments to land mobility block the transfer of land from larger to smaller farms either by sale or rental. On the side of the demand for land, there is little credit available to small farmers for land purchase. On the supply side, rental is often precluded by landowners' fear of squatting and by current agrarian reform laws which view rented land as proof of inadequate use and, thus, more liable to expropriation than unrented land. Moreover, there is an apparent preference by large landowners for engaging in relatively unprofitable, extensive cattle grazing rather than growing more lucrative crops which would require larger amounts of labor and more supervisory time. The result has been the allocation of too much

[3]Information on average factor returns is presented by R. A. Berry, "Farm Size Distribution, Income Distribution and the Efficiency of Agricultural Production: Colombia," *American Economic Review* (May, 1972), 402-8.

land to cattle production.[4] The combined effect of all of these distortions was to produce a nonoptimal allocation of land and an excess supply of labor in the small farm sector prior to mechanization.

In this factor market setting there occurred in the late 1940s and early 1950s a significant growth in mechanization on large farms. It was stimulated both by a decline in the relative price of imported capital goods (especially in the early fifties) which stimulated more capital-intensive technologies in all sectors of the economy and by a capital market subsidy which made the cost of capital for large mechanizing farmers lower than that for nonagricultural users of capital.[5] Aside from custom land preparation in a few regions, small farmers have evinced little demand for mechanized services and, therefore, have not benefited much from their greater availability and lower cost.

In light of the preceding initial conditions, mechanization may appear to be a promising second-best policy if the relevant policy choice were between accepting the *status quo ante* of unmechanized cattle raising or fostering the expansion of mechanized, but noticeably more labor-intensive, large-farm crop production. Resource allocation would improve as land on large farms was shifted from cattle to crops and as labor was shifted from smaller to larger farms. Unless final demand were price inelastic, the overall demand for agricultural labor could be expected to increase, and possibly some of the poorest groups in Colombia would benefit.

Although it is plausible, this result is not necessary because the argument considers only adjustments within the agricultural sector, i.e., it is based on a partial equilibrium framework. This study concludes that, when equity and efficiency are viewed from the perspective of the whole economy, the benefits of improved resource allocation within agriculture may be insufficient to make subsidized mechanization a desirable policy. The economy-wide repercussions of diverting capital to large crop farms from the rest of the economy raise the prices of capital and land (at least one type of land) relative to labor. Our best or preferred estimates indicate that this policy raises total capital income in the economy by about 16 percent. Our lowest, and most conservative estimate, places this gain at around 8 percent. Regardless of the exact size of the income increment received by capitalists, it appears that somewhere between 80 and 85 percent of this gain

[4] This statement is not equivalent to one which says that, *ceteris paribus*, large landowners are willing to settle for less income than they could obtain. The point is that the realized rate of return to capital is often lower in cattle than it would be in a number of labor-intensive crops. The large landowner, however, may be maximizing his own income if such intensive cultivation would cause a decline in his income from urban activities by more than any increase in agricultural income and if he views renting or reliance on a farm administrator as a high risk venture. From the point of view of the economy, however, total output would be greater if some additional land could somehow be reallocated from cattle to crops.

[5] Low interest loans from foreign lenders to purchase farm machinery, including World Bank credits, were converted by Colombian authorities into low interest domestic credit for large farm machinery buyers. These loans were tied to the purchase of farm machinery and, while available in theory to smaller farmers, were of interest only to large ones.

is achieved at the expense of labor incomes and the incomes of small-scale farmers. The remainder of this income shift is borne by landowners.

Section 2 describes the assumptions and comparative statics model employed. The third section discusses the solutions generated by the model; section 4 deals briefly with the origin of the parameter values used in the numerical simulations. Particular simulations are selected in the next section as the best illustrative measurements of relative price variation. Estimated changes in income distribution attributable to the mechanization subsidy are the subject of section 7. Some sensitivity analysis is also conducted in this section. A final section is addressed to the efficiency aspects of the subsidy and to some qualifications of the conclusions that are reached on the basis of this aggregate simulation analysis.

2. THE MODEL

Analysis of the distributive impact of subsidized farm mechanization relies on an extended version of the general equilibrium model of tax incidence developed by A. C. Harberger.[6] Instead of the usual two-factor, two-sector model, this analysis of mechanization is conducted at a more disaggregated level involving the four factors and four sectors mentioned in the previous section. The sectors, comprising small- and large-farm crop production, large-farm cattle, and nonagricultural output, together employ the four homogeneous factors–labor, capital, mechanizable land and non-mechanizable land. Although labor is employed in all sectors, capital is assumed to be an input used in only the nonagricultural sector and the large-farm crop sector. Mechanizable land is a unique input in the large-farm sector where it is used in either crop production or cattle raising. Land which is physically unsuitable for mechanization is used exclusively in the large-farm cattle activity. Land of either type used by small farms is assumed to be frozen at initial levels, a crude method of modeling the distortion in the market for land.[7] This disaggregation of the Colombian economy is roughly coincident with the major sectoral outlines observable in that country and the pattern of factor market distortions found among different sectors.

Because the model relies upon comparative statics, all of the equations in the model appear as first derivatives. This form facilitates comparison of the new equilibrium, after the capital subsidy is in effect, with the original equilibrium prior to the subsidy.

In the long-run context considered here, the capital stock is fixed in total amount, but malleable in form such that its services are perfectly mobile between the two capital-using sectors. The price of capital is defined as the cost of a unit of capital services where these are measured by the amount that one peso will

[6] A. C. Harberger, "The Incidence of the Corporate Income Tax," *Journal of Political Economy*, Vol. 80, (June, 1962), 215-40.

[7] Moreover, much small-farm land is neither mechanizable nor easily converted into grazing area.

buy. The government can be thought of as granting a subsidy to the cost of capital in large-scale agriculture and assuring that the supply of capital is adequate to meet the extra demand at this new price. When this diversion of capital occurs, the price of capital to the nonagricultural sector adjusts to clear the capital market in that sector.

Although imported farm machinery is one of the most visible and important components of the stock of farm machinery, it should be borne in mind that all forms of capital used in large-scale agriculture enjoy the same interest rate subsidy. If farm machinery is a reasonably fixed fraction of the total amount of such capital, the percentage change in the use of machinery will equal the percentage change in large-farm capital use that occurs in response to the subsidy.

The equations that link the different parts of the economy are listed below. The behavioral equations, which rest on the assumptions of utility and profit maximization are subsequently discussed in the order in which they appear. Some equations appear in differential form; others do not in order to aid their interpretation. A hat symbol ($\hat{}$) denotes percentage changes in a variable. In total, there are twenty-two independent equations:

$$\hat{L}_f = \sum_i \theta_i^f \sigma_{L_i}^f \hat{P}_i + \hat{F}_f; i = L,K,A \qquad (1)$$

$$\hat{K}_f = \sum_i \theta_i^f \sigma_{K_i}^f \hat{P}_i + \hat{F}_f; i = K,L,A \qquad (2)$$

$$\hat{A}_f = \sum_i \theta_i^f \sigma_{A_i}^f \hat{P}_i + \hat{F}_f; i = K,L,A \qquad (3)$$

$$\hat{A}_c = \sum_i \theta_i^c \sigma_{A_i}^c \hat{P}_i + \hat{C}; i = M,L,A \qquad (4)$$

$$\hat{L}_c = \sum_{i=1} \theta_i^c \sigma_{L_i}^c \hat{P}_i + \hat{C}; i = M,L,A \qquad (5)$$

$$\hat{M} = \sum \theta_i^c \sigma_{M_i}^c \hat{P}_i + \hat{C}; i = M,L,A \qquad (6)$$

$$\hat{F}_s = g_P(\hat{P}_s - \hat{P}_y) + g_{Ls}\hat{L}_s; g_P > 0; g_{Ls} < 0 \qquad (7)$$

$$\hat{F} = \theta_f \hat{F}_f + \theta_s \hat{F}_s \qquad (8)$$

$$\bar{L} = L_f + L_y + L_c + L_s \qquad (9)$$

$$\bar{K} = K_f + K_y \qquad (10)$$

$$\bar{A} = A_f + A_c \qquad (11)$$

$$P_M = \bar{P}_M ; \hat{P}_M = 0 \qquad (12)$$

$$\hat{K}_y - \hat{L}_y = \sigma^y (P_{K_y} - \hat{P}_L) \qquad (13)$$

$$\hat{P}_{L_f} - \hat{P}_f = 0 \qquad (14)$$

$$\hat{P}_{L_y} = \hat{P}_{L_f} = \hat{P}_{L_c} = \hat{P}_f \qquad (15)$$

$$\hat{P}_{A_c} = \lambda\hat{P}_{Af};\lambda < 1;\hat{P}_{Ac} = \hat{P}_{Af} = \hat{P}_A \quad (16)$$

$$\hat{P}_{K_y} = \hat{S} + \hat{P}_{K_f} \quad (17)$$

$$\hat{P}_y = \sum_i \theta^y_i \hat{P}_i; i = L,K \quad (18)$$

$$\hat{P}_f = \theta^f_K(\hat{P}_K - \hat{S}) + \theta^f_A \hat{P}_A + \theta^f_L \hat{P}_L \quad (19)$$

$$\hat{P}_c = \sum_i \theta^c_i \hat{P}_i; i = M,L,A \quad (20)$$

$$\hat{F} = E_{fy}(\hat{P}_y - \hat{P}_f) + E_{fc}(\hat{P}_c - \hat{P}_f); E_{fy}, E_{fc} > 0 \quad (21)$$

$$\hat{C} = E_{cf}(\hat{P}_f - \hat{P}_c) + E_{cy}(\hat{P}_y - \hat{P}_c); E_{cf}, E_{cy} > 0 \quad (22)$$

This set of equations is sufficient to solve for twenty-two endogenous variables: the amount of land used in large farm crops (A_f) and cattle (A_c); the amounts of labor employed on large crop and cattle enterprises (L_f and L_c), on small farms (L_s) and in nonagriculture (L_y); the amount of capital found on large crop farms (K_f) and in nonagriculture (K_y); the employment of nonmechanizable land (M); the price of land devoted to crops (P_{Af}) or to cattle (P_{Ac}); the price of nonmechanizable land (P_M); the unsubsidized price of capital used on large farms and in nonagriculture (P_K); the price of labor in all sectors (P_L); product prices for crop goods (P_f), cattle (P_c), and nonagricultural commodities (P_y); the quantity of crop production marketed in the large farm sector (F_f), the small farm sector (F_s), and from both sectors (F), and the quantity of cattle marketed (C). For the sake of convenience and easy reference, the definition of these variables and their notation are repeated in the appendix to this study.

The first three equations are percentage changes in the derived demand for land, labor and capital in large-farm crop production.[8] In each equation the first three terms are the factor substitution effects of factor price changes, output constant (σ^f_{ij} is the Allen partial elasticity of factor substitution), while the last term represents the scale effect of a changed level of output. Because constant returns to scale are assumed, no optimum farm size exists, and changes in the level of output produced by this sector can occur either through an adjustment in the size of original farms or alterations in the number of farms.

Equations 4-6 describe a similar production technology in the cattle sector, but one which utilizes a different trio of inputs: labor and two types of land (mechanizable and nonmechanizable). The output of cattle C refers to marketed

[8]The explicit form of these equations can be derived by differentiating the equilibrium condition equating the price of a factor to its marginal value product. One characteristic of these equations is that

$$\sum_j \theta_j \sigma_{ij} = 0$$

for any factors i and j, so a proportional change in all factor prices will not affect factor demands.

production which may or may not be the same as the flow of new beef production in a given time period.[9]

Equation 7 describes changes in the sale of crop output produced on small, nonmechanizing farms. These farms are assumed to produce perfect substitutes in consumption for the type of crop grown on large farms.[10] A major feature of the small farm sector is its role as a repository of surplus labor. An "unlimited" amount of labor is offered to other sectors at the constant real wage received by landless rural workers and labor employed in the nonagricultural sector. Moreover, labor which becomes unemployed elsewhere will be absorbed into the small farm sector, so there is no overt unemployment in our model. Perhaps because transfer payments or savings are inadequate to finance labor market search, it is assumed that migration from this sector occurs only in response to job opportunities elsewhere.[11]

Small farmers sell what they produce in exchange for nonagricultural goods, or retain their output for home consumption. This decision is assumed to depend on relative output prices and the labor intensity (ratio of labor to land) of small farms. Whenever relative crop prices increase, small farmers are encouraged to expand crop output and curtail their consumption of crops. Thus, the elasticity of marketed output with respect to changes in relative commodity prices (g_p) is positive. In addition, the presence of diminishing returns in crop production implies that an extra worker in this sector may contribute more to the demand than to the supply of crop output, or that he may be more profitably employed in producing other, noncrop, goods which are consumed by the farm family (e.g., home building, food preparation). In either case, the elasticity of marketed output with respect to small farm labor (g_{Ls}) is assumed to be negative.

Equation 8 recognizes that there are two alternative sources of crops supplied to the market and indicates that changes in total supply are a weighted average of the marketed output changes in the small and large farm crop sectors. The weights, θ_f and θ_s, are, respectively, the original shares of the market supplied by large and small farms.

Equations 9-11 express the overall constraint on resource supply in the labor, capital, and land markets given by the endowment of each factor. In the labor market there is surplus labor in the sense that the *ex ante* supply of labor exceeds

[9] By assumption, crops are not used to feed cattle so a declining crop price creates no incentive to substitute feed for land. The high price of crops compared to land makes this a reasonable assumption for Colombia. See D. Hedley, "An Economic Analysis of Corn Production in the Cauca Valley" (unpublished Ph. D. dissertation, Michigan State University, 1969).

[10] Thus, although four sectors comprise the model, there are really only three different consumer commodities: crop output, cattle and nonagricultural goods.

[11] Surveys of urban unemployment in Colombia indicate a low rate of unemployment among migrants. Cf., R. Nelson, P. Schultz, and R. Slighton, *Structural Change in a Developing Economy* (Princeton, N. J.: Princeton University Press, 1971), 151-52.

the demand for labor at a fixed real wage.[12] At this constant real wage labor in small scale agriculture stands ready to fill any new job openings in other sectors. This queuing characteristic of the labor market is consistent with current "cold storage" notions about the peasant sector as a reservoir of labor to be drained or filled according to varying demand conditions elsewhere. It is assumed that surplus labor is never exhausted, even if the total demand for labor is increased as a result of mechanization.

Moreover, land tenure conditions are assumed to have no bearing on the functioning of the labor market, or on the outcome of the analysis, since the rental of land in the large farm sector is probably analytically equivalent to the use of hired labor in that sector.[13] With flexible land rentals, a maximizing landowner would receive the same return on his land whether he hired labor to work it or leased it to tenants.

The capital constraint embodied in equation 10 requires careful interpretation. Since external, low cost, mechanization loans augment the real resources of the Colombian economy, equation 10 contains the assumption that, if Colombia had not solicited and acquired these loans for farm-specific capital inputs, it could have obtained loans of comparable value for the purpose of expanding the capital stock in non-agricultural sectors. Alternatively, it may be assumed that, even if Colombia had not obtained external financial support for mechanization, it would have pursued domestic policies to encourage larger imports of farm machinery at the expense of machinery imports for the nonagricultural sector. In either case, growth in large-farm capital requires a corresponding reduction in the capital stock of the nonagricultural sector.

Government control and regulation of financial markets effectively lowers the supply price of capital services in large-scale agriculture relative to their price in nonagriculture. The government also insures that the amount of capital supplied at this lower price matches the quantity demanded. With a fixed capital stock, this capital subsidy to large-scale agriculture is equivalent in its relative price ef-

[12] Surplus labor can be reconciled with an active rural labor market by appeal to Lewis-type sharing of land rents, legal minimum wages, or employers' desire to provide a living wage to landless workers. All of these types of behavior appear to operate in Colombia although the first is probably the dominant one.

[13] For more complete explanation, see S. Cheung, "Private Property Rights and Sharecropping," *Journal of Political Economy*, Vol. 76, (Nov./Dec., 1968), 1107-22. Because of rigid land rents, landlords in India and Pakistan have apparently reacted to profitable mechanization opportunities by pushing sharecroppers off the land and, in some instances, buying up land owned by small farmers. In Colombia the 1970/71 census of agriculture indicates a significant decline in small farms rented or share-cropped over the number reported in the 1960 census. How much of this decline could be attributed to mechanization is not yet clear. For the Pakistan case, see J. P. McInerney and G. Donaldson, *The Consequences of Farm Tractors in Pakistan: An Evaluation of IDA Credits for the Mechanization of Farms in Pakistan, 1966-1970,* World Bank, 1973 (Mimeo.); also see S. R. Bose and E. H. Clark, "Some Basic Considerations on Agricultural Mechanization in West Pakistan," *Pakistan Development Review*, IX (1969).

fect to a tax on the use of capital in nonagriculture. Although the cost and return to capital differs between sectors, within each sector competition is assumed to produce the same rate of return on capital. Competitive arbitrage between sectors is blocked through legal and institutional restrictions on the mobility of funds. Investors are unable to borrow in the low-cost portion of the capital market and invest in the higher return segment. Neither can savers shift easily from a low to a high return compartment of the capital market due to the fragmented nature of that market. These restrictions assure the absence of excess demand for agricultural credit and enable a reallocation of physical capital to large farms.[14]

The capital price relationship–equation 17– in this institutional setting states that the cost of capital services in large-scale agriculture is reduced relative to that in nonagriculture by the introduction of a fixed proportional subsidy $\hat{S}$. This subsidy is the single policy instrument in the model. All of the endogenous variables can be solved in terms of the value assigned to this instrument.

Equation 11 specifies a fixed amount of mechanizable land which may be used in either crops or cattle. Equation 16 indicates that initially this type of land earns a lower rental return in cattle than in crops, due to the failure of large-scale entrepreneurs to choose the profit-maximizing output mix between these two activities. The size of this distortion is assumed to be constant so that, in the differential form of equation 16, the distortion parameter vanishes and all units of mechanizable land increase or decrease in rent by the same percentage amount. By inducing a switch of land from cattle to crops mechanization may have beneficial effects on the global efficiency of land use. Reflecting Colombia's land frontier in the llanos region, equation 12 assumes that the supply of nonmechanizable land is perfectly elastic at some initial price P_M.[15]

By Walras' law, the supply and demand equations of nonagricultural output are redundant. Only the factor demand relationship for this sector is required and it appears as equation 13. The parameter σ^y is the elasticity of factor substitution between capital and labor for some constant-returns-to-scale production function. No supply function for large farm crop goods is necessary since it is implicit in the first three equations of the model.

Equation 14 defines the real wage in large-scale agriculture, which is assumed to be constant in terms of the price of agricultural crop goods. These goods are by far the most important single item in the consumption budget of low-income

[14]Note that complete compartmentalization of the capital market need not be assumed for a reallocation to occur. It is only necessary that, at the margin, controls be adequate to divert some capital into large-farm agriculture. In a recent book McKinnon has elaborated a theory of farm mechanization on a similar notion of capital immobility. See R. McKinnon, *Money and Capital in Economic Development* (Washington: Brookings, 1973). The absence of excess demand has also been commented upon by Dale Adams. See D. W. Adams, "Agricultural Credit in Latin America: A Critical Review of External Funding Policy," *American Journal of Agricultural Economics* L (May, 1971).

[15]If supply were less than perfectly elastic, owners of this land type would benefit from the impetus to mechanize, or at least experience smaller losses than the model suggests.

workers.[16] This assumption and that of perfect labor mobility between small-scale agriculture and other sectors imply that nominal wages in all sectors outside the small farm sector will move proportionately with changes in crop prices. It is also a helpful and natural simplification to take the real wage as the numeraire for the system in determining the relative price effects of subsidized mechanization, as is done in equation 14.

Equations 18-20 provide the link between factor price (cost) changes and commodity price changes. If firms price according to marginal cost, and output adjusts to eliminate pure profits, product price changes are a weighted average of factor price changes with the weights being the appropriate factor shares.

Finally, equations 21 and 22 show how the division of output among different sectors will depend on the final demand sensitivity of consumers (and producers as well, since input-output relations are ignored in the model) to changes in relative product prices. For example, the output-expanding effects of farm mechanization will assume importance only if the price elasticity of demand for crop output is large, in which case labor employed in mechanized, large-scale agriculture could conceivably increase despite the substitution of machinery for labor in production.

The demand equations 21 for crops and 22 for cattle ignore two different kinds of income effects which are theoretically capable of influencing the composition of final demand. Any redistribution of income among purchasers will ordinarily alter the pattern of demand unless all consumers spend an extra dollar in the same manner. Although average consumption propensities may (and, as we shall see, do) vary across individuals and income groups, it is assumed here that everyone manifests the same marginal propensity to consume each good. Secondly, the impact on demand of changes in real income resulting from a more or less efficient reallocation of resources is ignored on the grounds that it is probably not a very important omission.[17]

The positive sign for the income-compensated price elasticity of demand, E_{ij}, between any two of the three commodities reflects the assumption that all of the goods are considered by purchasers to be substitutes for each other. A separate demand equation for nonagricultural goods cannot be specified independently of the other two demand equations. This completes the description of the model.

3. SECTORAL RESPONSES TO SUBSIDIZED FARM MECHANIZATION

One of the costs of a complex model is an inability to solve the system of equations for neat and readily interpretable solutions. Numerical simulation is the best

[16] During the period from about 1945 to 1969, real wages in agriculture grew by less than one percent per year. Even this rate may be upward biased due to the increasing importance of higher paid tractor drivers and large-farm workers in the wage survey.

[17] For some evidence on this score, see J. G. Ballentine and I. Eris, "On the General Equilibrium Analysis of Tax Incidence," *Journal of Political Economy*, LXXXIII (1975).

one can hope to do under these circumstances. It is worthwhile, however, to examine some of the predictable reactions in individual sectors as an aid to interpretating the simulation results.

Introducing the subsidy lowers the cost of capital to large crop farms and the price of crop output falls as they expand their level of operations in response to their reduced cost of production. Capital is substituted for labor and the demand for complementary mechanizable land increases. As mechanizable land is bid from the cattle sector, its price rises and moderates the demand for capital, while encouraging greater labor use and the substitution of nonmechanizable for mechanizable land in the cattle sector. Since crops are more labor-intensive than cattle, this shift in output composition will lead to increased labor demand.

The diversion of capital to large-farm crop production will raise the rate of return to capital in the nonagricultural sector, leading in turn to an increase in the relative price of nonagricultural output and a fall in consumer demand for that output. Consumer demand for crops and cattle will consequently increase. If the contracting nonagricultural sector is relatively labor-intensive compared to expanding large-farm crops, the change in output composition will diminish the total demand for labor. Since nominal wage rates are tied to the price of crop goods, the decline in crop prices will reduce wage rates and stimulate greater labor demand in all sectors. While it can be safely predicted that the nonagricultural sector will become more labor-intensive, a similar prediction cannot be made for large-farm crops since both the cost of capital and the cost of labor will be reduced. Qualitative analysis can only go so far; a precise determination of these matters requires a solution to the model.

Before considering these results, the question of who pays the subsidy is examined. It is not a fiscal subsidy whose cost could be attributed to taxpayers. Rather, it results from a form of price control in which buyers benefit at the expense of suppliers. In other words, the cost of the subsidy is borne by owners of capital who receive a lower return on their assets than they otherwise would. In Colombia, it is probable that much of this loss is inflicted on low and middle income families who have fewer alternative outlets for their savings than higher income families.[18] Despite this loss imposed on capital incomes, it is possible for capitalists as a group to be better off because of the subsidy if it leads to a sufficiently higher rate of return on other assets.

To see this more clearly, let V_K^i be the value of capital income earned in either the nonagricultural (V_K^y) or large-farm crop (V_K^f) sector. Using the notation introduced earlier, the change in capital income, relative to labor, can be written as:

$$V_K^y(\hat{P}_K+\hat{K}_y)+V_K^f(\hat{P}_K-\hat{S}+\hat{K}_f)$$

[18]The Caja Agraria, a major source of institutional credit, has traditionally been financed in part by savings deposits, a low yield asset. But in view of the considerable fungibility in the financial system, other savers may lose as well.

With a fixed endowment of capital, $V^y_K \hat{K}_y + V^f_K \hat{K}_f = 0$, so that the condition for higher capital incomes becomes:

$$\hat{P}_K/\hat{S} > V^f_K/(V^f_K + V^y_K)$$

If the induced increase in the unsubsidized return to capital exceeds the share of large-farm crops in total capital income, capitalists as a group will benefit from the subsidy. For example, if there is no change in the rate of return to capital, capitalists will lose by the amount of the subsidy. As for landowners, it can be seen from equation 19 that, given the numeraire assumption,

$$P_A/S = -\theta^f_K/\theta^f_A(P_K/S-1).$$

Thus, if $P_K/S<1$ and the cost of capital in agriculture falls relative to labor, the relative price of land (mechanizable) will increase. Labor's fortunes depend upon the level of employment since the real wage is fixed. As the marginal product of labor in the reservoir small farm sector is below this wage, the total income of small farm families and hired workers will rise if employment outside this sector increases.

4. PARAMETER VALUES

In order to implement the model empirically and use it as a basis for further analysis of income distribution and resource alloation, it is necessary to have information on the size of twenty-eight parameters.[19]

For all of the 49 simulations that were tried some parameters did not vary. These were assigned the following values:

$\sigma^y_L = .63; \theta^y_K = .37; \theta^f_L = .18; \theta^f_K = .5; \theta^f_A = .32; \theta^c_A = .38; \theta^c_L = .24; \theta^c_M = .38;$

$g_p = .1; K_f/K_y = .27; L_f/L_y = .07; \theta_s = .66; \theta_f = .33; \lambda = .8; L_s/L_y = .5; L_c/L_y = .18;$

$\sigma^c_{\ell a} = .2; \sigma^c_{am} = 2.5; A_f/A_c = .3$

Table 8.1 lists the alternative values for the other parameters that were used in different simulation groups. Different simulations correspond to the range of serious doubts about the exact size of some of the parameters, especially the final demand and factor substitution elasticities. For each simulation group, the parameter σ^y varies in the range of zero to .5 (or to 1).

[19] Factor shares for nonagriculture are based on national accounts data adjusted for the incomes of unincorporated business. Income shares and employment ratios in mechanized agriculture are derived from national accounts data and a variety of other sources. For a discussion of the data and its sources, see W. R. Thirsk, "Income Distribution, Efficiency, and the Experience of Colombian Farm Mechanization," Program of Development Studies Discussion Paper no. 33, Rice University, Houston, Texas.

TABLE 8.1. Parameter Values in Different Simulations

Simulation Group	(1)	(2)	(3)	(4)	(5)	(6)	(7)	(8)
Parameter								
E_{fy}	0.5	0.4	0.5	0.4	1	1	0.5	0.5
E_{fc}	0.5	0.3	0.5	0.3	0.5	0.5	0.5	0.5
E_{cy}	0.2	0.3	0.2	0.3	0.5	0.5	0.2	0.2
E_{cf}	1	0.6	1	0.6	1	1	1	1
g_{Ls}	−0.2	−0.2	−0.1	−0.1	−0.2	−0.1	−0.2	−0.1
$\sigma^f_{k\ell}$	1.5	1.5	1.5	1.5	1.5	1.5	1	1
σ^f_{ka}	0.1	0.1	0.1	0.1	0.1	0.1	−0.1	−0.1
$\sigma^f_{\ell a}$	0.6	0.6	0.6	0.6	0.6	0.6	0.4	0.4

The demand functions satisfy two properties. One is homogeneity, or the absence of money illusion, which requires that own-price elasticies E_{ii} be equal to the negative sum of all cross-price elasticities E_{ij}. Thus, for crops

$$E_{ff} + E_{fc} + E_{fy} = 0$$

and for cattle

$$E_{cc} + E_{cf} + E_{cy} = 0$$

The second property is symmetry in consumer substitution so that $V_iE_{ij} = V_jE_{ji}$ where V_i, V_j are total consumer expenditure on commodities i and j. These restrictions are reflected in the chosen demand parameters (the ratio V_f/V_c is given a value of two).

On the basis of both interest rates charged by institutional lenders and empirical rate of return calculations, a plausible range for the size of the subsidy instrument $\hat{S}$ is between 0.35 and 0.5.[20] A value of 0.4 is chosen for the simulation results. Strictly speaking, these solutions are only valid for small changes in the value of $\hat{S}$. To the extent that the derivatives are not entirely independent of the size of the subsidy, another element of approximation is introduced.

5. SIMULATION RESULTS

In every simulation a sizeable expansion occurs in the employment of land, labor and capital in large-scale agriculture. Numerical results are reported in Table 8.2. The level of employment in small-scale agriculture displays considerable sensitivity

[20] S, it will be recalled, is the proportional reduction in the cost of and return to agricultural capital compared to what capital is paid in nonagricultural activities.

TABLE 8.2. Simulation Results

Simulation	A_f/S	K_f/S	L_f/S	P_K/S	L_c/S	L_s/S	M/S	P_A/S	P_y/S
(1) σ^y =0	0.957	1.07	0.930	0.826	0.004	0.445	0.241	0.270	0.355
0.1	0.879	0.985	0.854	0.836	0.010	0.240	0.233	0.254	0.359
0.2	0.799	0.899	0.776	0.847	0.016	0.030	0.224	0.232	0.364
0.3	0.718	0.810	0.696	0.858	0.022	−0.185	0.214	0.230	0.369
0.4	0.635	0.719	0.614	0.869	0.028	−0.407	0.206	0.202	0.374
0.5	0.549	0.623	0.531	0.880	0.034	−0.634	0.196	0.185	0.378
1.0	0.080	0.120	0.080	0.940	0.070	−1.900	0.150	0.094	0.470
(2) σ^y =0	0.734	0.847	0.707	0.826	0.071	0.323	0.307	0.270	0.355
0.1	0.659	0.765	0.634	0.837	0.075	0.119	0.297	0.252	0.360
0.2	0.582	0.680	0.558	0.847	0.080	−0.090	0.287	0.237	0.364
0.3	0.502	0.593	0.480	0.858	0.085	−0.305	0.277	0.219	0.369
0.4	0.421	0.504	0.400	0.871	0.091	−0.525	0.270	0.199	0.375
0.5	0.336	0.413	0.318	0.882	0.096	−0.751	0.256	0.182	0.379
(3) σ^y =0	0.864	0.969	0.839	0.838	0.011	0.400	0.231	0.251	0.360
0.1	0.829	0.931	0.805	0.843	0.014	0.214	0.227	0.243	0.362
0.2	0.793	0.892	0.770	0.847	0.017	0.027	0.223	0.237	0.364
0.3	0.757	0.853	0.735	0.852	0.019	−0.163	0.219	0.229	0.366
0.4	0.721	0.813	0.700	0.857	0.021	−0.356	0.215	0.221	0.368
0.5	0.685	0.773	0.663	0.862	0.024	−0.549	0.211	0.213	0.371
(4) σ^y =0	0.669	0.775	0.643	0.835	0.075	0.291	0.298	0.255	0.359
0.1	0.635	0.738	0.610	0.840	0.077	0.107	0.294	0.248	0.361
0.2	0.600	0.700	0.576	0.845	0.080	−0.079	0.290	0.240	0.363
0.3	0.565	0.662	0.541	0.850	0.081	−0.269	0.285	0.232	0.365
0.4	0.530	0.623	0.507	0.855	0.084	−0.460	0.281	0.224	0.368
0.5	0.494	0.584	0.472	0.860	0.086	−0.653	0.276	0.216	0.370

TABLE 8.2. Continued

Simulation	A_f/S	K_f/S	L_f/S	P_K/S	L_c/S	L_s/S	M/S	P_A/S	P_y/S
(5) σ^y =0	1.26	1.63	1.17	0.427	−0.232	0.831	0.547	0.887	0.184
0.1	1.23	1.59	1.14	0.435	−0.224	0.724	0.542	0.875	0.187
0.2	1.19	1.55	1.10	0.445	−0.217	0.613	0.537	0.860	0.191
0.3	1.16	1.51	1.07	0.454	−0.208	0.496	0.532	0.846	0.195
0.4	1.12	1.47	1.04	0.464	−0.200	0.375	0.527	0.830	0.200
0.5	1.08	1.42	1.00	0.475	−0.191	0.248	0.522	0.813	0.204
(6) σ^y =0	1.12	1.47	1.04	0.464	−0.200	0.746	0.527	0.830	0.200
0.1	1.10	1.45	1.02	0.469	−0.196	0.643	0.525	0.822	0.202
0.2	1.09	1.43	1.00	0.473	−0.193	0.537	0.522	0.816	0.203
0.3	1.07	1.41	0.990	0.478	−0.189	0.430	0.520	0.808	0.205
0.4	1.06	1.39	0.976	0.482	−0.185	0.321	0.518	0.802	0.207
0.5	1.04	1.37	0.960	0.487	−0.181	0.210	0.515	0.794	0.209
(7) σ^y =0	0.988	0.965	0.931	0.821	0.002	0.389	0.244	0.277	0.353
0.1	0.908	0.883	0.855	0.832	0.003	0.187	0.236	0.260	0.358
0.2	0.826	0.799	0.777	0.843	0.014	−0.022	0.227	0.243	0.362
0.3	0.742	0.712	0.696	0.855	0.020	−0.236	0.218	0.224	0.368
0.4	0.656	0.624	0.614	0.866	0.027	−0.455	0.208	0.207	0.372
0.5	0.563	0.533	0.529	0.878	0.030	−0.681	0.198	0.189	0.378
(8) σ^y =0	0.904	0.878	0.851	0.833	0.008	0.351	0.235	0.259	0.358
0.1	0.868	0.841	0.816	0.838	0.011	0.167	0.231	0.251	0.360
0.2	0.831	0.804	0.781	0.843	0.014	−0.019	0.227	0.243	0.362
0.3	0.794	0.766	0.746	0.848	0.017	−0.207	0.223	0.235	0.365
0.4	0.756	0.727	0.710	0.853	0.019	−0.398	0.219	0.227	0.367
0.5	0.718	0.688	0.674	0.858	0.022	−0.591	0.215	0.220	0.369

Note: The parameter assumptions for the simulations are in Table 8.1.

to the size of the factor substitution elasticity σ^y. Employment of labor in the cattle sector changes very little. The capital-labor ratio tends to increase in large-farm agriculture and to decline in nonagriculture. The land-labor ratio in large-farm agriculture becomes larger while the same ratio in small-farm agriculture mirrors the extent of the change in the amount of surplus labor. In all of the simulations the prices of land, capital, and nonagricultural goods increase relative to the price of labor. Since $\hat{P}_K/\hat{S}$ is less than unity in every case, the after-subsidy price of capital, relative to the wage rate, declines in large-scale agriculture.[21] The qualitative results do not seem to be highly sensitive to the possibility of errors in parameter values.

These results are also consistent with Harberger's earlier analysis of the impact of capital taxes. He found that a partial tax on capital income burdens all capital incomes. Here, a subsidy (or the equivalent of a negative tax) on the use of capital in one sector benefits capitalists in general. A major difference in result, however, is due to the existence of land used as a third factor in the sector receiving the subsidy. The induced expansion of the subsidized sector contributes to higher nominal incomes for owners of mechanizable land who, besides capitalists, are the major beneficiaries of the subsidy. As will be seen in the next section, these two groups also receive higher real incomes.

Assuming higher final demand elasticities E_{ij}, or a higher value for the labor intensity elasticity g_{Ls}, has the predictable impact of fostering a higher rate of expansion of large-farm crops. Simultaneously, the amount of surplus labor contained in small-scale agriculture increases. This result underlines the shortcomings of partial equilibrium analyses of the employment impact of farm mechanization. Many judgments about the desirability of farm mechanization are based on a comparison of post-mechanization large-farm employment levels with those in the pre-mechanization era. If the output expansion effects dominate the labor substitution effects and large-farm employment grows, mechanization is viewed favorably. The simulation results, however, indicate strongly that this partial equilibrium view is an inadequate indicator of whether or not subsidized farm mechanization is labor saving within the whole economy. Increased employment of labor in large-scale agriculture is compatible in some of the simulations with increased amounts of surplus labor in small-scale agriculture despite the increase in labor demand which occurs when land is switched from cattle to crops. Higher employment in large-scale agriculture may be achieved at the expense of an even greater decline of employment in other sectors. Although labor per unit of nonagricultural output increases (by an amount which depends on the value of σ^y), this effect is outweighed in many cases by the impact of a diminished output level in this relatively labor-intensive sector.

Some judgment concerning the most representative outcome is required if

[21] Note that as σ^y increases, $\hat{P}_K/\hat{S}$ becomes somewhat larger. Although a larger value for σ^y shifts more capital to agriculture and by itself dampens any tendency for P_K to rise, the induced expansion of agriculture, by reducing P_f and thus P_L more than offsets this effect.

these results are to undergo further analysis. Of the eight simulation groups, 5 and 6 employ the most improbable parameter values on the demand side since they assume quite large compensated own-price elasticities of 1.5 for both crops and cattle.[22] Simulations 7 and 8 have the lowest partial substitution elasticities and are also excluded because of the close similarity of their results to the remaining pairs: 1 and 3; 2 and 4. These pairs contain the middle and lower estimates of the final demand elasticities. For all of the simulations, except 5 and 6, the critical relative price variable $\hat{P}_K/\hat{S}$ moves in the narrow range of 0.8 to 0.85.

6. INCOME DISTRIBUTION EFFECTS

From benchmark information for factor shares (see Table 8.4, for example) it can be easily established that the ratio of large farm to total capital income is about 0.12. There is no simulation result which generates a value smaller than 0.2 for the relative price term $\hat{P}_K/\hat{S}$. In fact, as shown above, most values are substantially higher than 0.12. Therefore, the distributive impact of the subsidy is to raise the level of capital incomes relative to those of labor. Moreover, since $\hat{P}_K/\hat{S}$ is less than one in each case, the rental price of land relative to labor also increases. By reducing the cost of the wage good, the subsidy has the important effect, described by a large number of development models, of lowering the supply price of labor to the nonagricultural sector and raising the real return to capital employed there.

Different economic groups may gain or lose in two distinct ways as relative prices change. As already shown, changing relative factor prices adjust the money incomes of some groups at the expense of others. However, as relative product prices are changed, real incomes of different groups may rise or fall depending on the proportions in which various commodities are consumed by each group. For any particular group, changes in the sources of income may either offset or reinforce changes in *uses* of income.[23]

A national income accounting framework is a useful stage on which to examine these two effects. National income, net of any own-farm consumption, may be defined as the value:

$$P_y Y + P_f(F_f+F_s) + P_c C$$

from the side of total expenditures, and as

$$P_L(L_f+L_c+L_y) \quad + \quad P_{Ky}(K_f+K_y) \quad - \quad SK_f+P_A(A_f+\lambda A_c)+MP_M+P_{Ls}L_s$$

from the side of income generation. A new variable is introduced here, P_{Ls}, which is defined as the average product of labor working on small scale farms.

[22]The larger is the price elasticity, the smaller is the induced decline in food prices and hence the less the money wage falls relative to the price of capital, as can be seen from an examination of Table 2.

[23]For a lengthier discussion of these concepts, see R. A. Musgrave, *The Theory of Public Finance* (New York: McGraw-Hill, 1959), Chapter 10, especially pp. 217-22.

The change in national income from the side of the sources of income is, to a first-order approximation,

$$(K_y+K_f)\hat{P}_K - K_f\hat{S} + (A_f + A_c)\hat{P}_A + M\hat{P}_M + L_s\hat{P}_{Ls}$$

Since labor is the numeraire, $(L_y + L_c + L_f)\hat{P}_L = 0$. National income is measured here in terms of real wage units. If Y_i, F_i, and C_i represent the value of consumption by the ith income group for commodities Y, F, and C, respectively, an income distribution balance sheet can be drawn up portraying changes in income on both sources and uses sides for each group of factor owners in the economy. For each group in Table 8.3 the sources entry measures the loss or gain in nominal income from ownership of that factor. The entry on the uses side captures the change in the real purchasing power of nominal expenditure (or "cost-of-living") due to changes in relative product prices. For example, if a group were heavily specialized in the consumption of a good whose relative price rose, that group's real income gain would be much less than any gain in nominal income it might receive.

Because it is only a first-order approximation, the overall sum of the income changes in this model is zero. Ignoring any subsidy element in foreign loans, there is a strict zero-sum redistribution of income among different groups as a result of the subsidy to farm capital.

If P_y and $\hat{P}_c$ are positive, small farmers will be worse off to the extent they are not entirely self-sufficient in consumption. Otherwise, they are harmed by a relatively lower price for their output. If this sector also has to accommodate more surplus labor, it will experience a further loss on the output or income side. If the real wage previously earned by new entrants to this sector approximates the average product of labor in this sector, a sharing ethic of income distribution will diffuse any income loss in the form of a lower average product for all members. On the balance sheet this second-order income change is ignored on both the income and expenditure sides.[24]

As mentioned before, there is both a gain and a loss to the capitalist group. Savers in this group lose interest income to mechanizing landowners who enjoy the benefit of lower cost capital. Those who lose may be poor savers whose only medium for saving is the financial system. On the other hand, some capitalists gain from a higher rate of return to capital in the nonagricultural sector caused by the diversion of more capital to agriculture. These capitalists may indeed be the rich; consequently, the income measure fails to capture important redistributions of income within the capitalist group.

Table 8.4 on the sources of income presents the information needed to estimate

[24] A measure of this income change is provided by the elasticity of the average product on small farms with respect to labor. This may be expressed as $(MP_l/AP_l - 1)$ where MP_l, AP_l are the marginal and average products of labor. Absolute income of the original small farm population changes by the amount $dL_s(MP_l - AP_l)$ where $(MP_l - AP_l)$ is the difference between the extra production and the additional consumption claim of a new entrant.

TABLE 8.3. Functional Income Balance Sheet

Factor Owners	Sources	Uses
Mechanizable land	$(A_f + \lambda A_c)\,\hat{P}_A$	$-(F_a\hat{P}_f + C_a\hat{P}_c + Y_a\hat{P}_y)$
Capital	$(K_f + K_y)\,\hat{P}_K - K_f\hat{S}$	$-(F_k\hat{P}_f + C_k\hat{P}_c + Y_k\hat{P}_y)$
Labor	$(L_f + L_c + L_y)\,\hat{P}_L = 0$	$-(F_\ell\hat{P}_f + C_\ell\hat{P}_c + Y_\ell\hat{P}_y)$
Nonmechanizable land	$M\hat{P}_M = 0$	$-(F_m\hat{P}_f + C_m\hat{P}_c + Y_m\hat{P}_y)$
Small farmers	$L_s\hat{P}_{Ls} = 0$	$-(F_s\hat{P}_f + C_s\hat{P}_c + Y_s\hat{P}_y)$

the nominal income distribution effects implied by the simulation results.[25] Table 8.5 on the uses of income makes allowances for the wide diversity of consumption patterns among different income groups in Colombia. The figures on uses of income reflect the assumption that recipients of nonlabor income spend five precent of their income on each of crop and cattle products and the rest on nonagricultural goods. These expenditure percentages probably err slightly on the high side, but there is little information on which to base a judgment about the

TABLE 8.4. Sources of Income by Type and Sector, 1964 (Millions of Current Pesos)

Sector	Nonagriculture	Mechanized Agriculture	Cattle	Small Scale Agriculture	Total
Income Type:					
Labor	15,984	490	1,247	–	17,721
Capital	12,075	1,355	–	–	13,430
Mechanizable Land	–	875	1,378	–	2,253
Small Farm	–	–	–	5,298	5,298
Nonmechanizable Land	–	–	1,907	–	1,907
Value-added:	28,059	2,720	4,532	5,298	40,609

Notes: (a) This table is based on the National Accounts for 1964.

(b) There is no attempt to allocate small farm income between capital (land) and labor payments.

(c) Small farm output is total crop output (excluding coffee) minus the output of mechanized crops where the latter is defined as the sum of value-added for cotton, rice, barley, sugar, sesame, soybeans, 10 percent of corn and potatoes and 50 percent of wheat.

[25]Government and housing services are excluded from this table–they are considered to be exogenous to the model–along with coffee production, an important export activity in Colombia. Ignoring this and other export sectors does not distort the results above to the extent that suppliers and users of foreign exchange belong to the same income groups.

TABLE 8.5. Uses of Income by Type and Commodity, 1964
(Millions of Current Pesos)

Expenditure	Crops	Nonagricultural Goods	Cattle	Total
Income Type:				
Labor	3,696	11,274	2,751	17,721
Capital	670	12,087	673	13,430
Mechanizable Land	112.5	2,028	112.5	2,253
Nonmechanizable Land	95.5	1,716	95.5	1,907
Small Farm	3,444	954	900	5,298
Total	8,018	28,059	4,532	40,609

Notes: (a) The table utilizes the assumption that nonlabor income recipients have average consumption propensities of 0.9 for nonagricultural goods and 0.05 for crops and cattle. An own-consumption ratio of 0.65 is also assumed for small farmers.

(b) There is no attempt to allocate small farm income between cpaital (land) and labor payments.

degree of probable overestimation.[26] Even though they are informed guesses, these average consumption propensities can be justified as an improvement over any procedure which assumes uniform spending patterns across different income groups. Labor's average propensity to consume food of 0.36 might appear to be too low, but this is only because food prices are measured at ex-farm values which exclude processing and distribution margins included in the price of urban food purchases.

Simulation 1, with $\sigma^y = 0$, can be used to illustrate the typical redistributive impact of subsidized farm mechanization. The value of $\hat{P}_K/\hat{S}$ is .826. If $\hat{S} = 0.4$, $\hat{P}_K$, the percentage change in the unsubsidized rate of return to capital, is therefore 33 percent. The percentage change in the price of nonagricultural goods, P_y, is 0.33 (12,075/28,059) = 14.22 percent. $(P_K\text{-}S)$ is equal to -0.0696 and the change in the return to mechanizable land P is (1355/875) 0.0696 = 0.1078, while the increase in the price of cattle P_c is 0.304 (.1078) = 0.03277. Given these relative price measures, the real income gains or losses of different groups (in millions of pesos) are:

[26]Two studies shed some light on the matter. The 1953 urban family budget study used to calculate consumption weights for cost-of-living indices indicated blue-collar families spent on average about 50 percent of their income on food. A later study, *Encuesta de Presupuestos Familiares: Parte Primera* (Bogotá: Universidad de los Andes, Centro de Estudios sobre Desarrollo Economico, 1971) suggested that a proportion closer to 60 percent would be more accurate. Given that the ratio of retail to ex-farm prices is about 1.75 to 2.00, labor's food expenditure of 0.36 in Table 8.5 is consistent with the budget studies. This proportion plus the small farm own-consumption ratio of 0.65 imply that recipients of nonlabor income spent 10 percent of their income on food. Marketing margins of 40-50 percent are appropriate according to the DANE study, *Contribucion al Estudio del Desempleo en Colombia* (Bogotá: Departamento Administrativo Nacional de Estadistica, 1971), 58.

Owners of mechanizable land	\$2,253(.1078) – 2,028(.1422) = 112.5(.03277)=\$252.87–288.34–3.69	= \$ 49.16
Capitalists	\$13,430(.33)–1.355(.4)–12,087(.1422)–673(.3277) = \$4,437–542–1,718.53–22.05	= \$2,154.69
Labor	0–11,274(.1422)–2,751(.03277) = 0–1603.16–90.15	= \$1,693.31
Owners of nonmechanizable land	0–1,716(.1422)–95.5(.03277) = 0–243.98–3.12	= \$ 247.10
Small farmers	0–954(.1422)–900(.03277) = 0–135.66–29.49	= \$ 165.15
		0

In view of the narrow range of variation in $\hat{P}_K/\hat{S}$, the results of simulations 2, 3, and 4, or any simulation with alternative values of σ^y of 0.1 or 0.2, would yield relative price effects that are almost identical. Therefore, balance sheet calculations for these simulations would not differ materially from those above. To gauge the sensitivity of these results to the value of the elasticity of factor substitution in nonagriculture, the previous exercise for simulation 1 was repeated, assigning values of 0.5 and 1 to σ^y. Without showing the detailed results, these calculations indicated a similar pattern of redistribution. When σ^y has a value of 0.5 (1), capitalists gain \$2,322.34 (\$2,544.40), landowners as a group lose \$394.15 (\$524.32), small farmers lose \$164.87 (\$164.53), and labor as a whole loses \$1,762.67 (\$1,855.21). Augmenting the value of σ^y changes the distribution of functional income in two directions. First, as a fraction of capitalists' gain, landowners lose somewhat more and labor somewhat less as σ^y increases. Secondly, at higher values of σ^y there is less surplus labor than in the initial situation, so that the group of newly employed workers outside small farms (or, alternatively, the group of small farmers) gain, although labor as a whole becomes slightly worse off.

Still, these results indicate that both kinds of landowners together lose a small amount of real income and that capitalists invariably gain higher real incomes (by about 16 percent) with from 80 to 86 percent of their gains achieved at the expense of labor and small farmers who, along with owners of nonmechanized land, sustain the largest real income losses.[27] Even with the conservative results of simulations 5 and 6, capital income is increased by about eight percent. The income loss of small farmers is in addition to any loss that they may have to bear by absorbing more surplus labor. When nonlabor income is considered as a whole, the conclusion is inescapable that real income is transferred toward the richest groups in the Colombian economy or, alternatively, that these groups would lose if the subsidy were removed.[28]

[27] From a different perspective, about 4.8 percent of total income is redistributed to capitalists from other groups. The top ten percent of income savers receive almost one-half of total income and probably own at least two-thirds of all nonland assets. Thus, about three percent of total income would be transferred to this group from the rest of the economy, or, on the basis of the more conservative estimate above, slightly more than one percent of total income.

[28] The dynamic consequences may be much more favorable, however, if the redistribution of income raises the saving rate and serves to augment the future demand for labor.

This important conclusion is subject to some small upward bias arising from the exclusion of urban land and from the possibility that certain segments of the nonagricultural labor force may have the institutional market power to extract real income gains due to a lower relative price for crops. If the real wage of many nonagricultural employees were constant in terms of nonagricultural prices, the real income losses of labor would be smaller than those indicated (and the real income gains of nonlabor factors would be less). More generally, if labor is not perfectly mobile in the long run, the increase in agricultural labor demand will raise wages in that sector while wages will decline elsewhere. Finally, although land rents tend to increase in the agricultural sector, this increment in land income is probably matched by reduced land rents in the urban economy as nonagricultural output contracts. From a global perspective, the real income gains ascribed to owners of mechanizable land probably should be ignored to offset any bias that results from excluding urban land rents.

7. CONCLUDING REMARKS

Although its income distribution effects may not be desirable, the subsidy to farm mechanization may still be beneficial in improving the allocation of resources in the economy. Changes in the level of national income depend on whether resources are transferred to higher or lower productivity uses.

The allocative impact of the subsidy can be approximately measured as

$$W = \tfrac{1}{2} D_K \delta K_f - D_L \delta L_S + D_A \delta A_f$$

where W is the gain or loss in national income associated with mechanization.[29] This measure takes account of preexisting distortions in the land and labor markets and recognizes that prices for the same factors in different uses are unequal. δL_S, δK_f, and δA_f represent, respectively, the equilibrium changes in the allocation of labor to small-scale agriculture, and of capital and land to large-scale agriculture in response to a capital subsidy of given size. D_L, D_K, and D_A represent the size of the distortion in the different factor markets and measure the excess of marginal social benefit over cost per unit change in factor allocation. The first term in the expression for W is always negative (a loss of income); the second is also negative if surplus labor is augmented; and the third term is positive if land is switched out of cattle and into large-farm crops.

Using the simulation results for factor reallocations and a range of plausible estimates for the size of the distortion parameters, a number of calculations were performed which are briefly summarized here. In virtually every case there was a diminution in the level of national income due to a worse allocation of labor and capital that outweighs the positive effects on total income of an improved alloca-

[29] See A. Harberger, "The Measurement of Waste," *American Economic Review* (May, 1964), 58-76, for a more complete explanation of the use of this type of measurement.

tion of land. The income-reducing effects of the subsidy and the shift of more labor to the small farm sector more than offset the increment to total income associated with the transfer of some large-farm land to crops instead of cattle. As with most estimates of this nature, the seriousness of misallocation is not large, being less than one percent of GNP in all cases and approaching zero as σ^y reaches its highest value of 0.5 or one. Of course, if external lenders were footing the bill, this loss is not an absolute one but occurs only in comparison with a neutral subsidy policy.

One reason for not giving this result too much weight is that it does not take into account all of the relevant distortions in the economy. A proper accounting of the allocative implications of the subsidy would consider corporate income, property and commodity taxes, tariffs, and the existence of labor unions. With the possible exception of tariffs, these distortions dampen the growth of the nonagricultural sector and serve to raise the marginal social value of production there above marginal social cost. By discouraging nonagricultural output, the subsidy to farm mechanization may have a welfare cost much larger than that which is indicated.

Even if mechanization had favorable effects on national income levels, it would not necessarily be a desirable policy. Although this study makes no comparison of alternative policies, it may well be that for a given subsidy cost, a policy of encouraging the use of biochemical inputs in small-scale agriculture would yield considerable benefits in terms of income distribution and resource allocation.

From the preceding analysis it is concluded that the economic goals of greater equality in income distribution and higher levels of output are likely to be complementary in terms of subsidized farm mechanization. Eliminating the subsidy would both improve the distribution of income and, as a bonus, better allocate the economy's exisiting resources. Either a tax on agricultural capital use or a higher interest rate for loans to purchase large-farm capital would effectively remove this subsidy. Another way of achieving the same end is to grant a similar subsidy to the use of nonagricultural capital. A general subsidy would be neutral between sectors and have no allocative or distributive effects of the type modelled here. Redistribution would be limited in this case to that which occurs between owners and users of capital.

In weighing these results, it should be remembered that model building requires the suppression of a great deal of information about an economy. The preceding analysis has ignored much structural detail about the Colombian economy. The assumption of homogeneous sectors neglects the economic diversity which exists within each sector. The nonagricultural sector, for example, is a collection of heterogeneous industries whose shifting composition and access to capital resources could conceivably alter the factor intensity and factor substitution values that have been used in the analysis. Perhaps the single biggest weakness in this exercise is the assumption that a cutback in the supply of capital to nonagriculture would occur on an across-the-board basis. If only large firms in each nonagricultural activity were squeezed from the capital market, it is possible that nonagricultural employment would not decline in response to the mechanization subsidy. Large firms, however, are notable for being at the head of the capital market queue. Moreover, even if modern sector urban employment is diminished, this reduction could conceivably give rise to larger small-firm urban employment instead of greater small-farm rural employment. There is also some evidence to suggest that the impact of farm mechanization varies with the region of the country and with the changes in land utilization that accompany it. To some unknown degree, the conclusions are inevitably prone to aggregation bias.

This bias means there are a number of specific mechanization issues on which this study offers only minimal insight. While it is possible to express reservations about the wisdom of general mechanization, there may be particular crops for which mechanization is desirable, particularly those on the margin of exportability when there is a shortage of foreign exchange. If, at world prices, the elasticity of final demand is infinite, subsidized mechanization will have positive, and possibly quite large, effects on the demand for labor. Similarly, there may be some merit in mechanizing some, but not all operations, for a given crop. More research is needed on whether selective mechanization policies and the development of small-farm machinery may remove the conflict between farm output and employment gains in those crops where it now occurs. The analysis also provides no answer to the question of how a full scale land redistribution would affect the demand for farm machinery since the initial land distribution is taken as given. However, if the pattern of land ownership were significantly less concentrated, it is unlikely that mechanization would present a problem for economic policy since the demands for farm capital and machinery would be much more likely to accurately reflect the resource endowment of the country and would resemble more closely the Japanese pattern of mechanization (labor-using, land-augmenting mechanical practices) rather than the North American one.

APPENDIX

The definition of and notation for the variables and parameters used in the previous analysis is:

F = level of crop output supplied or demanded. F_f, F_s, denote large and small farm crop output respectively assumed to be perfect substitutes in consumption.

Y = level of composite nonagricultural output supplied or demanded.

C = level of cattle output supplied or demanded.

L = labor services. L_f, L_s, L_y, L_c are employment levels in large-crop farms, small-scale agriculture, the nonagricultural and cattle sectors, respectively.

K = capital services. K_y and K_f are the amounts of capital used in the non-agricultural and large-crop farm sectors, respectively.

A = mechanizable land used in the large farm (A_f) and cattle (A_c) sectors.
M = nonmechanizable land (hilly or uneven ground).
P_K = the unsubsidized price of capital services (cost of nonagricultural capital).
P_L = the money wage received by labor. For example, P_{Lf} signifies the money wage paid to labor in large-farm agriculture.
P_{A_f} = the rental price of mechanizable land in large-farm agriculture.
P_M = the rental price of a unit of nonmechanizable land in cattle.
P_f, P_y, P_c = output prices for commodities F, Y, and C, respectively.
θ_i^j = the income share of factor i in sector j.
σ_{ij}^k = the Allen partial elasticity of substitution between factors i and j. A superscript denotes each sector, Y, F, and C.
E_{ij} = income-compensated price elasticity of final demand between the products of sectors i and j.
g_p = constant elasticity of small farm marketed supply with respect to the percentage change in relative product prices.
g_{Ls} = constant elasticity of small farm marketed output with respect to percentage changes in small farm labor.
S = proportional subsidy to the cost of using capital in large-farm crops vis-á-vis the nonagricultural sector.
σ^y = elasticity of factor substitution in nonagriculture.
V_i = the value of output produced in the ith sector or the total payments made to the i'th factor of production.
P_{Ls} = the average product of labor in small farm agriculture, assumed to be equal to the real wage paid to labor in other sectors.

Chapter 9

INCOME DISTRIBUTION CONSEQUENCES OF AGRICULTURAL PRICE SUPPORTS IN COLOMBIA

Wayne R. Thirsk
University of Waterloo

1. INTRODUCTION

Colombia is not unique in pursuing protective agricultural policies. In many countries efforts are made to create and preserve the relatively small scale, family farm unit of production and the competitive market structure implied by the preservation of that unit. On the other hand, there are few countries which do not attempt to shield their agricultural producers from the rigors of competition at the international level. Most developed countries have adopted a protective scheme of either tariffs or deficiency payments as a means of insulating domestic producer prices and incomes from the vagaries and hazards of world price changes. Common Market countries, for example, rely on a common external tariff to elevate the prices of domestic cereals above the import price of a comparable item purchased on the world market. The United Kingdom, Canada and the United States have all to some extent depended on a system of deficiency payments and production controls to raise farm incomes beyond the level that would be determined by the untrammeled market for farm commodities. A number of less developed countries, among them Colombia, have also introduced policies seeking to inhibit the influence of international prices on domestic ones.

Although sometimes proposed as an aid to price stabilization, measures for supporting domestic agricultural prices have been more frequently justified on

*The author is grateful to G. Smith, Y.-M. Ho, and especially to R. A. Berry, for their comments on an earlier version of this paper. None of them, needless to say, bear any responsibility for its contents and remaining errors.

the income distribution basis of raising relatively low average agricultural incomes. Economic analysis of these programs initially focused on their efficiency implications and either ignored, or was less concerned with, their ability to meet distributional objectives.[1] These studies invariably seem to indicate a loss in economic efficiency will result from the imposition of price support programs. In general the loss arises from the fact that at the margin of production the cost of an extra unit of output diverges from its value to the consumer. Recently, however, there have been new efforts to determine the income redistribution effects of price support programs. In the U. S. Bonnen concluded that for a wide range of commodity programs it required from twenty to one hundred dollars of total program benefits to provide one dollar to the bottom twenty percent of farmers.[2] Schultze argued that subsidies accrue in the main to those whose incomes exceed the nonfarm average and do little for the low income farmer whose plight provided the original motivation for the programs.[3] Lidman, however, notes that these results were based on a model which failed to incorporate supply adjustments; it was implicitly assumed that supply elasticities (and, as well, demand elasticities) for all crops were zero.[4] Using a spatial linear programming model of the agricultural sector, Lidman estimates the price and output changes that would follow from the abandonment of the farm programs and finds that current farm programs probably augment the net incomes of farmers in different sales classes almost proportionately. He, too, criticizes the undesirable "trickling up" of benefits to the higher income groups. Almost all of the work to date in the United States and elsewhere has neglected to deal with the effect of price supports on the purchasing power of different income groups. When relative prices change, people in any income group can become comparatively worse or better off either because their nominal income is altered or because their consumption pattern is atypically weighted toward commodities whose relative prices have changed. This paper attempts to take account of the manner in which price supports in Colombia have operated on both the earning and expenditure sides of the income statements of different income groups.

The rest of this paper is divided into four sections. Section 2 discusses the history of agricultural price supports in Colombia and furnishes some details on the methods of support. Then a model is developed to measure the income redis-

[1] Two of the best attempts to ascertain the output losses or efficiency cost of these programs might be mentioned. These are T. D. Wallace, "Measures of Social Cost of Agricultural Programs," *Journal of Farm Economics* (May, 1962), pp. 580-94 and R. Dardis and E. W. Learn, *Measures of the Degree and Cost of Economic Protection of Agriculture in Selected Countries*, U. S. Department of Agriculture, Economic Research Service, Technical Bulletin 1384, November 1967.

[2] J. T. Bonnen, "The Distribution of Benefits from Selected U. S. Farm Programs," *Rural Poverty in the United States: A Report of the President's National Advisory Commission on Rural Poverty* (Washington, D. C., 1967), pp. 461-505.

[3] C. L. Schultze, "The Distribution of Farm Subsidies," *A Staff Paper* (Washington, D. C.: The Brookings Institution), 1971.

[4] R. M. Lidman, "The Distribution of Benefits of Major Agricultural Programs" (Unpublished Ph. D. dissertation, University of Wisconsin, 1972).

tribution arising from price supports followed by a brief description of the data. The counterfactual question posed is which income groups would benefit and which would lose if domestic crop prices were brought into line with either unadjusted or adjusted international values? Since abandonment of the price support program (though not necessarily its stabilization aspects) would involve a change in the efficiency of resource allocation, this effect is analyzed in a subsequent section. A final section summarizes the results and discusses some indirect effects of price supports which must be considered in an overall evaluation of such programs.

2. THE DEVELOPMENT OF COLOMBIAN PRICE SUPPORTS

Protection of Colombian agriculture dates from the depression of the 1930s when tariff legislation was introduced which sharply raised import duties on all agricultural products.[5] Subsequently, rigid import quotas were applied to basic foodstuffs both during and after World War II. In 1944 a semi-official marketing agency, INA (Instituto Nacional de Abastecimiento), was established for the purpose of setting minimum prices for rice, corn, beans, and wheat. As part of an overall import substitution strategy of economic development, the avowed goal of INA was self-sufficiency in agricultural production. Support prices for other crops were left in the hands of the various commodity organizations that were formed after World War II with government encouragement. Thus, the coffee growers federation supported coffee prices, the tobacco institute maintained tobacco prices, and the cotton development organization became concerned with the setting of sesame, cotton, cottonseed, and other oil seed prices.

INA became the national instrument for importing crop goods and used its control over imports to establish desired differentials between support prices and domestic market prices. Usually the latter were kept above the former to prevent an overloading of INA's limited storage capacity. In effect, INA's almost exclusive ability to import under a regime of foreign exchange licensing was used to validate its system of price supports. The level of support was based on the average cost, including a normal rate of return of producing the crop in Colombia. This process of establishing support prices prompted an observation in the early 1960s that "the difference between domestic and world prices has often been substantial, reflecting in part the strong motivation for saving foreign exchange through import substitution."[6]

INA's cost of intervention in the market, i.e., the costs of storage, operation, etc., was entirely underwritten by the sizeable profits achieved from importing commodities at world prices and reselling them at higher domestic prices, and from the arbitraging of domestically produced crops over time and space. In

[5] Much of the factual material in this and succeeding paragraphs borrows heavily from T. Goering, "Colombian Agricultural Price and Trade Policies," Facultad de Agronomia, Palmira Colombia; Universidad del Valle, 1961.

[6] D. Adams *et al.*, *Public Law 480 and Colombia's Economic Development* (East Lansing: Michigan State University, 1964), p. 39.

terms of its import replacement goal, INA was successful in helping to reduce dependence on foreign sources of supply for a number of crops, the only notable exception being wheat. In some instances producers were able to pressure INA into restricting imports whenever they felt price movements threatened the profitability of their activities.[7] With a limited storage capacity that in the early 1960s permitted the purchase of only about five percent of the total production of supported crops, INA never accumulated unsold surpluses that could only be sold abroad at a substantial loss. In fact, cotton represents a case in which an import substitution phase was followed by an export phase that required only a small and temporary subsidy before the crop was able to compete in world markets without assistance.

From 1951 to 1958 INA was known as the Corporacion de Defensa de Productos Agricolas. In 1968 it was superseded by a new government controlled body called IDEMA (Instituto de Mercadeo Agropecuario). In most important respects IDEMA closely resembles its predecessor except that its range of functions and powers is wider than before. Inventories of domestic crops and imports provide the supply-side control of domestic prices and constitute the source of the budget for IDEMA as in the past. At planting time IDEMA announces floor prices for a wider group of crops including rice, sesame, barley, edible beans, corn, sorghum, soybeans, wheat, potatoes, and anis.[8] IDEMA attempts to buy all that is offered at these prices but uses its import and export power to insure floor prices are less than domestic open market prices and the bulk of the crop is therefore handled by private interests. Floor prices are still pegged to average production costs inclusive of normal profit, are uniform for all parts of the country, and are based on delivery to purchase or storage points owned and operated by IDEMA (or, more precisely, by the storage affiliate known as Instituto Nacional Agropecuario–INAGRARIO). IDEMA is also empowered to offer especially attractive incentive prices (precios de fomento) to stimulate the supply of particular products. It may also purchase on-farm crop supplies at an intervention price somewhat less than the market price in order to restrain short-run price increases. Farmers are enticed to sell at these prices because IDEMA will lower its quality standards (accept a higher moisture and trash content) and absorb a portion of the farmer's transport costs. Normally most farmers must accept a higher transport charge because of the limited number of IDEMA purchase points.

In 1969 IDEMA purchases constituted approximately eleven percent of the value of the total output of those commodities enjoying price support. However, eighty-seven percent of the total purchases made by IDEMA during the 1968-70 period were concentrated on the three products, corn, rice, and wheat, which

[7]In the book by Adams *et al.*, *ibid.*, p. 212, a case in which the cereal growers organization, Federacion Nacional de Productores de Cereales (FENALCE) brought about the reversal of INA plans to import P. L. 480 foodgrains is documented.

[8]Another government agency, the Superintendencia Nacional de Precios, controls the price and absorption of agricultural products used as an input in manufacturing processes and also distribution margins in the case of milk and meats.

crops are, respectively, most important in terms of acreage, value and foreign exchange use. With the assistance of loans from the Inter-American Development and U. S. Export-Import Banks, IDEMA embarked on a program in 1969 of expanding its storage capacity by fifty percent. It was anticipated that by the end of 1973 IDEMA would be in a position to purchase about 20 percent of the annual output of major grain crops. This capacity, according to Food and Agriculture Organization (FAO) estimates, would be sufficient to guarantee price stabilization.[9]

This is not the place to attempt a detailed evaluation of the success of IDEMA in meeting its own goals. There are, however, some crude indicators of the successfulness of IDEMA's policies. First, prices for any crop may be judged too high if they induce significant import deficits in other crops and "large" export losses for that crop. Of course, when the exchange rate is overvalued, as it unquestionably has been in Colombia over most of the last three decades, there is a strong allocational argument in favor of general export subsidies, one form of which is the losses sustained by a government marketing system. Export losses would be inappropriate only if the degree of the implicit subsidy on export sales exceeded the extent of overvaluation. But there have been instances in which support prices have distorted production choices. For example, in Valle the policy of higher cotton prices in the middle 1950s led to a growth in cotton acreage and a consequent glut in cottonseed cake at the same time there was a reduction in corn-bean acreage and a shortage of corn.[10] Export subsidies have been substantial in other instances. In 1969, for example, rice and maize exports required a sizeable budgetary subsidy of 32.5 million pesos (about 1.82 million U. S.) which was granted in response to the growing accumulation of stocks in these two groups. It is difficult to judge whether these examples reflect an inevitable lack of foresight about the strength of internal and external demand or instead represent correctable defects of the price support policy.

A second criterion for judging the impact of IDEMA policies is the ability of IDEMA to reduce the seasonal variance in agricultural prices. One study of this matter concluded that, in the case of rice, government intervention through IDEMA has achieved little effect in reducing the variance of either farm prices or farm incomes.[11] Such a before-and-after comparison is not conclusive, however, for it cannot distinguish the effects of government intervention from other differences between the two periods that were considered. Thus, for example, it fails to consider improvements in transportation over time. Perhaps the only judgment possible is that from the perspective of achieving self-sufficiency and reducing price instability there is evidence of neither dismal failure nor clear success.

[9]This is an interesting case in which success breeds on itself. If market participants expect IDEMA to secure price stability their behavior will help to realize those expectations. Thus, the existence of larger IDEMA capacity may mean it is never fully utilized in achieving stabilization.

[10]This situation is described in greater length by Goering, *op. cit.*, pp. 9-10.

[11]N. Gutierrez A., *Costos Sociales de los Precios de Sustentacion en Arroz* (Bogotá: Instituto Colombiano Agropecuario, 1972), p.87.

3. AN INCOME DISTRIBUTION MODEL OF PRICE SUPPORTS

A number of alternative methods can be used to describe the distributional impact of a price support program. For example, one could compare benefits as a fraction of gross income for different income groups. Another possibility is a comparison of the percentage distribution of nominal income in the absence of supports with the percentage distribution of program benefits accruing to people at different income levels.[12] This approach would lend itself to easy interpretation since Gini coefficients could be calculated to determine what changes in income distribution were attributable to price supports. While these methods of evaluation are of some interest they are not used here because they focus exclusively on changes in nominal income and ignore the losses which must accompany any redistribution of income.

A more complete analysis of the problem is to consider changes in real income and to recognize that the real gains won by any income group must be realized at the expense of the other, less fortunate, income groups. This goal is simple to achieve if any income size class is treated as the unit of analysis and redistribution within any class is ignored so that only the net position of the group is allowed to count in assessing gains and losses.

The analysis begins with the straightforward proposition that the sum of the purchases of domestic output for all income classes, valued at producer prices, is equal to the income earned by all income classes. When certain behavioral assumptions are introduced, this accounting identity is converted into a useful vehicle for examing income redistribution.

To facilitate exposition, the following notation will be used:

C_{ij} = amount of crop j consumed by the ith income class, j = 1 . . m, 1 . . n
P_j = producer price for crop j, j = 1 . . . m
Q_{ij} = amount of crop j produced by farmers who belong to the ith income class.
M_{ij} = amount of imports of crop j consumed by the ith income class. Imports are sold to consumers at price P_j, the same as domestic output. Total purchases of crop goods by all income classes are distributed between domestic output and imports:

$$\sum_j^m \sum_i^n C_{ij}P_j = \sum_i^n \sum_j^m Q_{ij}P_j + \sum_i^n \sum_j^m M_{ij}P_j \qquad (1)$$

Ignoring the subscripts on the summation signs for the moment and taking first differences of equation (1) yields

[12] Methodologies of this kind have been adopted in the work of Bonnen and Schultze, *op. cit.*, for the United States. Bonnen concluded that the bulk of the expenditure on commodity programs eluded the pockets of the marginal farmer. A recent U. S. wheat sale to Russia illustrates the inadequacy of this approach to income distribution. The hue and cry raised by higher consumer prices for food was not considered at the time of the sale by the United States Department of Agriculture which was concerned only with improving nominal farm incomes.

$$\Sigma\,\Sigma\, C_{ij}\Delta P_j + \Sigma\,\Sigma\, \Delta C_{ij}P_j + \Sigma\,\Sigma\, \Delta P_j\Delta C_{ij} = \Sigma\,\Sigma\, Q_{ij}\Delta P_j + \Sigma\,\Sigma\, \Delta Q_{ij}P_j + \Sigma\,\Sigma\, \Delta Q_{ij}\Delta P_j + \Sigma\,\Sigma\, M_{ij}\Delta P_j + \Sigma\,\Sigma\, \Delta M_{ij}P_j + \Sigma\,\Sigma\, \Delta M_{ij}\Delta P_j \quad (2)$$

This last expression provides the basic accounting framework for the study of price supports. A number of assumptions need to be made in order to empirically implement this framework for Colombia. Since the alternative of primary interest to us is that of no price supports, the change in crop prices ΔP_j that is envisioned is one where domestic crop prices are allowed to move to world price levels. It is assumed that world prices of the various crops would be unaffected by the abandonment of the support program. The appropriate exchange rate to use is considered later on. Distribution margins between the prices paid by consumers and the prices received by producers are ignored throughout and assumed to be constant when domestic price supports are removed. Thus, the full extent of any change in producer prices is assumed to be passed on to the consumer.

Another assumption is that $\Delta Q_j = -\Delta M_j$ or that changes in domestic output are exactly offset by more or fewer imports. This is equivalent to assuming that only producers, but not consumers, are responsive to price changes since $\Delta M \equiv \Delta C + \Delta Q$. A special case is where $\Delta Q_j = 0$ or where there is a zero supply elasticity for that particular crop. Because all crop prices would be adjusted at the same time the structure of relative crop prices will not experience as much change as when only a single price is altered and so the assumption of no supply response may not be as extreme as it appears. It could in any event be removed if estimates of supply elasticities were available. The same rationale can be used to justify the assumed price insensitivity of consumers. Notwithstanding the dearth of demand elasticity estimates in Colombia, the fact that a large number of crop prices are permitted to vary in the same direction makes the assumption that $\Delta C_j = 0$ not too extreme.

When these restrictions are imposed on equation (2) the result is

$$\Sigma\,\Sigma\, C_{ij}\Delta P_j - \Sigma\,\Sigma\, M_{ij}\Delta P_j = \Sigma\,\Sigma\, Q_{ij}\Delta P_j \text{ or } \Sigma\,\Sigma (C_{ij} - M_{ij})\Delta P_j = \Sigma\,\Sigma\, Q_{ij}\Delta P_j \quad (3)$$

Equation (3) is a first-order approximation of the income redistribution resulting from a change in crop prices. Two features of this equation may not be entirely obvious. For any income group the term

$$\sum_j C_{ij}P_j\ \Delta P_j/P_j$$

measures the changes in income on the uses side while the term

$$\sum_j Q_{ij}P_j\ \Delta P_j/P_j$$

measures the income change on the sources side. The difference between these two measures indicates how the real income of a particular group is altered. Moreover, if imports are negligible, the sum of the real gains and losses spread over all groups is zero and the hypothesized price change will, therefore, generate a pure

TABLE 9.1. Market, Support and World Prices by Crop (Pesos), 1954-1970

	Rice (Paddy)			Wheat			Barley			Soybeans		
Year	Support Price	Market Price	World Price	Support Price	Market Price	World Price	Support Price	Market Price	World Price	Support Price	Market Price	World Price
1954	–	470	400	571	710	–	385	380	395	–	–	–
1955	400	475	542	642	650	197	415	400	271	–	–	–
1956	440	485	520	642	680	190	470	425	–	–	–	–
1957	512	615	–	725	760	402	498	480	–	–	825	–
1958	840	750	–	856	870	509	620	580	690	550	850	–
1959	840	770	845	921	940	494	684	630	608	650	1,050	653
1960	840	883	–	921	880	505	684	624	–	800	800	559
1961	1,006	954	843	921	975	598	760	637	567	800	850	635
1962	1,006	919	–	921	957	651	–	642	575	850	900	631
1963	1,260	1,046	–	1,098	1,052	807	–	828	–	–	1,200	1,039
1964	1,260	1,347	–	1,428	1,394	732	–	898	720	–	1,600	1,042
1965	1,260	1,703	1,650	1,428	1,525	806	–	999	739	1,460	1,700	1,044
1966	1,720	1,884	–	1,714	1,755	1,020	–	1,284	1,162	1,460	1,850	1,446
1967	2,050	1,914	1,896	1,714	1,756	1,052	–	1,274	1,262	1,680	1,930	1,818
1968	2,050	2,106	–	2,100	1,956	1,100	–	1,490	1,148	1,680	–	–
1969	2,000	1,866	1,450	2,100	2,059	1,150	2,000	1,600	1,260	2,000	1,600	1,260
1970	2,250	1,850	1,785	2,100	1,933	1,265	2,000	1,592	1,415	2,000	1,592	1,415

Notes: (1) Information on support prices came primarily from the government marketing agency IDEMA but was supplemented in earlier years by the published material of other government organizations. Market prices for each crop are published regularly by the Banco de la Republica. Numerous sources accounted for the data on world (CIF, Atlantic port of Colombia) prices including special reports on Colombia of the World Bank (IRBD), the Anuario de Comercio Exterior of the National Statistical Agency DANE, unpublished IDEMA data, annual reports of FAO and scattered bits of individual research on Colombian agriculture. Breaks in any price series indicate in most instances the unreliability of the data rather than its nonavailability.

TABLE 9.1. Continued

Year	Corn			Potatoes			Beans			Sesame		
	Support Price	Market Price	World Price	Support Price	Market Price	World Price	Support Price	Market Price	World Price	Support Price	Market Price	World Price
1954	280	330	279	318	319	192	–	1,140	621	–	588	–
1955	280	300	–	311	211	159	–	1,070	566	–	686	–
1956	319	350	–	311	312	575	–	1,360	559	–	833	–
1957	319	430	347	311	311	–	–	1,440	1,837	–	1,323	–
1958	440	385	–	360	370	621	1,280	1,440	1,490	1,350	1,323	–
1959	440	450	384	360	304	371	1,280	1,400	–	1,350	1,323	1,250
1960	440	474	300	360	350	555	1,280	2,000	–	1,550	1,519	1,280
1961	560	629	511	–	504	699	1,760	2,277	1,640	1,550	1,617	1,319
1962	750	526	600	–	291	–	–	2,066	1,873	1,560	2,250	1,562
1963	850	794	–	–	730	863	–	2,419	2,555	2,100	2,450	2,309
1964	925	1,040	590	–	1,050	1,047	–	2,987	2,342	2,100	3,283	–
1965	925	903	–	–	612	–	3,200	3,477	2,764	2,100	3,283	–
1966	1,020	1,104	901	–	983	–	3,200	3,662	2,630	2,900	3,682	2,052
1967	1,250	1,203	–	–	876	–	3,200	3,393	–	3,500	3,934	–
1968	1,020	1,294	942	–	822	–	6,800	5,230	4,697	3,700	3,817	3,670
1969	1,300	1,319	994	–	1,260	–	4,500	4,995	4,596	3,700	4,371	–
1970	1,350	1,490	1,000	–	1,040	–	4,500	4,774	–	3,700	4,799	–

Notes: (2) The following grade classifications were meant to apply to the support prices: Type I, Category A for paddy rice, high grades for wheat (hard wheat) and barley, average grades for soybeans, yellow and white high grade corn, and Type II, Category A (Calima, Nima varieties) for beans. Market and World prices were impossible to control on a consistent quality or grade basis and much of the apparent unreliability of the data could be related to this problem.

or zero-sum redistribution of income among the various income groups. Conversely, there is a real net loss if the price of a commodity in excess demand increases. Finally, with respect to own-consumption of crops, the effects cancel in their impact on distribution as any change in the value of production is matched by an equal change in the value of consumption.

The data needed to implement this approach are contained in Tables 9.1, 9.2, and 9.3. Price information on the eight crops that were considered is presented in Table 9.1. Obtaining a consistent set of price data over time for any crop is difficult in view of the uncertainties and potential distortions that result from variability in the composition of crop grades, from different time intervals for the availability of particular prices, and from conflict among various sources which often occurs when the same data are reported for different geographical locations. An attempt has been made to secure comparability of the price series by excluding data which could conceivably introduce significant quality variations. Gaps in any year for support prices, CIF (Credit, Insurance and Freight) import prices or for market prices received by producers reflect either the absence of any information or a vote of nonconfidence in it. The reliability of the CIF values is most worrisome since that series derives from a number of diverse sources, quality was difficult to standardize and the crop definitions and classifications used by any single source often underwent bewildering revisions.

From the point of view of a buyer in a free market (a miller or a wholesaler) his options consist of purchasing the crop at its landed CIF price or relying on the sales of domestic farmers. If the transportation cost between the port of entry and the buyer is roughly the same as that between the domestic farmer and the buyer, the relevant price comparison is CIF vis-à-vis ex-farm or market prices. There is no need in this case to adjust either the CIF or the market prices for transport margins in determining the alternative prices that would be received by producers with the price support program and without it.[13]

Another matter that requires some consideration is whether to use the actual exchange rate or an estimated shadow rate to make value conversions. In most Latin American countries the adoption of import substituting industrialization strategies of economic development has led to the erection of high barriers to trade in industrial goods. The result of these policies is a decline in the nominal exchange rate with respect to domestic price levels and the creation of an artificial inducement to import food products which discourages domestic agricultural production. Colombia is no exception to this pattern. World prices for agricultural commodities are lower than domestic values at least in part because of the protection granted to the industrial sector.

If the system of price supports were abandoned, it is possible that any balance of payments effects would be offset by compensatory policies. Any tendency towards larger agricultural imports might prompt either greater efforts to export

[13] Where the assumption of offsetting transport costs is obviously incorrect, the market price should be compared to the CIF price plus transport costs to point of use less transport costs from a Colombian farm to the same destination.

or attempts to curtail other kinds of imports. Under these circumstances domestic prices would fall to international levels converted at the existing exchange rate if price supports were removed. This is the first counterfactual situation considered. Alternative situations can be encompassed by making a simple proportional adjustment to the estimates presented for this alternative. For example, if the exchange rate depreciated when supports were removed and the fall in domestic prices was only one-half of that postulated by the first alternative, the degree of income redistribution would decline by the same proportion.

There is also some intrinsic interest in determining the income distribution implications of moving to a more efficient allocation of resources. In an open economy a particular resource allocation can be deemed efficient if the domestic resource cost of earning or saving a unit of foreign exchange is the same for every activity. In Colombia as of the late 1960s this criterion implied that price supports should avoid surpluses that could be sold only at a subsidy larger than the fifteen percent CAT subvention available to minor exports and also should avoid import replacement if the required degree of protection exceeded the 30-35 percent average tariff on industrial goods.[14] Since abandoning a system of price supports would result in larger purchases of imports rather than the loss of export sales, the domestic resource cost of saving a unit of foreign exchange would be equal, on the average, in all parts of the economy if the nominal CIF price of crops was increased by about one-third. Assuming that the policy of tariff protection is a permanent feature of the economy, the appropriate shadow rate of exchange is also about one-third higher than the level of the nominal exchange rate.[15] In this alternative calculation of the income redistribution arising from the price support program observed market prices were compared to nominal CIF prices that were augmented by thirty percent. Because this relative price relationship fluctuated from one year to the next, the most typical differential nearest to the year 1968 was chosen for the income redistribution calculation. The year 1968 was singled out for special attention since the price data on the sources and uses of income refer to that year.

[14] This degree of protection is mentioned in the Colombian Ministry of Agriculture document OPSA-016, December 1969, entitled, "Financing Considerations for the Agricultural Exports of IDEMA." It agrees with other estimates. Note that this average tariff conceals a great deal of dispersion in the tariff rates for different industrial goods and that the average tax on imports is still substantially larger than the average subsidy on exports so that it costs more resources to save a dollar of foreign exchange than to earn a dollar. Thus, if resources for agricultural exports were drawn from the protected industrial sector, subsidization on a scale larger than fifteen percent (up to 30-35 percent) would be justified. Otherwise, the 15 percent CAT (Certificado de Abono Tributario) available to minor exports would apply as indicated in the text.

[15] This second-best measurement of shadow exchange rates is discussed in more detail by A. C. Harberger, "Survey of Literature on Cost-Benefit Analysis for Industrial Project Evaluation," *Project Evaluation* (Chicago: Markham, 1972), and by D. Schydlowsky, "On the Choice of a Shadow Price for Foreign Exchange," *Harvard University Economic Development Report No. 108* (Cambridge, Mass.: Development Advisory Service, 1968).

Table 9.2, which presents the data on the sources and uses of income by crop and income class, relies on data that was extracted from a recently developed input-output table for Colombia.[16] The data in turn are constructed primarily from the 1970 survey of urban households which disaggregated all families into five income classes. Having only five income size categories is somewhat confining for economic analysis since the income variation within each broad income class is neglected and therefore the total variance of earned income is understated. However, there is presently no substitute for the information contained in the input-output table which is so far unique in linking uses and sources of income by income size and type of production activity. Another shortcoming of this data is that the aggregate distribution of income suggests more equality than is in fact likely to exist. In the input-output table the two bottom income groups, which together comprise 72 percent of total income earners, receive about 46 percent of total income while the DANE (National Statistics Agency) data, on which the table is based, indicated that the income share of these two groups was only 32 percent.[17] Nonetheless, after certain adjustments are made to the raw data in the table the pattern of sources and uses by income class is highly plausible. For all of the crops considered, an extra dollar added to the price of the crop would result in greater increases in expenditures than in earnings for the low income groups and larger increments to earnings than to expenditures for the higher income groups.

The adjustments to the raw data in the input-output table used in deriving Table 9.2 were twofold. The uses data in Table 9.2 represent the sum of direct and indirect uses in the input-output table. Potatoes, beans, and soybeans were the only crops with no indirect uses. Wheat and rice were used indirectly in milling. Sesame was used entirely in oils and in other foods. Corn and barley were used as inputs in the livestock activities of eggs, milk, pork, cattle, and cattle raising. Because the consumer purchases gross output while the producer on the sources side receives that amount less intermediate input purchases, total uses of any crop always exceed the amount of total sources. In Table 9.2 the sources have been adjusted proportionately so that total sources equal total uses. This adjustment is in keeping with the earlier assumption of a zero supply elasticity when all crop prices are changed and presumes that purchases of intermediate goods would remain unchanged as the consumer pays an extra dollar more (or less) for crops whenever price supports are introduced (or abandoned). A similar rationale

[16] S. Daines, J. Ricardo, C. Gleason, and G. Poyner, "Input/Output Matrices Condensed for Analysis of Primary Agricultural Sectors–116 Principal Product Sectors at Producer Prices," *Statistical Working Document No.2* Agency for International Development, March, 1972.

[17] Most of the error, however, appears to be associated with income in the nonagricultural sector. In agriculture the bottom two income groups (90 percent of all income earners) receive 52 percent of the total income while, according to Berry, they receive 48 percent. See R. A. Berry, "Land Distribution, Income Distribution, and the Productive Efficiency of Colombian Agriculture," in *Food Research Institute Studies in Agricultural Economics, Trade and Development*, Vol. XII, No. 3 (1973).

TABLE 9.2. Sources and Uses of Income by Crop and Income Class (Thousands of 1968 Colombian pesos)

Income	Uses					Sources				
Class:	I	II	III	IV	V	I	II	III	IV	V
Crop										
Potatoes	272,891	243,788	112,268	33,207	86,223	255,575	173,952	107,371	69,931	141,348
Beans	78,373	69,949	28,202	8,008	20,908	65,614	47,267	31,727	20,441	40,391
Corn	387,103	346,787	174,236	60,813	196,450	335,472	275,423	197,762	122,691	214,041
Rice	502,688	453,624	211,281	77,323	144,042	363,833	299,384	242,466	156,240	327,035
Wheat	452,060	405,510	185,148	71,347	127,517	37,282	30,227	24,146	15,726	33,482
Barley	37,193	33,589	19,285	6,575	25,954	28,341	22,872	18,449	11,560	41,374
Sesame	44,517	39,933	14,293	4,906	8,236	36,758	25,633	16,374	10,592	22,528
Soybeans	88,549	79,431	28,430	9,760	16,399	58,930	48,445	37,588	24,424	53,182

Notes: (1) This table is based on data contained in *Input/Output Matrices Condensed for Analysis of Primary Agricultural Sectors–116 Principal Product Sectors at Producer Prices*, S. Daines, J. Ricardo, C. Gleason, G. Poynor, Statistical Working Document #2, Agency for International Development, March 1972.

(2) Intervals for the five income groups in pesos per month are defined in the following manner: Group I - less than 500 pesos, Group II - 501 to 1,000 pesos, Group III - 1,001 to 1,500 pesos, Group IV - 1,501 to 3,000 pesos, and Group V - more than 3,000 pesos.

(3) Total uses give a sum which closely approximates gross output value and total sources have been adjusted to agree with total uses for purposes of analysis. The gross output figures contained in the input-output table are in close agreement with independent estimates made by J. Atkinson, *Changes in Agricultural Production and Technology in Colombia*, Washington, D. C., U. S. Department of Agriculture, Economic Research Service, Foreign Agricultural Economic Report No. 52, June 1969.

is employed in the effective protection literature where the influence of tariff changes on an activity's value-added is examined. In the case at hand the adjusted sources trace the assumed income changes which accrue to the on-farm resources of land and labor in response to changes in price supports.

For potatoes, beans, corn, rice, and barley the foregoing procedures were felt to lead to reasonable adjustments in the data since the sum of direct and indirect uses closely approximated the value of gross output in each crop.[18] However, this was less true for sesame and soybeans whose relatively large assignment to the inventories category could not be directly traced to any income class. In the case of these two crops, both the uses (in oils and other foods) and sources of income were adjusted proportionately to match the level of gross output.

The remaining difficulty concerns the disposition of wheat. Wheat poses special problems for the analysis of price supports because, unlike the other crops, it is a significant import commodity.[19] By the end of 1971 domestic wheat production was only two-thirds its level in 1962 and accounted for only about fifteen percent of domestic consumption. It was explained earlier how IDEMA finances its operations through its ability to import wheat at world prices, or even lower prices in the case of United States P. L. 480 wheat, and sell these products at higher domestic prices. In effect, the budgetary funds for IDEMA are raised from a regressive sales tax on food consumption. If this peculiar tax were removed, a substitute source of finance would have to be found—presumably from the regular tax system. In Table 9.2 the uses of wheat far exceed the sources of income from wheat, reflecting the importance of initial wheat imports. If wheat prices fell to adjusted international values consumers in all income classes would experience real income gains due to the repeal of this regressive consumption tax. However, since the budget of IDEMA would have to be met by increases in other forms of taxation, the gain in real income through lower prices would be offset by lower disposable incomes. This offset is not taken into account in subsequent calculations because there is no reliable way of determining which taxes would be compensatorily raised. Nonetheless, it is unlikely the government would replace this regressive sales tax with another equally regressive so the price-cum-tax change would be expected to result in a redistribution of income from rich to poor. As it will be seen, this redistributive effect would be similar to those realized for the other crop price changes.

Table 9.3 presents alternative estimates of consumption patterns by crop and by income position. Each estimate, including the one which utilizes the same data found in Table 9.2 on sources and uses of income, suggests the expected pattern, a monotonic decline in the fraction of income spent on each crop as income in-

[18] Total uses did not exactly equal gross output value due to the omission of some extremely small indirect uses of the crop.

[19] Small and sporadic imports of corn, rice, and barley have occurred but there has been no consistent tendency to import any of these crops. Recently, barley has been a more frequent entry on the side of imports but the amounts involved have been a negligible fraction of domestic output.

TABLE 9.3. Alternative Estimates of Consumption Ratios by Crop and Income Class (per cent)

Income Class: a)	I		II		III		IV		V
b)		I'		II'		III'		IV'	
Crop									
Potatoes	1.27		1.17		0.91		0.55		0.28
		4.0		2.27		1.11		0.46	
Beans	0.37		0.33		0.23		0.13		0.07
		2.74		1.73		0.98		0.37	
Corn	1.81		1.66		1.41		1.01		0.64
		1.34		0.77		0.42		0.07	
Rice	2.35		2.17		1.71		1.29		0.47
		9.2		6.84		4.08		1.3	
Wheat	2.11		1.94		1.49		1.19		0.42
(bread)		3.9		2.4		2.38		0.98	
Sesame	2.91		2.67		1.62		1.14		0.38
Soybeans	0.41		0.38		0.23		0.16		0.05
(oil)		0.74		1.55		1.50		0.83	
Total Crops	11		10		7.5		4.4		2.64
		19.4		14		9.38		3.5	

Notes: (1) The columns representing the income classes I through V use the data described in Table 9.2. Columns I' through IV' represent data contained in the *Final Report of the Rural-Urban Intermarket Project (PIMUR)* based on a consumer survey in 1968 of people in Cali and the department of Valle and published by Michigan State University in 1970. The income intervals in this study differ significantly from those in the first study making the comparison of consumption ratios across the studies impossible. Differences in crop definition also add an element of noncomparability.

(2) Only one other attempt to measure food consumption patterns by income class has been made. This is the CEDE study by R. Prieto entitled *Estructura del Gasto y Distribucion del Ingreso Familiar en Cuatro Ciudades Colombianas 1967-1968, Parte Tercero*, University of Los Andes, Bogotá, May 1971. Unfortunately this study treats crops at only an aggregate level and cannot be decomposed for the study of particular crops. However, for the aggregate entity cereals and derivatives the pattern of expenditures is similar to that in Table 9.3 for total crops as the lowest income group spent 15.3 per cent of its income on cereals and derivatives compared to 4.7 per cent for the richest income group.

(3) Each entry refers to the per cent of total income spent on a particular crop for any income group.

creases. The data derived from AID sources indicate that the ratio of combined expenditure on all crops to income is 4.17 times greater in the lowest income bracket than in the highest income bracket. Allowing for the fact that the definitions of highest and lowest income bracket differ, the comparable ratio for the Rural-Urban Intermarket Project (PIMUR) data is 5.5, while that for the Centro de Estudios sobre Desarrollo Economico (CEDE) data is about 3.3. The overall consistency of the AID data with other sources of information establishes some degree of confidence in the distributions of Table 9.2

Table 9.4 summarizes the income distribution calculations using the data in the preceding tables. Price relationships prevailing in 1969 were used for rice, barley, corn, and beans while the price changes for wheat and soybeans refer to the years

TABLE 9.4. Price Supports and Income Redistribution (Thousands of 1968 pesos)
Price Reduction and Associated Income Change

Crop and Income Class	(1)	(2)
Rice	**ΔP: 22.3%**	**0%**
I	$ 30,965	–
II	34,390	–
III	-6,950	–
IV	-17,598	–
V	-40,807	–
Wheat	**ΔP: 43.7%**	**26.9%**
I	$181,258	$111,575
II	163,999	100,951
III	70,358	43,310
IV	24,306	14,962
V	41,093	25,294
Barley	**ΔP: 21.25%**	**0%**
I	$ 1,881	–
II	2,277	–
III	178	–
IV	-1,059	–
V	-3,277	–
Soybeans	**ΔP: 16.7%**	**4%**
I	$ 4,946	$ 1,184
II	5,175	1,239
III	-1,529	-366
IV	-2,449	-587
V	-6,142	-1,471
Corn	**ΔP: 25%**	**2.4%**
I	$ 7,908	$ 759
II	17,841	1,713
III	-5,882	-565
IV	-15,470	-1,485
V	-4,398	-422
Beans	**ΔP: 11.3%**	**-14.3%**
I	$ 8,768	$-11,095
II	16,159	-20,449
III	-2,352	2,976
IV	-6,425	8,131
V	-16,150	20,437

[1]For each crop the percentage price change reflects the following price comparisons: Market prices with unadjusted world prices in the first column; and market prices with adjusted world prices in the second column.

[2]Percentage price changes rely on data in Table 9.1. The product of the percentage price change and the difference between sources and uses for each income class in Table 9.2 gives the income change for each crop.

1968 and 1970, respectively. No satisfactory price data were felt to exist for potatoes and sesame so these crops were excluded in Table 9.4 A glance at Table 9.1 confirms that had other years been chosen instead—assuming that the data on sources and uses in Table 9.2 would be appropriate for these years—the estimates of income redistribution would have displayed considerable variation. Despite the annual variability of relative prices the calculations shown in Table 9.4 are probably of the right order of magnitude.[20] Two kinds of price comparisons are shown in Table 9.4. The first estimate compares market prices with unadjusted CIF values while the second estimate allows for thirty percent overvaluation of the exchange rate.

Because low income groups invariably spend more on a crop than they earn in producing it, and the opposite is true for higher income groups, abandoning the price support program would, with one exception, result in clear-cut equity gains. Only in the case in which market prices for rice and barley coincide with adjusted international values would no change occur if price supports were dismantled. Beans provided the only instance in which income transfers would move the other way because adjusted international values for this crop exceeded actual market prices. For wheat all consumers would be better off if the price support was discarded, but much larger gains would accrue to the bottom than to the top income groups. In terms of absolute magnitude, this policy change would do more to improve the incomes of the poor than if all the other crop prices were adjusted in a similar fashion. Generally speaking, the main feature of the price support program in the late 1960s was a transfer of real income from groups with below average incomes to groups which enjoy incomes above the mean. Taking account of the position of both producers and consumers at each level of income, most of the burden of price supports was borne by low income consumers while most of the benefits were conferred on high income producers.

If the monetary gains of the bottom two income groups I and II are summed for the different price alternatives, it can be seen that they would receive a total gain of 476,113 thousand pesos if market prices fell to current world prices and 185,877 thousand pesos if market prices fell to adjusted world prices. While it is impossible to objectively determine at what point a transfer becomes significant for policy purposes, judgment of this matter is aided by some notion of the relative magnitude of these income transfers. According to the input-output table, the bottom two income groups received 42,344,303 thousand pesos. Therefore, depending on the price alternative in question, these groups would receive a benefit from abandonment of the supports that would be worth between slightly less than one-half of one percent of their initial income and slightly more than one percent. As a fraction of national income (about 42,605,883 thousand pesos) the amounts redistributed would be even smaller, between 0.2 and 0.5 percent according to the choice of exchange rate regime.[21] Income redistribution on this scale may not be an inconsequential concern for economic policy.

[20] For example, the largest redistributions occur in the case of wheat; a ten-year average of the market price–unadjusted world price differential from 1961-70 is 39.7 percent compared to the 43.7 percent figure used in Table 9.4.

[21] These losses would be somewhat larger if decent price data for potatoes and sesame were available.

The sensitivity of these results to the maintained assumptions of zero supply and demand elasticities can be gauged by referring to Diagram 1 below. In this diagram price supports are shown to be sufficient to raise domestic prices from OF to OG and achieve self-sufficiency in production. The extra rent accruing to producers is measured by the area GFIA while the loss inflicted on consumers is represented by the area GFCA. Equation 3, used to calculate the amount of redistributed income, is equivalent to the area GFBA. Thus, that equation overestimates the change in income on the sources side (by the triangle ABI) and underestimates it (by the triangle ABC) on the uses side. If the elasticity of demand n_d and the elasticity of supply n_s are the same for all crops and income groups, the extent of overestimation ($1/2\ \Delta Q \Delta P$) may be expressed as $1/2\ (P_oQ_o)(\Delta P/P)^2 n_s$, and the degree of underestimation as $1/2\ P_oQ_o\ (\Delta P/P)^2 n_d$. The error in equation 3 arising from the restrictiveness of its assumptions is the second-order term $1/2(\Delta P/P)^2\ (P_oQ_o)\ (n_d-n_s)$ while the distribution of this error across i income groups is given by $\Sigma\ 1/2(\Delta P/P)^2\ [n_d(C_i-M_i)P_j-n_sQ_iP_j]$. The size of this error increases with the size of the price change that is envisioned. It is also apparent that if the price elasticities of supply and demand are equal there is no error in the amount of income redistributed through price supports. Equation (3) in this case is amended to

$$\sum_i \sum_j \Delta P_j/P_j\ [(C_{ij} - M_{ij})P_j - Q_{ij}\ P_j] + \sum_i \sum_j 1/2\ (\Delta P_j/P_j)^2 n_s[(C_{ij} - M_{ij})P_j - Q_{ij}P_j] \quad (3)'$$

Inspection of this equation reveals that, since sources exceed uses in the higher income brackets and vice versa in the lower brackets, the addition of the extra term reinforces the earlier result of redistribution from poor to rich when prices are supported.

It could be argued, however, that it is as restrictive to assume price elasticities of demand and supply are equal as to assume they are zero. The case which stands

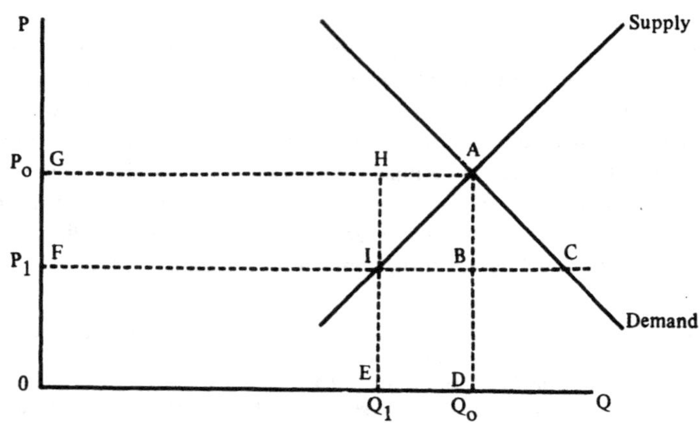

Figure 9.1

the best chance of disturbing the previous results is the one where the supply elasticity exceeds the demand elasticity. To test this possibility, the amended version of equation 3 was used assuming that extreme values, $n_s = 1$ and $n_d = .1$ held.[22] From the totals reported in column 1 of Table 4 it was found that $39,226 should be deducted for income group I, $29,875 for group II, $24,790 for group III, $15,376 for group IV, and $28,015 for group V. Thus, it may be concluded that the results of Table 4 are quite insensitive to the assumptions made with respect to the responsiveness of producers and consumers to price changes.

Before turning to an examination of the efficiency aspects of price supports, some discussion of the functional income distribution changes associated with supports would seem desirable. This topic has been explored elsewhere by Floyd and others and the conclusions reached in their analysis are directly applicable to Colombia.[23] Because the demand for agricultural products is inelastic, the imposition of above-equilibrium prices through price supports will raise total expenditure on the supported commodities. The distribution of this extra expenditure between land and nonland factors will depend on the configuration of supply elasticities for these factors and the size of the elasticity of factor substitution. Those factors least elastic in supply will experience the largest price increase provided it is not easy to technically substitute other factors for them. Since in the long run (and perhaps in the short run, as well) the supply of labor and capital is apt to be perfectly elastic to agriculture and the substitution elasticity between land and other factors is likely less than one, the impact of higher product prices will probably raise the return and the income share of inelastically supplied land. Aggregate data for Colombia tends to confirm this description of the economy. Over the period 1950-1968, average per capita incomes in agriculture were rising at an annual rate of about two percent while the real wage stayed virtually constant.[24] Data stretching over a slightly longer interval also indicate that the income shares of land and capital have risen at the expense of labor. A higher land share in income would be a predictable outcome of price supports in Colombia. Because

[22] Few empirical studies have concluded that n_s is as high as unity for large farm aggregates. For example, Heady and Tweeten rely on econometric techniques to reach the result that for the United States the elasticity of supply for all farm products is 0.10 after two years, 0.15 in four years, and 0.6 after twenty years of adjustment. See E. Heady and L. Tweeten, *Resource Demand and the Structure of Agricultural Industry* (Ames, Iowa: Iowa State University Press, 1965), chapters 8-9.

[23] The seminal article is by J. E. Floyd, "The Effects of Farm Price Supports on the Returns to Land and Labor in Agriculture," *Journal of Political Economy*, Vol. 73, (April, 1965), pp. 148-58. Floyd relied on a two-factor neoclassical framework to investigate how factor returns and employment respond to various price support schemes. His work has been extended by Finis Welch to consider technological change. See F. Welch, "Some Aspects of Structural Change and the Distributional Effects of Technical Change and Farm Programs," in *Benefits and Burdens of Rural Development*. Some Public Policy Viewpoints, by the Iowa State University–Center for Agricultural and Economic Development. (Ames, Iowa: Iowa State University Press, 1970), chapter 9.

[24] These income trends and other evidence pointing to an elastic supply of rural labor are discussed in R. A. Berry, "Land Distribution, Income Distribution and the Productive Efficiency of Colombian Agriculture," *op. cit.*

the ownership of land is much more highly concentrated than the ownership of nonland factors, the higher land share would be translated into a larger dispersion of nominal incomes. Another way of illustrating this result is to note that the least labor-intensive farms would gain the most from a program of price supports. Farms with low labor intensity tend to be larger farms so that these farms having higher initial income would tend to be the primary beneficiaries of price supports.

This brief excursion into functional distribution reinforces the previous results for the size distribution of incomes. It was implicitly assumed in the earlier analysis that all income recipients involved in the production of a given crop gained in the same proportion from price supports. We have just argued, however, that this particular pattern of benefits is unlikely to be true. Some groups, such as hired labor, with a highly elastic supply of services will probably not share in the income benefits at all. If, as seems likely, these groups are concentrated at the bottom of the size distribution of income, our previous results likely understate the redistribution associated with the introduction of price supports. It is difficult to avoid the conclusion that the operation of price supports has contributed to income inequality in Colombia.

An important caveat to the preceding finding is that it ignores compositional changes within the whole agricultural sector. If a system of price supports encourages a shift of economic activity toward supported and away from nonsupported lines of production, income distribution will be influenced by factor intensity differences between these two types of activity. For example, if supported products are labor intensive relative to unsupported ones, introducing a system of price supports will tend to increase the demand for labor and raise labor incomes. If it were strong enough, this effect could conceivably outweigh the effect of farm size variation and result in an increase in labor's share within the agricultural sector. How important this phenomenon might be in Colombia is difficult to ascertain in the absence of information on the degree of substitutability among outputs in production. Nonetheless, it deserves to be pointed out that cattle raising employs much less labor per hectare than crops grown on either large or small crop farms, and it is therefore possible that a cattle-to-crop production shift in response to crop price supports will attenuate the measured income transfer to high income producers on the side of the sources of income.

4. PRICE SUPPORTS AND ECONOMIC EFFICIENCY

The efficiency problem of price supports has received far greater attention in Colombia than the question of income distribution. Henning was among the first to propose that for efficiency reasons support prices should be pegged to international prices adjusted for a shadow rate of foreign exchange.[25] He correctly emphasized that the alternative of tying price supports to average production costs

[25] R. G. Henning, "A Suggested Agricultural Price Policy for Colombia," IDEMA, Bogotá, October, 1971.

fails to encourage efficient production practices for any crop and also fails to stimulate the mix of crop commodities in which Colombia enjoys a comparative advantage in world markets. Gutierrez undertook the measurement of the social costs of price supports in rice production.[26] Using a cobweb model of production in which the rice market does not clear either with or without government intervention, he estimates the value of the lost consumer and producer surplus that results from IDEMA price supports. For different years this cost fluctuates between 0.06 percent and 16.5 percent of the value of rice output.

Dudley has made a careful examination of price support policy in the case of wheat.[27] Invoking the principle that to minimize the total cost of obtaining wheat the marginal social costs of domestic production and importation must be the same, Dudley adjusts CIF prices of wheat for distribution costs, a thirty percent overvaluation of the peso, and a twenty-five percent deduction from private domestic production costs to allow for zero opportunity costs of unskilled labor and land used in wheat growing. The determination of the optimum price support is most easily seen in diagram 2 below. PMC and SMC refer to private and social marginal costs, respectively, of domestic production. P_M represents the CIF price adjusted upward for the estimated extent of overvaluation of the peso and for a distribution margin. The optimum support price is given by the intersection of P_M and SMC which determines optimum domestic output of Q* and, thus, the required support price of P_s needed to elicit the amount of Q* from producers. There is only one questionable feature of this exercise and this is the inclusion of a distribution-transport margin in the adjustment of import prices. According to the discussion of this issue in the previous section, this margin probably ought to

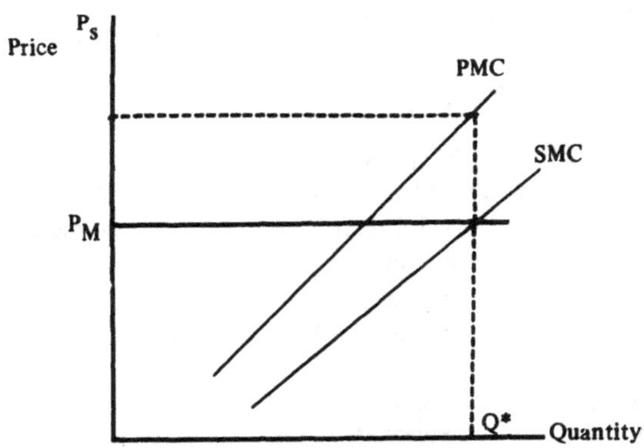

Figure 9.2 Determination of Optimum Price Supports.

[26] N. Gutierrez A., *Costos Sociales de los Precios de Sustentacion en Arroz* (Bogotá: Instituto Colombiano Agropecuario (ICA), August, 1972).

[27] L. Dudley, "An Analysis of Alternative Policies for the Wheat Market in Colombia," National Planning Department of Colombia (Planeacion), Bogotá, July 25, 1972.

be excluded from the calculation. It should also be noted that losses imposed on consumers due to a higher price (a loss of consumers' surplus) are ignored in this particular case because the demand elasticity of wheat is assumed to be zero.

In a subsequent paper Dudley and Sandilands probe the conflict between the pricing policy of a profit conscious marketing agency and the prices needed to minimize the social costs of procuring wheat.[28] They show that a profit-maximizing marketing agency will in general fail to price imported commodities high enough to insure optimal results. Their conclusion is that IDEMA sold imported wheat at a price low enough to drastically cut back domestic production but still high enough to yield sizeable profits from the imports replacing domestic output. As a result 1.4 million tons of wheat were imported which could have been produced by domestic sources at lower opportunity costs. This pernicious and unintended by-product of PL 480 imports made the value of this component of foreign economic aid barely positive.

In the remainder of this section, an attempt is made to assess the efficiency implications of price supports using a slightly different approach suggested by Johnson and Krueger.[29] Their framework hinges on the concept of the domestic resource cost (DRC) of saving a unit of foreign exchange through import substitution versus the DRC of earning a unit of exchange via more exports. An economy has achieved an efficient allocation of resources when the cost is the same for each alternative method of obtaining a unit of foreign exchange. With a shadow rate of foreign exchange this condition implies that no foreign exchange generating activity would have a DRC ratio in excess of unity. Inefficiency then is defined by the extent of the dispersion in DRCs for different activities contributing to the supply of foreign exchange.

If the following conventional, but somewhat restrictive, set of assumptions is made, the efficiency loss attributable to price supports can be measured according to the formula

$$P = \sum_i [(-P_f)/P_d)]_i V_i$$

where P_d is the price (cost) of domestic crop output, P_f is the import price adjusted by the extent of overvaluation (30 percent), and V_i is the value of the domestic crop output at domestic prices. For this measure to have some validity it is necessary to assume that private factor costs adequately reflect opportunity costs, international terms of trade are fixed, costs of production are independent of output levels, each crop employs the same amount of direct and indirect imported inputs, and that home production would

[28] L. Dudley and R. J. Sandilands, "The Side-Effects of Foreign Aid: The Case of P. L. 480 Wheat in Colombia," *Economic Development and Cultural Change*, Vol. 23, No. 2 (January, 1975).

[29] H. Johnson, "The Cost of Protection and the Scientific Tariff," *Journal of Political Economy*, Vol. 68, (August, 1960), pp. 327-45; A. Krueger, "Some Economic Costs of Exchange Control: The Turkish Case," *Journal of Political Economy*, Vol. 74, (October, 1966), pp. 466-80. DRC is defined as the ratio of value-added per unit of ourput at domestic opportunity costs plus the accounting value of non-traded inputs to the difference between foreign exchange earned (or saved) and the amount of foreign exchange used.

be entirely replaced by imports if P_d exceeded P_f. If these assumptions are met, the formula for P corresponds to Johnson's concept of production cost in which the size of P measures the value of domestic resources at domestic prices which could be extracted from the economy through resource reallocations and trade without affecting final consumption of all goods and services. This measure of extractable surplus would be zero if every domestic crop price equalled the adjusted import price. As a measure of welfare loss it understates the true cost of price supports since it ignores costs resulting from substitution in consumption. However, this omission may be counterbalanced by the presence of rent elements in domestic costs and, if this were the case, the expression above for P might provide a closer measure of the total than merely the production cost of price supports.

Using the data on uses of income in Table 9.2 and the precentage price differences in Table 9.4 for the excess of domestic over adjusted world prices, the production cost of Colombian price supports is estimated to be 74,812 thousand pesos or about 4.85 percent of the total value of output for wheat, soybeans, and corn. Only these three crops had domestic prices in excess of adjusted world prices. The domestic prices of rice and barley equalled adjusted world prices while the domestic price of beans fell slightly short of the adjusted world price. It seems to be a safe conclusion on the basis of this somewhat crude calculation that the efficiency cost of the price support program in Colombia is not high.

5. CONCLUSIONS

The main findings of this study are twofold. First, the operation of Colombia's price support program appears to have exacerbated the inequality of income distribution in that country. The costs of this program have been borne by low-income earners as a group while most of the benefits have been obtained by higher income groups. Second, the structure of relative prices generated by the price support program imposed an efficiency cost on the economy resulting from an inappropriate allocation of the economy's resources. Although the size of the income redistribution effect, and especially the size of the efficiency cost, involve less than one percent of national income, it is difficult to justify inefficient inequality on the grounds that it is "small."

In weighing the desirability of the present price support program it should be recognized that some indirect effects of the program have been neglected. These effects would need some consideration in a complete evaluation of the program. In the likely event that the benefits of price supports are capitalized into land values, higher land values, by adding to the wealth of large landowners, may make it easier for this group to gain access to rationed credit while at the same time savings incentives for this group are diminished. Higher land prices also reduce the purchasing power of the budget for the land reform agency INCORA and make it more difficult for that organization to redistribute land to smaller farmers. Moreover, the windfall loss of wealth that would result from terminating the program may hurt those who paid the capitalized land price and raise complaints of capricious income redistribution. Another indirect effect is the redistribution of income among agricultural producers arising from the position of cereal growers as input suppliers to the livestock sector (cattle, pork, poultry, and eggs). Because of this input-output linkage there is little doubt that higher support prices would harm livestock producers by raising input costs.

Alternative ways of measuring equity might give a somewhat different picture of the distributive effects of price supports. For example, if producers who receive price supports are located in only a few areas, regional income disparity may be increased. Nonetheless, on the fairly crude methods employed in this study the disappearance of the price support program appears to offer the chance of simultaneous improvement in both the level of total output and its distribution.

Chapter 10

URBAN BUILDING AND INCOME DISTRIBUTION IN COLOMBIA: SOME RELEVANT ASPECTS*

R. Albert Berry
University of Toronto

Ronald Soligo
Rice University

THEORY, CONCEPTS, AND BACKGROUND

Under the Pastrana government the construction of urban housing was elevated to the position of being a major element in the overall employment and income distribution strategy;[1] it was expected to effect a rapid increase in the quantity of employment available in urban areas for relatively low skilled workers. In principle the objective could be viewed as achieving either an increase in the number of jobs in construction and similar activities with workers moving to these jobs from lower paying ones, or an increase in the real wage rates for these jobs with the number being relatively constant. In other words, the objective was to substantially increase the wage bill for low skilled urban workers. A component of the strategy was to foster rural to urban migration as a means of increasing real incomes of people who were in rural areas.

The proposition that residential construction could play the role of a leading sector in the growth process is based on the arguments that i) the demand for housing is substantially income and price elastic, ii) house construction is one of the most labor-intensive activities in LDCs, and iii) there is a considerable supply

[1] National Planning Department, *Guidelines for a New Strategy* (Bogotá, 1972).

*Reprinted with permission of Studies in Comparative International Development.

of underemployed labor in most LDCs.[2] These factors suggest that a policy which promotes the construction of houses could produce significant increases in output and employment and have a beneficial effect on the distribution of income.[3] On these grounds the International Labor Organization (ILO) commission report on Colombia recommended that international aid agencies make "seed" money available to credit institutions specializing in financing house purchases in order to initiate what would eventually be a self-supporting process of continued expansion in the house construction industry.[4] The building sector was favored by the Planning Commission over other labor-intensive sectors such as small-scale manufacturing, commerce and agriculture partly on the grounds that the policy instruments to activate its growth appeared to be more readily accessible and partly because it was more consistent with other aspects and objectives of the Plan.

One basis of the ILO recommendations and the policy which was eventually implemented in Colombia was that residential construction was being held down[5] because of insufficient mortgage credit, due in turn to the modest nominal and low or negative real rate of interest paid to depositors in the Banco Central Hipotecario (BCH)–the primary source of mortgage credit to the private housing sector. A low deposit rate was matched by a low rate for mortgage loans, leading to a disequilibrium in the mortgage credit market so that credit had to be allocated on an administrative basis.

The policy adopted was to create a new savings institution and asset (Unidad de Poder Adquisitivo Constante, or UPAC) which would pay depositors and charge borrowers a fixed real rate of interest. The new attractive financial asset was expected to raise savings and, while (nominal) interest rates would be much higher under the new system, it was anticipated that they would still be suffi-

[2] Further, a disproportionate share of the unemployed are usually linked to (e.g., had their last job in) the construction sector. In Colombia the 1970 household survey recorded an unemployment rate of 14 percent for the construction sector, as compared with 7.4 percent in the economy as a whole and 10 percent for the urban sector. (Departamento Administrativo Nacional de Estadistica (DANE), *Boletin Mensual de Estadistica*, No. 238 [May, 1971], pp. 63 and 79.)

[3] The emphasis on urban building contained in the plan (*Guidelines..., op. cit.*) did not encompass self-contracted or noncommercial housing–the phenomenon discussed by S. Bender in Chapter 11. It was felt that such housing generated relatively little paid employment (since considerable family labor was involved). Bender, however, concludes that the income distribution effects of such housing have probably been significantly beneficial.

[4] International Labor Office, *Towards Full Employment: A Programme for Colombia* (Geneva: ILO, 1970), pp. 127-36.

[5] Strassman found housing construction accounted for 2.5 percent of Gross Domestic Product (GDP) in a set of seven underdeveloped countries, and 4.6 percent in five middle income group countries. Colombia's ratio as of 1970 was about 2.5 percent, suggesting the possibility of a substantially higher share of GDP in this sector in the future, since Colombia is approaching the middle level group of countries. (See W. P. Strassman, "The Construction Sector in Economic Development," *Scottish Journal of Political Economy* (November, 1970), pp. 391-409.)

ciently low to induce borrowers to borrow a larger amount than was available under the previous (low interest) system.

In the discussion which follows, we focus mainly on the new system as originally designed and put into practice in late 1972. In the remaining two years of the Pastrana government it was amended in various details (which for example lowered the real pretax return on UPAC's below the original 5-5 1/2 percent). The Lopez administration made substantial changes, which essentially ended the experiment; these included limiting the degree of indexing enough to push the real rate of return below zero under the existing inflation rates. The growth of real deposits ended in 1974 and the building boom ended soon thereafter.[6]

Distributive Aspects of the Colombian Housing Strategy

The two most obvious mechanisms by which the building strategy would affect distribution are (i) the impact on returns to monetary assets, related to the way in which new housing is financed; and (ii) the effect on factor use and, hence, factor incomes.

The creation of the UPAC system affected distribution directly in two ways. First, the higher interest rates paid to depositors increased their incomes. Secondly, those who gained access to mortgage credit as a result of the greater funds channeled into mortgages under the UPAC system gained while those who would have had access to such credit under the previous low interest rate system were worse off since they were required to pay the higher interest rates. Unfortunately, it is difficult to determine with much precision what groups in Colombian society correspond to these categories. In the absence of hard data one can only speculate on whether the net gains tended toward more or less equity.

Higher deposit rates would be expected to benefit mainly the higher income groups, both because they hold most of the nation's wealth and because they have greater access to the new financial assets. This differential access reflects both the physical proximity of urban as opposed to rural persons to the new savings institutions and the greater degree of sophistication and information required to invest in UPACs. To the extent that substitutions by some wealth holders towards UPACs from other financial assets (in particular, from bank deposits) raises the returns on those assets, their holders would benefit. In fact, the savings account interest rate as well as other controlled rates were increased when the UPAC was introduced, reflecting the anticipated and actual substitution towards the UPAC; however, since these rates are in nominal terms the accelerated inflation of the succeeding years made the real returns negative and variable in contrast to the UPAC. The main beneficiaries from the UPAC (relative to their in-

[6] For a detailed chronology of the changes in rules governing the UPAC system, see R. Sandilands, "Indexing in Colombia, Brazil, and Chile with Special Reference to Housing Finance," Ph.D. dissertation, University of Strathclyde, Glasgow, 1976.

comes were probably not the wealthiest strata but rather the middle and upper middle income groups which are likely to hold a higher proportion of their wealth in financial assets (including UPAC). The highest income groups have greater accessibility to investments in real capital goods and presumably would continue to hold substantial portions of their wealth in this form. Also, for groups in high tax brackets the advantage of UPAC was reduced by the fact that real income earned from them was taxable while tax exempt bearer bonds were available from BCH and Instituto de Credito Territorial (ICT), for example. Being anonymous bearer bonds the latter also constituted a good way to conceal undeclared income. These advantages help to explain why the demand for such assets remained fairly strong after the introduction of the UPAC.[7]

On the borrower's side, the new system has probably contributed to greater equity within the top half of the income distribution. Under the previous system, the allocation of low (real) interest BCH credit required rationing and favored the higher income groups; among loan candidates they could offer the greatest security and some may have had personal ties with those deciding on the loans. Under the new system the corresponding group pays a higher interest rate. Persons slightly lower in the income distribution gain from the UPAC system since they are now able to obtain long-term financing on "reasonable" terms for the purchase of housing.[8] The extent to which the higher income candidates are worse off depends on the access they have to low interest credit from other financial institutions such as the commercial banks; they may be able to substitute such (short-term) borrowing for the longer-term mortgage credit and avoid the higher interest charges. However, if they borrow large sums from the commercial banks for other purposes (e.g., working capital) it is not possible in practice to isolate the extent to which such borrowings are substitutes for long-term mortgage credit.

To sum up, the introduction of the UPAC system has probably led to greater equality within the upper income groups, predominantly the top half of the urban income distribution. But the discrepancy between that group as a whole and the poorer groups is likely to have been widened since the lower income and rural groups gain little (directly at least) from the financial innovations.

The direct employment and distributional implications of increasing the volume of construction of houses are examined empirically in Part B. These depend largely on the supply elasticity of construction workers. While there may be a large pool of underemployed labor in Colombia, it is not clear how quickly it can be mobilized. Even construction work requires some skills which take time to develop; further, much of the underemployed labor may still be in rural areas.

[7] Sandilands, *op. cit.*

[8] This argument presumes that under the BCH system there was an excess demand for the low cost credit it dispensed. That this was the case seems to be strongly supported by the large excess of loan applications relative to available funds in the UPAC system by 1974. Even allowing for some duplications, the 3:1 ratio by mid-1974 is striking (Sandilands, *op. cit.*). Since the system was essentially dismantled by the end of 1974, the fascinating question of how large was the excess demand for either the reasonably priced UPAC system credit or the subsidized BCH credit cannot be answered with any precision.

Thus, while the long-run elasticity of supply of labor to construction may be quite high, in the short run elasticity may be much less. Interestingly enough, the availability of housing space for migrants, which could be reduced by a shift to construction of middle and upper income housing, could be an important variable in determining the willingness of labor to migrate.

If the short-run supply elasticity of construction workers is small, an increase in construction activity will generate higher wages but not too much additional employment. Conversely, the larger the elasticity the greater the increase in employment and the smaller the increase in real wages per worker. In terms of the overall distribution of income for the country as a whole, either outcome would be equalizing in the sense of increasing the share of total income going to the lower income groups. However, the two outcomes differ in terms of how they distribute increments to income among the low income groups.

A complete analysis of the distributional implications of the housing strategy would include consideration of its effects on rural-urban migration and the implications of this migration for distribution; the distributive effects of changes in the level of output in other sectors which result from increased urban construction; the distributive effects of related changes in relative prices and the rate of inflation; the effects on the self-contracted housing sector; and the supply price of construction workers. It would also be necessary to evaluate the effects of the higher rates of return on savings on the level of savings by income group[9] and ultimately on the long-run distribution of wealth and the functional distribution of income. Some of these effects are fairly "direct" while others can only be handled within a more general equilibrium framework.

Bender's hypothesis in Chapter 11 that the emphasis on middle and upper income housing has resulted in higher prices of building materials which in turn have cut the rate of investment in self-financed housing by lower income groups exemplifies the sort of relationship which would have to be taken into account. His hypothesis implies that the increased demand for labor generated by the housing strategy would be partially offset by a decrease in employment provided by the subcontracting of work in the self-financed sector. More importantly, a substitution of the construction of middle and upper income housing for that of lower income groups would imply a relative decrease in the rate of capital accumulation by these latter groups. Thus, the wage income of lower income groups could be temporarily augmented by higher levels of employment in the construction industry while capital income, in the form of income in kind from owner-occupied housing and cash income from renting or using the home for commercial purposes, could be reduced permanently. Whether this occurs de-

[9]There is as yet no consensus on the effects of the new financial institutions on total savings. An OAS study concluded there was no net increase (Organizacion de los Estados Americanos, *Incidencia de Un Incremento en el Ahorro Destinado a la Financiacion de Vivienda en Colombia* [Washington, D.C., 1975]); a Planeacion study concluded just the opposite, that a substantial increase in total savings had resulted (D.N.P. *Evaluacion de la Economia Colombiana 1970-74* [Bogotá: Unidad de Programacion Global, 1974]).

pends on whether the positive effect on self-contracted housing of the increased incomes of poorer groups does or does not outweigh the negative effect of the increased materials prices. This paper does not attempt this sort of comprehensive analysis.

Factor Proportions: the Short Run vs. the Long Run

The empirical analysis of this paper is limited to the direct effects of housing on factor demands and, thereby, on income distribution. Within that focus, however, it is important to distinguish the short run, during which the labor intensity of the building activity is expected to cause a positive distributional impact from a shift toward that sector, and the longer-run where the distributional impact is less obvious. More precisely it is necessary to distinguish a period during which the demand for building services is rising relative to other final goods and services, and a later period when this is no longer the case. If the increase in building activity is once and for all, the first period is quite short. Housing is a capital good with long length of life; accordingly, the acceleration principle implies that mild changes in the final demand pattern can generate much stronger fluctuations in the demand for the production of the capital good, in this case buildings.

It appears that the wide range of opinions with respect to the labor intensity of housing results from the tendency to focus on one or the other of the two stages in the production of housing services: the construction activity, which is more labor-intensive than almost any other important sector of the economy; and the subsequent stage during which the houses produce a service (lodging) where the labor intensity is relatively low. This difference makes it imperative to decide exactly what the relevant concepts of "labor intensity" and, correspondingly, factor shares are.

Labor intensity (L/K ratio) will normally differ among the various stages in the production of a final good or service, including both the production of current inputs (taken account of in input-output tables) and of capital goods, either of which may or may not be produced in the country. A relevant ratio is one which summarizes, in some way, the "typical" ratio characterizing the whole of the production process. If the ratio varies substantially over the production process, and if that process is a long one, the time sequence of the variation can be important.

Figure 10.1 illustrates the various stages for the housing sector. Suppose, for simplicity, that the machinery used is in each case imported. The period t_1 to t_2 corresponds to the construction of a capital good—the house, t_2 representing the moment of completion. Up to that moment the amount of capital invested in the construction process *per se* (measured at each point of time by the height of the curve DA) rises continuously with the purchase of inputs (including physical inputs, labor, and management); from that moment the value of the capital diminishes (as indicated by the falling price of the house), arriving eventually at

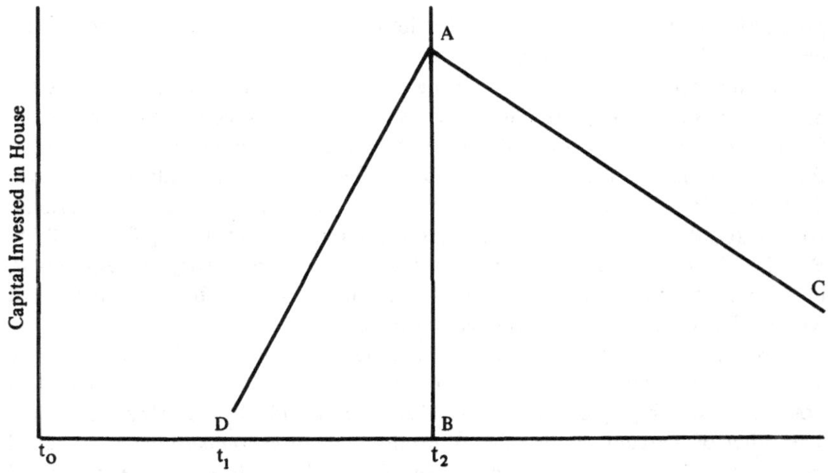

Figure 10.1.

scrap value unless repairs permit the house a perpetual life.[10] A third process of relevance is the production of inputs to the building process—cement, rocks, etc. This must occur before the actual construction, and is here arbitrarily assumed to take place during a period designated in Figure 10.1 as t_0 to t_1.[11]

To determine the long-run distributional implications of a "housing strategy" let us contrast the demands for labor and capital in two stationary equilibria, one characterized by a higher production of housing services than the other, but with production maintained at a constant level over time in each case. Assume that the typical house lasts 50 years and has no economic value at the end of this period, the net rate of return to owning a house is 10 percent, annual repairs correspond to 1 percent of the original price of the house and involve a 0.75 to 0.25 split of income generated (both directly and indirectly) in favor of labor, and finally that machinery used in construction is imported.

If P_v is the price of a new house, then annual capital income in the form of rent (net of depreciation allowances) is about $0.10\ VP_v/2$ and that from repairs is $0.0025\ VP_v$.[12] Labor income from repairs is $VP_v(0.0075)$. In this last stage of

[10]In situations involving speculation, increased price due to location, restriction of new production, and so on, it is possible that the value of a house does not diminish over time, even in real terms. In such situations a theoretical problem of defining the amount of capital involved arises, as the present value of the services which that capital will render in the future is greater than the cost of construction less the services already rendered. But when markets and predictions are perfect these two measures would always be equal and from a normative point of view the relevant calculation is the one involving historical cost.

[11]Theoretically, of course, this time sequence can go far back in time, when one considers inputs for the inputs, etc. But the savings involved are much less at these earlier periods and we neglect them.

[12]The average value of a house over its lifetime is roughly $P_v/2$, so that aggregate annual rent, net of depreciation, would have to be 10 percent of $VP_v/2$.

production of housing services, the distribution between capital and labor would be about 7:1 in favor of capital.

Maintenance of the flow of housing services hypothesized here involves the production of V/50 houses annually, which generates additional income. In Colombia about 40 percent of the price of a house corresponds to value added in the construction industry itself, and about 60 percent to value added in the production of inputs. With respect to the former, the division tends to be quite favorable to labor, with the labor income/capital income ratio being 0.75 to 0.25. Roughly 60 percent of value added in the construction activity corresponds to blue collar construction labor and 14 percent to skilled labor, architects, and white collar workers; the rest is payment to capital.

Given these numbers, the annual income flow corresponding to the value added in construction would be $VP_v/125$ (40 percent of the annual value of new housing) of which $VP_v(0.74)/125$ would go to labor and $VP_v(0.26)/125$ to capital. The other 60 percent of the value of production corresponds to the value added in the production of materials purchased from other industries. The functional distribution of income so generated is harder to estimate, but data for the industries producing the most important inputs (cement, bricks, wood, and metal products) suggest that the income (value added) resulting indirectly from housing is divided more or less equally between labor and capital with the blue collar share of labor income being about 60 percent. Under these assumptions, the labor share in the total building process including production of inputs, would be approximately 60 percent.[13] Of the labor income, roughly two-thirds goes to blue collar workers in both construction and the input industries; the rest goes to professionals and white collar workers.

Putting these pieces of information together, we conclude that the capital and labor shares of maintaining a given stock of housing are 0.76 and 0.24, respectively. The relatively labor-intensive construction and maintenance processes are overwhelmed by the capital intensity of the final production stage: the provision of housing services. Hence, the overall set of activities is unquestionably capital-intensive.

Table 10.1 illustrates this conclusion using the actual value added in construction of urban building in Colombia in 1969. The remainder of the numbers in the table are calculated from this datum using the assumptions and other data outlined above. As the table shows, only 24 percent of income generated in the housing process goes to labor. In contrast, the paid labor share of gross domestic product at factor cost for Colombia in 1970 was estimated as 41.1 percent in the national accounts; in manufacturing the comparable figure was 40.0.

If we compare two stationary states, one of which maintains a relatively large housing stock while the other has a lower stock of housing and greater production in all other sectors, the labor share would be smaller in the first, if the assumptions used above are reasonably accurate. In other words, the long-run implication

[13]The share of labor is $0.4(0.74)+ 0.6(0.5) = 0.60$.

TABLE 10.1. Illustrative Calculation of the Functional Distribution of Income Generated in the Provision of Housing Services with a Constant Stock of Houses and Value Added in Urban Building at the 1969 Levels (millions of 1969 pesos)

Source of Income	Labor Income	Capital Income	Total Income
Current stock of buildings			
rent	0	9,100	9,100
repairs	1,365	455	1,820
total	1,365	9,555	10,920
Construction of new buildings	1,092	364	1,456
Production of inputs for construction of new buildings	1,092	1,092	2,184
Total	3,549	11,011	14,560
Percent of Total	0.24	0.76	100.0

Note: It is important to note that the figures for repairs are guesswork and that the overall functional distribution of income is rather sensitive to them. For example, if repairs are assumed to be 1.5 percent of P_V each year instead of the 1.0 percent assumed in the table, the labor share would be 0.27. If repairs are 0.5 percent of P_V, the labor share would be 0.21.

Methodology: The figure for value added in construction of urban buildings (1,456 million pesos) is from the national accounts. The others are based on that figure and the assumptions outlined in the text.

of a strategy to increase investment in housing and to maintain a larger stock of housing is a lower labor share. Although the assumptions used here could be somewhat wide of the mark, the assumption that houses last only 50 years seems conservative, and it is improbable that much more than 1-2 percent of the initial value of the typical house is spent in repairs every year. The range of error in these figures is not so great as to make credible a labor share in the housing process as high as 50 percent.

The picture becomes cloudier again when one takes account of items complementary in consumption to housing, e.g., vigilance, cleaning services, etc., since some of these are quite labor-intensive.[14] Thus, even after the house is finished, the production of the bundle of housing and related services may not be as capital-intensive as indicated above. This empirical point, one of those which must be cleared up before we can reach any overall conclusions as to the income distribution implications of housing expansion, has received little consideration to date.

As of 1970, average earnings of workers in urban building were probably about 65-75 percent of those in the urban economy as a whole. The distributional impact of an increase in the demand for this relatively low income labor would

[14] When making comparisons between different types of houses, it may be relevant to distinguish those houses big enough to induce or to necessitate domestic service from those which do not.

presumably be more positive, given the labor share, than if the workers were highly paid and therefore already high up in the income distribution. Since the wages of most of the people working either in building repair or housing related services like domestics are also low, the labor share in these activities would likewise understate the importance of them in determining the overall degree of equity in the economy.

Analysis of Accelerated Production of Housing. The above comparison of two stationary systems with different levels of housing services is not the appropriate framework for a discussion of the Colombian strategy. For here the goal was to increase the relative size of the building sector; accordingly, the transition from a system with a lower share of output in the form of housing services to a system with a higher share must be analyzed. During that transition, the income flows generated in the production of inputs and in the building activity itself, a relatively high share of which goes to labor and especially blue collar labor, dominate; the large capital income flow in the future (from the rent on the houses) is of less importance. In the short run, and while this production is being accelerated relative to that in other sectors, the effect on functional distribution would be to increase the labor share. Assuming that the income elasticity of demand for housing services does not keep rising, acceleration would eventually end or reverse itself. If the curve S_T in Figure 10.2 represents the proportion of income going to labor in an alternative development strategy involving a smaller production of houses and a larger production of everything else, the effects of the choice of a strategy with a heavier emphasis on housing, initiated at time t_1 are (a) a positive effect on the labor share over a certain period of time, and (b) subsequently a negative effect on it; this is illustrated by the curve S_{TV}. The new long-run equilibrium level for the labor share would be below that of the alternative strategy.

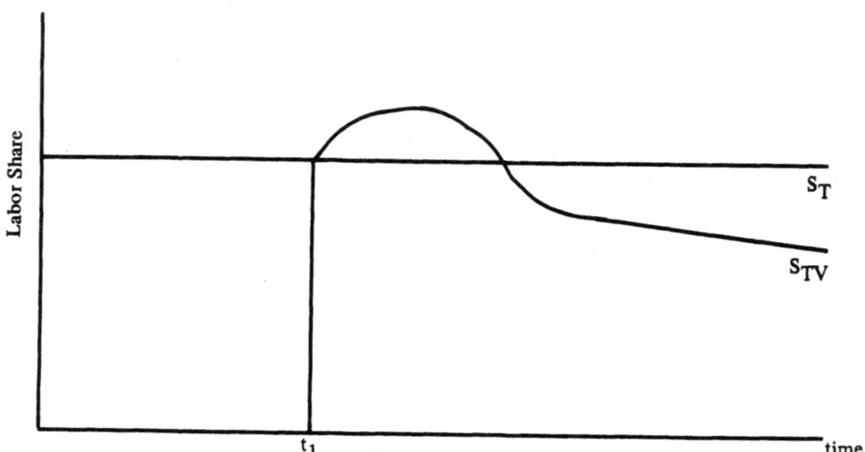

Figure 10.2.

The transitory positive effect on the labor share and hence on the distribution of income may be important, e.g., one might believe that if distribution could once be changed it would not then revert easily to its present level of inequality.

EMPIRICAL EVIDENCE RELATING TO THE IMPACT OF THE EXPANSION OF HOUSING ON FACTOR DEMANDS

This section considers the direct effects of increased house construction on factor demand, using two types of evidence: (i) observations on employment and wage trends; and (ii) quantitative evidence on the structure and factor proportions of the building and related industries. The former evidence has two defects: first, it is incomplete, especially that on employment; second, since building is not one of the larger sectors in terms of employment or output (and was not even during the Plan), it is difficult to distinguish its effects from those of other unrelated phenomena. The weakness of any analysis which is built on the factor proportions in construction and related industries lies in the inadequacies of this data *per se*, and the possible invalidity of the assumption that average factor proportions (the only figures available) are a good predictor of the (marginal) factor proportions corresponding to new or additional output. It is, therefore, important to complement each type of information with the other as much as possible. We turn first to the evidence on factor proportions.

The basic logic which underlay the urban building strategy is reflected in Table 10.2 which compares the labor-output ratio and income shares for urban building,[15] its input industries, factory manufacturing, and the economy as a whole. As discussed earlier, urban building is shown to be much more labor-intensive than the urban economy or the economy as a whole.[16] These data create a

[15] A few other estimates have been made of this ratio. Strassman (W. Paul Strassman, "Measuring the Employment Effects of Housing Policies in Developing Countries," *Economic Development and Cultural Change*, Vol. 24, No. 3 [April, 1976] used an implicit labor productivity of 13,900 (1969 pesos) per worker in the value of low income buildings and site improvements, and 33,900 for high income buildings, 33,000 for Bogotá and 30,700 for other Colombian cities (see pages 624 and 627). The average figure implicit in Table 10.2 is only 16,000 pesos, i.e., a little over half as high as Strassman's estimate. His was based on Mexican data, which were derived from "designs, handbooks, and interindustry tables" and likely to be "good practice" estimates.

[16] The quantification of the direct and indirect demands used to at least illustrate the magnitude of the needs associated with this plan are presented in Eduardo Sarmiento P., *Aspectos Cuantitativos del Plan de Desarrollo,* Planeacion (Bogotá: Canal Ramirez-Antares, 1973). In a Keynesian world with some underutilization of every resource, the direct and indirect increases in demand associated with an increase in final demand would become increases in total output and employment. In fact, one cannot presume this is true, but must proceed to analyze the supply response to the demand increases implicit in the input-output figures.

TABLE 10.2. Data Related to the Distribution of Labor Income by Sectors, 1970

	Building		Input Industries[c] for the building sector		Building Plus input industries		Factory[c, e] industry		Urban nonagricultural sector		Whole economy	
	A Man-Years per million pesos of value added	B Income shares of gross value added	A	B	A	B	A	B	A	B	A	B
Blue Collar	83-95[a]	0.60	24.7	0.31	48.0-52.8	0.43	10.7	0.21	10	0.08	19	0.16
White Collar[d]	3-4	0.14	7.8	0.21	5.9-6.3	0.18	2.7	0.14	23	0.40	12	0.24
All Workers	86-99	0.74	32.5	0.52	53.9-59.1	0.61	13.4	0.35	33	0.49[b]	31	0.40
Blue Collar Share of total paid labor income		0.81		0.60		0.70		0.60		0.18		0.40

[a] Blue collar income assumed to be 60 percent of value added. The annual average blue collar income is assumed to be between 6,300 and 7,200, based on an average daily wage of 30.33 pesos and 40-45 hours paid per week.

[b] Extrapolated from value 0.48, corresponding to 1969.

[c] Small industry excluded (less than 5 workers and 24,000 pesos output).

[d] Note that the definition of "white collar worker" is broad–it includes all sales persons, etc.

[e] Figures calculated from DANE, *III Censo Industrial, 1970* (Bogotá: DANE, 1976). The labor shares are somewhat downward biased due to an overestimation of value added in DANE's figure.

strong presumption that growth of the sector would increase incomes of low income workers.

The effect of an increase in building activity on employment and labor share may vary according to the type of structure built and the type of builder (type of technology). However, it does not appear that there are significant differences in the factor proportions by type of structure; the possibility that different types of construction firms and different producers of inputs are characterized by different factor proportions must be taken more seriously. A construction boom built on the expansion of the most capital-intensive of the producers in these two categories could generate much less employment than a proportional expansion of all types. Whether something of this happened when construction expanded in 1973 and 1974 is not yer clear.[17]

Unfortunately, Colombia's input-output tables have not been disaggregated by size of firm, a variable closely associated with factor proportions. Accordingly, it is not possible to say much about the range in which the direct and indirect employment effects of the program might vary according to the characteristics of the firms where the growth was located.

The extent to which the building boom would be expected to affect macroeconomic variables such as employment depends also on the importance of urban building in the economy. During the period 1966-74, the value of urban building was between 5 and 6 percent of gross urban product in 1958 prices, and somewhat higher in current prices.[18] However, building accounts for a higher share of the urban labor force (probably about 7.5-10 percent in the census years of 1964 and 1973),[19] and a much higher share of urban male paid blue collar workers (about 22 percent in 1974). It is likely, therefore, that a rapid expansion of the sector would have significant effects on the labor market of which construction workers are a part.

Various indicators might be expected to reflect these developments; most directly, one would expect either employment or wages in the urban building

[17]Strassman (Measuring..., *op. cit.*, p. 631) has reached the conclusion that the employment effect of a given value of low income housing is 2 to 3 times as great as that of high income housing in Colombia (data based on Bogotá, Barranquilla, Medellin, and Bucaramanga). The conclusion, however, is based exclusively on Mexican data, partly from designs and handbooks, partly from interindustry tables. While it creates some presumption that such a difference might exist in Colombia, the issue must be researched there, and with *ex post* rather than *ex ante* data on labor and output ratios. The direction of the difference seems plausible; the magnitude is harder to judge.

[18]For more details on the relative share of urban building, see R. A. Berry and R. Soligo, "Urban Building and Income Distribution in Colombia: Some Relevant Aspects," Program of Development Studies Discussion Paper No. 84, Rice University, 1978.

[19]The DANE *Encuestas* of 1970 and 1971 showed 4.7 to 5.6 percent of employed persons as in construction. This would imply that about 7-9 percent of the urban labor force was attached to that sector. A majority of these would be in urban building, and to these are added workers in the building input industries.

sector and the industries producing inputs to rise.[20] Information is still incomplete with respect to the impact of the building boom of 1973-74. Value added in building construction, which had grown by only 12.5 percent over the period 1967-72, grew by 47.7 percent over the 1972-74 period.[21] The increase was associated with the new financial system, and there were decreases in the amount of building done by or financed through the ICT and the BCH.[22]

Wage information from both DANE and CAMACOL indicates a continuation during those years of a downward trend in real wages which began, at least for the four largest cities, in the late 1960s or around 1970. (See Table 10.3.) In all four cities, both series indicate lower real wages in mid-June, 1974, than in 1971. What effect the expansion of housing had on real wages is hard to judge; the major hypothesis with respect to the decline over these years is that the accelerating inflation led to a wage-price lag and pushed real wages down. This is suggested by the general decrease in wages for the economy as a whole during this period.[23] Wages of construction workers appear to have fallen by about the same amount as those of most other sectors. Over 1971-75, Instituto Colombiano de Seguros Sociales (ICSS) data show a decline of about 10 percent in the real median wage of those covered. This is possibly an overstatement of the actual decline since the data fail to include fringe benefits whose share of total labor costs may have risen.

On the most important question of employment, data are unfortuantely deficient. DANE household surveys beginning in 1970 provide hints, but they fail to distinguish between workers in the building industry and in other construction; they span the housing boom without providing an observation in the middle of it; and their universe changes from sample to sample. A comparison of figures for June 1974 and for September-October 1972 suggests considerable increases in Cali, Medellin, and Barranquilla but a decrease in Bogotá.[24] These data by themselves do not prove that a large employment increase occurred in construction as a whole.[25] But given the slow growth of output in "other construction" over 1972-74, employment there probably stagnated, in which case the increase

[20]The most direct impact of the Plan is to raise the demand for labor in these industries; if the supply curve to them is quite elastic, one would not expect an increase in wages in those specific industries, although if the demand increase was sufficiently large one might expect the wage rate of the types of workers involved to be pulled up generally (i.e., in all sectors). If labor were more specific to construction and the input industries, the increased demand should pull wages up. Either effect could be considered as beneficial from the point of view of low income persons.

[21]Banco de la Republica, *Cuentas Nacionales, 1970-75.*

[22]Sandilands, *op. cit.*

[23]See A. Berry, "The Effects of Inflation on Income Distribution in Colombia: Some Hypotheses and a Framework for Analysis," Chapter 4 in this volume.

[24]Bogotá had a high level of employment in construction before the boom; Cali's high figures for early 1971 reflect the construction activity prior to the Pan-American Games held in that city.

[25]They are far from adequate to measure the employment effects of the housing strategy. For example, the seasonality of housing and of other construction probably plays some role in the variations observed.

TABLE 10.3. Real Unit Labor Cost in Construction: Indices, 1967-68 to 1976, DANE and CAMACOL Series (1971=100)

	BOGOTÁ		MEDELLIN		CALI	
	DANE	CAMACOL	DANE	CAMACOL	DANE	CAMACOL
Jan. 1960				80.4[a]		
1967-68		81.6		113.4		
1969		81.7		107.8		108.0
1970		88.7		105.3		106.8
1971	100.0	100.0	100.0	100.0	100.0	100.0
1972	96.7	102.5	96.5	98.2	92.6	93.2
1973	91.9	92.3	90.4	90.2	86.0	88.8
June, 1974	90.2	82.3	84.9	97.6	88.2	83.5
April, 1975	90.1		87.2		88.5	
Sept., 1975	97.4		88.1		87.6	
Feb., 1976	92.4		87.9		81.5	
Percent change:						
1967/8 to June, 1974		+0.9		-14.0	-11.9	
1972-June, 1974	-6.7	-19.7	-12.0	-0.6	-4.8	-10.4

TABLE 10.3. Continued

	BARRANQUILLA DANE	BARRANQUILLA CAMACOL	BUCARAMANGA DANE	CUCUTA DANE	MANIZALES DANE	CARTAGENA DANE	NEIVA DANE	PASTO DANE
Jan. 1960								
1967-68		101.2						
1969		102.1						
1970		99.1						
1971	100.0	100.0	100.0	100.0	100.0	100.0	100.0	100.0
1972	95.5	104.5						
1973	88.4	93.3	87.5	81.7	103.2	108.2	101.1	103.1
June, 1974	83.0	77.8	89.4	84.2	111.1	89.2	110.8	95.3
April, 1975	72.6		90.4	89.8	108.7	89.0	87.2	94.8
Sept., 1975	65.7		89.0	86.0	110.7	84.4	84.0	94.3
Feb., 1976	79.4		84.5	90.4	112.0	80.0	84.7	89.8
Percent change:								
1967/8 to								
June, 1974		-23.1						
1972-June, 1974	-13.0	-25.6						

[a]Based on data presented in CAMACOL, Antioquia, *Estudio Sobre la Demanda de la Edificacion en Medellin y Municipios Vecinos* (Medellin, 1970), Cuadro 1.7.

Sources: For 1967-68 to 1974, Centro Estadistico Nacional de la Construccion (CENAC), *Estadisticas del Costo de Construccion en Colombia*, CEN-04-74 (Bogotá: CENAC, 1974), p. 73 and 82. Wage indices in nominal terms from this source were deflated by the blue collar cost of living series for the respective cities except in the case of Cucuta where the Bucaramanga cost of living series was used, Cartagena where that of Barranquilla was used, and Neiva where that of Cali was used. The DANE data were originally from DANE, *Boletin Mensual de Estadistica* (Mayo-Junio, 1973) and unpublished DANE tabulados. Data for 1975 and 1976 are from DANE, *Boletin Mensual de Estadistica*, No. 297-98 (Abril-Mayo, 1976), and No. 291 (Oct., 1975). Apart from other differences between them, the DANE and CAMACOL series are distinguished in that the former is collected on a monthly basis while the latter apparently is not, judging from the fact that it tends to remain constant over several months or quarters. According to a Planeacion study (*La Mano de Obra en Construccion y Alternativas Para Un Programa de Formacion y Capacitacion Acelerada*, Documento URH-994 [Nov., 1972], p. 20), the CAMACOL data is supplied by the construction companies; since the labor contractors or subcontractors are the ones who deal directly with the workers, these figures may not be very accurate. In 1971, the wage levels reported by DANE tend to be below those reported by CAMACOL, except in Cali. DANE presents data separately for maestros, officials, and peones rasos; in the sources cited above these were averaged into one series.

in building employment between 1972 and 1974 would be greater than suggested by the figures of Table 10.4. Allowing for this, and the rapid increase of output in urban building, a reasonable guess would be that the associated increase in employment was probably 1-3 percent of the urban labor force between late 1972 and the peak of the boom, perhaps in early 1974.

Of crucial importance, of course, is the extent to which the net increase in persons employed in the building sector would otherwise have had less productive and/or remunerative jobs. This cannot be ascertained from available data, though some circumstantial evidence can be brought to bear. In a sample taken in 1975 in urban Colombia, it was observed that 56 percent of the construction workers had begun their careers in that sector; another 23 percent had been agricultural workers, and only 4 percent had been manufacturing workers.[26] This observation is consistent with the general impression that there is considerable mobility between agriculture and construction and that the ultimate source of most additional workers in construction would be agriculture.

TABLE 10.4. Share of the Construction Sector in Total Employment: Urban Areas

Year	Urban	Bogotá	Atlantic region	Eastern region	Central region	Pacific region
1970 (June-July) (EH1)	5.60	6.17	4.50	5.74	5.89	5.69
1971 (March-April) (EH3)	7.09	8.18	5.77	6.53	6.72	8.10
1971 (July-August) (EH4)	7.00	9.41	5.99	5.91	6.07	7.40
1971 (Nov.-Dec.) (EH5)	6.42	8.30	5.92	6.07	6.93	6.20
1972 (Sept.-Oct.) (EH6)	6.15	9.74	3.71	7.66	5.68	5.20
1974 (June) (EH7)	7.17[d]	7.04	4.97[a]		8.06[b]	8.02[c]
1974 (Oct.-Nov.) (EH8)	6.53	7.28	6.48	6.34	6.18	6.25
1975 (Sept.-Oct.) (EH9)	6.52[e]	6.72	5.37[a]		6.51[b]	6.54[c]

[a]Barranquilla only.
[b]Medellin only.
[c]Cali only.
[d]Data are for the four largest cities only.
[e]Data are for seven cities only.
Sources: DANE, *Encuesta de Hogares, 1970*; DANE, *Encuesta Nacional de Hogares*, Etapas 3, 4, 5, and the subsequent publications of the same title for etapas 6, 7, 8, and 9.

[26]B. Kugler, A. Reyes, and M. I. Gutierrez de Gomez, *Educacion y Mercado de Trabajo Urbano en Colombia; Una Comparacion entre Sectores Modernos y No Modernos* (Bogotá: Corporacion Centro Regional de Poblacion, 1978, p. 109.

TABLE 10.5. Unemployment in the Construction Sector Before and After the Housing Boom, Urban Area

Year	Persons Looking for Work in Construction as a Percent of All:			Construction sector unemployment rate[c]	Total unemployment rate
	Cesantes[a]	Aspirantes[b][c]	Unemployed[c]		
1971 (Nov. - Dec.)					
EH5	15.67	7.30	11.59	16.05	11.55
1972 (Sept. - Oct.)					
EH6	13.03	7.11	10.64	14.81	10.03
1974 (June)[e]					
EH7					12.68
1974 (Oct. - Nov.)					
EH8	11.19	4.11	8.14	11.43	10.42
1975 (Sept. - Oct.)[d]					
EH9	14.86	3.78	10.90	15.44	10.58

[a] Those currently unemployed who have worked previously and are currently looking for work.
[b] Those who have not worked before and are seeking their first job.
[c] Figures shown exclude persons who do not designate sector where they are looking fcr work.
[d] Seven cities.
[e] Four largest cities.

Source: DANE, *Encuesta de Hogares*, 1970; DANE, *Encuesta Nacional de Hogares*, Etapas 3, 4, 5, and the subsequent publications of the same title for etapas 6, 7, 8, and 9.

Another possibility, of course, is that construction workers come from the pool of unemployed. However, as Table 10.5 shows, the aggregate unemployment ratio did not decline between September-October, 1972 and October-November, 1974, but rather increased slightly from 10.0 percent to 10.4 percent.[27] The share of unemployed looking for jobs in construction did decline (Table 10.5), as did the unemployment rate in construction, as defined by those seeking work there divided by the sum of those working, plus those seeking work in that sector. Both these ratios moved back in 1975 to about the same levels they had in 1971. It seems fairly clear, therefore, that part of the increase in construction employment did come ultimately from the pool of unemployed, in the sense that that pool became smaller during the housing boom. If the unemployment rate in the construction sector fell, say, from 15 percent to 10 percent (one must again speculate due to the lack of observations during the heart of the boom), this would imply the creation of about thirteen thousand urban jobs, assuming the urban construction labor force reported in EH6 of September-October, 1972. In other words, a substantial share of the new jobs were filled by previously unemployed; judging from the previous paragraph, many of the rest probably came from agriculture. Consistent with this conclusion are the facts that (a) the level of unemployment for persons with no education appears to have fallen during the housing boom period, although since it appears to undergo considerable fluctuation, this may be coincidence; and (b) the unemployment rate of blue collar workers was sharply lower in mid-1974 than earlier or later; between September-October, 1972 and June, 1974, it fell by several percentage points while that of white collar workers rose.

SUMMARY

Colombia's development strategy over 1972-74 placed a heavy emphasis on urban building as a motor of growth and a generator of employment for relatively low income people. Data on the labor intensity of the sector suggest that its employment creating potential should have been substantial during a period of output acceleration. While data are too imperfect to permit a good measure of the effects of the strategy, they suggest that:

(a) a significant increase in employment in building did occur, with some employees coming (directly or indirectly) from jobs in other sectors, especially agriculture, and some from the pool of unemployed. While the employment effect was not large as a share of the total urban labor force, it may have been large for male blue collar paid workers.

[27]The peak of the housing boom occurred in mid-1974 so that the October-November figures measure unemployment rates at a time when urban building was declining.

(b) any effects on the lower skilled blue collar wage rate were probably positive but not large enough to offset other forces (especially the accelerating inflation) which were at the time exerting downward pressure on real wages in general.

These effects on employment and wages were temporary because of changes by the Lopez administration which effectively terminated the program at the end of 1974. However, as was pointed out in the first part of the paper, an acceleration of the rate of increase in building can increase the labor share only in a transitional period until a new and higher equilibrium stock of buildings is reached. In the long run an economy with a larger stock of buildings and a correspondingly smaller stock of capital in other activities will have a lower labor share than an economy which has a smaller stock of buildings and a larger stock of other capital.

Chapter 11

LOW INCOME HOUSING DEVELOPMENT AND INCOME DISTRIBUTION: THE IMPACT OF GROWTH AND CHANGE

Stephen O. Bender
Associate, Rice University

INTRODUCTION

Much has been written concerning clandestine[1] community development in Latin America, with particular emphasis on formation and land tenure. It is generally accepted that such communities, composed of low and moderate income families, are created in response to a lack of alternatives for resolving housing needs within the conventional, legally sanctioned housing markets (commercial and government). This paper attempts to assess the economic benefits derived from development of such settlements and how they affect income distribution in Colombia. To do so it is necessary to consider the process through which housing is developed in these settlements; if other investment alternatives are present, whether they are more advantageous; and finally, the impact of this type of housing development on families with similar income levels who have not been able to invest in housing development.

Our first step is to examine the stimulus behind the growth of the clandestine settlements, define the role they have played in the accelerated urban growth of Bogotá, and identify the main reasons why the lower income classes have invested in them. Second, we analyze characteristics of all lower income settlements, whether clandestine or legal in origin, in order to understand what difference land tenure makes and what common aspirations of settlement dwellers are ful-

[1] Clandestine communities are understood to include (for the Bogotá, context): 1) *Piratas*—settlements not legally recognized because they include land sales of unserviced lots, and 2) invasions—settlements developed through the illegal taking of land.

filled through housing development. (As we see below, apart from their formation and land tenure aspects, the similarities between clandestine and legally accepted settlements composed of comparable income groups are more notable than the differences.) It will then be possible to present in some detail the benefits derived from settlement development (both clandestine and legal) and the economic dependence low income families have on that development. Income distribution may be improved quite directly by low real costs of low-income urban housing. Less obviously, owning a house may constitute a better investment for low income families than other investment alternatives and may be a source not only of income in kind but of cash income from rental space and commercial activities. We attempt a rough estimate of the possible impact of clandestine community development on the income distribution of Bogotá and of Colombia.

SETTLEMENTS IN AN URBAN GROWTH AND CHANGE CONTEXT

Clandestine settlements have been the dominant force in shaping the large urbanized areas in Latin America, including Bogotá. They are to a great extent a result of the rapid migration from rural and semirural areas, a phenomenon viewed variously as a reflection of rapid overall development and structural change (the pull factor), of a stagnant rural labor market (the push factor), or some combination of the two.

The inner core of the expanding urban areas had been developed during colonial times as the residential center of those who controlled both agricultural production and the commercial arena. Imported advances in transportation and communication, and massive public works projects later allowed those inhabitants to establish residential enclaves on the perimeter leaving the colonial cores as business centers. Vacated colonial dwellings were quickly converted into dense low cost rental units and were rapidly occupied by the immigrant influx. When the existing housing stock was fully committed and occupied, migrating families were forced to seek housing solutions elsewhere. Housing institutions, both private and the newly established public agencies, supplied dwelling units to the middle and upper economic classes, but they did not respond adequately to the needs of these lower income groups—who had, therefore, to seek alternatives outside the existing social, legal, and physical order. The common solution was provisional shelter, rudimentary in nature, built illegally and in a clandestine manner on publicly or privately held land by migrant families (sometimes acting individually, but often in groups numbering in the thousands). Frequently, as in Bogotá, land could be attained from private entrepreneurs who, capable of withstanding social, legal, and political pressure, would sell parcels for illegal development.[2] These areas grew quickly, often at a faster rate than that of the total urban population. Housing was (and is) the immediate and most pressing need of these migrants, a need which they were both able and accustomed to fulfill by themselves.

Official reaction was varied. On the one hand, the growth of invasion and "illegal" housing settlements was condoned, perhaps even secretly supported, by governmental agencies and political parties hoping to gain the political support of the migrants, silence their demand for housing, and avoid facing the major problems of urban development directly.[3] At the other extreme were the official political and professional positions declaring such settlements to be festering sores—rings of poverty, filth, and political radicalism that encircled and threatened the peaceful and orderly social, economic, and physical operation of cities. Settlements were decried as illegal, unplanned, dangerous growths that blighted the environment and whose only solution was eradication.[4,5] More balanced observers recognized both potential promise and danger in the rapid growth of these settlements and sought to create standards and master plans to guide and control that growth.

During the 1960s, as the serious study of the origins and organizations of these settlements began, the view of clandestine settlements changed to one of marginality—a group of homogeneous developments characterized by illegal land tenure and owner-built housing, with a migrant base, but necessarily outside the mainstream of urban life. Studies emphasized the internal organization of the settlements and their roles in the urbanization of peasants as the last step of the rural to urban, colonial core to fringe settlement migration pattern.[6] The importance of the acquisition of housing to the families involved was recognized, and the redeeming social and physical graces of clandestine settlements and their part in providing housing were explained.

The "festering sore" view of clandestine settlements demanded overt control of urban growth by traditional means, including forceable removal and replacement by institutionalized housing solutions. The "marginality" view suggested

[2]This form of development, *piratas*, is especially prevalent in Bogotá, accounting in 1970 for an estimated 41 percent of all dwelling units in Bogotá; invasion settlement dwellings accounted for only about one percent of the total. See J. Valenzuela and G. Vernez *Actividad Constructora Popular: Analisis General y Elementos Para Una Politica de Apoyo* (Departamento Administrativo de Planeacion [DNP], April 1972), p. 68.

[3]See Collier, "Squatter Settlement Formation and the Politics of Co-optation in Peru," Ph.D. Dissertation, University of Chicago, 1971.

[4]See W. Mangin, "Latin American Squatter Settlements: A Problem and a Solution," *Latin American Research Review*, 1, 3 (Summer, 1967), pp. 65-98.

[5]This parallels policy and planning thinking in most western, industrialized nations, particularly in the United States, laying the groundwork for vast urban renewal projects in deteriorated urban areas, and massive public expenditures to house the urban poor.

[6]J. C. Turner, "Housing Priorities, Settlement Patterns, and Urban Development in Modernizing Countries," *American Institute of Planners Journal*, 34, 6 (November 1968), pp. 354-63.

that the settlement phenomenon was separate—especially physically—from its larger urban context, and residual to urban growth as a whole. Neither view has proved adequate. Clandestine settlements are diverse in their characteristics. Their formation takes place in a variety of patterns that respond to social and political organization, leadership availability, economic status, and ability to operate effectively in the larger urban environment. Migration to the settlements often takes place directly from rural or semirural areas without participation in an urbanization process.[7] Although their adult population is still predominantly migrant, many squatter settlements will soon be composed largely of first generation urban dwellers.

Land tenure is more complex than was originally presumed. Invasions and illegal formation of settlements form the basic land acquisition methods, later complemented by organized and complex systems of buying, selling, and renting land parcels. The development potential of squatter settlements has been recognized not only by the inhabitants, but also by the more traditional and institutional land development interests, who have sought entrance into the market.[8]

Self-help housing[9] (*autoconstruccion*) has generally characterized clandestine housing developments, but such construction might better be described as owner-contracted, since a variety of subcontractors are usually engaged for fees or in-kind services by the owner. In Bogotá during the 1960s such construction approached conventional housing in number of units and represented a substantial part of total consumption of construction materials.[10]

The development of clandestine settlements responds to locational factors such as land availability and accessibility to places of work in much the same fashion as do other sectors of the housing market. Because of their magnitude, they have dramatically altered the growth patterns of many cities, extending beyond the existing infrastructure of the city, thus dictating where future transportation and other services must be located. Substantially altering master plans, their growth demands a review of existing construction standards, zoning and building ordinances, and housing policies and programs. Clandestine settlements are the most dynamic, adaptive physical environment in the urban setting, reflecting a determination and ability to grow and change.[11]

While having as their basis the provision of shelter, clandestine settlements satisfy other needs as well, including security of ownership, productive invest-

[7]A. Berry, *Algunas Caracteristicas del Sector de Auto-Construccion de Vivendas: Proyecciones de Su Importancia Relativa en El Futuro* (DNP, 1972), p. 9; hereafter cited as Berry.

[8]R. Losada and H. Gomez, *La Tierra en el Mercado Pirata de Bogotá* (Bogotá, Fedsesarrollo, June, 1976).

[9]The term usually applied to owner-built dwelling units.

[10]Valenzuela and Vernez, *Actividad Constructora Popular*, p. 13.

[11]See Centro para el Desarrollo Economico y Social de America Latina (DESAL), *marginalidad en America Latina*, I and II (Santiago, Chile 1967). For a critical analysis of this concept, see J. Nun, "La Marginalidad en America Latina," *Revista Latinoamerica de Sociologia*, 5 (July, 1969).

ment in capital, the opportunity to supplement family income with home-based business, and the need to establish and identify the dwelling as a personal possession.[12] The process begins with the creation of minimal physical accommodation, and over a period of time that shelter is evolved into a permanent, valuable, and much sought after dwelling unit. Housing construction done in an evolutionary manner allows the settlement family to match available resources closely with family housing needs and investment potential. The typical dwelling unit is developed in four or more phases during at least a six-year period,[13] until a permanent structure of reinforced concrete with brick or block is completed. Materials can be gathered as it becomes possible to acquire them and labor can be utilized in accordance with skill, needs, and availability. During this evolution the original aggregation of shelters is transformed into a stable, growing community with a complement of public and private services. Commercial uses are quickly introduced into any settlement; more gradually infrastructure is upgraded or established if not already present. A transformation takes place which allows for integration into the larger urban context.

Land tenure status does not sharply differentiate clandestine and government settlements in terms of the investment and development process followed by the communities' inhabitants. Variables such as age of the settlement, stage of evolution of the dwelling units (including number of rooms, type of construction, length of construction period), location of the settlement, and family income have a much greater impact on housing development and the economic benefits derived therefrom.

LOW INCOME HOUSING DEVELOPMENT

The preponderance of low-income families find housing solutions through owner-contracted (self-help) means whether in the invasion, *pirata*, or government sectors of the housing market.[14] To assess the relevance of this phenomenon in income distribution, it is necessary to examine the income characteristics of those families and the importance of the dwelling unit as a source of income.

According to DANE estimates, 50 percent of all Bogotá households earned less than 2,500 pesos per month in 1970.[15] The relationship between family income and type of housing solution, as estimated by Valenzuela and Vernez, is shown in Table 1. The dwelling units occupied by families with monthly income below 2,500 pesos were primarily single family attached units built over an extended period (excluding the commercial submarket); Table 1

[12] Turner, "Housing Priorities," pp. 354-63.

[13] Berry, *op. cit.*, page 7.

[14] Some government programs, for example, require the recipient to finish the unit while being provided with a shell or core house.

[15] Departamento Administrativo Nacional de Estadistica (DANE), *Encuesta de Hogares* (E-H2) (unpublished tables); see Departamento Administrativo de Planeacion Distrital, *Mercadeo de Tierras en Barrios Clandestinos de Bogotá* (April, 1973), p. 10.

TABLE 11.1 Housing Submarket by Family Income

Monthly family income (pesos)	Invasion	Pirata	Government	Commercial	Total units	Percent
0-500	653	9,392	1,930	21,530	33,505	7.4
501-1250	2,863	87,897	8,673	21,850	121,283	26.9
1251-2500	1,333	85,143	21,419	13,431	121,326	26.9
2501-4000	104	21,847	10,295	61,382	93,628	20.8
>4000	–	–	6,426	74,934	91,360	18.0
Total	4,955	204,182	48,740	193,124	451,102	100.0
%	1.1	45.3	10.8	42.8	100.0	

Source: Valenzuela and Vernez, *Actividad Constructora Popular: Analisis General Y Elementos Para Una Politica de Apoyo* (DNP, April, 1972), page 27.

implies that 79.4 percent of families with monthly incomes of 2,500 pesos or less were finding their housing solution as owners, renters, or roomers in self-contracted units.[16] In all housing submarkets except the commercial the majority of families owned their dwelling (see Table 2).[17] Renters occupy the majority of commercial submarket units and approximately one-fifth of the *pirata* units, but are not found in the government submarket (government housing for this income category offers ownership rather than rental programs). For the pirata and government submarkets, roomers account for a significant portion of the households and most likely represent the portion above unity (.2 to .3) of the ratio of the number of households per dwelling unit (1.2 to 1.3).[18]

The major contribution of settlement housing to the family's income comes through the relief from rental payments that possession of a dwelling unit (with or without legal title) represents, the quantity of living space potentially available, and the security associated with possession of land. Since the most critical step in the process of clandestine housing investment and dwelling unit development is access to land, purchasers in clandestine settlements are willing to reduce housing services to the level of simple, provisional shelter in order to gain access to land.

Government programs, on the other hand, generally *reduce* the size of the dwelling unit and the corresponding lot, reflecting its emphasis on providing finished housing solutions rather than increasing the access to the "evolutionary"

[16]Roomers include the "inquilinatos" or those who rent rooms from a household, sharing common sanitary facilities. As will be discussed later, the government housing solutions offered in this income category are of a self-contracted nature, with the family making modifications and/or additions to the units they build or buy through the government programs. See Valenzuela and Vernez, *Actividad Constructora Popular*, pp. 27 and 30.

[17]*Invasion* settlements are eliminated from the discussion because of their minor role (1.8 percent of total families) in housing in this income category (see table 1).

Renters and roomers represent 65.3 percent of the families in the commercial submarket. Moreover, this submarket houses the poorest segment of the population—76.0 percent of the families in the submarket have household incomes of 1,250 pesos or less.

[18]See DAPD, *Mercadeo de Tierras*, p. 78.

TABLE 11.2 Household Distribution by Housing Submarket and Housing Tenure

Housing submarket	Tenure			Total percent
	Owners	Renters	Roomers	
Pirata	52.9	19.7	27.4	100.0
Invasion	61.8	0.0	38.2	100.0
Government	85.7	0.0	14.3	100.0
Commercial	34.7	65.3		100.0

Source: Valenzuela and Vernez, *Actividad Constructora Popular: Analisis General Y Elementos Para Una Politica de Apoyo* (DNP, April, 1972), page 30.

housing market for low-income families. Investors in either the clandestine or the government settlements have chosen these for economic reasons. Ownership of property and better housing conditions are believed to be available at a lower price.[19] Only in the minority of cases (less than 30 percent) are factors such as proximity to employment, friends and family, transportation, or security selected as the principal reason for moving to the settlement.[20] The lower the income, the more the economic factor appears to dominate. Among the settlements studied, with the average family income (excluding imputed rent on owner housing) of about $4,600 in the *pirata* settlement, $2,000 in the government settlement, and $1,300 in the invasion settlement, the opportunity to own housing or to improve housing conditions was cited as the principal reason for investment in 70, 76, and 86 percent of the cases, respectively.[21]

Berry's previous studies of housing expenditures in Bogotá indicate that for the *pirata* settlements, 51 percent of the households paid nothing for housing services in 1970,[22] a figure approximately equal to the 52.9 percent of the households who are owners in this housing submarket. In invasion settlements, dwellers most often pay nothing for housing services (other than construction costs). For those settlement owners who have monthly expenditures, their housing costs are comparable in amount to those of families to whom they rent, yet they consume two to three times the quantity of housing services (number of rooms). The amount that this housing expenditure relief represents as a percentage of total income can only be estimated roughly with the data presently available, but it is evidently considerable, especially in the lower income categories. (See Table 3.) While there is probably some upward bias in these figures,[23]

[19] Berry, *op. cit.*, p. 8: and G. Vernez, *Distribucion Espacial de la Poblacion-Colombia*, Corporacion Centro Regional de Poblacion, 1976, p. 160.

[20] Survey conducted by the author and T. O Gauhan, 1973-74.

[21] *Ibid.*

[22] Berry, *op. cit.*, p. 12.

[23] Income is likely to be underestimated, whereas the imputed rental figure per room was estimated directly. One might guess that the imputed rental per room should be lower for lower income families, but data on estimated value of houses (divided by number of rooms) do not suggest this

TABLE 11.3 Imputed value of Housing Services as a Percent of Total Monthly Family Income[a]

Barrio	Monthly Monetary[b] Family Income					
	<1250	1250-2500	<2500	2500-4000	⩾4000	Total
Pirata	67.0[c]	44.3	46.8	28.3	14.2	22.0
	(13)	(44)	(57)	(48)	(78)	(183)
Invasion	56.1	26.8	44.9	35.0	24.1	41.3
	(69)	(37)	(106)	(9)	(3)	(118)

[a]Including imputed rental income.
[b]Excluding imputed rental income from housing services.
[c]Figure includes a number of families who reported zero income.
( ) = Number of observations
Source: Data from the survey by Bender and Gauhan.

they strongly suggest that families in these barrios consume more housing services[24] than they would have, with comparable income levels, had they been renting. For those households in the low income category (2,500 pesos or less per month) that pay for housing services, the cost is generally 20-25 percent of monthly incomes.[25] As of 1970, actual payments seldom exceeded 500 pesos or were less than 150 pesos[26] with a median cost of 200 to 250 pesos.[27]

If families who possess dwelling units in these settlements were forced to seek housing on the rental market, it would be extremely difficult for them to duplicate the services that they are now consuming. They, like the families to whom they rent, would be forced to locate in fewer rooms, lose the income resources the dwelling unit represents, and pay a significant portion of their real income for rent. The lower share of income paid in rent by families without their own dwelling, relative to the share of income from imputed rent received by home owners, suggests that such a squeezing does occur.

The attractiveness of clandestine settlements depends partly on the cost advantages of self-contracted housing and partly on relatively low land prices. Land prices in clandestine settlements are indirectly subsidized by the government through its inability (or unwillingness) to control illegal *pirata* land sales. Without the legally mandated public services (potable water, sewerage system,

[24]Since housing units in the barrios studied averaged from 3.7 (invasion) to 6.1 (*pirata*) rooms per dwelling, imputing a rent of 250 pesos per room implies that in 1973 for dwelling units without rental space the value of monthly services consumed averaged 935 pesos in invasion barrios (3.7 rooms per dwelling), and 1,530 pesos in *pirata* barrios (6.1 rooms per dwelling). (Bender and Gauhan, Survey, 1973-74. These figures correspond to 31 m^2 [invasion] and 58 m^2 [*pirata*] as described by Valenzuela and Vernez, *Actividad Constructora Popular*, p. 78.)

[25]DAPD, *Mercadeo de Tierra*, p. 25; and R. Losada and H. Gomez, *La Tierra en el Mercado Pirata de Bogotá*, Fedesarrollo (June, 1976), p. 112.

[26]Consultecnicos, Ltda *Estudio de Normas minimas de Urbanizacion, Servicios Publicas y Servicios Comunitarios: Informe Basico y Complimento* (Bogotá: Consultecnicos, 1971).

[27]DAPD, *Mercadeo de Tierras*, p. 48.

electric power), lot prices in clandestine settlements are 50-67 percent less than comparably priced land in "urbanized" commercial settlements.[28, 29]

Clandestine settlement has the additional advantage of lower construction costs. The involvement of family labor in the construction process has long been cited in this connection and has led to the extensive use of the term "self-help" housing to imply erection of the dwelling unit solely with family labor, with or without technical assistance. In the case of initial or first phase dwelling units, which are provisional in nature, that term is probably correctly applied. For permanent construction, however, skill levels are needed which, while present in the settlement, may not necessarily be present in every family. The availability of unskilled family labor is not an important source of the lower construction costs of clandestine settlements. The cost of materials for commercial housing construction represents 50-65 percent of total construction cost.[30] While some portion of these materials may be produced in low income settlements (principally masonry and wood products), the great majority have to be purchased. Labor represents approximately 30 percent of construction costs; 35 percent of the labor hours correspond to skills built up with experience and/or knowledge of the trade (and tools). Unless these skills are found in the family, they are purchased or traded for goods or services that can be provided by the family itself. The hourly cost of skilled labor is at least double that of unskilled so those unskilled labor costs which could be avoided by the use of family labor represent no more than 15 percent of the total construction cost.[31] Given the extended costruction period, and the relatively small size of construction projects undertaken at any one time (1-2 rooms) the number of hours of unskilled labor input at any time is small and the opportunities for participation by the family on own-account construction are quite low. In summary, then, while it is probable that construciton costs in clandestine settlements are less than in the commercial submarket, this is due far more to the elimination of fees and services (public fees and licenses, professional fees, insurance, profits, and interests on loans,[32]

[28] Losada and Gomez, *op. cit.*, p. 32.

[29] A somewhat similar phenomenon occurs in government settlements which typically utilize public lands whose original purchase price rather than market value at time of development is used in determining the dwelling unit price. Because of political and economic pressures which demand that government housing projects accommodate specific income groups, financing costs are also usually subsidized; this, together with a reduction of housing services (number of rooms, size of lot, quality of construction, etc.) allows dwelling unit costs to be kept within reach of target income groups.

[30] J. Valenzuela and R. Kiedrowski, *Indices de Costo de la Construccion de Vivienda Urbana en Colombia–Modelo y Bases para la Muestra* (Centro de Investigaciones para Desarrollo [CID]: Universidad Nacional de Colombia, 1970), pp. 67-68.

[31] The use of family labor does not, of course, fully offset the cost of commercially supplied labor. Rather, family labor should be valued at its opportunity cost, the savings over commercial labor being the difference between the market wage and the family opportunity cost.

[32] Centro de Estudios sobre Desarrollo Economico (CEDE), *op. cit.*, p. 90. Fifty-eight percent of the modifications or additions made to dwelling units in Ciudad Kennedy were financed from personal savings.

which together amount to 20-30 percent of the cost of commercial housing),[33] than to the use of own-account labor.

Some of the housing services at the command of owners are rented to other families. The fraction of households per dwelling unit over unity (0.2 to 0.3) can be attributed to roomers in owner-occupied or rented dwelling units given that families who rented to roomers were reported to be approximately 25 percent of the total number of families in *pirata* and government settlements.[34] A more recent study by Bender and Gauhan limited to three distinct settlements–invasion, *pirata*, and government–at different levels of development and in distinct locations in Bogotá, indicates a similar occurrence of roomers. The percentage of dwelling units with roomers was 38, 22, and 3 for the government, *pirata*, and invasion settlements, respectively. The government and *pirata* settlements were more than 85 percent developed into permanent structures.[35]

Rental income from roomers as a percentage of total monthly family income for all families represented perhaps 9 percent for the government settlement, 8 percent for the *pirata* settlement, and 5 percent for the invasion settlement. When considering rental income in relation to the total monthly family income of only those families with roomers, rental income represented 18 percent of the total income for the government settlement, 26 percent for the *pirata* settlement, and 29 percent for the invasion settlement.[36]

The study also indicates that the roomers occupied an average of 0.71 rooms per dwelling in the government settlement and 0.47 rooms per dwelling in the *pirata* settlement (excluding baths, patios, and storage areas). In 1975, 36 percent of the original single family dwelling units in Ciudad Kennedy housed roomers.[37] Although these samples are not necessarily representative of the entire urban situation, the figures serve to corroborate the estimate based on Bogotá-wide 1970 data and underscore the importance of renting as an income source to those primary occupants with the ability to develop and expand their dwelling unit to other uses. It is interesting to note that the majority of dwelling units at the point of occupation in both clandestine and government settlements are basically single family units. In both cases, during development of the dwelling

[33]Valenzuela and Kiedrowski, *op. cit.*, pp. 64-65.

[34]Berry, *op. cit.*, p. 12.

[35]1973-74 survey of three settlements by S. O. Bender and T. O. Gauhan, Progam of Development Studies, Rice University, Houston, Texas. The invasion settlement was less than 30 percent developed into permanent housing. It is located 350 meters above the city in the hills to the southeast of the central business district and was a 35 minute bus ride from the city's center.

[36]These figures are approximate due to inconsistencies in reporting income. They may be underestimates if other income (particularly wage income) was more accurately reported than rental income. In general, under-reporting of all income categories is common.

[37]CEDE, *op. cit.*, p. 53. It is interesting to note that in contrast to the single family attached units, of all the multifamily units (low-rise apartments) in Ciudad Kennedy, only 2.6 percent housed roomers in 1975.

unit the option is exercised to consume less than the total available amount of housing services in order to generate income.[38]

Migration patterns reinforce the importance of this supply of housing services in low-income migrant families. Vernez estimates that between 50 and 80 percent of the immigrants arriving in Bogotá in the late 1960s became roomers in *pirata* and invasion settlements. Only 7 to 27 percent of the immigrants arriving go first to the city's center, their traditional destination,[39] the remainder going directly to low-income settlement areas. Many migrants pay a portion of their income as rent to other families who are investing that income in developing housing services. Self-contracted housing, then, includes self-financing, and contributes to the income of both low-income owners and low-income renters.

Not only is it quantitatively significant, but the income derived from rental dwelling unit space can be increased (by squeezing the family's own living quarters) according to family contingencies. Investment can be matched to available resources in any given period, providing a flexibility that is not offered by other investment opportunities. It is doubtful that the available funds and labor of low-income families can be invested in other sectors so effectively and efficiently. In a study of a large government settlement (Ciudad Kennedy) in Bogotá, only investment in a retail business (*tienda* or *almacén*) was considered preferable to investment in housing expansion for rental space to roomers (*inquilinos*).[40] Savings accounts, investment in a taxi or bus, and stocks and bonds (in descending order) were all considered less attractive than housing investment. There was a clear preference shown for investments over which the investor could exercise the most control. It must be noted also that the preference for investment in a retail business would, based on consumption of dwelling unit space for nonresidential uses mentioned earlier, most likely include developing additional space (investment in the dwelling unit) or a reduction of consumption of presently available housing services. While no data are available on the asset structure of the clandestine settlement owners, it appears that housing, both the initial cost and subsequent extensions, are systematically chosen over alternatives.

A second important source of cash revenue for low-income families is utilization of the dwelling unit for nonresidential purposes. Given that underemployment or occasional rather than permanent employment is prevalent among low-income families, the opportunity to supplement wage income with rental of dwelling unit space for nonresidential uses or the use of space by the family for

[38] The need to reduce housing expenditures is also evident in the commercial sector of the housing market in Bogotá (those dwelling units built in legal urbanizations under licensed construction for upper-middle income groups and above). As an example, during the 1974-75 period, a 35 percent decrease was noted in the amount of housing square footage constructed, while a 6 percent increase in the total number of dwelling units built was recorded. Camara Colombiana de la Construccion (CAMACOL, *Boletin Anual* [January, 1976], No. 9, p.8)

[39] Berry, *op. cit.*, p. 16.

[40] CEDE, *Estudio Sobre Los Inquilinatos en Bogotá*, Segunda Parte; Documento No. 034 (June, 1976), p. 92.

business or commercial concerns deserves attention. A small sample study in Bogotá and Cali indicates that goods-producing shops represent the principal income for 14-25 percent of the families.[41] In Ciudad Kennedy in 1965 (2 years after competion of the project) 20 percent of the single family dwellings housed commercial establishments.[42] (Small amounts of commercial space in government-sponsored settlements appear to be inadequate as evidenced by the rapid growth of businesses in the dwelling units, which are in type and quantity comparable to clandestine settlements which start with no exclusive commercial space.) Settlement dwellers are providing needed goods and services as their communities evolve, and the establishment of commercial and producing businesses are a natural outgrowth of development. Their presence in the community should not be viewed with surprise nor as due solely to economic necessity, although economic incentives are certainly present. It is partly the absence of larger retail and wholesale enterprises in these low-income settlements which allows such a quantity of small businesses to operate. These businesses have two important characteristics, however, which aid their proliferation. First, because of the space limitations of the dwelling units where they are housed, their growth is constrained; few capture large segments of their particular market. Secondly, and most importantly, the implicit rent on the space they use may in many cases be rather low, helping to keep their prices down, to the benefit of their customers (almost exclusively settlement dwellers).

A land use inventory of the three previously mentioned settlements and an additional *pirata* and invasion settlement (both more than 85 percent developed into permanent construction), done by the author in 1973, shows that 7-21 percent of all dwelling units quarter some type of nonresidential use.[43] The percentage of different types of nonresidential use is shown in Table 4. The most

TABLE 11.4 Nonresidential Uses in Five Low Income Settlements (Bogotâ): Percent Distribution

Settlement	Small food store	Small prod. shop (goods)	Small retail shop (goods & ser.)	Restaurant	Office	Total
Pirata	30.3	21.4	22.3	16.5	9.5	100.0
Invasion	38.0	27.5	19.7	11.3	3.5	100.0
Government	25.2	18.9	30.8	9.4	15.7	100.0

Source: Bender Settlement Land Use Inventory, 1973-74.

[41] Berry, *op. cit.*, p. 8.

[42] ICT, *Informe 1965 al Senor Ministro de Fomento*, p. 113.

[43] The invasion settlement mentioned earlier (see note 35, page 256) showed only 7 percent of the dwelling units having some type of nonresidential use. This would appear to be due to the recent establishment of the settlement (1967), the still-provisional condition of most of the construction present, and the lower family income characteristic of the settlement. Of all dwelling units in the government and *pirata* settlements, 19 and 21 percent, respectively, of the units had nonresidential uses.

prevalent activities found are those which provide commercial goods and services to the community (small food stores, small retail shops, and restaurants). These are probably operated by someone other than the head of the household—the women and children in the family—who combine the businesses with their domestic tasks. The other two activities (small production shops and offices) are most likely carried on by the heads of households, and in some cases offer employment to nonfamily members.[44]

Income from the group of activities conducted by nonheads of households represented 15.9, 21.7, and 25.5 percent of the families' total wage income in *pirata*, invasion, and government settlements, respectively. Income from those activities conducted by heads of households was 19.5, 24.9, and 13.4 percent, respectively, of total wage income of the families in question; the low percentage in the government settlement is probably due to the income requirements of the government housing programs, which tend to accept heads of households with stable employment.

Of the nonresidential uses identified in the three-settlement study, less than 13 percent occur in rented rooms, indicating that these activities are usually carried on by the primary occupants of the dwelling unit.[45] Comparing the percentage of total income that these business activities represent and the rental value of the space they occupy, it appears that the return is approximately the same for the two uses. Since some shops provide the family with goods at wholesale prices, nominal income understates the value of having a business in the dwelling unit.[46] There would also appear to be more family satisfaction in operating a business, in that it gives the appearance that the family is progressing and economically active. Finally, business activities may interfere less with family life than the presence of roomers who must share sanitary facilities.

Almost all income-producing use of dwelling unit space takes place in units which are of permanent construction. Rental of space to roomers is most commonly found in smaller units and is associated with households with lower incomes. Nonresidential activities are most generally found in households who own rather than rent the units they occupy, and they usually have higher incomes than those families who rent to roomers.

Summing the dwelling units with nonresidential uses and those with roomers, 10 percent of the invasion settlement, 43 percent of the *pirata* settlement, and 57 percent of the government settlement dwelling units surveyed utilized some

[44] Berry, *op. cit.*, p. 8.

[45] Less than 2 percent of those dwelling units with roomers indicated that they also rented space for nonresidential uses. Specific data is not available as to whether or not roomers are also present in those dwelling units with businesses operated by dwelling units' principal occupants. From the above, it would seem that it is improbable. Since dwellings in these settlements have an average of 5.77 rooms and 7 persons per unit, it can be assumed that no more than 1 to 1.6 rooms per dwelling would be devoted to non-family use (the family occupying a living area, kitchen, and two sleeping areas).

[46] Berry, *op. cit.*, p. 5.

space as an income-producing source, representing 13 to 29 pecent of the total monthly monetary income of the families involved.

LOW INCOME HOUSING AND INCOME DISTRIBUTION

The direct effect of low income housing development on income distribution can be estimated on the basis of (a) the various contributions such settlements make to the real incomes of the lower income families involved, and (b) the location of those families in the overall income distribution. Table 1 presents for Bogotá an estimate of the income distribution of families by type of housing solution, and shows the tendency for self-contracted housing to be more prevalent in the bottom 60 percent or so of the income distribution. Less information is available for Colombia's other urban centers, but a plausible though rough guess for 1970 would be that 40-50 percent of urban families lived in such dwellings. Other cities are generally poorer than Bogotá, but it is not clear whether the mechanisms for *pirata* developments are as well developed as in Bogotá.

The fact that urban families generally have higher incomes than rural families means that any given urban family would lie in higher deciles in the national income distribution than in the urban one. Table 5 summarizes our best estimate for the distribution of all families (urban and rural) in invasion and *pirata* barrios in 1970. It suggests that most of the benefits from this type of housing accrue to deciles two through seven, but that disproportionate benefits accrue to the third quintile.[47]

The data discussed above permit some feel for the effect of low income housing development on the incomes of the owners and renters of such houses or of rooms in them. The income benefits to owners may be broken down into (a) reduced cost of and/or increased quantity of housing or shop services and (b) income from space rented out to roomers or for nonresidential use, yielding a greater return than the next best alternative form of investment. When, as here, we prefer to express the income gains in terms of current flow (rather than present value), allowance must be made for the fact that the owners of settlement dwellings had to lower their consumption at some point in the past to build the houses. One estimate of the amount by which their current income has been raised is the difference between the actual income flow and the flow which would have resulted from the same amount of investment in each past period, but in the next best alternative. The investment sequence (i.e., amount invested each period) would presumably have been different had the families not built houses, so this may be either an over or underestimate of the true effect of the housing option. But it is a handy initial benchmark.

[47]Using nominal pesos to compare urban and rural incomes may overstate the former, due to price differentials, greater underreporting of rural income and other factors. There is thus some likelihood that more of the benefits of low income urban housing accrue to families towards the bottom of the (true) income distribution than is indicated in Table 5.

TABLE 11.5 Share of all Families (Urban and Rural) in Invasion or *Pirata* Barrios by Income Level, 1970

Families, ranked from lowest income				
Lowest	11.3%	.11	.25	.25
Next	37.4%	.29		
Next	25.6%	.40	.32	
Next	14.6%	.16		
Highest	11.1%	0		

Source: Based on Table 1 and a comparison of rural and urban income distributions for 1970, as presented in DANE, *Boletin Mensual de Estadistica* #237, p. 59. The estimates are rough, since the DANE table only presents data for distribution by income earners. It is assumed here that the relation between rural and urban distributions is the same in the family distribution as for the income earners' distribution.

Consider a family whose house yields cash or imputed income (from rental and use) equal to 33 percent of other income, i.e., 25 percent of total income. If these benefits constituted a rate of return of 20 percent on past investment, and the next best alternative would have yielded 5 percent, then the housing option has permitted a current income stream higher by 19 percent of total income (¾ x 25 percent). None of the ratios in question are known with any precision, even for Bogotá. But, as noted earlier, families with incomes below 2,500 pesos per month, who pay for housing services, spend 20-25 percent of their incomes this way. It seems very probable that owners receive a higher share of their income (imputed housing services are part of their income) from their houses—they clearly consume more housing services than families who must pay for them. Meanwhile, other investment options for such families are usually poor, especially under inflationary conditions. For many, achieving even a zero return is difficult; many would not save were it not for the high return opportunity presented by self-contracted housing (and the pressure it puts for further saving once the process is started). For the present comparison, non-saving has the same result as saving which yields a zero return. Note, also, that when the return to alternative investment opportunities is near zero, the estimate of the gains in current income from housing is not sensitive to the rate of return on investment in that housing, a rate which appears to be high but is not known with real precision.

The effect of clandestine housing on a single family's income, other things held constant, is one thing; the effect of the phenomenon *in toto* is another. Were there no such housing, one must presume that the commercial and government housing sectors would be larger, and that somewhat fewer families would have migrated from rural areas. Assuming that other types of housing solutions would on balance be more expensive, the price of comparable housing services would be higher than in fact it is, and low income families in general would be worse off as a result; the higher income families who would rent or sell commercially produced dwellings would be better off. The quantitative effect of self-contracted housing on the price of housing services can only be guessed at. Given its importance, however, it seems unlikely that these services would be less than 20 percent more expensive; the upper level is harder to guess at, and we assume 50 percent by way of illustration. The representative owner of a self-contracted dwelling who now receives, say, 25 percent of total income from his house would have an income as much as 60 percent below the current level if his return on alternative investment was zero and he paid 50 percent more for the same amount of housing services. In fact, he would doubtless reorganize somewhat his consumption pattern and thereby avoid part of this loss, but it could easily be 30-40 percent of current income.

Those families who are now renters of low income housing would also be hurt by the higher rents, with income loss related to the rent difference. The loss will generally be a smaller percent of income than for the present low income owners.

Table 6 presents high and low estimates for various income groups of the share of their current income which may be attributed to living and investing in *pirata* and invasion housing. That share is of major significance for the second to sixth deciles. While the assumptions used to generate these figures involve much guesswork, especially about the effects of the absence of this housing on the cost of rental housing, there is no doubt that development of *pirata*/invasion housing

TABLE 11.6 Illustrative Estimates of the Percent of Current Family Income Attributable to the Existence of Invasion and *Pirata* Housing, by Income Groups, Bogotá, 1970

Monthly family income	Accruing to occupants (1)	Accruing to owners who rent to others (2)	Total (3)	Percent of families (4)	Percent of total income[a] (5)
0-500	4.3-7.1	.09	5.2-8.0	7.4	0.9
501-1250	10.4-15.2	2.91	13.31-18.11	26.9	7.6
1251-2500	9.6-13.4	4.74	16.44-20.24	26.9	15.4
2501-4000	2.8- 4.0	1.31	4.11- 5.31	20.8	21.1
>4000	0	0	0	18.0	55.0
Total	2.9- 4.1	1.1	4.0 - 5.2	100.0	100.0

Sources and Methodology: Col. (1) is based on the assumption that for owner occupants the following percentage of income is due to the low income housing: 30-40; 25-30; 25-30, and 15-20, for the four income categories where such housing is found, beginning with the bottom one. For renters and roomers benefits are assumed to constitute 6-15; 5-12.5, 4-10, and 2.6-9 percent of income. These benefits are attributed to the shares of each income category living in the houses in question.

Col. (2) is based on the assumption that the housing rented to the 46.8 percent of families not having their own house provide net benefits to the owners one-third as large as those provided to owner-occupants, and that the benefits are distributed somewhat higher up on the income scale. The owner receives the payoff to this space as an investment; especially in the case of roomers, the space will be smaller than the average lived in by owner-occupants.

[a]Rough estimates based on Table 1.

is of great importance in Bogotá. Like many phenomena which might be encouraged with a view to improving distribution, it does not reach a high share of the families with the very lowest current incomes; its effects are, however, felt close to the bottom of the income scale. In fact, when permanent or long-run income is the measure used to array families, many of the lowest income group distinguished here would not be so low; the inquilinos recently arrived in the city (having very low current incomes) often move to squatter settlements later. In other words, these settlements do affect the incomes of many of the poorest families at some stage of their lives. And the apparent magnitude of the effect is greater than can be expected from most distributional policies.

Postscript

With the expansion of upper middle and upper income housing construction since 1971, and the associated scarcity of building materials, there may have been a decrease in the starts per year destined for low income families. This would help to explain the growing incidence of roomers in low income (particularly government) settlements which, when they came on to the market, had no roomers. The demand, then, for roomer situations would appear to be growing. At the same time, increasing numbers of low income families are totally dependent on low-income settlements for housing as publicly sponsored rental projects for low-income families are nonexistent, and the commercial sector has neither the need nor the incentive to provide low-income housing.

For Bogotá, the issue is not what share of the production of low-income housing will be assumed by the participating public and private sectors, be they legal or illegal, but rather whether these sectors will be able to continue to deliver the opportunity for low-income families to participate and gain from evolutionary housing (settlement) development. Access to land and construction materials at affordable prices and provision of public utilities are necessary if low-income settlement development is to continue. These issues are, however, controlled by forces external to the settlements themselves. There is no guarantee that the resources necessary for settlement development will continue to be provided and the benefits derived therefrom present.

INDEX

For Product Safety Concerns and Information please contact our EU representative GPSR@taylorandfrancis.com
Taylor & Francis Verlag GmbH, Kaufingerstraße 24, 80331 München, Germany

www.ingramcontent.com/pod-product-compliance
Lightning Source LLC
LaVergne TN
LVHW011119300926
849160LV00008B/439
9780367171360